*Literature and
Nation in the
Sixteenth
Century*

Literature and
INVENTING
Nation in the
RENAISSANCE
Sixteenth
FRANCE
Century

TIMOTHY HAMPTON

Cornell University Press
ITHACA & LONDON

Copyright © 2001 by Cornell University

All rights reserved. Except for brief quotations in a review, this book, or parts
thereof, must not be reproduced in any
form without permission in writing from
the publisher. For information, address
Cornell University Press, Sage House,
512 East State Street, Ithaca, New York 14850.

First published 2001 by Cornell University Press

Printed in the United States of America

Library of Congress Cataloging-in-
Publication Data

Hampton, Timothy.
  Literature and nation in the sixteenth century : inventing
Renaissance France / by Timothy Hampton.
    p. cm.
  Includes bibliographical references.
  ISBN 0-8014-3774-1
    1. French literature—16th century—History and criticism. 2.
Nationalism in literature.   I. Title.
  PQ239 .H26 2000
  840.9'358—dc21

                                    00-010240

Cornell University Press strives to use
environmentally responsible suppliers
and materials to the fullest extent possible in the publication of its books. Such
materials include vegetable-based, low-
VOC inks and acid-free papers that are
recycled, totally chlorine-free, or partly
composed of nonwood fibers. Books that
bear the logo of the FSC (Forest
Stewardship Council) use paper taken
from forests that have been inspected
and certified as meeting the highest stan-
dards for environmental and social responsibility. For further information, visit our
website at www.cornellpress.cornell.edu.
         Cloth printing
          10 9 8 7
           6 5 4
            3 2
             1

for my mother,
who encouraged me to go to school

Contents

Preface

This is a book about edges. It is about the edges of community and the edges of literature. It concerns itself with moments when communities face those who are their neighbors or adversaries, and it analyzes what happens when these moments are represented in literary texts. It considers the consequences of such moments of limitation, both for the representation of community and for the language and formal conventions of literature.

Literature and Nation in the Sixteenth Century explores the relationship between a series of ideological struggles over the meaning and limits of community in Renaissance France, and the emerging secular literary culture that reflects and responds to those struggles. The question of the edges of the nation and of the political and cultural vulnerability of France more generally is a central, though rarely analyzed, theme of French Renaissance literature: in this book, I trace the ways in which anxiety about the edges and definition of France places pressure on the conventions and the language of literary representation. And I show how the generic and rhetorical multiplicity that marks much of early modern French literature functions as a form of mediation, as a way of responding imaginatively to the breakdown of community.

In recent years students of early modern European culture have paid increasing attention to the cultural and political origins of the modern nation-state. In a sense, this marks a kind of sea change in the study of the period. The fertile and long-established concern with the relationship of "ancients and moderns," with such issues as imitation, classical authority, and the reception of ancient texts that dominated the field of Renaissance studies a decade or so ago, has slowly begun to give way to an increasing interest in the ways in which communities and cultures define themselves with regard to other communities and cultures. A synchronic focus is replacing a diachronic one. Such books as Richard Helgerson's *Forms of Nationhood: The Elizabethan Writing of England*, and Richard Marienstras's *Le proche et le lointain: Le drame Elisabethain et l'idéologie anglaise aux XVIe et XVIIe siècles*, consider how cultural and political collectivities in Renaissance Europe mark out their identities and spaces. As the titles just mentioned suggest, this strain of thought has found Renaissance England, with its geographical insularity, its powerful queen, and its religious independence, a particularly fruitful object of study. France, however, surely provides the most widely influential model, in a European context at least, of the close bonding of literary culture and national spirit. Indeed, the blending of nationalism with the sanctification of literature is a central feature of French identity that has been exported with great success. One of my aims in writing this book is to trace the pre-history of the relationship between secular literary culture and national identity in France. Moreover, in the context of an emerging field of European studies, I hope, by focusing on the turbulent case of France, to offer a model for thinking about the relationship between culture and politics in the Renaissance that would counterbalance the conventional versions offered by scholars oriented toward more centralized and irenic collectivities such as England and Spain.

"I am driven to the conclusion that no 'scientific definition' of the nation can be devised; yet the phenomenon has existed and exists," writes Hugh Seton-Watson in his book *Nations and States*. How much more difficult, then, to try to define the relationship between literature and national identity. For if the "nation" itself can nowhere be pointed to, how is one to trace the ways in which it interrelates with literary and cultural production? To be sure, there is no lack of national literary histories, and such scholars as Colette Beaune, Claude-Gilbert Dubois, Anne-Marie Lecoq, and Walter Stephens have written compellingly about the symbols and myths that inform French nationhood. In a slightly different tradition, other scholars have focused on the images through which collective experience is defined. Thus, for example, in his study *Children of the Earth*, Marc Shell focuses on the metaphor of the nation as family and traces it through a number of literary texts from different periods. Jacques Derrida's *The Politics of Friendship* does something similar for the notion of political subjectivity as friendship. Less attention has been paid, however, to the problem of the simultaneous emergence of new images of the nation and new forms of secular literary representation. My book examines the dynamic and multifarious productions that mark a historical moment when neither literature nor national identity is clearly defined, when both texts and communities are in struggle, when many forms and figurations jostle for domination.

Any attempt to grasp and describe the relationship between the making of nations and the making of literary texts thus faces a difficult methodological challenge, since the two objects of study—nations and texts—define and shape each other. Scholars of the Renaissance have tried to meet this challenge in a variety of ways. One approach is to absorb literature into the larger category of "culture," and simply read it as one discourse among others (law, cartography, etc.) that together are seen to construct a national consciousness. This approach occasionally produces fascinating interconnections between different spheres of writing. A comprehensive study of such discourses, however, would imply nothing less than a complete anthropological and historical reinvention of the period under consideration. To offset the massiveness of such a task, scholars produce new ways of dividing culture into manageable chunks. Thus, for example, in *Forms of Nationhood*, Helgerson wisely chooses to focus on a specific generation: the generation of male writers born in England between 1551 and 1564. These men, he argues, are the men who "write" the nation. This approach necessarily takes for granted certain preconditions (political stability, a set of cultural institutions, etc.) that frame the ideological construction of nationhood. It presumes that the nation must already be somehow "there" before it is given form in language by a specific generation of writers.

My book shows that the privileging of a particular group as a kind of synecdoche of the larger problem of culture and nationhood is impossible for the student of France during the period. For whereas England enjoys a certain political stability, France undergoes a complete political and social collapse in the last years of the sixteenth century. French identity is always at risk during the Renaissance, never quite able to take coherent shape. One cannot "write" the French nation because, haunted as it is by discontinuity, violence, and fragmentation, it escapes representation. And it is over and against this fragmentation that one may grasp the ideological significance of the notion of literary form. For while literature may be just one discourse among many, it does provide a set of rhetorical strategies, formal conventions, and self-conscious play with fictionality that makes it a particularly important site for thinking about the fictions and mystifications that underpin the imagination of nationhood.

This book argues that community is represented in French Renaissance literature as a concept in danger. It is depicted chiefly through moments at which it is threatened by some enemy or stranger. Such threats to community are legible in literary texts at both the level of theme, and, more powerfully, the level of genre. The breakdown of community is also a breakdown of genre, a point at which literary conventions run up against the limits of their capacity to represent. In the works of such generically promiscuous writers as François Rabelais, Joachim Du Bellay, Marguerite de Navarre, and Michel de Montaigne, I argue, one may read the stakes of the struggle over community, as they stage the death of old literary forms and the birth of new ones. Thus literary discourse seeks to mediate a crisis of community through the production of new forms. On this level, this is a book about the ideological work done by literature in a particular set of political contexts.

But, in fact, the book traces out several interwoven trajectories. It provides a loosely chronological account of the relationship between literature and politics in the French Renaissance. Each chapter considers a different theoretical problem underpinning the representation of nationhood, from the definition of national character to the representation of territory. Moreover, the unfolding of the argument turns around a series of identity-threatening encounters between the French and the non-French—the Turks, the Americans, the Spanish, the Italians, the English. Finally, each chapter considers the relationship between an author of major influence and a particular ideological or political context. Through the exploration of these connections, the book seeks to articulate a model for thinking about the relationship between different literary genres and the literary construction of nationhood.

The crises of community on which I focus in this book often involve violence. On a thematic level, they feature scenes of torture, physical mutilation, madness, and confusion. The violence they depict is also linguistic, involving strange shifts in perspective, logical incongruities, and rhetorical exorbitance. I will be paying a great deal of attention to these moments of rhetorical energy, as a way of grasping the linguistic dimension of literary nationhood. Certainly, one can say that linguistic flux is a characteristic of Renaissance culture generally, from the puns in Thomas Wyatt and Shakespeare to the discussions between Don Quixote and Sancho Panza over the correct meaning of particular words and phrases. In the French tradition the linguistic exuberance of Renaissance literature has usually been seen either as a moment of exhilarating freedom before the fall into the constraints of *classicisme*, or as a mark of a more general "productivity" that seems to characterize all texts. Without denying the importance of either of these perspectives, I will be arguing that much of the linguistic violence of Renaissance French literature is deeply historical, that it is a symptom of the crisis of community that afflicts French culture more generally during the period. As such, I will be particularly attentive to the ways in which tropes, figures, and genres distort and transform the terms of ideological discourse, often in ways that cannot be accounted for by the study of authorial intention. I will be trying to trace the ways in which literature is caught in the paradoxical contingencies of its worldliness.

The trajectories offered by this book are presented with the goal of opening a new perspective on the formative moment in modern French literary culture, pointing to the ways in which literature both reflects and redefines collective identity. The project of reconsidering French literature in its relationship to different communities and nations has recently acquired a certain urgency. The pressure exerted on traditional notions of European national identity by the new Europe emerging after the Maastricht Treaty suggests the need for new ways of imagining literary and cultural history. The new Europe demands an account of French culture that would focus on the borders of France and the edges of French identity. It calls for approaches not generally exploited by either conventional French literary history or the traditional categories of comparative literature. What is required is a history of the cracks and fissures in European culture, of the seams that shape community. In fact, one might say that our own historical moment makes the study of myths and forms of community urgent indeed, since we seem to be living through a paradoxical overlapping of the affirmation and the destruction of national communities. It is clear that the nation-state is reaching the end of its history, and that the precise definition of any type of "grouphood," be it national or ethnic, is virtually impossible in a post-modern, racially mixed, global economy and culture. Yet we live at this very moment among increasingly violent Balkanizations, essentialist affirmations of group identity (often produced, understandably, against the leveling effects of globalization) sprinkled across both the political map and the cultural landscape. The texts studied here may alert us to some of the cultural forces that shape moments of paradox like our own.

T. H.

Berkeley, California

xiii

Acknowledgments

Since this is a book about the relationship between intellectual activity and its various contexts, it is a particular pleasure to thank the institutions, colleagues, and friends who have supported, encouraged, and challenged me during work on this project.

First, I would like to thank Bernhard Kendler and the staff of Cornell University Press for their expertise and courtesy during the publication process.

I would also like to thank the John Simon Guggenheim Foundation of New York, and the Humanities Sabbatical Supplement program of the University of California, Berkeley, for fellowship support.

Portions of the book have appeared in earlier (though now, in all cases, revised) forms, as articles in the following publications. A section of chapter 2 appeared in *Representations* 41 (1993): 58–82. Sections from chapter 4 appeared as "Examples, Stories, and Subjects in *Don Quixote* and the *Heptaméron*" in *Journal of the History of Ideas* 59, no. 4 (1993): 597–612 (© 1993 by the *Journal of the History of Ideas*, Inc.; reprinted by permission of the Johns Hopkins University Press), and as "On the Border: Politics, Genre, and Cultural Geography in the *Heptaméron*" in *Modern Language Quarterly* 57, no. 2 (1997): 517–44. Part of chapter 6 is reprinted by permission from the *Romanic Review* 18, no 2 (March 1997): 203–28, copyright by the Trustees of Columbia University in the City of New York, and also appeared in *The Project of Prose*, edited by Roland Greene and Elizabeth Fowler (Cambridge: Cambridge University Press, 1997), 80–103; reprinted by permission of Cambridge University Press. Permission to reuse this material is gratefully acknowledged.

My work on this book has benefited from support and criticism by colleagues, friends, and students in a number of contexts. First off, I want to thank my students, both graduate and undergraduate, in the Departments of French and Comparative Literature at Berkeley, who have helped me think through many of the problems engaged here. It has been a privilege to have such interlocutors. Colleagues in the Bay Area Pre- and Early Modern Studies Group and in the Townsend

Acknowledgments

Center for the Humanities at Berkeley listened to earlier versions of several chapters and offered good feedback. The members of my reading group, Katherine Bergeron, Robin Einhorn, Leslie Kurke, Celeste Langan, Michael Lucey, and Nancy Ruttenburg have generously commented on rough versions of much of this material with a combination of good spirits and intellectual rigor that is rare indeed. Albert Ascoli generously read the entire manuscript and provided important perspectives and corrections. Also at Berkeley, Paul Alpers and Victoria Kahn have offered valuable advice and critical commentary. And Louisa Mackenzie took precious time from her own dissertation work to prepare the bibliography and helped, both intellectually and materially, in numerous ways. Farther afield, I have been helped by insights and questions from colleagues at a number of universities. I would like specifically to thank Terence Cave, Lisa Freinkel, Andrea Frisch, Michael Harrawood, Constance Jordan, Ullrich Langer, Seth Lerer, Patricia Parker, and Timothy Reiss. Special thanks go to David Quint and François Rigolot for their friendship and guidance, and for many valuable suggestions and insights. At home, I have been constantly inspired by the patience, good humor, courage, and love of my wife, Jessica Levine, and by the sweet presence of my daughter, Emily Xiao-Mei Hampton, who arrived just in time to see this book finished.

*Literature and
Nation in the
Sixteenth
Century*

Chapter One

Garden of Letters:
Toward a Theory of Literary Nationhood

this best garden of the world,
Our fertile France . . .
—SHAKESPEARE, *Henry V*

Speaking Frankly

The first edition of Etienne Pasquier's *Les recherches de la France* appeared in 1562. The *Recherches* is a compendium of facts, legends, geographical descriptions, and anthropological minutiae about the customs and history of the French. Throughout his life Pasquier, who was a learned humanist and jurist and a friend of Montaigne's, would expand and revise his text until it filled several large volumes. A landmark of historical and ethnographic writing, the *Recherches* are the first modern scholarly study ever devoted to the French. The book begins slowly. Chapter 1 asserts the importance of the undertaking, gives a plan of what is to follow, and assures Pasquier's readers that he will not stuff his work with references to writers he has not read. Then, in chapter 2, he turns to his main topic, "our France," which he introduces by refuting the label of "barbarian" that writers from other countries have attached to the French. He is especially resentful of the Italians, who have a long tradition of cultural arrogance toward their neighbors to the north. Julius Caesar had once called the Gauls "light" (an epithet that sixteenth-century French writers return to bitterly again and again), and more recent Italian writers, from Petrarch to the historian Paolo Giovio, have scorned the French for their lack of refinement. To demonstrate both the misapprehensions of the Italians and the excellence of the French, Pasquier offers an anecdote (the first of the hundreds to appear throughout the work), in which he recalls a scene that originally appeared in the *Geography* of the Greek writer Strabo. Strabo recounts how Alexander the Great fought the Thracians and invaded the country of the Getae. There he was met by ambassadors from the Celts (or, as the Romans called them, the Gauls), who sought his friendship. Alexander

< *Garden of Letters* >

greeted these ambassadors with a question. As Strabo puts it, "The king received them kindly and asked them when drinking what it was that they most feared, thinking they would say himself, but . . . they replied that they feared no one, unless it were that Heaven might fall on them, although indeed they added that they put above everything else the friendship of such a man as he."[1]

For both Strabo and Pasquier the Gauls' reply to Alexander is a sign. In the language of the ancestors of the French both writers discern the trace of collective identity. For Strabo, that identity involves what one might call ethnicity; for Pasquier, it might be called national character. Yet the meaning of this sign of identity is far from clear. For Strabo, the Gauls' reply connotes their open character. It is one of a series of examples that he adduces to illustrate the "*haplótes*," or "straightforwardness" of barbarian peoples. "*Haplótes*" implies simplicity, unity, frankness, the coherence of something with itself. It is contrasted by Strabo with "*poikilia*," which the Greeks are depicted as having introduced into barbarian lands. "*Poikilia*" is rendered by most modern translations as "cunning," but it also connotes variegation, complexity, dissimulation, subtlety. The "*haplótes*" of the Gauls prefigures one of the commonplaces used by French writers to describe the French during the sixteenth century. This is the notion that the French are characterized by "frankness" or "franchise"—by honest virtue, which is frequently contrasted with the duplicity or sophistication of other national groups (again, principally the Italians). Such "frankness" is often linked through false etymology to the very name of the French or Françoys, as well as, in a famous pun, to the "frank" personality of the Valois king Francis I. Indeed, given Pasquier's own insistence at the outset of his book on his rejection of empty erudition and pretentious learning, the quality of "*haplótes*" might even extend to his own writing in the *Recherches*.

However, frankness may not always be as straightforward as it seems, especially in translation. Strabo's anecdote is retold by the Italian humanist Pietro Crinito in his *De honesta disciplina* of 1504, a series of exempla on moral and political themes. It is through Crinito, perhaps, that the anecdote comes down to Pasquier. At any rate, it is Crinito whom Pasquier mentions by name, as an example of Italian arrogance and stupidity, when he evokes the scene. Crinito recasts the exchange between Alexander and the Gauls as a warning to princes, and places emphasis on the Macedonian's foolish arrogance. In passing he suggests that the Gauls' response is a proof of barbarian

< *Garden of Letters* >

simplicity or "simpleness of mind" ("for they are men who are simple in mind and barbarian" ["ut homines sunt ingenio simplici atque barbari"]).[2] His translation of *"haplótes"* by "ingenio simplici" is what irks Pasquier. For Pasquier assumes that Crinito intends "simple in mind" to mean "idiotic." In fact, he enhances the mildly negative connotation of "ingenio simplici" by translating Crinito's own translation of *"haplótes"* as "lourdauds," that is, clumsy, rustic, maladroit:

> Crinito . . . thinks he has done his duty if, each time that he puts forward the name of the Gauls, he adds the surname of clumsy, or barbarian . . . These Gauls (says this Italian) like those who are naturally heavy, clipping the arrogant presumption of Alexander, answered only that they feared that this great vault of heaven might fall on their heads.

> [Crinit . . . à chaque propos penseroit avoir fait corvée, lorsqu'il met le nom des Gaulois en avant si d'une mesme suitte il ne l'accompagnoit d'un surnom ou de lourdaut, ou Barbare . . . Ces Gaulois (dit cet Italien) comme ceux qui de leur nature sont lourds, escornans l'outrecuidée presomption d'Alexandre, respondirent seulement qu'ils craignoient que ceste grand voulte du ciel tombast sur leurs testes.[3]]

If the Gauls are too light for Caesar, they also seem to be too heavy for Crinito. In Pasquier's mind, Crinito's depiction of the earliest French aims to ridicule them as slow-witted fools ("he, who in this passage imputes these words to clumsiness" ["luy, qui en ceste endroict nous impute ceste parole à la lourdise"]). The truth, however, he goes on, is that the Gauls' response was a brave gesture, a sign, not of idiocy, but of virtue: "we can see here a trace of the courage and magnanimity of our ancestors" ["nous pouvons descouvrir je ne scay quoy de la prouesse et magnanimité de nos ancestres"]. In fact, he continues, the response was a clever one, since, as even the Italians admit, it left the normally self-possessed Alexander completely confused.

All agree that the phrase uttered so long ago by the Gauls is an important and revealing statement, a sign, in effect, of some essence, of some "je ne sais quoi" (Pasquier's term) that is peculiarly French and that, like the phrase "je ne sais quoi" itself, defies translation. Yet it is an essence that appears to mutate according to the perceptions of the observer. For Strabo the Gauls' response connotes "straightforwardness." For Crinito, it signifies a "simplicity" that may be "simple-mind-

< *Garden of Letters* >

edness." For Pasquier, it is good classical virtue. What is more, in his insistence on the intelligence of the Gauls and their ability to "confuse" Alexander, Pasquier evokes another dimension of the scene, which he hints at but never pursues. This is the way the Gauls' answer suggests a kind of political sagacity, or craftiness. Because it confuses the powerful Alexander, this unexpected and unusual answer, like Hamlet's madness, may even be a kind of ploy, a stratagem employed by the weak and vulnerable to confound the strong. Yet if it is indeed a ploy, it is not a mark of "simplicity" or "frankness" at all, but an instance of the very cunning or "*poikilia*" that Strabo asserts is the characteristic of the Greeks, not the barbarians. Under the pressure of Crinito's translation of Strabo, Pasquier's gloss suggests that the Gauls' answer to Alexander means precisely the reverse of what Strabo says it means. Because he is struggling to make the Gauls *not* simple, Pasquier makes them more complicated than Strabo or he might want them to be.

Pasquier's attempt to define the essence of the Gauls is central to the ideological stakes of his own project. As one of the so-called "Politiques," a contingent of moderate, humanist-trained writers who sought to propose a "political" (that is, a civic and monarchic) solution to the religious conflicts that disrupted late sixteenth-century France, Pasquier is interested in writing a history that would be collective and national, instead of heroic and dynastic. For Pasquier, traditional models of history based on the great deeds of kings or families inevitably lend themselves to rhetorical exaggeration and falsification. Historians in the pay of the powerful cannot avoid distorting the facts. In contrast to such distortion, which evokes the rhetorical excesses of the French religious conflicts and the ceaseless, ideologically motivated, election of heroes and martyrs on both sides, Pasquier makes the "nation" the protagonist of his history. He locates the essence of France not in conquest and violence, but in institutions. Yet his difficulty in grappling with the ambiguities of the Gauls' response to Alexander shows the ways in which his project runs up against the limits of its own generic innovations. His claim that the Gauls' simple response signifies a kind of classic heroism suggests that any attempt to constitute a "nation" as the object of history must reduce a variegated community to a single essence—a kind of collective version of McAuliffe answering "nuts" to the Germans at the Battle of the Bulge or Admiral Farragut shouting "damn the torpedoes." Such a reduction not only draws inevitably on the rhetoric of the very

< *Garden of Letters* >

heroic history Pasquier is rejecting; it raises infinitely the political stakes of the interpretation of the past.[4]

Given his anxiety in the face of Crinito's gloss, it might be easy to write Pasquier off as just another in a long tradition of paranoid Frenchmen, from Roland to Charles de Gaulle. Yet the scene raises a number of issues which will inform the discussion to follow. Any consideration of communal identity must simultaneously address two problems: the question of the edge of the community, of its relationship to its borders, and the question of how centralized forms of power act on subjects to define the group's limits and distinguish it from its neighbors. Both of these issues are at play in the episode just analyzed, where an encounter with a potential enemy poses the problem of what, specifically, makes up the "essence" of the Gauls and binds them together. Of course, communities often define themselves through a relationship to some type of Other, or stranger.[5] However, these relations of alterity are never stable, and have their own history. Colette Beaune has shown that medieval French identity, and the very invention of the notion of the French "nation," was predicated on a persistent depiction, in the thirteenth and fourteenth centuries, of the English as threatening Other.[6] Yet in the Renaissance, with the onset of new forms of political centralization and increasing communication among national spaces, this fear of the Other becomes generalized, and is a persistent, though rarely analyzed, theme of virtually every major writer in the period. The moment of the encounter with non-French figures, be they Spanish, Turkish, Italian, Brazilian, Mexican, or English, functions as a point of departure for analyzing the ways in which French identity is configured. Thus, much of the focus of the later chapters in this book will be on moments at which major works of French Renaissance literature turn their attention to the relationship between French territory or community and the territory or community of rival groups. These moments of encounter with various Others offer sites at which the limits of community become legible. They provide a gauge for analyzing the representation of community in literature. Their presence in founding works of several major genres, and in the texts of the authors who shape the later history of French literature, locate them at the genesis of modern French literary culture.

Pasquier's reading of Crinito reading Strabo is a forgotten moment of intellectual history that might not be worth our attention were it not that Pasquier's text founds the long and rich tradition of writing

< *Garden of Letters* >

seeking systematically to "describe" France—from the literary projects of Michelet, Balzac, and Léo Mallet, to the films of Erich Rohmer, and such recent massive scholarly enterprises as Pierre Nora's *Les Lieux de Mémoire*, Pierre Bourdieu's *Distinction*, and Fernand Braudel's *The Identity of France*. The persistence of this tradition of systematic description—the notion that it is somehow possible to describe France exhaustively—and the fact that it seems to be a peculiarly French phenomenon, suggest its importance in any consideration of French culture. Pasquier's book shows that, from the very outset of this tradition, the attempt to define national identity faces a certain number of rhetorical dilemmas. The most obvious of these, as the Strabo anecdote suggests, is that the synecdochic logic of representation is already unstable, since the single sentence that is taken as the embodiment of a larger "character" depends upon an uneasy mix of metaphysical piety (fearing the gods) and political success (confusing Alexander)—two forms of activity that may or may not be equivalent. Yet even more interesting, in this case, is the way in which the famous trope of French "frankness" becomes paradoxical the moment it is depicted in action—for simplicity only becomes legible when it is expressed through words or deeds directed to an Other who is not "simple." Yet if it succeeds in impressing or confounding that Other (as it inevitably does), it begins to look suspiciously like cunning. In other words, the true essence of the French can only be identified by the non-French, yet at the moment it is seen, it dissolves. In this particular episode, furthermore, the instability of French identity is magnified by the fact that the relationship of alterity is doubled. It first involves the relationship between the Gauls and Alexander, and then, as Pasquier attempts to read that relationship, it extends to include his own antagonism toward Crinito. The Gauls and Alexander are a kind of allegorical prefiguration of Pasquier's relationship to powerful and arrogant Italians who look down their noses at the French. Yet whereas Strabo sees the Gauls as merely quaint, as defined merely by their difference from the overly subtle Greeks, Pasquier tries to build history on them. He wants to turn their contingent utterance into a mark of some invisible essence that can form the basis for a narrative linking present and past. However, in order to claim the Gauls' answer to Alexander, and to marshal their frankness for his own project, he must already acknowledge that frankness has many names, and that, in effect, it is rhetoric, not virtue, that defines the reputations of nations.

6

< *Garden of Letters* >

In 1517 Erasmus praised France's "supreme" power and integrity, noting that it was at peace with itself and "pure" in its religion, suffering from none of the impurities brought on by contact with such threatening Others as Jews (who, he says, "corrupt" Italy with commerce), Turks, or Marranos (who presumably threaten the unity of Spain).[7] And yet, sixteenth-century French writers are obsessed with borders and frontiers, with threatening enemies and aliens. Indeed, as Emmanuel Le Roy Ladurie has noted, the notion of the "vulnerability" of France is a recurring motif in French political writing from the end of the fifteenth century to the middle of the seventeenth, and in the pages below we shall see its persistence in literature.[8] I shall argue that it is through this obsession that the particularity of French nationhood in the Renaissance takes form. In contrast to the strongly institutional dimensions of both English and Spanish nationhood, which rely on processes of consolidation aimed at ridding these states of alien elements, the sense of France during this period is constructed dialogically, by engagement with what is alien.

On one level, the French concern with borders may be traced to the political and geographical situation of France itself at the onset of the modern age. France's central location in Western Europe, surrounded on all sides by hostile states and lacking the natural boundaries that set off the island state of England and the peninsulas of Iberia and Italy, meant that the question of the integrity and definition of France had to be constantly addressed by the French throne through treaties and agreements with all manner of allies. The first attempts by Charles VIII, Louis XII, and, later (and more aggressively), by Francis I to centralize political power and unify France brought with them a whole sequence of border skirmishes, annexations, negotiations, and military standoffs. Beginning in the mid fifteenth century, the concrete political domination of the court of "France" over other ducal and regional powers (principally Burgundy) involved the domination and annexation of a number of regional spaces, from Roussillon and Cerdagne in the south to Brittany in the north. Later, at the turn of the sixteenth century, the focus shifted to Italy, with the French making incursions into the peninsula, all the while entering into a complicated set of treaties with, among others, the English, the German princes, and the Turks. With the onset of religious conflict in the later decades of the century, there was increasing concern about the influence of rival states such as England and Spain backing either Protestant or Catholic factions and

< *Garden of Letters* >

threatening the territorial integrity of France. Throughout this period, French foreign policy was characterized by an aggressive expansionism that makes France the dominant paradigm of state-building during the period—both for contemporary observers and for later historians of nationalism.[9] Neither the politically decentralized space of Italy, nor the geographically and politically centralized spaces of England or Spain, France is engaged in a constant dialogue between center and periphery, between identity and alterity.

Meanwhile, the principles of internal coherence that defined France were themselves undergoing a violent transformation. France was perhaps unique in the century in living the religious disruptions brought on by the Reformation as full-scale political catastrophe. Medieval France had articulated its unity through the promotion of the unique status of the Gallican church, as rival to Papal authority. The Gallican image of the French king as "Most Christian" ("Roy Très Chrestien"), and the ideal of a unified nation marked by a single faith, law, and king ("Une Foy, une Loy, une Roy") were exploded by the onset of Protestantism and the processes of political centralization undertaken by the Valois. Political exigency and, on occasion, personal conviction found the king at odds with the faith of many of his subjects, and the role of law as a mediation between subject and king had to be redefined. The relationship between king, faith, and law became precisely the issue in struggles over communal identity, as writers sought to determine how these three traditional components of French identity might fit together. The crisis produced the genesis of the modern secular nation-state. With the repression of Protestantism by the monarchy, Protestants tended to turn their allegiance to the "nation," which they set in opposition to the abuses of the "Catholic monarch." Toward the end of the century, the eventual rejection of the Catholic extremism of the Guise family by the monarchy led Catholics to carry out the same shift of allegiance, leaving the Guises isolated, as the "servants" of Spain. Thus, as Hugh Seton-Watson writes, "at the accession of Henri IV both Catholics and Protestants claimed to be fighting for the nation: national unity was being treated as a greater good than religious truth."[10]

The modern notion of "nationalism" is essentially an invention of the Enlightenment.[11] By contrast, the sense of literary "nationhood" that I explore in this study constitutes a kind of pre-history of the national. If nationalism implies a communal existence based on (in Re-

< *Garden of Letters* >

nan's famous formulation) "a spiritual principle," then nationhood, in the sense in which I understand it here, may be seen to concern itself with the material origins of that spirituality.[12] If nationalism is produced out of the idea that individual identity is shaped and given purpose by a concept of community of which a common language is the medium, territory the seat, and shared character the stimulus, the history of nationhood, as a pre-history of nationalism, might be said to involve the struggle to determine language, space, and character, and to define their interaction. My concern is the *literary* (as contrasted with the historiographical, institutional, or iconographic) construction of nationhood. And in literature, this struggle may be traced by studying the representation of community. The literary sense of nationhood involves the way in which literary texts register the conflicts between the different models of community that compete in the emergence of the nation-state, and the different representational practices that accompany those models. The most influential texts of sixteenth-century French literature are themselves explorations of the nature of collective experience, from the expansive narratives of Rabelais, through the dialogues on community in Marguerite de Navarre's *Heptaméron*, to the "civic" consciousness of such poets as Louise Labé, the coterie culture of the Pléiade, the partisan theological rhetoric of d'Aubigné, and the failed "national" epic project of Ronsard's unfinished *Franciade*. Indeed, even Montaigne's *Essais*, that most "self-centered" of books, is also, as scholars of Montaigne have only recently begun to show in detail, a vast meditation on the politics and social fabric of France, and on how different forms of collective experience overlap and conflict in their construction of subjectivity. One of the tasks of the following chapters will be to trace how literary discourse registers the shifts of language and representation that accompany the large political realignments marking the century. For, as the Pasquier anecdote suggests, any attempt to define or describe the relationships linking myths of national identity must raise issues of representation, rhetoric, and authority, because the myths themselves are expressed in literature. The imaginative writing that we moderns call literature emerged, in its secular form, at the same time as the political struggles sketched above. French political culture and French literary culture grew up together. However, what has been less noticed and analyzed by literary historians is the extent to which the emergence of secular literary culture is intertwined with political crisis and, in many ways, presents itself as a response to it.

< *Garden of Letters* >

This book traces the process by which the shifting languages of "community" and "nation" in a tumultuous political sphere not only provide content for literary discourse, but are shaped by the forms of its expression.

In our own time, Richard Rorty has suggested that communities can be thought of as shared vocabularies, as sets of terms that make discussion possible. At moments of rapid change, these vocabularies are placed in question. "Progress, for the community as for the individual," writes Rorty, "is a matter of using new words as well as of arguing from premises phrased in old words."[13] In early modern Europe, this takes the form of a complex intertwining of a language reflecting personal alliance and vassalage with a language structured around the common experience of membership in an emerging nation-state.[14] The overlapping of communities produces overlapping vocabularies. Rorty's formulation has resonance for the work of the Savoyard political philosopher Claude de Seyssel. In his *Monarchy of France*, written in 1515 and dedicated to Francis I, Seyssel praises the uniqueness of France among nations, singling out its institutional organization and the strength of the three estates that structure French society. This seemingly traditional praise is surprising in the way it reconfigures the vocabulary of statecraft. Whereas traditional thinkers had used the notion of "three estates" to indicate the clergy, the nobility, and the burgers, Seyssel asserts that the clergy is an element of each of the other three estates, which he then designates as rich (*gras*), middle class (*moyen*), and poor (*peuple menu*). Seyssel uses precisely the same "old words" evoked by Rorty, but redefines them. In the process he opens the way toward an incipient vision of France as a collection of social classes and shifts the institutional importance of the clergy into a supporting role.

Seyssel's text has interesting parallels with another description of French uniqueness written some twenty years later by the Florentine expatriate poet Luigi Alamanni, an important cultural presence at the Valois court. In his immense georgic "La Coltivazione," written in the 1530s and dedicated to Francis I, Alamanni praises France as a land of peace, in which all the people, specifically the nobles and the peasants, are united by a spiritual bond: "in charity joined/The richest lords and the ignoble plebes/Live together, each keeping his own fortune/Without harm to the other" [" 'n carità congiunti,/I piû ricchi signor, l'ignobil plebe/Viverse insieme, ritenendo ognuno/Senza oltraggio d'altrui le sue fortune"].[15] Alamanni bases French identity on

< *Garden of Letters* >

the spiritual bond of "charity." Yet he seems to conceive of charity as a spiritual bond that is manifested in secular political and social terms. Love of one's neighbor here suggests a love of one's neighbor's status, a simple lack of covetousness, a kind of acceptance of the same social roles described by Seyssel.

Both Seyssel and Alamanni describe France in a language that evokes traditional forms of community. Seyssel's description draws on the language of allegiance and vassalage that characterizes late-medieval political discourse. Alamanni deploys the theological vocabulary of Christian charity, which involves loving one's neighbor as a way of loving God. Yet both of these writers endorsed and supported Francis I's attempts to centralize French politics, and both seem to gesture, from within their conventional language, toward a model of political organization based more on modern political contract than traditional vassalage. Both seem to be groping for a way of expressing new forms of collective experience from within a vocabulary rooted in institutions that were either disappearing or becoming increasingly hard to define. This lexical fluidity reflects a larger shift which, I will argue, marks literary representations of community in Renaissance France. Alamanni's use of the word "charity" to describe political relations reflects a general tendency among early French humanists, often under the influence of Erasmus, to conceive of political organization in the vocabulary of the New Testament, as a community bonded by charity, implying an inclusive, at times almost egalitarian, regard for one's neighbor. However, as the century unfolded, political conflict within Europe and increasingly frequent encounters with cultures from outside of Europe placed in question the usefulness of Christian charity for describing collective experience. In the face of threatening strangers, charity shows its limits. In place of this theological vocabulary, new vocabularies emerged—economic, courtly, ethical—that found their ways into the discourse of literature and helped shape literary texts, not only thematically, but rhetorically and generically as well. New relations of identity and difference require new words, new images of the body and community, new forms of representation.

Speaking French

Historians of collective experience in early modern Europe conventionally distinguish between two objects of study. On the one hand, there is the history of the set of images, myths, and practices shared

< *Garden of Letters* >

by those born in the same community or region. This sense of "nationhood" is suggested by the etymological connection of "nation" to the Latin *nascor* (to be born). The vagueness of this definition reaffirms what Pasquier's text has already hinted at: that any precise definition of "nation" is always shifting and transitional. Indeed, in the sixteenth century the term described everything from students at the University of Paris (organized into various nations), to speakers of given languages, to those who shared a certain set of customs, to geographical territory. It is in contrast to this shifting terrain that historians frequently define the centralizing processes of the "state" or of "state building," which impose new forms of power and organization on traditional communities. More than one influential account of the emergence of modern political organization understands it to be a process whereby the second of these two forces (the emerging state) overwhelms and appropriates elements of the first (the traditional community of the nation), which it then reinvents in its own image.[16]

This process of reinvention has important consequences for the language of literature. Writing of the emergence of what he calls the "nation form" (that is, the modern nation-state as a structure) Etienne Balibar stresses the way in which the pre-history of nationalism includes a number of phenomena and events that imply no connection whatsoever to what we now think of as the nation-state. Rather, they often occurred in the context of such non-national structures as the city-state or the empire, and only later became constitutive of the nation-state:

> The fact remains that all these events, on condition they are repeated or integrated into new political structures, have effectively played a role in the genesis of national formations. This has precisely to do with their institutional character, with the fact that they cause the state to intervene in the form which it assumed at a particular moment. In other words, non-national state apparatuses aiming at quite other (for example, dynastic) objectives have progressively produced the elements of the nation-state or, if one prefers, they have been involuntarily 'nationalized' and have begun to nationalize society [*sic*].[17]

For Balibar, the power of the "nation form" exists in the way it appropriates forces not properly its own and turns them to its own purposes. Practically, this involves such phenomena as the "institutionalization" of Roman law or the domestication of the feudal aristocracies

< *Garden of Letters* >

(two of Balibar's examples of this process). The ideology of the nation-state then rewrites or reinterprets these past events and discourses as inevitable steps in a narrative of the nation-state's own genesis. The nation-state, then, seems to be constructed out of energy refracted from other, theological, dynastic, or civic struggles.

To say that nationalist ideology takes past events and turns them into constitutive elements of its own narrative is another way of saying that nationalist ideology allegorizes the events it appropriates. Just as kings and battles of the Old Testament are retrospectively transformed by allegorical Biblical exegesis into figures of Christian fulfillment, so does the nation-state pry "pre-national" events loose from local or municipal struggles to give them histories they never knew they had. Indeed, Henri Lefebvre makes a point similar to Balibar's when he notes that the emergence of national states and empires brings a "general metaphorization" of space, where figural expressions such as "reason of state" mask the displacement of specificities, places, and localities.[18] And yet, as any reader of the history of Biblical typology knows, one of the obstacles the allegorization of history constantly faces is the tendency of signs, texts, and events to retain traces of their original identities, the vestiges of their historical roots. Similarly, new national identity is forged out of earlier identities, which nonetheless leave their traces—as a kind of resistance—in the text. As I shall show, this resistance is felt in literature as a problem of language, and specifically of figural language. The traces of earlier identities find expression as the stubborn persistence of a literal meaning that contrasts with and calls into question the figurations that give shape to the emerging nation-state. This linguistic resistance works to expose the violence inherent in figuration, and in the nationalist project itself. The new community of the modern nation state thus comes at the expense of some earlier community or shared sense of identity. Literature measures the costs of this transition.

One can see this process at work in the writing of the most important French poet of the early sixteenth century, Clément Marot. In 1526, in one of the most disturbing episodes of his adventurous life, Marot was imprisoned in the Châtelet. The charge was that he had "eaten lard during Lent." Since this activity was by no means a usual pretext for imprisonment, scholars have seen in the official charge a disguised reference to some other, probably more personal, vendetta against the poet. After his release, Marot composed a poem, the "Enfer" ("Hell") in which he recounts his experience. The poem depicts

< *Garden of Letters* >

the poet at the mercy of various lawyers, figured as "demons" of the underworld. It draws on traditions of anti-legal satire current in late medieval literature; one sees similar dismay about the obscurantism of lawyers in Rabelais. Yet since it is precisely the excellence of the same French judiciary satirized by Marot that is often celebrated by apologists of the reign of Francis I (like Seyssel) as one of the signs of the excellence of France, I would like to look at the issues Marot's poem raises issues about the relationship between the subject and juridical power.

At the center of the "Enfer," Marot is asked by the infernal judge Minos to identify himself, tell his estate and the place of his birth. He names himself by evoking Virgil, whose family name of Maro is recalled by Marot's own surname. He then offers praise of the king, Francis I, the patron of arts and letters, whom he calls a new Maecenas. He points out how Francis has transformed the very cultural soil of France, once dessicated and barren, into a veritable literary paradise: "The beautiful, abundant, orchard of letters,/Reproduces for us its flowers in clusters/[Flowers] once faded and dry/By the cold wind of ignorance" ["Le beau verger des lettres plantureux/Nous reproduit ses fleurs à grandes jonchées/Par ci-devant flétries et séchées/Par le froid vent d'ignorance"].[19] The idea of the "rebirth of learning", a cliché of Renaissance humanism, is here applied to France itself, the history of which is split in two, between the flourishing present and a barren past.

This horticultural language, however, is then repeated, a moment later, in a more striking depiction of a somewhat different orchard. Marot speaks longingly of his place of birth, Cahors, in Quercy, in the southwest of France, which he describes as a site of temperate climate, filled with fruit and flowers. And it was from the garden of Cahors that Marot was taken as a child by his father, the court poet Jean Marot, to lead the hard life of the itinerant poet. The ancestral home of Quercy rhymes ironically with the depiction of the court as the site of longing ("pour venir querre icy"[v. 395]), and the "thousand fruits" of Cahors give way to the thousand miseries of the courtier's life.[20]

What is striking about this moment of self-definition is the contrast that it sets up between two models for understanding the poet's relationship to his country and his past. The metaphorical "orchard" or "garden" of letters is a trope of royal propaganda, a sign of the entire operation of centralization undertaken by Francis I to form a unified France. Yet at the very moment he evokes this royal allegory,

< *Garden of Letters* >

Marot leaves it to recall a garden that seems to interest him much more—the land of his youth. The contrast between the two gardens is bridged by Marot himself, whose life is split, like that of France, into a "before" and an "after," between a youthful identification with the south and the mature life of an itinerant court poet who adorns the king's new garden of letters. The pairing of the two garden images reveals the uneven prision of the trope of royal power on the subject.

The garden image is of course a cliché for describing France. Like all clichés, its meaning is heavily over-determined. Colette Beaune has shown that the image goes deep into the Middle Ages, where it was linked to the notion that France was the most Christian of nations, "the Garden of Christ, where all virtues bloomed."[21] This allegorical tradition, moreover, becomes intertwined with the traditional medical discourse that asserts a link between climates and human temperaments. Thus, Robert Gaguin, often called the first French Renaissance humanist, stresses in a letter to Carolo Sacco of 1472 that the difference between the Spanish and the French stems from differences in climate. Whereas the Spanish are choleric because of the dry climate in which they live, the mildness of the French climate, he notes, makes of France a garden, filled with innumerable fruits ("Gallie fructus . . . numerem pene innumerabiles"), and of its people a well balanced group.[22] This image achieved great currency in the fifteenth century, as the French strove to distinguish themselves from more aggressively mercantile groups such as the Italians.

Of course, the figure of the garden is not applied only to France during this period. Everyone wants to conceive of his country as naturally fertile: Shakespeare's *Richard II* famously compares the state to a garden, and Jean Lemaire de Belges' poetic reflection on the differences between France and Italy, the *Concorde des Deux Langages* (1511), plays on the image of Florence as the seat of flowers. Yet the figure of the garden is widely recognized as central to French communal identity and to the relationship between community and land, and the pertinence of the image as a figure for France seems to have been widely accepted internationally. This is demonstrated most authoritatively by Shakespeare, that great master of cultural clichés, who, in *Henry V* (a play centrally concerned with the issues of borders and communities that will be our focus as well), has Burgundy describe France as "this best garden of the world,/Our fertile France" (V.2.36), and then repeats the image in the play's Epilogue, where he laments the later English loss of "the world's best garden."[23]

< Garden of Letters >

Obviously, there is no room here to attempt a complete taxonomy of the uses of the figure of the garden at the close of the Middle Ages, from literary depictions of the *locus amoenus* to the iconography of the *hortus conclusus* and the uses of "garden" and "field" to describe collections of poetry.[24] Indeed, the history of the image is specifically not our concern. What is important for our purposes, however, is the way in which Marot's manipulation of the figure raises issues about the status of French identity and the relationship of literature to politics in the sixteenth century. Indeed, Marot's notion of an "orchard" or "garden" of *letters* draws upon a tradition different from those just mentioned. The image comes from Tacitus's *Dialogue on Oratory*, where rhetoric in the state is compared to a plant in a field. While it is unlikely that Marot ever read Tacitus, the parallel between the public sphere and the garden in which "flowers of rhetoric" bloom is a humanist commonplace. In this context, the connection between the two images, between rhetoric as garden and France as garden, may be linked to the ideology of the Valois monarchy. The garden image mediates between Francis's role as "patron of letters" and his political power.[25] One finds the parallel in many forms and contexts. Hugues Salel writes an allegorical poem on the illness of Francis I's son in which he expands the moral and political implications of the image, giving the monarch voice as the *"Jardinier Françoys"* tending his *"jardin gallicque."*[26] Luigi Alamanni's georgic, "La Coltivazione," mentioned earlier, is built around the same conceit, with the prince as eloquent gardener, and his subjects as well tended plants. The Lyonnais humanist doctor Symphorien Champier links politics, culture, and horticulture in praising the new cultural fertility of France at the outset of his *Hortus Gallicus*, of 1533, a book that purports to show how all of the medicinal herbs of the East mentioned in the writings of the ancients have their counterparts in France. For Champier, the metaphorical image of rhetoric as flower is re-literalized, as it were; transplanting flowers becomes translating empire, and vice versa.[27]

Marot's fusion of the traditional image of France as garden with the Tacitean humanist description of political rhetoric recalls Balibar's claim that the nation-state defines itself by appropriating material from other contexts and redefining it in its own terms. Here, a discourse that is traditionally both theological and climatological becomes a trope of royal ideology. Yet it is precisely on the level of trope that Marot resists this appropriation. For the contrast he sets up between the two gardens defines the relationship between subjectivity

< *Garden of Letters* >

and political ideology as a question of figuration. The tension between Marot's home of Quercy and "France" is the tension between figural language and literal language, between a metaphorical "garden of letters" that transmits French royal propaganda and the "real" personal garden (though perhaps no less idealized) of childhood memory. That is, the garden of Quercy can be visited and strolled through; the "garden of letters" cannot. The image of the garden stands as the battle ground between an official version of French history and geography, and the personal memory of the uprooted subject. In this context, Marot's description may be seen as a reflection on rhetoric and power, on the way in which the language of the king inscribes itself on the land and its inhabitants. Marot's frustrated depiction of his own suffering (however much he may have generally approved of and profited from Francis I's cultural politics in other ways) sets up a confrontation between two types of rhetoric: between rhetoric as a tool of power, and rhetoric as a constitutive element in the imaginative writing that we call literature. As royal ideology appropriates the tropes of "Frenchness," literature redoubles and parodies that ideology. The poet's very authority as one of the flowers in the new garden lends him the rhetorical power to express his own misery.

Marot's use of the garden image suggests a conceptual nexus for exploring the *literary* dimension of the emergence of the nation-state described above by Balibar. The figure of the flower not only relates to images of France; it is a traditional figure for rhetoric itself, and is central in the history of the self-conscious figurations that we call literature. The image of the "garden of letters" thus figures a particular tension in the relationship between politics and literature—a tension that we will see in a variety of guises throughout this book. Its importance stems from the way it figures forth the intertwining of a "national" collective identity (already hinted at in the Pasquier scene analyzed earlier) and the self-conscious play of literary rhetoric. National ideology involves the construction of a collective identity, a "garden," in language. Yet the very flowers it deploys are simultaneously the tools of a literary rhetoric constantly reinventing community in ways that may have nothing to do with emerging nationhood. Indeed, to push the argument a step further, the image of the garden might even be said to contain within its many late-medieval and Renaissance shapes one of the paradoxes of the representation of community. If the representation of community, as noted earlier, involves

< *Garden of Letters* >

both the question of how power binds together disparate subjects with myths of identity and the question of how borders distinguish one community from another, one might wonder whether the garden of France is a *locus amoenus*, a temperate space in which all subjects share a character "naturally" produced by climate, or whether it is a *hortus conclusus*, a walled space defined only by its difference from enemies. To be sure, the tension between these models informs considerations of French identity in the Renaissance.

To stress the linguistic dimension of these issues, one might consider Marot's assertion, a moment later, that, upon leaving Quercy, he was obliged to give up his native dialect (or "mother tongue") and learn the tongue of the king: "Not yet ten, I was brought to France/There where, since, I have travelled so much/That I forgot my maternal language/And badly learned the paternal tongue,/The French tongue, esteemed in the great courts."[28] The opposition here between the maternal and the paternal confirms the distance between the literary and the political, establishing the gendered contrast between a "female" nation and a "male" state organization that will become a commonplace for later writers on nationhood. Here, moreover, the description of these domains in terms of different tongues underscores the sense that the use of language is a form of resistance between two zones of experience.

The irony here is that Marot's "wandering" is itself a complex and politically significant activity. He depicts himself leaving home and mother to follow his father, the court poet Jean Marot, who seems to have led an itinerant life, finding employment in several different ducal courts. By the time of Marot's own maturity, however, he has become attached to the court of Francis I, which itself "wanders" through France. Yet the mobility of the French court (which contrasts with the more sedentary models of kingship in Spain and England) was by design a strategy for unifying the country and affirming Valois authority. Thus, between the generation of Jean Marot and that of his son, the poet's itinerance becomes the mark, not of the fragmented nature of France, but of a strategy of political centralization. It is in this "wandering," Marot goes on to tell us, that he has mastered French, "[I learned] my French, which has finally become somewhat polished,/By following the King Francis, first of that name."[29] Following his father turns into following his king. Wandering with the court gives Marot the French language, the very medium he uses to express his anguish at what he has lost. And indeed, even

< *Garden of Letters* >

as Marot depicts the tension between personal history and collective (in this case, political) identity through a contrast between two types of language, literal and figural, he also links the two gardens. He makes them part of the same conceptual space through narrative, through the story of his own life. What the rhetoric of royal ideology severs—the relationship between individual experience and "official" history—Marot attempts to reconnect. This double strategy underscores the importance of what Homi K. Bhabha has called, following Volosinov, the "hybrid" nature of ideologies of nationhood.[30] That is, even as nation-states construct narratives of their genesis and rise, they simultaneously produce rhetorics of forgetfulness, strategies for excluding events, meanings, and people who don't fit the myth of community. The image of the garden figures both royal propaganda and personal tragedy; it simultaneously praises the cultural politics of the monarchy and empties that praise of its power. This duality is part of the literariness of Marot's text, and we will see it repeated, in different forms and by different authors, in the chapters to follow. The surplus value in this literary gesture might not serve the ideological needs of the court. But it might, in another register, be productive of nationhood.

Speaking Naturally

Benedict Anderson has argued that one of the preconditions for the emergence of nationalism, in its modern form, is the definition of discrete vernaculars, which emerge in the Renaissance to mark out national identities below, as it were, the universal culture of Latinity, and above the limited language worlds of local dialect. Anderson points out that national vernaculars were originally administrative languages, connected to courtly elites but owing their diffusion and thus their nationalizing effects to the rise of print capitalism.[31] To be sure, scholars of France have long insisted on the importance of the vernacular as a unifying feature of French political, social, and cultural life. Francis I's edict of Villers-Cotteret in 1539, which made French the official organ of juridical and fiscal activity, is often taken as a classic example of the imposition of centralized power "from above," as the first of the many linkings of political power and language that characterize French history.

However, here, a consideration of the specifically *literary* dimension of the rise of a national language can open perspectives not available to cultural or institutional history. The domain of the literary,

< *Garden of Letters* >

through the rise of new forms of authorship and new genres, is where the dignity of the vernacular is affirmed, and where the most enduring (and presumably profitable) products of print culture are generated. It is in fact impossible to trace the immediate impact of official gestures like the edict of Villers-Cotteret on collective experience. Literature, by contrast, mediates the encounter between administrative vernaculars and everyday language in ways that can be analyzed with some specificity.

Certainly, Marot's claim that his journey from Quercy to "France" has entailed the replacement of his "maternal" patois by "French, esteemed in the great courts," points to the intertwining of the emergence of the French vernacular with the definition of new forms of authorship and new types of political community. Indeed, his reference to "the great courts" in the plural form, evokes the still fragmented topography of a France divided into duchies, even as it acknowledges the French language as a potentially unifying element. Yet the proximity of Marot's lament about language to his complaint about the loss of his "garden" homeland suggests that the literary construction of nationhood encompasses both the question of how figural language functions in political rhetoric (in this case, the trope of the garden), and the politics of the emergence of the vernacular. Or, to be more precise, it concerns the ways in which figuration affirms the authority of the emerging vernacular, even as the emerging vernacular deploys its own resources to shape new images of community.

One can begin to grasp the stakes of these linguistic questions by turning briefly to Joachim Du Bellay's treatise on French poetry and language, the *Deffence et Illustration de la Langue Françoyse* (1549), one of the major documents of the emergence of vernacular languages in Europe. Toward the end of the first half of the *Deffence*, Du Bellay considers a question raised also by Pasquier and Marot—the question of the relationship between the newly emergent "national" culture of modern France and its predecessors. Du Bellay states the problem in more classically humanist terms than do the other writers, by asking whether the moderns can equal the ancients. He recalls several important inventions of antiquity, and compares them with such then recent developments as the printing press and gunpowder to suggest that the moderns are fully capable of doing excellent things. This judgment leads him to propose that the French language can be as accomplished and as beautiful as Greek and Latin, not only in the ideas it expresses, but also in its sound. "As for sound, and I

< *Garden of Letters* >

know not what natural sweetness (as it is called) resides in their tongues, we have no less of it, according to the most delicate ears. It is true that we follow the conditions set up by nature, which has only given us a tongue to speak with" ["Quant au son, et je ne sais quelle naturelle douceur (comme ils disent) qui est en leurs langues, je ne vois point que nous l'ayons moindre, au jugement des plus délicates oreilles. Il est bien vrai que nous usons du préscrit de nature, qui pour parler nous a seulement donné la langue"].[32] And there follows a whole list of similes that describe the languages of other nations through a series of caricatures. The French, we are told, don't vomit their words "from the stomach, like drunkards," they don't strangle them in their throats, "like frogs," they don't cut them off at the palate, "like birds," and so on. If such distortions are what constitute the sweetness of languages, he concludes, French is indeed rough and ugly.[33]

This is one of the few passages in the *Deffence* that met with the approval of Du Bellay's most stringent critic. Soon after the publication of the *Deffence*, Du Bellay's ideas were savagely attacked by the Lyonnais writer Barthélemy Aneau, in his "Quintil Horatien." Aneau criticizes virtually every aspect of the *Deffence*, from the way Du Bellay identifies himself to his theories about culture. In Aneau's consideration of this passage, he corrects Du Bellay's claim that nature has given us only a tongue with which to speak by citing writers who mention other organs as well. But he goes on to say that, "The part which follows," that is, Du Bellay's discussion of French pronunciation ("la ronde parole Française") and his caricatures of how others speak, is "very good," since it evokes other nations without naming them ("notant les nations sans les nommer"). "There," concludes Aneau, "I recognize you for a good Frenchman" ["Là je te reconnais bon Français"].[34]

Literary history has concurred with Aneau in recognizing Du Bellay as a "good Frenchman," and making his verse a cornerstone of French patriotism to this very day. Indeed, Aneau's praise underscores the importance of this moment in the *Deffence*. Du Bellay takes as his general premise the idea that French culture is weak, and that its greatness lies ahead of it. In fact, this is the only feature of French culture in the book that Du Bellay sees as a current strength. Here, at the point where Aneau "recognizes" Du Bellay as a "good Frenchman," Du Bellay's text defines a model of French identity. Given his humanist training it is not surprising that Du Bellay first compares the

< *Garden of Letters* >

French to the Greeks and Romans. However, the movement of the passage takes us from a comparison between moderns and ancients to a contrast between French and various types of "non-French" speech, from diachronic to synchronic binarisms. This shift from history to alterity is effected through a play on the word "langue," or "tongue," which is first taken to refer to the languages of the Greeks and Romans ("leurs langues"), and then to a particular body part ("pour parler [nature] . . . nous a seulement donné la langue"), which introduces the caricatures of the bodily function of speech among other peoples. Diachronically, this shift from one meaning of "tongue" to the other produces a narrative link between the French and the Greeks; synchronically, it makes possible the satirical jibes at the "bodily speech" of neighboring nations. The pun on "tongue" locates "Frenchness" through a play of both identity (diachronic) and difference (synchronic). It connects an "essential" trait (the ability of the French to produce sweet sounds) to a satirical rejection of all non-French nations. Even as the pun takes us from language as collective social institution to language as corporeal trait, it defines all other nations as grotesques who speak through the wrong body parts. Yet at the same time the movement of the passage mystifies the true genesis of French identity. And to glimpse that mystification one must read the movement of the passage, as it were, backwards. After all, Du Bellay has no firsthand knowledge of how the Greeks and Romans spoke (as he readily admits). All he has experienced is the speech of other contemporary Europeans. It is from his rejection of these Others that he constructs his version of the essential beauty of French, which is then connected, through the pun on "langue," to the glory of the ancients. As in the Pasquier anecdote, the natural essence of the French may be nothing but the sum of a series of differences. Yet whereas Pasquier's attempt to locate that essence in a single phrase leads to ambiguity, Du Bellay seeks to ground it in nature through a pun linking body and language.[35]

Du Bellay's irenic assertion of the importance of the body in defining the relationship between language, history, and community takes on its fullest resonance if it is paired with a somewhat different treatment of the same topic, some twenty years earlier, in Rabelais's *Pantagruel* (1532). Whereas Du Bellay is interested in the problem of defining Frenchness in contrast to other national groups, Rabelais confronts the question of the emergence of a unified French language community out of discrete regional identities. Chapter six of *Panta-*

< *Garden of Letters* >

gruel bears the heading, "How Pantagruel Met a Limousin Who Counterfeited the French Language" ["Comment Pantagruel rencontra un Limosin qui contrefaisoit le langaige Françoys"].[36] Here, Rabelais depicts the young prince (Pantagruel) on a walk with his friends outside the walls of Paris. They meet a young student from the Limousin region, who responds to Pantagruel's greetings in an affected Latinate French (or Frenchified Latin) mimicking the jargon of Parisian intellectuals. Pantagruel fails to understand the boy's answers, and curses at him, muttering that he is a "sorcerer," and a "heretic." When the boy persists in his jargon, Pantagruel threatens him outright: "You skin Latin," he says, "by Saint John, I'll make you skin the fox; for I'll skin you alive" ["Tu eschorches le latin; par sainct Jean, je te feray eschorcher le renard, car je te eschorcheray tout vif"]. And he picks him up by the throat—at which point the young man cries for help in his native dialect and soils his pants in fear. "Now you speak naturally," ["A ceste heure parles tu naturellement"], says Pantagruel, throwing him down in disgust.[37]

It may not be by accident that Pantagruel swears by Saint John, who began his Gospel with the phrase "In the beginning, was the Word"—for the student's crimes seem to be both that he is out of place, and out of language. Pantagruel says that he "counterfeits" being a Parisian; on one level, then, he is a pretentious provincial who has the temerity to pretend to be from the capital. Yet we are also told (in the chapter title) that he "counterfeits" French and (by Pantagruel) that he "skins" Latin. Indeed, it is impossible to tell whether what he is speaking is a kind of French or a kind of Latin. Neither normal French nor normal Latin are ever uttered by him, and he seems to move between a provincial language space of which he is ashamed, and a rarefied jargon which he has affected. When Pantagruel casts the boy as a "heretic" and a "sorcerer," turning a harmless student into a figure worthy of the stake, one cannot know whether it is social temerity or linguistic abuse that is at issue. Would it be all right for him to speak jargon if he were a "real" Parisian? Should he simply admit that he is a provincial? Could he save himself by speaking either good French or good Latin? None of these questions is answered, but none is excluded. By making them all possible but leaving them all open, the scene asks us to think about the relationship between language, power, and territory.

Here, as in Du Bellay, language is corporeal. Just as Du Bellay links the the sweetness of the "round French word" and French dig-

< *Garden of Letters* >

nity to French tongues, so here do excrement and the Limousin dialect come forth at the same moment, and it is impossible to know which of them Pantagruel has in mind when he says that the boy now speaks "naturally." Moreover, the relationship of language and body involves that dimension of language which I analyzed earlier in Marot—the power of rhetorical figures. "Skinning Latin," the charge leveled against the Limousin by Pantagruel, recalls an idiom whereby those who used Latin incorrectly were said to "skin" it. Because he "skins" Latin, the boy is forced to "skin the fox," a popular expression for vomiting. When Pantagruel threatens to skin the student and make the student skin the fox for skinning Latin he moves between language and body. He takes a corporeal metaphor applied to language ("skinning Latin") and violently applies it back to the body.[38]

This linking of rhetorical figuration to the body suggests that proper linguistic usage is the mediator connecting language and national community. Indeed, perhaps the greatest irony of the passage lies in the fact that one can't say, precisely, whether what the Limousin schoolboy is actually "skinning" is Latin or French, since he speaks a language which is patently neither. And this linguistic indeterminacy makes Pantagruel's violent gesture all the more telling. One could not define the student as a "skinner of French," since, at this early moment in modern French nationhood, the vernacular has no fixed rules of "proper" usage that can be "skinned." Pantagruel's anger toward the uppity "heretic" can only be expressed by first locating him in a particular language community (that is, by "fixing" his identity as a speaker of Latin) and then by defining him as a transgressor against the rules of that community. Yet the title of the chapter, which claims that he is counterfeiting French, simultaneously places him in different language community from the one evoked by Pantagruel. Thus the scene leaves us between two languages, Pantagruel's French and a "proper" Latin that never gets spoken.[39]

Pantagruel's response suggests the violence involved in the clash of different languages at the moment of struggle over the emerging vernacular. The Limousin's displaced "counterfeiting" of Parisian jargon stands in contrast to Pantagruel's own mobility, as the young prince has just completed a tour of all of the universities of France. The episode draws on the resources made possible by the overlapping of languages by taking a metaphor from one language community ("skinning Latin") and "literalizing" or "corporealizing" it in another. Through that literalization, the subject can be put in his place, as it

< *Garden of Letters* >

were, in the emerging world of vernacular culture. The national nuance to the scene is hinted at yet again a moment later when it is revealed that the Limousin eventually died "the death of Roland," that is, of thirst. Whereas Roland, the great protagonist of Carolingian literature, dies fighting Saracens, the religious and cultural Others, Pantagruel constructs the socially ambitious schoolboy as a "heretic" and a "sorcerer," suggesting that he is the embodiment of an alterity that already inhabits France, and that must somehow be controlled. His ultimate death of thirst, which puts an end to his sorcery, makes him a kind of martyr to linguistic struggle. Indeed, the episode concludes with a moral, that one should avoid linguistic flotsam ("les mots espaves"[247]), as the captain of a ship avoids reefs. Presumably, the proper solution for the Limousin would have been to steer between the Scylla of jargon and the Charybdis of his local patois, into the clear seas of either good Latin or good French.

But what is most important here for a more general consideration of how literature constructs nationhood are the curious slippages from metaphorical to literal language, and then from sign to referent, in Rabelais and Du Bellay. For both of these writers the literalization of metaphor seems to be a strategy for attaching language to the body, for imputing a particular form of identity to the subject. Du Bellay connects the French to the Greeks and Romans and distinguishes them from other modern nations by emphasizing "*langue,*" the homonymous link between the organ of speech and the social medium of language. Rabelais humiliates the Limousin by bringing a dead metaphor ("skinning Latin") to life, and imposing it violently on the boy's body. Both of these moments involve the definition of new national linguistic communities. Conversely, Marot's bitter complaint about his dislocation and bad fortune articulates itself through a carefully defined *disjunction* between the figural and the literal, between a metaphorical national garden and a "real" personal one.

All of these passages suggest that, at times of political and social transformation, the changing relationship of individual and collective is represented though rhetorical distortion, through a kind of violence done to decorum. In their study of Kafka, Deleuze and Guattari have stressed the violence done to language and the body at the moment when a "minor" language and literature seek to define their own authority from inside a "major" language community. They read the Kafkian trope of metamorphosis, the literalization of metaphor seen in the tale of the cockroach Gregor Samsa and in such stories as

< *Garden of Letters* >

"The Penal Colony," as the strategy of the oppressed minority seeking to define the edges of its cultural space.[40] However, as the Rabelais anecdote suggests, these displays of figural distortion seem to accompany any episode in which the edges of community and the definition of literary nationhood are at stake. The development of a discourse of "national" community in sixteenth-century France, with its royal propaganda, its emerging vernacular, its territorial reorganization, and so on, is made legible at such moments of tension or crossing between the figural and the literal (Marot's two gardens), or, more exorbitantly, between sign and referent (Rabelais's metaphors' becoming bodies).

To some extent, the "naturalization" of tropes is of course characteristic of all ideological discourse.[41] And certainly, the kind of mobilization of figures just analyzed is but one aspect of the rhetorical *enargeia* which characterizes much of Renaissance European literature, from Shakespeare and Nashe to Góngora. However, I would argue that the dizzying movement between figures and bodies that characterizes so much of Renaissance French literature is also politically marked. It reflects the violence that accompanies the transformation of community, both at its edges and from its center. In the case of *Pantagruel*, at least, rhetorical distortion registers and mediates the confusion that ensues when one form of collective experience collides with another, when displaced subjects appropriate the languages of communities to which they "don't belong."

The problem of reading these rhetorical crossings haunts any consideration of the French Renaissance; for at times of violent upheaval, communities tend to imagine themselves as utopian spaces, as gardens or harmonious convivia, masking the violence and collective anguish that often give them shape. And precisely because of the violent political history of sixteenth-century France, the literature of the period abounds in figures of ideal communities, be they Evangelical congregations, humanist academies, "gardens of letters," utopias, feminine coteries, friendship societies, pastoral choruses, peasant gatherings, courtly festivals, or carnivalesque drinking parties. The richest texts of the period feature multiple moments at which different collectivities are depicted, each evoking a different generic register or ideological context, often in seeming competition with each other. One of the challenges of reading French Renaissance literature is to know how seriously to take such moments of represented communal harmony. And, of course, the privileging of

< *Garden of Letters* >

one gathering over another, though often generative of remarkable insight, tends inevitably to reflect the presuppositions of the critic. Thus, at one level, the history of readings of French Renaissance literature is a history of how readers have tended to take the utopianism of this or that figure of communal harmony at its word, as an emblem of the whole text.

Such harmonious tableaux persist even to our own day in, for example, Rorty's description of communities as "vocabularies" or "conversations." And one must be as skeptical of such formulations as of Rabelais's happy drinkers or Du Bellay's fraternity of poets. Indeed, what Rorty's formulation fails to acknowledge is that the layering of old "vocabularies" and new ones, of outmoded systems of signification and emerging discourses, is precisely a terrain of struggle and of the production of ideology. This book will argue that such utopian scenes may best be taken as moments of mystification. The most useful way to approach them is to consider, not the organizational principles of their communities, but their limits and the limits of their representation. Their historicity and contingency become legible when we turn our attention to the points at which communal representation seems to break down. This might also, one hopes, provide a hedge against these texts' Medusa-like power to fascinate critics with the spell of theological, textual, or political utopia. The history of literary nationhood must thus begin with a consideration of how depictions of communal identity are haunted by the awareness of their own contingency and arbitrariness. For, as the passages cited a moment ago suggest, it is there that private and public meet, that political metaphors like the "garden of letters" are confronted by private memories, and there that the clichés of language use ("skinning Latin") become symbolic forms of political violence. At the edges of communities, where representations reach their limits, is where literary nationhood may be read.

I have been arguing that the struggles over the identity and constitution of community that accompany the emergence of modern nationhood may best be grasped, not merely through thematic studies of imagery or iconography (dominant in the French tradition of work on this topic), or through histories of the institutions that shape culture (characteristic of much recent good work on English nationalism), but at the level of language itself. It is through the deployment of figuration, through crossings and distortions of metaphorical language, that bodies are roped into imagined communities, and com-

< *Garden of Letters* >

munities are sutured into national states. Yet our argument requires a final step. For merely to focus on the emblematic representations of collective life (France as "garden of letters"), or the encounters between various groups from different communities (Alexander and the Gauls) is merely to make the necessary but obvious point that literature can redefine the language of politics by playing with it. In order to account for the ideological work that literature does in reconfiguring community and producing new images of collectivity, the interest in borders and communities must be brought into line with a focus on literary form itself. This means that we must link the concern with rhetoric and image to a concern with literary *genre*. For it is through the notion of genre that one may grasp the collective dimension of literary form, the power of form to shape collectivity by molding the experience of time and space. Genres are the bearers of collective values and fantasies. They are, as Fredric Jameson has noted, the "institutions" of literature.[42] Yet genres are also crisscrossed by other genres, by conventions and commonplaces linked to other forms of collective experience. The raw materials with which nations build their stories inevitably bear the traces of earlier stories. The local or dynastic struggles that provoke the "institutional" imposition of the nation-state (to recall again Balibar's terms) are themselves already inscribed in their own local or dynastic histories, each of which brings with it its own set of conventions, clichés, and topoi. These other types of narratives embody the values (dynastic, civic, or other) that the nation-state seeks to appropriate. Thus, to return for a moment to our opening example, for Crinito, who is writing advice literature in the "Mirror for Princes" genre, Alexander's encounter with the Gauls is a moral exemplum about arrogance. For Pasquier, who is seeking to invent a new form of national history, it becomes a parable of collective identity. Crinito's interest is in abstract rules of comportment for princes, whereas Pasquier's is in circumventing traditions of imperial rhetorical history and establishing a narrative link between modern France and ancient Gaul. In the case of Marot's "Enfer," the depiction of the subject's anxious journey on the hard road to fame draws on an entire multiplicity of generic codes, from the medieval "consolatio," through confessional literature, to satire. In other words, not only is the ideological sign always Janus-faced, but the representation of the raw material of history is always a competition between differing modes or genres of representation.[43] And when forms of collective experience are threatened or in rapid transformation, the

< *Garden of Letters* >

genres that embody the values, and the sense of space and time congruent with that experience, break down. The crisis of communal identity brought on by encountering the Other is expressed in a crisis of literary genre. The promiscuous overlap of different identities, dramatized in Rabelais and Marot by the physical mixing of the people who claim them, incites a similar generic promiscuity. The threat to community is represented as a reflection on the limitations of henceforth discredited generic conventions. And it is precisely as symbolic responses to or resolutions of these social and political crises that new genres emerge. Though one often hears the nation-state described in literary terms as a "narrative" or "narration," it seems more accurate to speak of it as *narrations*, as a process whereby the same raw material is refracted through competing generic lenses. In sixteenth-century France, political and social change inscribe themselves on literature as a crisis of genre, and literary nationhood takes the form of a struggle between different generic conventions. The emergence of secular French literary culture during the sixteenth century involves the way in which new, "hybrid" literary texts such as the narratives of Rabelais and the essays of Montaigne stage the death of old forms, and dramatize the often painful birth of new ones.

Certainly, any discussion of nationhood and genre in the Renaissance invites a consideration of the most imperial of all genres, the epic. From the time of Virgil, after all, epic has provided the narrative model for defining new communities and building national identities.[44] However, one of the most distinctive features of French literary history in the sixteenth century is that it never produced a secular, Virgilian epic to parallel the works of Spenser, Tasso, Camoens, or Ercilla. Pierre de Ronsard struggled mightly to write such an epic, in his failed, incomplete, *Franciade*, and Agrippa d'Aubigné's *Les Tragiques*, the only reasonably successful French epic from the period, is aimed specifically at displacing secular literature and nationhood in the name of an international Protestant community. Ronsard will be discussed in a bit more detail below. However, at one level, the chapters in this book might be seen as a series of analyses demonstrating why the ideological and political struggles of sixteenth-century France make impossible the conditions for writing a national epic in which narrative form, history, community, and geography are blended into a coherent whole. In contrast to the centralizing politics of epic, I show, the French sixteenth century produces a whole series of powerful, generically multivalent texts, whose very heterogeneity

< *Garden of Letters* >

may be linked to the problem of defining the contours of community. This is not to suggest, of course, that generic hybridity is *only* connected to the emergence of nationhood (or, still less, that only these authors at this particular moment construct generically hyrid texts). Rather, my aim is to trace the particular work done by that hybridity in a specific set of contexts where the nature of community is at issue—a project which takes on added resonance when one recalls the dual obsession with national consolidation and generic purity that marks the period immediately following this one in France.

Each of the chapters to follow may be read as consideration of a different theoretical problem involving the edges of community and the edges of genre. Each chapter considers a different intersection of genre and history, building an argument that brings a major author together with other figures, both literary and non-literary. And each concerns itself with French anxiety toward a particular Other. Taken together, however, these chapters also define a trajectory that intertwines with the political evolution of French society during the period, and that delineates the development of new literary genres. At one level, of course, my choice of texts, like all such choices, is made in light of the argument. I have selected a number of works that pose the problems I want to explore as central to a theory of literary nationhood. At the same time, however, it is surely no accident that virtually all of the authors discussed here have been centrally influential in the later history of French culture both as inventors of new forms of literary representation and as exemplars of particular types of "Frenchness." The relative brevity of my consideration of an otherwise major figure such as Ronsard (to take but one example) is linked to the fact that he did not particularly concern himself with the issues of alterity and representation that are my focus. However, it may be no accident that his one gesture in that direction (again, the incomplete *Franciade*) both failed to grasp the relationship between genre and community and was the great disappointment of his career.

Chapters 2 and 3 concern themselves with how the first glimmerings of modern nationalism were produced out of representations of the "universal" Christian community. The focus here is on Rabelais, who confronted these issues directly and whose linguistic creativity and influence on subsequent French literary culture make him the obvious point of departure for any number of reasons. Moreover, since the history of Rabelais interpretation is a particularly vexed and

< *Garden of Letters* >

contentious one, it is also here that the interpretive stakes are highest. Rabelais's tales are great narratives of spiritual and political community, in which the very fate of Christendom is at issue, and where the themes of language, collective experience, and personal identity intersect with extraordinary complexity. In chapter 2 I will consider his first book, *Pantagruel*, in the context of the transformations in Christian thought during the first decades of the sixteenth century. The rise of "Christian humanism" and French Evangelicanism, under the influence of Erasmus, Briçonnet, Marguerite de Navarre, and others, defined a context of Christian renewal that had a powerful influence on the development of literary culture. My discussion of *Pantagruel* examines the ways in which that discourse of renewal, which based its very authority on its universality, was thrown into crisis when it came up against the limits of Christendom, in an encounter with the Islamic civilization of the Ottoman Empire. My reading of *Pantagruel* focuses on the paradoxes that emerged when the Rabelaisian community encountered the Islamic Other, and considers the implications of such paradoxes for the generic registers (history writing, travel narratives, etc.) on which Rabelais draws.

Chapter 3 turns from the limits of Christian universality to the relationship between nationalism and humanism. In it, I analyze Rabelais's second published book, *Gargantua*, in light of both the rivalry between Francis I and Charles V, and the humanist political theory that attempted to respond to increasing tensions between national states in Europe. I will show *Gargantua* to be in dialogue with a series of writers and philosophers whose work lay the foundation for what would later be modern political theory. An analysis of the multiple generic registers in Rabelais's book locates it within the ideological struggles surrounding the emergence of a new imperial French identity, and shows how Rabelais's much-discussed "Christian humanist" project is contingent on fantasies of French imperialism.

In chapter 4, I consider the literary delineation of national space, analyzing the depiction of the border in the writings of Francis I's sister Marguerite de Navarre. My discussion centers on the *Heptaméron*, Marguerite's collection of framed tales, which I read in the context of anti-Spanish sentiment, and the aggressive political centralization that marked the Valois monarchy in the middle years of the century. Marguerite's text stages a conflict between images of a wandering international aristocracy (registered through motifs taken from the genre of romance), and the increasingly circumscribed space of

< *Garden of Letters* >

French court society. The last section of the chapter explores the relationship between the *Heptaméron* and one of its literary descendents, Madame de Lafayette's *La Princesse de Clèves*, written a century later and often thought of as the first modern French novel. At issue here is the relationship between the figuration of national space and the fictional space of the novel.

The patriotic and national themes foreshadowed by such writers as Rabelais and Marguerite de Navarre were a central preoccupation of the generation of writers that followed the death of Francis I. In Chapter 5, I will consider the problem of national character, looking at the poetic coterie known as the Pléiade, the first avant-garde movement in French letters, and the apologists for a full-scale French imperialist poetics. My focus here will be the poetry and theory of Joachim du Bellay, whose work I read in light of mid-century debates over French identity and the anxiety about the cultural dominance and political influence of Italy. In this chapter I will show how Du Bellay's manipulation of the various generic registers of lyric poetry, and of the sonnet collection in particular, work to locate him in a set of contradictory relationships to different communities. Through his deployment of his liminal position at the edges of both France and Italy, I argue, Du Bellay (in contrast to his friend Ronsard) invented a new notion of French character. Du Bellay's marginality made possible the invention of a character that became canonical for later generations of French readers.

The final chapter of this book considers the relationship between literary authority, national identity, and history during the religious wars that marked the late sixteenth century. Through a reading of Montaigne's *Essais*, I will show how the breakdown of homogeneous political space disrupts the imagination of history and subverts the claim to speak for community. A close reading of Montaigne's description of the encounter between Europe and the New World shows how the experience of alterity is intimately linked to Montaigne's imagination of history, and to his definition of his own literary authority. This chapter concerns itself less than the others with the symbolic violence that underlies the construction of community, precisely because it focuses on representing and coming to terms with the real violence of civil struggle and colonialist murder. Moreover, it provides a somewhat more irenic, if provisional, counter to this violence. In response to the moral and epistemological dilemmas posed by European atrocities in the New World, I show, Montaigne defines

< *Garden of Letters* >

a problematic, multiple location for himself in language, with the discourse of the new genre of the essay emerging to respond to the new representational tasks posed by the experience of cultural diversity. Montaigne's self-location permits him to explore the limitations of the European philosophical tradition by imaginatively recreating the experience of the Other.

Thus the various chapters pursue the role of genre in the literary construction of political identity, space, national character, and history. This conjunction of concerns brings me back to Strabo and Pasquier, the authors with whom I began. Their depictions of the Gauls' answer to Alexander's leading question, I noted, are fraught with ambiguities. For, indeed, it appears that the Gauls' mysterious utterance may be read as either the sign of simplicity or the sign of prudence. These two interpretations give us two distinct models of the relationship between language and community. In the first, language is transparent, a direct communication from the heart of the "simple" Gauls. In the second, language is a deflecting mirror. However, none of the readings of the scene that have been considered so far is able to give full weight to both of the elements in the anecdote, to the fact that the Gauls both fear the falling heavens and succeed in confusing the greatest general of their day. If one assumes, with Strabo, that they speak "honestly" and really do fear only the falling heavens, one must assume that they are barbarians, that is, lacking the power of reflection, and that their success against Alexander is a mere accident. If, on the other hand, one assumes that they evoke the falling heavens to trick Alexander, it is difficult to reconcile their political cunning with their cosmological naïvete. Perhaps the inability of writers such as Strabo and Pasquier to account for the seeming variegation of the Gauls is itself evidence of their own generic limitations. For the only truly comprehensive reading of the scene of which I am aware comes in a very different genre, with a very different set of conventions. This is the reading offered in no less authoritative a text than Goscinny and Uderzo's popular comic book series, *Astérix*. The Gauls of *Astérix* are indeed "complex," but their complexity is social, not spiritual or mental, as Strabo would have it. In *Astérix*, it is the king of the Gauls, Abraracourcix, who "has only one fear . . . that the sky may fall on his head tomorrow," while the everyday footsoldiers concern themselves with tricking and confusing the Other—in this case, the legions of Rome.[45] Cosmic terror becomes comic terror, and is represented in the satiric discourse of the comic book as the neuro-

< *Garden of Letters* >

sis of the ruling elite. Astérix himself, the hero of the series, uses neither persuasive speech nor mere trickery to drive away the enemy. Instead, showing the courage that Pasquier sought to find in the Gauls' answer to Alexander, he uses the strength of his arm. However, he also relies on a magic potion that makes him, like the heroes of Rabelais, stronger than mere mortals. Only in the multi-voiced discourse of the popular comic, it seems, can the Gauls be both fearful and brave, both simple and cunning. Whether one should read Astérix's magic potion as a metaphor for the essential force of "Frenchness," or nationalist images like the "garden of letters" as elixirs for motivating the traditionally irresolute Gauls, is a question that, for now, at least, must remain open.

Chapter Two

The Limits of Ideology:
Rabelais and the Edge of Christendom

If the lion had a consciousness, his rage at
the antelope he wants to eat would be ideology.
—ADORNO, *Negative Dialectics*

Humanism and the Politics of Charity

In the previous chapter, I argued that the emergence of nationhood
has a linguistic and literary dimension, which may be traced through
the deployment of figural language and in the power of genre to
shape and represent community. In response to the encounter with
the Other, the edges of community become legible, at the level of literary form, in the breakdown of generic conventions, in the intersection of genres. And the violent border encounter between diverse
identities is often demonstrated in language as rhetorical distortion
or violence done to linguistic decorum. I would now like to consider
how these issues are played out in what is certainly the greatest communal crisis of the period, the breakup of a unified Christendom in
the early sixteenth century. It was from this crisis of Christian unity
that new models of distinctly national political identity began to
emerge displacing traditional notions of Christian identity—even as
the breakup of Latinity resulted in the development of the modern
national vernaculars. This is, of course, an immense topic, of which
only one aspect can be addressed here. My concern will be with the
impact on literary representation of the sense, urgent in the early sixteenth century, that the Christian community was in danger and
needed reinvention. This problem has often been approached
through analysis of such topics as Reformation politics or the institutional history of the rise of Protestantism. A new perspective, however, may be opened up, in keeping with our interest in borders and
liminality, by focussing on the edges of Christendom; for it is there
that one can trace how a growing awareness of the limits of Christian
identity made itself felt in the language of literature.

The notion of charity must be central to any consideration of how

< *The Limits of Ideology* >

collective identity is figured in the Christian tradition. Charity forms the very conceptual basis of that community, beginning with Paul's promotion of the concept in his letters to the Corinthians, and Augustine's assertion that charity "embraces both love of God and love of neighbor."[1] Indeed, charity is the strongest, and, one might say, the most imperial of all Christian concepts, since it mediates the relationship between spirituality and social relations. The idea took on particular importance in the early sixteenth century, when both Catholic and Protestant thinkers were attempting to reimagine the nature of community. "This is what Paul calls charity," says Erasmus in his widely-circulated handbook, the *Enchiridion*, "to edify our neighbour, to consider everyone as members of the same body, to regard everyone as one in Christ, to rejoice in the Lord at your brother's prosperity as if it were your own and to heal his misfortunes as if they were your own . . . in a word, to devote all your resources to this one end, that you benefit as many as you can in Christ."[2] And for the great reformer Jacques Lefèvre d'Etaples charity is what structures one's very being in the world with others: "Faith makes Jesus Christ ours; charity makes us our neighbor's."[3] However, charity is no less linked to courtly and more properly political notions than it is to specifically theological contexts. Rabelais's friend, the humanist Symphorien Champier, wrote in a treatise on the meaning of nobility that it is charity toward the weak and captive ("des hommes pris et vaincus qui demandent mercy") that characterizes the true knight; "And if the knight has no charity, how can he be part of the order of chivalry?" In a more "national" French context, the term was centrally linked to the special status of the French king as "Most Christian."[4] Yet precisely because charity mediates between the social and the spiritual, it holds within itself the tension between a universal notion of Christian community, and an emergent national identity.

Rabelais is centrally concerned with these issues by virtue of his proximity to the so-called "evangelical" or "évangélique" tradition of French thought which came to prominence in the 1520s and 1530s under Francis I, and included the group around the Cardinal Briçonnet (among others, the king's sister Marguerite de Navarre and the poet Clément Marot). These thinkers, like their sometime mentor Erasmus, sought to redefine Catholic practice from within the ambit of the Church. They refused both the traditional rigidity of the Sorbonne and the radical Protestantism of Luther and Calvin in favor of a pious, moderate humanism. Despite the king's initial sympathy to-

< *The Limits of Ideology* >

ward their project during the 1520s, their moderation ultimately failed in the face of the increasing polarization of Catholics and Protestants. However, their importance in the emergence of secular literary culture in Renaissance France cannot be overestimated.

The workings of charity in social relations are a central theme in Rabelais's works. We can see them in one of the most famous meetings in all of Renaissance literature: the encounter between Pantagruel and Panurge in the ninth chapter of Rabelais's *Pantagruel* (1532). While strolling outside the walls of Paris with his friends one day, the young giant Pantagruel meets a raggedly dressed but handsome stranger: "He met a man of handsome build, elegant in all his features, but pitifully wounded in various places, and in so sorry a state that he looked as if he had escaped from the dogs, or to be more accurate, like some apple-picker from the Perche country" ["rencontra un homme beau de stature et elegant en tous lineamens du corps, mais pitoyablement navré en divers lieux, et tant mal en ordre qu'il sembloit estre eschappé es chiens, ou mieulx resembloit un cueilleur de pommes du païs du Perche"].[5] We later learn that the stranger is called Panurge—a name that suggests the Greek word *panourgos*, and means, among other things, "crafty," "prudent," "resourceful."[6] Pantagruel asks Panurge, in French, the same questions that are always asked of handsome strangers in literature: "Who are you?" "Where do you come from?" "Where are you going?" "What are you seeking?" Panurge responds, however, in thirteen different languages, ranging from Spanish and Italian to Lanternese and Utopian, until it becomes clear that both characters are native speakers of French. At this point Pantagruel informs the stranger that he is already attracted to him: "I've already taken such a liking to you, in faith, that if I have my way you'll never stir from my side" (201) ["par ma foy, je vous ay ja prins en amour si grand que, si vous condescendez à mon vouloir, vous ne bougerez jamais de ma compaignie" (269)] He offers him food and drink, and they become fast friends.

Commentators on this scene have often seen Panurge as a figure of Babel. His linguistic pyrotechnics offer an emblem of both the scattering of meaning and the fragmentation of community that characterize life in the fallen world. Yet it is precisely this fragmentation that is repaired, at least momentarily, by the close of the scene. For the kindly Pantagruel's acceptance of the stranger transcends the chaos represented by Panurge's linguistic profusion and replaces solitude and need with community. The glue that holds this community

< *The Limits of Ideology* >

together is the notion of charity, here represented by the initial gesture of pity toward Panurge's "pitoyable" misery. Charity makes communication possible. It precedes the acknowledgment of a common language ("I've *already* taken such a liking to you": "je vous ay *ja* prins en amour"). Commentators have stressed the importance for the scene of Paul's first letter to the Corinthians (13.1), in which the apostle proclaims, "If I speak in the tongues of men and of angels, but have not charity, I am a noisy gong or a clanging cymbal." Christian charity overcomes the confusion of many tongues to create a community in which the superficial marks of difference between human beings are erased. The letter kills and separates; the spirit of charity unifies and heals.[7]

The meeting of Panurge and Pantagruel evokes traditions both secular and saintly. The literary topos of the meeting of strangers draws parodically on countless similar meetings in medieval romance, where two knights who meet at a crossroads or in a forest must reveal their identities. Yet the depiction of one man helping another in need also recalls one of the best known passages from the New Testament, the tenth chapter of Luke, in which Christ tells the following story: "A man was going down from Jerusalem to Jericho, and he fell among robbers, who stripped him and beat him, and departed, leaving him half dead." Christ goes on to recount how two wealthy men, first a priest and then a Levite, came by but refused to help the wounded man. Only a Samaritan, the third passerby, was willing to help: "But a Samaritan, as he journeyed, came to where he was; and when he saw him, he had compassion."[8] The Samaritan bound the man's wounds, took him to an inn, and paid his bill. Christ tells his disciples to go and do like the Samaritan. Because of the inequality between Pantagruel and Panurge—one is a well fed prince, the other a starving vagabond—Rabelais's scene parallels this narrative of power and charity. Pantagruel takes the role of the Samaritan in helping his needy neighbor.

Yet there is an important feature of Christ's parable that raises issues rarely pursued by students of Rabelais. The passerby was a Samaritan, and Samaritans were shunned by Jews in the ancient world. Though Samaritans worshiped God and used the Pentateuch, Jews saw them as an alien race to be despised. Jesus himself, when he sent forth his disciples to preach (Matthew 10.5), forbade them from entering Samaritan villages. Thus Christ's version of the old literary topos of the meeting of two strangers is inflected with

< *The Limits of Ideology* >

what might be called an anthropological dimension. The meeting on the road isn't only about travel, or power; it is also about cultural difference and cultural identity, about what constitutes a community, and about how members of one group relate to those of another.

In this chapter, I want to consider what happens when Rabelais's text moves beyond the European ambit of Christian humanism, with its ideal fraternity of pious tipplers, to encounter an Other much less easy to appropriate and understand than the wily Panurge. This Other is the Ottoman Empire, whose presence on the eastern edge of Europe was a source of political panic and moral confusion for Christian intellectuals during the sixteenth century. To be sure, it is common for readers of Rabelais to stress the importance of themes of community in his work. It is less often recognized, however, that the representation of community is often extremely problematic. Indeed, Rabelais's text is marked by scenes of extraordinary violence against anyone who is not a French male Christian of noble birth. A consideration of Rabelais's representation of the Turks will show that the imagination of community in Rabelais is shadowed by images of political violence and cultural paranoia. "Proprietatem Christiana caritas non novit," writes Erasmus in the *Enchiridion*. That is, "Christian charity knows no exclusivity"—though one might just as well translate "proprietas" as "property," "propriety," or "particularity."[9] In its universality charity is everywhere. Yet it is this very universality that is threatened on the edges of Christendom, when charity runs up against forms of representation and action that are very "exclusive" indeed.

The stakes here are high. For in a sense, the problem of Rabelais is the problem of literature itself. Humanism, whether it be the Christian humanism of the Renaissance or any of the various literary humanisms that have followed it down to the present, involves a conviction that the reading and writing of fictions are ethical and moral activities. Yet whereas the influence of Christian humanist thought on Rabelais has been widely recognized at least since 1942, with the publication of Lucien Febvre's study, *Le problème de l'incroyance au seizième siècle: La religion de Rabelais*, the precise ways in which humanist ideology imposes itself on the language of his texts remain a source of contention and puzzlement for readers. The encounter of Pantagruel and Panurge suggests that we are faced, here at the dawn of modern literary culture, with a theoretical problem that will continue to haunt the relationship between ideological discourse and fictional

< *The Limits of Ideology* >

representation. That is, even if one accepts the close alliance between Rabelais's text and the theological and political ideals of Christian humanism one must still consider how the *representation* of ideological themes in fiction is transformed in the face of alterity. I will suggest that Rabelais's text constantly projects models of harmony and virtue while dramatizing, in its very language, the difficulty of realizing them. Yet in response to that dilemma, the Rabelaisian text also presents itself, its own rhetorical energy and self-conscious fiction making, as the mediating force that can reconcile ideology and representation. Rabelais's writing is engaged in a ceaseless struggle to work out a relationship between language and community. That struggle emerges from the crisis of Christian and French identity that marks the early decades of the sixteenth century. In response to that crisis, Rabelais simultaneously lives off the language of Christian humanism and points to its contradictions. Every moral message Rabelais presents seems to be undone by his own writing, yet every undoing has a moral.[10]

Thoughout this chapter and the next I will read Rabelais in dialogue with his Christian humanist contemporaries, principally his friend and mentor Erasmus. I have chosen this course not only because Erasmus was the major European intellectual of the day, but because the contradictions and conflicts faced by the humanist attempt to inject moral concerns into the brutal world of politics come most clearly into focus through his work. In the discussion below I will look carefully at a number of texts in which Erasmus and his fellow humanists offer advice on the proper form of political action. Since this type of writing tends to bring moral admonition together with the depiction of ideal forms of behavior or government and commentary on current affairs, I will be especially interested in the conflicts or tensions between what writers like Erasmus project as ideal behavior and what they say about specific contemporary situations. In other words, where are the pressure points, where do theory and practice seem to be not quite in harmony? And how do Rabelais's consideration or representations of similar themes, images and topoi transform or redefine the terms set up by humanist argument? I will show how the advice literature and moral counsel for which Erasmus is famous is marked by various contradictions or inadequacies in the face of the complexity of the political and theological crises to which it seeks to respond. It is in response to those contradictions, as a kind of aesthetic solution to them, that one may understand certain of the

< *The Limits of Ideology* >

representative strategies of Rabelais's narratives. Thus, literary form saves humanism from its own contradictions.

To read the famous encounter between Pantagruel and Panurge as the demonstration of a moral message, a kind of precept about friendship and charity, is to follow guidelines set up by the Renaissance humanists themselves. Moral allegory is central to humanist hermeneutics. In what is probably the most programmatic of his many writings on education, the *De ratione studii* of 1516, Erasmus stipulates that every text should be read four times: once for its general sense; once with attention to grammar and vocabulary; once with an eye to its rhetorical figures; and, finally, once to seek a moral example that might be applied to daily life, "for example, the story of Pylades and Orestes to show the excellence of friendship; that of Tantalus, the curse of avarice."[11] According to Erasmus, moral allegories or lessons of comportment are to be sought in all texts, whether sacred or profane, literary or historical.

Yet what is never quite articulated in the Erasmian model of reading is how the moral lessons that the reader is to draw from texts are to be applied to specific, contingent forms of action—most specifically to political action. From the time of the *quattrocento* Italian humanists, rhetorical and literary study had as its goal the promotion of virtuous and prudent public action, the effective execution of statecraft. As the northern heir to that pedagogical tradition, Erasmus seeks to blend the rhetorical interests of the Italians with a Christan piety based in New Testament morality.[12] Yet Erasmus's very moralism and commitment to Pauline ideals constantly runs up against the harsh realities of sixteenth-century politics. It is not enough, in reading Erasmus, simply to suggest that his moralistic discourse envisions a purely psychological or spiritual (that is, internal) response to the text. After all, charity, as noted, involves social and political relationships. For Erasmus the male companionship of, say, Pylades and Orestes (recalled in the relations between Pantagruel and Panurge) is a model of both the demonstration of charity and the dynamics of political organization. Erasmus opens his most influential book, the *Adages*, with a series of adages on friendship, the first of which is the proverb—found as well in both Aristotle and Plato—that "Between friends all is in common." He glosses this maxim by drawing a parallel between politics and friendship. And he contrasts to it the disruptive power of possession and, ultimately, avarice (figured above by

< *The Limits of Ideology* >

Tantalus), which destroys both the exchange between friends and the commonwealth more generally: "Plato . . . says that a state would be happy and blessed in which these words 'mine' and 'not mine' were never to be heard. But it is extraordinary how Christians dislike this common ownership of Plato's, how in fact they cast stones at it, although nothing was ever said by a pagan philosopher which comes closer to the mind of Christ."[13] Erasmus's discussions of charity evoke the point where spiritual dispensation and public action meet. They include both the individual believer and the collective experience of the polis. The conjunction of charity, friendship, and politics, however, depends on a specific meeting of personalities. For if Erasmus defines political harmony in terms of charitable relationships among friends, he also points out, both in the very next adage and in the *De ratione studii*, that friendship generally springs up between people who resemble each other: "The deepest form of love coincides with the deepest resemblance."[14] And it is in this praise of similitude that the Christian humanist merging of politics and moral philosophy begins to run into problems. For it offers no terms for defining action in a world *not* characterized by friendship among likes.

In addition to the theme of language, which is the obvious center of concern in the encounter between Pantagruel and Panurge, the scene also raises questions about the importance of vision—suggested by Pantagruel's willingness to help Panurge on sight. This motif is also central to Christ's parable about the good Samaritan. For it stresses that charity and pity stem not from language, but from vision: "and *when he saw him*, he had compassion." Rabelais's contemporaries return again and again to the connection between vision and charity. Thus, for example, Rabelais's friend, the poet Clément Marot, writes a verse epistle from prison to his friend Lyon Jamet. Marot retells Aesop's fable of the Lion and the Rat—a story which, like Christ's parable, deals with pity for a suffering neighbor from another "social group." Aesop recounts how the lion helps the rat and the rat helps the lion; the powerful must not neglect the weak. Marot, too, explores the relationship between vision and language. He adds to Aesop's story the detail that the lion first sees, and then helps the rat: "This lion . . . /Saw once that the rat could not/Escape where he was" ["Cestui lion . . . /Vit une fois que le rat ne savait/Sortir d'un lieu"]. He then extends the motif of vision to include the reader, as he turns, in the final lines, to ask for help by saying "come and *see* me," ["viens me *voir*"] (my emphasis).[15] The

< *The Limits of Ideology* >

same motif of vision is stressed throughout the Pantagruel/Panurge meeting: "When he *caught sight* of this fellow from the distance, Pantagruel said to his companions: 'Do you *see* that man coming along the road from the Charenton bridge?' " (196) ["De tant loing que le *vit* Pantagruel, il dist es assistans: '*Voyez vous* cest homme, qui vient par le chemin du pont Charanton?' " (263, my emphasis)]. Yet a consideration of this motif in light of questions of cultural and political difference would have to take into account not only the vision that sparks charity, but the gaze through which the Other is perceived and judged.

Rabelais himself seems to sense that the relationship of charity to vision is not as simple as it might appear. The very introduction of Panurge into the text already raises questions about how strangers are perceived. To recall again the narrator's description, "Pantagruel . . . met a man of handsome build, elegant in all his features, but pitifully wounded in various places, and in so sorry a state that he looked as if he had escaped from the dogs, or to be more accurate, like some apple-picker from the Perche country" (196) ["Pantagruel . . . rencontra un homme beau de stature et elegant en tous lineamens du corps, mais pitoyablement navré en divers lieux, et tant mal en ordre qu'il sembloit estre eschappé es chiens, ou mieulx resembloit un cueilleur de pommes du païs du Perche" (263)]. The narrator's description underscores the contrast between Panurge's exterior misery and his physical beauty. This relationship of outside to inside will be reversed as the book proceeds, as Panurge becomes an elegant blade of questionable moral character. More important, the narrator then offers two possible explanations for Panurge's appearance. He looks like he has just escaped from a pack of dogs, or "to be more accurate," like an apple picker from the Perche region. In describing Panurge as an escapee from a pack of dogs, the narrator is judging him according to the criteria of vision, as he appears. However, it is a strange description, even in such a strange book as this, and the narrator immediately replaces it with a more precise, familiar, proverbial description. Panurge appears to be an apple picker, more "properly" than a man escaped from dogs. Yet this shift from the unfamiliar to the familiar is deceptive; for we soon learn that Panurge *has* just escaped from a pack of dogs, as he himself goes on to narrate. The initial description comes from a visual impression which turns out to be accurate. Yet since neither he nor Pantagruel yet knows anything about Panurge, the narrator is also transmitting information that he cannot possibly

< *The Limits of Ideology* >

know. The description of Panurge as an escapee from dogs offers a visual impression that is arresting by its strangeness, but true. The more "familiar" and "proverbial" description ("an apple picker from the Perche") turns out to be deceptive. The text sets up a split between what it proverbially "knows" about the Other and what it later demonstrates to be "true." In a gesture that will recur a number of times in this book, the text slips into fiction as it encounters alterity. Indeed, one might suggest that the tension within Christ's parable between the Samaritan's "alterity" or "outcast" status and his charity is played out in Rabelais through the shifting opinions of the narrator himself.

These issues of community, alterity, and charity unfold in complicated ways as Panurge recounts his escape from the Turks to Pantagruel. This scene, in chapter 14 of *Pantagruel*, comes immediately after Pantagruel has demonstrated his great sagacity by resolving a seemingly impossible law case between Humevesne and Baisecul. The shift from a parody of justice to a scene of escape marks an abrupt transition; by evoking the Turks Panurge calls to mind a major political crisis of the 1520s. During this period (and most especially during the years directly preceding the writing of *Pantagruel*), the Ottoman empire, under the rule of Suleiman the Great and the daring corsair Barbarossa, posed a constant threat to the security and stability of Christian Europe. Suleiman's navy dominated the Mediterranean, and his army twice invaded Hungary on its way to attacking Vienna itself.

The political crisis of the "Turkish question" was also a moral crisis. The morality of a war against the Turks was a favorite topic of humanist-influenced writers during the first decades of the century. Opinion varied on the question, from the claim that the Turks must be wiped out through a new crusade, to the notion that they were a scourge sent by God to teach Christian Europe about its own sins. Luther, to take but one example, moved between these extremes, suggesting in his *Explanations of the Ninety-Five Theses* of 1518 that the Turks were heaven-sent and should not be resisted. He then reversed himself in a 1529 treatise on the Turkish question, claiming that war against the Ottomans might be morally acceptable if it were led by the Holy Roman Emperor.[16]

It is, however, in the work of Erasmus that this ambiguity toward the Ottoman threat takes its most complex form.[17] Erasmus argues his position on the question of the Turkish threat in a variety of texts,

< *The Limits of Ideology* >

from the adage "Dulce bellum inexpertis" ("War is sweet to those who have not tried it") of 1515 and through the *Education of the Christian Prince* of 1516 and the *Complaint of Peace* of 1517, to a treatise titled *On the Turkish War* published in 1530—only a few years before Rabelais's *Pantagruel.* Throughout his writings Erasmus criticizes both those who want to massacre the Turks and those who claim that the Turks are a divine plague that should not be resisted. His general position is that the Turks may be fought, but only as a last resort. The real problem raised by the Ottoman invasions, he says at several points, is less the conflict between civilizations than the spiritual fragmentation and disarray of Christendom itself. When the princes of Europe squabble among themselves, he wonders, how can they ever hope either to conquer or to convert the Turks? For though the rulers of Europe call themselves Christians, they behave toward each other with anything but Christian charity. The successes of the Ottoman armies should offer a warning to Christendom to set its house in order both morally and politically. Otherwise, suggests Erasmus in a particularly somber moment, the Christians may degenerate into Turks before they can make the Turks into Christians.[18] In fact, so great is the lust for power among Christian princes that they are beginning to look very much like the enemy, and "it is as Turks that we are fighting Turks."[19]

As these last anxious warnings suggest, Erasmus's own depiction of the Turks is contradictory in ways that take us to the center of the issues raised by our reading of Christ's parable of the Samaritan. Erasmus vacillates over what exactly it is that, politically and morally, distinguishes Turks from Christians. He infuses the question with which I began—the relationship between otherness and community in Christian humanist thought—with an explicitly political dimension and suggests its importance for thinking about the pre-history of nationhood. Erasmus's attempt to defuse anti-Turkish hysteria while avoiding the suggestion that Christians should allow themselves to be martyred leads him to paint a curious hybrid Turk—a Turk at once totally alien and strangely familiar. For if, on the one hand, the Turks are to be seen as barbarians, as figures into which decadent Christians might degenerate unless they mend their ways, they (the Turks) must consistently be painted as threateningly different from Christians, as completely Other, as defined by marks of cultural difference that can never be erased. This is the tack taken by Erasmus in many of his most moralistic moments, where he pulls no punches in

< *The Limits of Ideology* >

vilifying the Turks. Thus, for example, in *On the Turkish War*, he presents a Turk who is at once a bloodthirsty warrior and a gutless voluptuary. "Barbarians, of obscure origin" ["gens barbara, obscurae originis"], the Turks, says Erasmus, are a people without virtue, effeminate and enamoured of wealth ("Gens est effoeminata luxu"). "They owe their victories," he warns, "to our vices." Yet at the same time he insists on the terrible cruelty and "monstrosity" that has marked Turkish treatment of Christian captives.[20]

This portrayal of a Turk at once cruel and decadent is, of course, already a cliché. Yet Erasmus goes beyond these conventions. For even as he rails against the Turks, Erasmus attempts to appropriate and "humanize" them. If his rhetorical distancing of the Turks makes possible moralistic warnings that Europe must be spiritually renewed, his desire to resist the bellicose posturing of those who would seek an immediate holy war leads him to offer a very different image. He says in the adage "Dulce bellum inexpertis" that because of their piety, "those people whom we call Turks are to a great extent half-Christian, and probably nearer true Christianity than most of our own people."[21] In *On the Turkish War* he echoes this astonishing phrase. He admonishes those who call the Turks dogs (as Christians had been doing at least since Petrarch). Then he praises the Turks' pious commitment to their religion and calls them "first of all men, then half-Christians."[22]

The Turks operate in Erasmus's discourse as both the Other and the same. Their political and cultural otherness makes it possible for them to be presented as images of barbarism and decadence; they offer negative examples to Christian rulers. Yet their pious commitment to the law that defines that otherness turns them into positive examples. Their humanity makes them figures who need to be converted and shown charity instead of massacred. "If we want to lead the Turks to the Christian religion," says Erasmus, "let us first be Christians."[23]

Erasmus's wavering description suggests the pressure placed on the rhetoric of moderation at a particular moment of political hysteria. Yet it also points to the limitations of Christian humanism itself, as it seeks to preach a doctrine of charity, of acceptance of the Other, while at the same time trying to ground its work in the political and spiritual unification of a Christian Europe threatened by strangers far more menacing than Panurge. Erasmus's rhetoric strains under the burden of trying to accept otherness while upholding a community based on absolute truth.[24]

< *The Limits of Ideology* >

If the universal European intellectual Erasmus articulates a contradictory attitude toward the Turks, the situation is even more complex for Rabelais, as a Frenchman writing under the dominion of Francis I. For Francis's policy toward Turkish ambitions in the West was curious indeed. If Suleiman I became a major player in the political maneuvering between Charles V and Francis I for the domination of Europe, it was largely through his special relationship with Francis, who liked to be known as the "Defender of the Christian Faith." Soon after the defeat in 1519 of Francis's bid to be Holy Roman Emperor, the French ruler enlisted Suleiman as an ally against his rival Charles. In fact, even during his imprisonment in Spain in 1525 Francis continued to make diplomatic overtures to the Turkish leader in the form of a series of personal letters. His encouragement and affirmation of his support for Turkish interests are generally acknowledged as factors behind the Sultan's second invasion of Hungary. At the Battle of Mohács, in 1527, thousands of Christian troops were massacred by Turkish forces. This disaster was the major European military encounter with the Turks until the Battle of Lepanto in 1571. Yet even after Mohács Francis continued his friendly overtures to the Sultan. And just as the Turks threatened the very gates of Vienna in March of 1532—only a few months before the autumn publication of *Pantagruel*—Francis sent an ambassador named Antonio Rincón to discourage Suleiman from invading Central Europe (which would have threatened French interests in Germany) and to encourage him to attack Italy (which would have weakened Charles V and permitted Francis to invade the peninsula as savior and champion of Christendom).[25]

Panurge on the Spit

The introduction of Panurge's tale of his escape from the Turks is abrupt and strange. After his resolution of the legal dispute between Baisecul and Humevesne, Pantagruel is rewarded with a barrel of good wine, and leads the company in a party. Panurge offers a toast and marvels at the excellence of the wine, which has the curious effect of producing thirst in those who drink it: "the more I drink of it, the thirstier I am" (214) ["plus j'en boy, plus j'ai de soif" (288)]. And he goes on to assert that Pantagruel's shadow makes "thirsty men" ("alterez") the way the moon makes catarrhs, at which the company begins to laugh. When Pantagruel asks why they are laughing, Panurge offers an explanation that appears to be a non sequitur: " 'My

47

< The Limits of Ideology >

Lord,' he replied, 'I was telling them how very unfortunate these dev-ilish Turks are not to drink a drop of wine. If there were no other evil in Mahomet's Koran, I still wouldn't put myself under its law, not for a moment' " ["Seigneur, (dist il), je leur contoys comment ces diables de Turcqs sont bien malheureux de ne boire goutte de vin. Si aultre mal n'est en l'Alchoran de Mahumeth, encores ne me mettroys je mie de sa loy"]. Of course, this is wrong. Panurge has just been offering a toast and a praise of a wine that makes those who drink it thirstier. The text is careful to point out that the laugh of the crowd came di-rectly from Panurge's joke about the moon and Pantagruel's shadow. Why, then, would Panurge claim that his joke about wine was in fact a story about the drinking habits of the Turks and the inconveniences of their "law"? And what does that curious misdefinition have to do with the tale of escape that Pantagruel then urges him to recount? The opening of the episode suggests that wine, community, and storytelling are intimately related.

Panurge's account of his escape from the Turks is marked by a number of interesting features. First, it is one of the very rare mo-ments anywhere in Rabelais in which someone other than the narra-tor recounts a story. The nature of this story, however, is puzzling. On the one hand, Panurge introduces himself to Pantagruel by say-ing that he has just had adventures "more marvelous than Ulysses" (201). His evocation of the classical hero most famous for his telling of untruths suggests that he is in the realm of pure fabrication.[26] Yet he repeatedly claims that not a word of the tale he tells is a lie ("je ne vous en mentiray de mot" [289]). And he takes pains to root the story in the world of contemporary politics. Panurge says he was captured "during the ill-fated attack on Mytilene" (201) ["quand on alla à Metelin en la male heure]" (270). This is a reference to the bungled French attack against the city of Mytilene on the Isle of Lesbos in 1502, in which ten thousand Frenchmen perished. Such explicit top-ical allusions are very rare in Rabelais (I will consider another one in my discussion of *Gargantua*), and this one serves to set Panurge's story somewhere between fiction and history. It recalls the topos of Odyssean adventures, yet juxtaposes that topos with a specific inci-dent in a political crisis of vital importance to European identity—an incident conveniently located on an island midway between East and West.[27]

Since the details of Panurge's escape will be important in what fol-lows, I recount the episode here. As the scene opens, the Turks have

48

< *The Limits of Ideology* >

tied Panurge to a spit, placed him under armed guard, and are roasting him over a fire. Around his waist they have wrapped strips of bacon, since, presumably, they plan to eat him, and, as Panurge says, he was so skinny that his body would have made "bad meat" without some flavoring. Recognizing that his predicament clearly recalls the martyrdom of Saint Lawrence, Panurge prays for deliverance. Sure enough, the guard suddenly falls asleep—through the intervention of either God or Mercury (who put Argus to sleep in the legend of Io). While the guard sleeps Panurge is able to seize two burning sticks with his teeth. He throws one stick onto a pile of straw, which immediately ignites, and the other into the lap of the guard—thereby scorching his genitals. The guard leaps up, runs toward his captive, and begins to untie him. He is stopped, however, when the pasha or master of the house appears and immediately puts the negligent soldier to death, presumably for having fallen asleep at the guard. By this time the fire has ignited the pasha's entire house. Seeing that the situation is desperate, the pasha decides to commit suicide. Panurge offers to help him, in exchange for his purse. When the master agrees to this offer Panurge ties him up, hangs him from the spit (thus exactly reversing the roles of a moment earlier), runs him through and leaves him to roast. Now the fire has begun to consume the city (though Panurge says "don't ask how"). As he flees through the smoke-filled streets, Panurge meets a group of escaping townspeople, who first cool him off by dousing him with water and then offer him food, most of which he refuses. With the city now completely in flames, he meets two other refugees, a "villainous little Turk, with a hump on his chest"(217), who tries to chew on the strips of bacon that still adorn his waist (Panurge slaps him away) and a courtesan who offers to give him an aphrodisiac—until she sees that his penis, like that of the guard, has been scorched in the fire and now, says Panurge, hangs no lower than his knees. Panurge escapes the flaming city and pauses only briefly to look back from the hilltop above—a gesture that he compares to Lot's wife's parting glance at Sodom and Gomorrah, as if the parallel were not already obvious. He is so happy at seeing the conflagration, he says, that "I almost shat myself with joy"(217). Yet, he is quick to add, his laughter is punished by God. For it is then that he notices he is being pursued by a pack of dogs fleeing the fire. To save himself from being devoured, the wily Panurge unties the savory strips of bacon that still adorn his waist and throws them to the hounds. They stop to gobble up the meat and he escapes, hav-

< *The Limits of Ideology* >

ing in the bargain been cured by the fire of his sciatica, a common symptom of syphilis. And he adds that by throwing the bacon to the dogs he found a remedy for toothache, or "le mal des dens." When his listener Pantagruel wonders why he should still have had toothache after having been cured of all other ailments including sciatica, Panurge points out that the teeth in question are not his own, but those of the dogs who wanted to bite him "can teeth give you any greater pain than when dogs have you by the legs?" (217). "Long live roasting," he shouts, and with this joke the episode ends.

Panurge's first-person narrative inevitably evokes the conventions of travel literature and accounts of escapes from terrifying aliens that were popular during the period. And because the tale involves the representation of that which is alien or other in narrative, it inevitably raises issues about naming, about the labels with which the unfamiliar is made familiar. This conjunction of problems of otherness and problems of naming places us in the realm of rhetoric. To name that which is different is to create an arbitrary link between the unknown object and known language. To speak of the Other is to produce a scenario in which a familiar signifier names something in the world that is not its normal referent. This scenario, in effect, enacts the logic that underlies the production of figures, the construction of tropes. To speak of the Other is to make metaphors.[28]

From its very beginning Panurge's story sets in relief the relationship between rhetoric and otherness. Its first lines are marked by three moments at which the Other is named. As he introduces his tale Panurge assures Pantagruel that what is noteworthy about the Turks is that they drink water instead of wine: "My lord . . . these devilish Turks are very unfortunate not to drink a drop of wine" (214). Thus at the moment that they are introduced the Turks are named with a cliché, as devils. A moment later, as he begins the story, Panurge offers figural descriptions of both himself and his captors: "The rascally Turks had put me on a spit, all larded like a rabbit" (214) ["Les paillards Turcqs m'avoient mys en broche tout lardé comme un connil"] (289). The adjective or noun "paillard," translated here as "rascally," refers, by metonymy, to someone who sleeps on a mattress of straw or "paillasse." The term connotes sexual licence. A sentence later, Panurge names his captors a third time, as he prays to God to deliver him "Lord God, help me! Lord God, save me! Lord God, release me of this torment which these treacherous dogs are inflicting on me for holding fast to Thy law!" (214) ["Seigneur Dieu,

< *The Limits of Ideology* >

ayde moy! Seigneur Dieu, saulve moy! Seigneur Dieu, oste moy de ce torment auquel ces traistres chiens me detiennent pour la maintenance de ta loy!" (289)]. It will remain to be seen what Panurge might mean by "Thy law," since he has just claimed that the absence of wine would keep him from ever embracing the law of Islam.

Thus at the very outset of the story the Turks are defined by three epithets: "devilish Turks"; "rascally or straw-dwelling [paillard] Turks"; "treacherous dogs." These metaphors may be dead metaphors, but Rabelais brings them to life again, for they are the terms that generate the narrative. The fire that destroys the city is ignited when Panurge's guard, the "paillard Turcq" who keeps watch over him, falls asleep. And it is Panurge himself who makes the metonymic connection between the "paillard" and his "paillasse," or straw mattress, by throwing not one, but two burning sticks, one onto the guard and the other onto the nearby pile of straw ("under a camp bed, which stood near the fireplace, and on which was the straw mattress [paillasse] of my friend, the Roaster" [215]). This metonymic movement is then continued in the progress of the fire: "Immediately the fire caught the straw, and from the straw caught the bed, and from the bed the floor . . ." Similarly, as soon as the fire has taken hold, the master of the house, one of the "devilish Turks," returns home, finds the house in flames, and calls upon devils to come to his rescue: "he gave himself over to all the devils, naming Grilgoth, Astaroth, Rappallus, and Gribouillis, each nine times" (215). This ceremony of devil worship terrifies Panurge, who has heard that devils love to eat bacon and fears that they will go for the strips around his waist ("these devils are fond of bacon" [216]). He calls on God to drive them away. When no devils appear the master of the house realizes that all is lost and resolves to kill himself.

Finally, and most fantastically, Panurge's metaphorical description of the Turks as "treacherous dogs" is neatly literalized in the last passages of the episode, as the prisoner looks back on the burning city and finds himself chased by a pack of hounds. The "Turkish dogs," as they are called in the famous cliché used by everyone in the period from Erasmus to Luther to Petrarch, have turned into real dogs. Panurge, who described himself early on as "greased up like a rabbit," keeps his own form but runs from the pack like the frightened prey of a hunt. In this violent scene of anti-Turkish paranoia Frenchmen are metaphorical rabbits running from real infidel dogs.

Thus the action of the episode is dominated by three narrative

< *The Limits of Ideology* >

moments (the fire, the suicide of the pasha, and the appearance of the pack of dogs), each of which is motivated by one of the metaphors used by Panurge to describe the Turks at the outset. Moreover, the movement from one trope to the next offers a kind of gradual intensification of the capacity of rhetorical figures to spill over into reality. First, the connection between the "paillard" and his "paillasse" is made by Panurge himself, when he throws one burning stick onto the straw and one onto the guard. Next, the metaphorically devilish pasha seeks vainly to invoke real devils. Finally, we shift directly from metaphor to literalization when the dogs miraculously appear at the close of the episode. Notwithstanding Panurge's repeated claims that he is telling nothing but the truth, the narrative structure of the episode is in fact produced out of its own figures. The Turk becomes his label—a dog, a lusty sleeper in the straw, a devil worshiper. Tropological naming functions both *rhetorically*, to freeze or capture the Other in figural language, and *ideologically*, to produce a particular culturally constructed notion of the Turks. Narrative becomes the process whereby the dead metaphors used to describe the Other are revivified. The rhetorical distortions I posited in my introduction as characteristic of the struggle to define the edges of community here turn up at the edge of Christendom itself.

Yet this scene of rhetorical distortion, with its anxious representation of the Other, butts up against a much more benign model of the relationship between language and otherness—a model intended to diffuse fear of strangers. This is the charitable attitude evoked in the encounter of Panurge and Pantagruel. Rhetorical freezing of the Other in language stands in tension with the Christian humanist notion of a charity that transcends superficial differences. The theme of charity makes its appearance after the suicide of the devilish master and before the encounter with the dogs, when Panurge meets the group of townspeople carrying pails of water to put out the fire. When they see him, "half roasted," as he says, "they took pity on me naturally and threw all their water over me, which was the jolliest refreshment, and did me a great deal of good" (217) ["Me voyans ainsi à demi rousty, eurent pitié de moy naturellement et me getterent toute leur eau sur moy et me refraicherent joyeusement, ce que me fist fort grand bien" (292)]. When these Moslem refugees offer the Christian Panurge food and water they are, much like the Good Samaritan of Luke 10, taking pity "naturally" on a stranger in need—the closest that infidels can come to something like Christian charity. Yet Pa-

< *The Limits of Ideology* >

nurge responds to this gift of food and drink with ingratitude "But I hardly ate, for they offered me nothing but water to drink, as is their custom" (217) ["mais ne mangeoys gueres, car ilz ne me bailloient que de l'eaue à boyre, à leur mode" (292)]. Panurge's response to the kindness of the Turks (a kindness offered with less hesitation, it should be noted, than the aid given by Pantagruel when he first meets his friend) is simply to note the insufficiency of their gift, which is water instead of wine.[29]

The Pleasures of the Flesh

Panurge's ingratitude articulates a moral message of the type promoted in the Erasmian humanist hermeneutic evoked earlier. The external sign of difference, abstinence from wine, blinds Panurge to the generosity demonstrated by the "devilish," "canine" Turks. The crucial issue here is not the theological limitations of pagan generosity (mere pagan pity, rather than true Christian charity) but Panurge's failure to recognize it and respond with charity of his own. Here, as in the encounter between Panurge and Pantagruel, Saint Paul's first letter to the Corinthians offers a useful gloss that stresses the crucial role of charity in encounters with one's neighbors. For it is this apostle who admonishes his readers, "If I give away all I have, *and if I deliver my body to be burned*, but have not charity, I gain nothing" (1 Corinthians 13:3; my emphasis). Not only does Panurge *not* recognize the generosity of those who help him, but he rejoices at his own destruction of their city. Moreover, if Erasmus worries that Christians may look a lot like Turks, Rabelais underscores the difficulty of telling Turk from Christian by making the guard and the pasha doubles of Panurge. Both Turk and Christian are scorched and tied up.

Clearly, the scene evokes the central political and moral dilemma addressed in the debates over the Turkish question during the 1520s—whether to be martyred by the invaders, or burn their cities. Yet the Pauline subtext suggests a moral dimension to Panurge's relationship to his own flesh. For though Panurge sees the parallel between his situation and the death of Saint Lawrence, he refuses the martyrdom his prototype accepted. His desire, in fact, is to deliver his body *from* being burned, instead of submitting it to be burned. Panurge is alert enough to recognize that his situation parallels Saint Lawrence's death on the grill, but he refuses to accept martyrdom at the hand of the infidel. Indeed, he turns the situation to his material

< *The Limits of Ideology* >

advantage by relieving the pasha of his purse—though, as if in echo of Paul's precept about giving away what one owns, he informs Pantagruel that the purse has vanished like the snows of yesteryear.

The question of the flesh—important throughout the scene—is emphasized in the final moment. Panurge's allegorical flight recalls the story of the wife of Lot, who, in Genesis 19:26, looks back (against God's commandment) on the burning cities of Sodom and Gomorrah and is in punishment turned into a pillar of salt. The Biblical scene is a conventional locus for discussions of the problematic nature of the flesh in Christian moral philosophy. The most influential late medieval Biblical glossator, Pierre Bersuire, provides an influential reading of the story of Lot's wife by taking it as an allegory about the sinful soul's reluctance to sever itself from the flesh (symbolized by the cities of the plain) in order to ascend to the mountain of contemplation.[30]

However, given the humanist emphasis on the relationship between reading and moral philosophy discussed earlier, one should not be surprised to find that Panurge's moral error is based on a hermeneutic distortion, on a mistake of interpretation. In a Pauline context carnality is associated with the letter, which kills as the spirit gives life. Panurge's immoral attachment to his own flesh is paralleled, in the sphere of interpretation, by a literal-mindedness that ignores the spirit of charity and distinguishes Turks from Christians according to such superficial signs as whether they drink water or wine. Panurge recognizes only literal differences between Christians and Turks but fails to see the deeper link defined by charity, and by Christ's commandment to love one's neighbor. To stress this moral point, the very metaphor that Panurge uses to describe the Turks (as dogs) is itself literalized and returns to attack the flesh with which he is so powerfully obsessed. This carnality explains the strange appearance of the "villainous little Turk" and the courtesan near the end of the scene. They offer two possible versions of how one lives in the flesh—through gluttony or through sex.

Panurge's blindness to generosity, then, can be linked to a failure to read, within the allegorical spirit of New Testament charity, the signs produced by the Other. And it is in the context of the hermeneutic literalism signaled by Panurge's fleshliness that one can see the ambivalent importance of his initial description of the Turks. For when, in the very first sentence of his story, Panurge calls the Turks unfortunate because they drink only water, he says more than he knows. In

< *The Limits of Ideology* >

New Testament terms the distinction between drinking water and drinking wine signals the theological distinction between living under Old Testament law and New Testament grace, as well as the hermeneutic distinction between reading literally and reading spiritually. Thus Panurge's lament that the Turks drink no wine is really a lament that they live under the law, rather than under the umbrella of grace. The catch, however, is that in order to see this allegorical message hidden in Panurge's description of the Turks, one must read his words figurally, that is, in terms of the spirit, which gives life, instead of the letter, which kills. Yet it is this very allegorical mode of interpretation that the fleshly, literalistic, Panurge is incapable of practicing. For him, the misfortune of the Turks is precisely and literally that they drink only water and not wine. Thus Panurge's discourse must be read for what it does, against, as it were, his own intentions—just as I am arguing that Rabelais's own language works to respond to certain ideological pressures on his text.

This concern with figuration can now help us understand the opening of the scene in which, as noted above, Panurge slides from praise of a vintage that makes one thirstier the more one drinks it to a joke about the Turks' refusal of wine. His description parodies yet another famous cross-cultural encounter in the Bible, Christ's response to the Samaritan woman at the well in John 4:13: "Everyone who drinks of this water will thirst again, but whoever drinks of the water that I shall give him will never thirst; the water that I shall give him will become in him a spring of water welling up to eternal life." The drink that makes one thirsty for more is precisely not wine. It is the "literal" water of the Old Testament. And the thirst that recurs can only be quenched by the "new" water given by Christ. That is, the water drunk by the Samaritan woman before she follows Christ is replaced by the water of the spirit. That water, however, is in turn symbolized by the wine of the sacrament, which holds the Christian community together. The literalist Panurge reverses the relationship of wine and water when he describes the wine he drinks with a language more appropriate to "old" water. In other words, he turns literal wine back into symbolic water. His literalistic echoing of Christ's utterance leads into his joke about the Turks, where he stresses the literal dimension of their abstinence. By literally misreading the nature of the Turks' literalism, Panurge not only fails to overcome the difference that separates him from them; he erects a barrier where none exists. For the Christian who, like Erasmus, knows how to read figu-

< *The Limits of Ideology* >

rally, it is enough that the Turks don't drink the wine of the spirit. That they drink no wine is of no consequence.

The episode of Panurge's escape from the Turks is marked by a conflict between two distinct models of the relationship between rhetoric and otherness. In the first of these models language is magical. The figure that defines the Other is miraculously literalized, as the metaphorical dog becomes a real dog, and the word becomes flesh. This model works to keep the Other at bay, so to speak, to dehumanize him. At the same time, however, the central importance of the theme of charity emphasizes Panurge's carnality and literal-mindedness. Panurge relates to the Other according to the flesh and the letter, focusing on such marks of difference as the drinking of wine instead of water—in complete blindness to the charity that Christian humanism claims should inform the relationship between self and Other. Rhetoric dehumanizes and distances the Other, while the Christian humanist ideal of charity accepts him through a hermeneutic based on figural reading. Erasmus's double representation of the Turks as both threatening and half-Christian is dramatized in the very rhetorical fabric of the scene, which sets trope and moral precept at odds with one another. Earlier, I suggested that rhetorical distortion shapes the edges of communities and nations. Here, that distortion simultaneously exploits and undermines the discourse of Christian identity.

The Pleasures of Narrative

The pressure that this encounter with the Other seems to place on humanist ideology may be expanded to involve the nature of literary representation itself. In his identification with the wife of Lot, as well as in his failure to recognize generosity and extend charity, Panurge is placed at odds with both Old Testament divinity and New Testament precept. He stands as a negative exemplar, as a model of how not to treat one's neighbor. Panurge himself makes the connection between divine law and the dogs seemingly sent to punish him. He realizes, after the fact, that he has erred. Unlike the wife of Lot, however, he saves himself by throwing a piece of bacon. This is the action that takes Panurge from history to literature, liberating him from the Turks and bringing him to the famous meeting with Pantagruel.

It is a powerfully overdetermined gesture. On one level it simply literalizes a well-known sixteenth-century proverb. "To throw one's lard to the dogs" ["Jetter son lard aux chiens"] meant to waste one's re-

< The Limits of Ideology >

sources, to spend one's money imprudently—as Panurge seems to have done by using up the contents of the purse given him by the pasha. On another level, it is a cliché of emblematic literature, recalling conventional depictions in bestiaries (and going back to Pliny) of the figure of the beaver, who bites off his own genitals and throws them to pursuing hunters—a gesture conventionally allegorized as an emblem of peacemaking.[31] This would seem to suggest castration. Yet the cross-cultural context of the scene suggests that what may be at issue here is less castration than circumcision, with the piece of bacon as a substitute foreskin and Panurge's hasty gesture a kind of dramatization of the notion that, in his literalism, he resembles the circumcised Turks he flees. That is, the beaver's self-castration is deflected by the cross-cultural context into a kind of symbolic circumcision. Either way, the bacon seems to be a kind of proxy for the genitals. And when Panurge flees the pack of Turkish dogs, he runs to save his very flesh. By throwing the bacon he saves that fleshly member which he most prizes. Temporally, the scene predates the meeting with Pantagruel, so virtually the first demonstratation anywhere in Rabelais of Panurge's celebrated *panourgia* or craftiness is his gesture of throwing to the threatening dogs the piece of bacon that hangs suggestively from his midsection.

The place of Panurge's gesture within the episode itself is important for a consideration of Rabelais's manipulation of narrative form. Let us recall again the sequence of events. Panurge calls the Turks dogs. He fails to recognize their generosity. At the top of the hill he looks back on the flaming city and laughs at their disaster. Yet God punishes him, as Panurge himself realizes, by sending a pack of dogs to chase him. Now, the obvious Christian humanist response to this ostensible divine punishment would be a moral transformation, a conversion that would turn viciousness into charity, literalism into spirituality. But this moral rebirth, which is called for by Christian humanist ideology and which should take place on the hilltop, is denied Panurge by the scene's very narrative movement. For by the time Panurge realizes his moral error the Turks, whom he needs to embrace, are no longer Turks—in Erasmus's words, "first of all men and then semi-Christians." They have become dogs. By making the double logic of Erasmian discourse unfold through a series of events, by *first* accepting the Turks (they are generous), and *then* dehumanizing them (they are dogs) at the moment when Panurge realizes that he has erred by not recognizing their generosity, Rabelais forecloses

< *The Limits of Ideology* >

the possibility of any immediate, politically charged response to the patent moral message that he is offering. In this way he deflects the tough moral dilemmas implied in the political context that the scene so obviously evokes. The text's humanist themes and Biblical sub-texts suggest the demonstration of a moral message of charity. Yet because the Turks have become dogs no charity need ever actually be shown. The moral message is inscribed in the text, but not on the body of the subject Panurge. The response to the limitations of the humanist rhetoric of otherness turns out to be narrative itself, which makes it possible both to kill and to flee from the Turks, yet, unlike Erasmus, his humanist colleagues, and even Francis I himself, advocates nothing.

Panurge's gesture of escape, moreover, suggests the distance between the "pre-national" world of Rabelais and the more centralized political systems that will emerge under the regime of nascent capitalism and absolutism in the seventeenth century. As Deleuze and Guattari have noted, it is precisely the harnessing of the erotic and linguistic energy of a "deterritorialized" humanity that capitalism achieves in instituting the regime of Oedipus and the power structures of the modern nation-state. Here, it might appear that we are dealing with a drama of castration in the Freudian tradition. Yet it is even more probable, as I've noted, that the bacon is a kind of emblem of the foreskin. Thus even as Rabelais uncannily prefigures the Freudian dramas that will accompany the rise of the absolutist state, it seems clear that the issue is cultural and religious difference, rather than sexual identity. The concept of repression so crucial to the Freudian schema seems to have no role here. Indeed, Panurge escapes precisely because he is *not* castrated by the God who seems to punish him. Threats of castration and punishment in general seem to roll off Panurge like water.[32]

Writing of the process whereby literature offers aesthetic solutions to real historical struggles, Fredric Jameson notes that "the literary work or cultural object, as though for the first time, brings into being that situation to which it is also, at one and the same time, a reaction."[33] Panurge's encounter with the Turks shows up the limitations of Christian humanism by displaying the contradictions that become legible when "humanism" is no longer dealing with Christians. It "brings into being," to use Jameson's terms, the contradiction between the rhetorical protection enlisted by a threatened Christendom, on the one hand, and the morality of reconciliation offered by human-

< *The Limits of Ideology* >

ism, on the other. It inscribes this contradiction into its very "message." Like Erasmus, Rabelais makes the Turks both like Christians and unlike them, both sympathetic and terrifying. Yet the contradiction in the Erasmian schema is resolved in Rabelais by the aesthetic object itself. The text itself "resolves" the ideological contradiction it has made legible by the way it orders events. Here, in the formative moments of modern secular literary culture, narrative form redeems humanist ideology.

However, if narrative seems to save ideology from the violence of history, yet another dimension of the episode concerns the epistemological status of Rabelais's own text. Consider the bacon. The piece of bacon that hangs from Panurge's waist is the site at which the two models for thinking about the Other at work in the scene—distancing the Turks through naming and accepting them through charity—overlap. Panurge's body is the site of carnality and literalism, of the dog-eat-rabbit world in which the only relationship to the Other is either cannibalism or lust—the "little Turk" or the courtesan. Yet Panurge's wily solution to his predicament brings us in a roundabout way back from the literal to the figural. At the close of the scene Panurge's dilemma is either to die a fleshly death, that is, to be eaten by the literalized metaphorical dogs that are chasing him, or to embrace them in the spirit of charity, overlooking the literal difference of their flesh and religion and recognizing their humanity. His response is to seek a midpoint between flesh and spirit, between the literal and the figural, by throwing the dogs a piece of flesh. It is a piece of flesh whose meaning is overdetermined tropologically as well as topologically. It is twice a replacement for the penis; it is a penis through the logic of both metaphor and metonymy. Literally, physically, it is a piece of bacon. Yet it is a figural penis, a substitute or fetish-object related to the real thing by virtue of its metonymical proximity to it— they both hang from the midsection. It is also, however, in its French name, a "lardon." And Rabelais's favorite expression to describe sexual intercourse is "frotter le lard" ("rub your bacon"). Thus the punning logic of metaphor makes the penis a "lardon" and the "lardon" a penis. This overdetermination resolves the tension between a rhetoric that works through the literalization of metaphors and a hermeneutics that shuns the letter and the flesh for the figure and the spirit. The piece of bacon is a substitute penis both physically and linguistically, a physical metonymy and a linguistic metaphor.[34]

But this tropological "resolution," central to the moral message of

< *The Limits of Ideology* >

the episode, depends upon another rhetorical distortion—a distortion of history itself. For the various layers of signification at work in the depiction of the bacon are all built upon the most obvious and outrageous irony in Panurge's story—the fact that Turks do not eat bacon, which is forbidden them for religious reasons. Only dogs eat bacon—or, more precisely, Turks only eat bacon when they have been turned into dogs. On the level of the evidential truth which Panurge, as witness to a real historical event, claims to tell, the "lardons" cannot possibly be eaten by Turks—even though Panurge is clearly about to be cannibalized. Either the bacon is an absolute fiction or the Turks must be made dogs if he is to escape. Yet the strips of bacon are absolutely essential to the scene, since the entire motif of physical mutilation from which the Christian humanist moral about charity takes its power depends on the pun that links "lardons" to penises. Thus the most obvious literal mark of cultural difference, the piece of bacon, becomes, when figured as a penis, the very sign that makes possible a moral message about the risks of being uncharitable to one's neighbor. The very same object which, on a literal level, separates groups of human beings, produces, when it has become a metaphor, a fable about uniting them. Depending upon whether it is a figure or an object, a word or a thing, the bacon is the marker of either otherness or community.

The moral fable, however, only works when the Turks' actual cultural difference (manifested in dietary prohibition) has been overcome by the effacement of their humanity. Both Panurge and the Turks need something, a kind of dietary supplement, to help them ingest their food. For the Turks it is the bacon that adorns Panurge's inedibly skinny body; for Panurge it is the wine that washes down the refugees' prandial gift. Yet whereas the wine can be ingested even by bad Christian readers like Panurge who ignore its figural meaning, the bacon cannot be ingested by Turks. The bacon is an absolute sign of difference, a literal mark of cultural otherness. Its presence underscores the moral contrast between Panurge's literalism and the Turks' literalism. Panurge's literalistic interpretation of the wine is defined negatively, as the mark of willful fleshliness. The Turks' literalistic obedience to dietary laws, on the other hand, is the very sign of their piety—a piety that makes them, in Erasmus's words, spiritual enough to be "half-Christian." To neutralize a Turkish literalism that is both admirable and stubbornly resistant to Christian theology Rabelais must either change the bacon or change the Turks.

< *The Limits of Ideology* >

The transformation of the Turks into dogs resolves an ideological dilemma no less than Panurge's stratagem averts physical catastrophe. And in the cultural context of Renaissance humanism there is a language to describe this, too. For both of them exemplify yet another proverbial phrase, the so-called "rule of Mytilene," evoked first by Aristotle in his *Nicomachean Ethics*. Instead of making their buildings according to a fixed measuring stick, the inhabitants of Mytilene were famous for adjusting the measuring stick to fit the stone at their disposal. Aristotle defines the rule in terms that uncannily prefigure Rabelais's exploration of the relationship between cultural contingency and narrative form. He notes that when the particularity of a legal case resists the universality of the law (just as, here, the literalism of the Turks limits the universality of Christian charity) the task of the judge is to become a kind of narrator, to invent a tale, "to say what the legislator himself would have said had he been present, and would have put into his law if he had known."[35] In an adage built from the proverb, Erasmus underscores its relevance for Rabelais. He transmutes Aristotle's legal language into moral terms, suggesting that the rule of Mytilene involves the bending of moral law to the contingency of facts, the adaptation of theory to practice, rather than vice versa.[36] On one level, this is precisely what the amoral Panurge does throughout Rabelais's works. But Rabelais is doing it too, in his play with narrative form. Like the Aristotelian legislator, he uses narrative fiction to resolve a contradiction between the contingency of history and the requirements of moral philosophy. His narrative trick parallels, on the level of literary representation, Panurge's prudence in escaping from the hounds.

Panurge's escape takes us from a concern with the contradictions of humanism at a moment of cross-cultural encounter, to a consideration of the epistemology of Rabelais's narrative itself. A humanist moral lesson is created by a scene itself produced out of tropological distortion. Yet that which is produced by troping (in this case dogs) in turn makes visible, when set into narrative form, the fragility and limits of humanist morality, which has to be saved by the incongruous bacon. A Christian humanist reading of the text as moral allegory is both absolutely essential to the scene and subverted by its rhetorical complexity. This impossible relationship between precept and trope may in turn be seen as the effect of the text's curious epistemological status. The episode draws upon a whole range of generic conventions. The evocation of the invasion of Mytilene suggests that

< The Limits of Ideology >

one is dealing with *reportage*, with the kind of eyewitness account of Turkish customs that flourished in the fifteenth and early sixteenth century. However, this tradition of travel writing relies on a discourse of witnessing clearly undermined by Panurge's questionable insistence that he is telling the absolute truth, and by the fantastic depiction of the bacon. Indeed, in his late sixteenth-century *History of a Voyage to the Land of Brazil*, the Protestant writer Jean de Léry criticizes cartographers who decorate their maps with images of New World natives roasting human flesh. This, Léry says, is no more believable than the tale of Panurge's escape.[37] Léry's statement reminds the reader that Rabelais is drawing on traditions of travel literature, and that such texts often did sound a lot like Rabelais. In any event, these two generic poles—"ethnographic realism" and the self-conscious fictionality of the bacon—cannot coexist; yet they must, if the episode is to deploy the moral discourse required by humanist ideology. Or, more precisely, the generic register of humanist moralism (which accepts the Turks' humanity) and the tradition of the traveler's tale or captive's narrative (which recounts the alterity of the Turks) can only coexist through the presence of the bacon, through the sign of the self-conscious fictionality that characterizes the discourse we call literature. Rabelais's text deploys a kind of generic mixing as a way of resolving the ideological problem of representing the Other. The multiplicity of generic registers not only mirrors the multiplicity of cultures. It is essential to the ideological work done by the scene.[38]

By posing the risk of excessive literalism as a problem both for reading the text and for reading the Other, Rabelais thematizes the unstable relationship between humanist idealism and literary representation in the face of cultural multiplicity. It is impossible to claim either that Rabelais is merely offering a humanist moral tale, or that he is simply showing how language undoes humanist ideology. To be sure, the scene subverts humanist clichés about charity. However, if we assume that that subversion somehow renders those clichés irrelevant, we have already failed to grasp the way the text asks us to move beyond its literal surface. To ignore the complexity of the issues of moral philosophy and politics that Rabelais is addressing here, to just read this as a mere "joke," would be to read Rabelais as reductively as Panurge reads the Turks. Yet, by contrast, to ignore the fact that humanism is being turned against itself is to miss the fact that the plot, at its most basic level, asks us to think about figuration. Moreover,

< *The Limits of Ideology* >

such a reading would fail to account for the violence done to humanist ideologies of community by the fact of cultural difference.

Although the escape from the Turks may at first appear peripheral, by virtue of both its geographical location (on the "margin" of Europe) and its brevity, to what scholars often see as the main themes of Rabelais's work, it is, in fact, central to understanding the dynamic relationship between community and otherness in Rabelais. For the encounter with the Turks is merely the most extreme expression of a series of concerns about literalism and moral allegory, letter and spirit, that permeate *Pantagruel* from its outset. In the prologue, the narrator distinguishes his book from the pamphletary *Chronicque Gargantuine*, which is evoked as a predecessor text. The book we are about to read, he asserts, is of the same type as the chronicle, only more believable, "a little more reasonable and credible than the last" (168) ("un peu plus equitable et digne de foy que n'estoit l'aultre"[218]). And he goes on to evoke the example of the Bible:

> But do not suppose—unless you wish to be wilfully deceived— that I speak of it as the Jews do of the Law. I was not born under that planet, nor have I ever come to lie, or to affirm a thing to be true which was not. I speak of it as a lusty Onocrotary—no, I mean Crotonotary of martyred lovers and Crocquenotary of love. *Quod vidimus testamur.* (168)

> [Car ne croyez (si ne voulez errer à vostre escient), que j'en parle comme les Juifz de la Loy. Je ne suis nay en telle planette et ne m'advint oncques de mentir, ou asseurer chose que ne feust veritable. J'en parle comme un gaillard Onocrotale, voyre dy je, crotenotaire des martyrs amans, et crocquenotaire de amours: *Quod vidimus testamur.* (218)]

The difference between *Pantagruel* and the *Chronicque* seems to be the difference between the Old Testament and the New. The Jews are seen here to be in error, and to speak falsely because they take their law to be universal truth. In the language of Christian Biblical typology, that law is *historical* truth, it is *literally* true, but it has been surpassed by a new law. The Jews are literal, but wrong. The Christian lives by a new literal truth, one embodied in the life of Christ, but one that retrospectively turns that old literal truth into figure. The Exodus is not only history; it is moral philosophy—the tale of the self's passage from error to truth. It is this new law and new way of reading that Rabelais claims for his own text when he quotes John's exclama-

< *The Limits of Ideology* >

tion, "We attest to what we have seen." *Pantagruel* is literally true, because it has been seen, but its importance lies in its moral significance for the reader. In theological terms, this significance ultimately involves the will of the reader. "If you think I am speaking only literally," he says, "you err, willfully" ("a vostre escient"). And yet the episode of Panurge's escape places these categories in question. Certainly, the narrator's first description of Panurge as looking like he's just escaped from a pack of dogs—a detail which, as I noted, is true but which he cannot know—suggests that even the testimonial veracity of his "quod vidimus testamur" may be in question—not because his will is weak, but because vision itself is weak when it confronts difference. For weakness of vision is the central problem of humanism in the presence of the Other.[39] This uncertainty is exaggerated throughout the rest of the episode, as Panurge's complex depictions of the Turks suggest that any attempt to avoid mere literalism may lead to an epistemological impasse. Indeed, the epistemological danger introduced by the Turks underscores the difficulty with which humanism allegorizes the Other. The problem of appropriating the strange or alien is paralleled in the theological literalism of the Turks themselves, who resist, by their very being, the Erasmian tendency to turn all cultural material into the pretext for moral allegory.

It may be the difficulty of appropriating topical material from contemporary politics for humanist moral reflection that leads Rabelais, in the final chapters of *Pantagruel*, to forsake altogether the dangerous area where cultures and communities collide. Both Panurge's prayer for deliverance and his blindness toward Turkish generosity are recalled at the end of the book. Here, we see Panurge's friend Pantagruel enter into battle with a hostile invader named Anarche. Pantagruel's victory over and subsequent charitable treatment of Anarche suggest a humanist fantasy in which the hostile Turk is rendered impotent and the human community can be restored to its wholeness. The "positive" exemplar Pantagruel redeems, in the final chapters, the moral errors of the "negative" figure Panurge. Yet this reaffirmation of humanist *ideology* comes at the expense of a shift in the form of *representation*. Anarche and his men bear a trace of the cultural alterity contained in the Turkish threat when they shout "Mahomet, Mahomet" as they enter battle. Yet the cry is a literary cliché which places them in a line of stereotypical pagans reaching back to the *Song of Roland*. Thus whereas the scene discussed above plays with the reality of the invasion of Mytilene and the conventions of escape narra

< *The Limits of Ideology* >

tives, the end of the book is purely allegorical, with the good king Pantagruel defeating the transparently named embodiment of anarchy. It takes place in a different register altogether, as if Rabelais's humanist message could only be articulated by forsaking the anxious zone of cross-cultural contact, where the discourse of humanist charity runs up against the contingency of the political world.[40]

Panurge's escape from the Turks thus has a number of interesting implications for a consideration of literature and nationhood in the French Renaissance. First, it suggests that the language of Christian humanism, which scholars have long seen as central to the cultural moment of the Valois monarchy, is already threatened by an increasing pressure from the experience of alterity, from the awareness of the difficulty of defining the Christian community in language—both at its "edges," and (as I shall show in more detail in the next chapter) at its center. Second, it underscores that the moment of the threat to community is also a moment of rhetorical distortion and exorbitance, of the creation of phantasmic images and scenes that seem to mediate the impossible relationships between different spaces and symbolic systems. Third, it points to the way in which these large ideological and epistemological conflicts seem to find momentary textual "solutions" in the strategies of form present in the self-conscious fictionality of literature itself.

Chapter Three

Nation and Utopia in the 1530s:
The Case of Rabelais's
Gargantua

Jewgreek is Greekjew.
—JAMES JOYCE, *Ulysses*

The importance of Rabelais's writing as a gauge of the forces shaping the emergence of French national identity in the third and fourth decades of the sixteenth century involves not merely his literary authority and range. It also has to do with what might be called his timing. The publication of his first two books, *Pantagruel* (1532) and *Gargantua* (1534), came at a moment of extreme fragility in French political and cultural life. Produced in the years leading up to the famous "Affaire des Placards" (1534), the works reflect the increasing interaction in French public life between theological ferment and political power. They appeared at a moment when threats to *Christian* unity were beginning to be perceived as threats to *French* unity. Francis I had initially seen the spread of Protestant "errors" in France as the work of "people of low status and lower understanding."[1] However, by the early 1530s, it had become clear that the new movement was also infecting intellectuals at the highest level of achievement and standing. Following the Affaire des Placards, Francis's early toleration of religious dissent hardened into a more rigid orthodoxy. And the problems of theological identity raised by Reformation thought had begun to be construed in more properly political terms. Indeed, as early as 1523, Francis had staged a spectacle in Paris to celebrate national unity and orthodoxy which concluded in the execution of six Protestants—for *both* heresy and treason. Religious dissent was already recognized as a national issue. Two weeks after this event, as Donald Kelley writes, "Francis declared to the Protestant princes of Germany (whom he was already courting because of rivalry with Charles V) that his displeasure was directed not against Lutheranism as such but against the seditious behavior of those who, behind their

< *Nation and Utopia in the 1530s* >

theological 'paradoxes,' were subverting French society. Even more than his treaty with the Turks of this same year, this act of the French king signified . . . the replacement of the religious question by politics."[2] Thus royal anxiety about religious dissent resulted in a political pronouncement directed toward rival princes.

This link between a crisis of theological community and a crisis of the political body takes a slightly different form elsewhere in French foreign policy. However, the terms are reversed, and political rivalry is interpreted as theological crisis. For the same historical moment also sees an intensification of the antagonism between Francis I and the Holy Roman Emperor Charles V. Indeed, as the papal nuncio noted at one point, Francis's hatred of Charles in the late 1520s and 1530s had reached such extremes that "he seems to make it his business to provoke the emperor."[3] Furthermore, Francis's captivity in Madrid during the middle years of the 1520s, following his defeat at the Battle of Pavia, had brought on a crisis of French identity, as the country saw itself thrown into a regency under the king's mother, and placed in a position of extreme political fragility. These tensions between princes were analyzed by many humanist writers, as we shall see in detail in a moment, as a crisis of the Christian body.

As an associate of Francis's most trusted diplomat, Jean Du Bellay, Rabelais was well positioned to appreciate the shifts in the domestic and international political scene of the late 1520s and early 1530s. These tensions provide the backdrop to his second book, *Gargantua*, which recounts the adventures of Pantagruel's father. *Gargantua* is the most explicitly political and patriotic of Rabelais's books. His increasing concern for the political sphere may reflect a new sense that Christian renewal could not be achieved without an increased attention to secular political affairs—that spiritual transformation required a political base. In any event, *Gargantua* provides a case history for tracing the interweaving of theological and political issues at a moment of fateful turning in French history. It offers a perfect example of the ways in which the themes of Christian universalism analyzed in the previous chapter become threatened from within the Christian community itself, in the emergence of new representations of national community. Having considered, in the previous chapter, the ways in which the edges of Christendom are figured in literary representation, we can now turn to the representation of an emerging political community.

Gargantua presents a landscape different from the one seen in *Pantagruel*, both in terms of the political problems it confronts and in terms

< *Nation and Utopia in the 1530s* >

of the rhetorical strategies it uses for addressing these problems.[4] For one thing the politics of the book engage, not a threat from outside Europe, but contemporary conflicts within the Christian community. Nor do we find the kind of tension between the specific embeddedness of historical event (the invasion of Mytilene) and the dramatic *deus ex machina* resolution seen in *Pantagruel*. Topical references to contemporary history are much more frequent in *Gargantua*, which seems to be in dialogue as much with contemporary political theory as with the theological idealism deployed in *Pantagruel*. Yet the political concerns of the book are again linked, even more explicitly than in *Pantagruel*, to language. The prologue to *Gargantua* compares the book to the figure of Socrates, whose ugly exterior hides a beautiful interior. The beautiful inside that we must uncover through the process of interpretation promises to reveal "certain very high sacraments and horrible mysteries, concerning not only our religion, but also our political state and domestic life" (38).[5] The destiny of France, the state of politics and religion, are linked to the language of the text, and to the act of reading.

In this chapter, I will suggest that there is a rhetorical and ideological tension in the text between the representation of what the prologue calls "religion," on the one hand, and "our political state and domestic life," on the other. *Gargantua* is caught between the reaffirmation of the unity of Christian Europe and a patriotic defense of a threatened Valois monarchy. Christian utopian themes consistently advocate a renunciation of the violence and antagonism that is evoked in the book's treatment of political relations; however, even as Christian humanist themes point toward the imagination of new forms of action and community, those same ideals, when they are represented in action, depend upon precisely the very language and violence that they seem to reject. Rabelais resolves this seemingly intractable ideological and rhetorical double bind through a variety of exorbitant rhetorical strategies, which are the property of that imaginative discourse that will come to be called literature. Thus, certain aspects of literary form may be read as an attempt to mediate between "religion" and "our political state."

These concerns are highlighted in the centerpiece of *Gargantua*, the story of the Picrocholine war, in which Gargantua and his men defeat their neighbors, the men of Lerné. This vast tale of violence and heroism is Rabelais's most accomplished narrative sequence. With amazing assurance, it leaps from camp to camp, sweeping from fresco-like descriptions of battle to the minutiae of the body. Yet it

< *Nation and Utopia in the 1530s* >

has traditionally posed interpretative problems for commentators. Not the least of these involves its very geography—the terrain on which the war unfolds. For the war against Picrochole functions on a number of seemingly distinct planes at once. The figure of Picrochole, who furiously invades Gargantua's home territory, has a triple provenance. On one level, as his name ("the choleric one") implies, he is a kind of emblem of psychic and physiological imbalance. In this regard, he recalls the allegorical figure of Anarche whom Pantagruel defeats in the first book. Yet on another level, Picrochole is the object of political satire; he has been seen as a figure for the feared and hated emperor, Charles V. This topical connection is underscored by Picrochole's frequent exhortation to his men to "go beyond" ("passer oultre")—a joking translation of Charles's motto "plus ultra." However, on yet another level, commentators have pointed out that the terrain of the war—in and around Rabelais's hometown of Chinon—recalls details of a quarrel between Rabelais's father and one of his neighbors, Gaucher de Sainte-Marthe. Thus, through a kind of zoom effect, the narrative moves from the allegorical world of the physiology of the humors, to the stage of world politics, to local anecdote.[6]

What is at issue on each of these levels, however, is the question of how to deal with one's neighbor. The theme of charity, of such importance in *Pantagruel*, is here projected into the field of politics proper—indeed, into the realm of what we might call European foreign policy. In this chapter, emphasis will no longer be on the fact of *cultural* difference, as it was in the preceding section, but on how *political* difference, the simple rivalry between princes, threatens representations of "universal" Christian identity.[7] *Gargantua* explores a theme of central concern to political philosophers during the period—the tension between charitable action and political expediency. As the political philosopher Claude de Seyssel put it in his *Monarchy of France*, the task of foreign policy was to preserve one's territory against enemy attack by any means necessary, while, nonetheless, keeping oneself within "the rule of charity" ("gardant toujours l'ordre de charité").[8] In *Pantagruel*, the order of charity was threatened by an encounter between the Christian community and the non-Christian. Here, when Rabelais links the politics of charity to the depiction of conflict between neighbors, he raises questions about the nature of community itself. *Pantagruel* explores how humanist ideology responds to threats from outside Christendom, *Gargantua* considers the meaning of difference within the Christian community.

< *Nation and Utopia in the 1530s* >

The most authoritative exploration of the relationship between secular community and spiritual community comes in a text that Rabelais would have known by heart, and that is central to all European Christian humanist thought—Paul's Epistle to the Romans. In this, the most political of his letters, Paul defines a contrast between two models of collective identity. On the one hand, in the world of the Old Testament, in the domain of the law, humans are defined by their membership in a nation, by a disposition separating Greek and Jew. After the coming of Christ, those identities are forgotten and replaced by a community in which "there is no distinction between Jew and Greek; the same Lord is Lord of all and bestows his riches upon all who call upon him. For 'every one who calls upon the name of the Lord will be saved' " (10:12–13). The leap from ethnic specificity into a new membership in a universal community is underscored by Paul's last phrase, which cites and distorts the Book of Joel's claim that at the moment of the destruction of Jerusalem some Jews will be saved by calling on God. When Joel says that "every one who calls upon the name of the Lord will be saved," he means, in context, every Jew. Paul means everybody.

It is worth examining the dynamics through which this leap from contingent ethnicity into Christian community is represented, both in Paul and in the Renaissance. Paul stresses that the law of the Jews has been fulfilled through the coming of Christ: "Now we are discharged from the law, dead to that which held us captive, so that we serve not under the old written code but in the new life of the Spirit" (7:10). However, the easy distinction between past identity and present identity, between letter and spirit, between Jew and Christian, becomes complicated when Paul turns, in Chapter 11, to consider how the supercession of the law affects those Jews who have not embraced Christ. He begins by asking if the incarnation of Christ means that God has rejected the people whom He chose as His own so long ago. "By no means!" Paul insists. God has retained a remnant, "chosen by grace, not by works," who have accepted Christ's message. The hearts of the rest of the Jews have been hardened. Of course, this formulation leaves Paul in a difficult rhetorical position, since he is preaching the universal accessibility of Christianity while suggesting that it is not equally accessible to all Jews. And it is in the gap between these two groups, between those who have accepted Christ (whether previously Greek or Jew) and the "hard-hearted" Jews, that Paul locates his own language. He claims that his mission, though di-

< *Nation and Utopia in the 1530s* >

rectly aimed at the gentiles, also obliquely targets the Jews. Since Paul cannot convert the Jews by preaching to them directly, he must do so indirectly, by preaching to the gentiles. The conversion of the Jews will then come about in mediated form, through their relationship to the gentiles. Entry into the Christian community becomes an issue of the interaction among nations.

There was some dispute among Rabelais's contemporaries about how, precisely, this complex mechanism of conversion was supposed to work. The Vulgate reads, "Quamdiu quidem ego sum gentium Apostolus, ministerium meum honorificabo, si quomodo ad aemulandum provocem carnem meam, et salvos faciam aliquos ex illis;" that is, "Inasmuch as I am an Apostle to the Gentiles, I do honor to my ministry if I somehow provoke my own flesh [i.e. the Jews] to emulation, and thus save some of them."[9] Some commentators on this passage claimed that what was at issue was a process of emulation, as is suggested by the verb "aemulari." Through a kind of exemplary imitation the Jews would see the happiness of the Christians and follow them. However, Erasmus takes issue with the notion that the Jews will be converted through emulation. This may be because emulation is classically depicted (most authoritatively in Aristotle's *Rhetoric*) as a noble impulse, the sign of heroic virtue—making the idea inappropriate in a discussion of the hard-hearted Jews. Erasmus insists in his *Paraphrase on Romans* that what is at issue here (as modern English versions suggest as well) is jealousy, a more ignoble impulse, and precisely, for Aristotle, the opposite of emulation.[10] For Erasmus, the Jews will come to Christianity not because they want to follow the Christians in their discovery of the truth, but because they are jealous of them. Yet whereas jealousy is an emotion that might be said to be produced out of differences between peoples, Erasmus locates it in Jewish identity itself.

Erasmus interpolates a line not in Paul's text: the Jews will follow the Christians through "a kind of envy and jealousy," he says, because "the Jews are a jealous race" ["zelotypum genus"].[11] If the French, for Strabo, are "simple," the Jews, for Erasmus, are "jealous." Now, of course, this is wrong. The Jews are nowhere described as "a jealous race." They are only described as having a jealous God. However, in displacing jealousy from God to people, by suggesting that the Jews' impetus to convert will come from a jealousy that is somehow ingrained in their very ethnicity, Erasmus suggests that their ethnic identity and their loss of that identity are closely intertwined. What

< *Nation and Utopia in the 1530s* >

makes the Jews Jews, historically and morally, according to Erasmus, is their jealousy. And it is that same collective characteristic, ingrained in custom and tradition, that will also make them no longer Jews. Through his preaching Paul will make what he calls "my own flesh" ("carnem meam") jealous of Christians. The common passion that makes them a nation will also make them cease to be a nation. Thus the Jews, the "different" race par excellence in Paul's scenario, are identified with the passion that produces differences. That same passion then powers the effacement of difference; it leads to the absorption of the Jews into a community in which they are no different from the Greeks. At the meeting point of communities, the force of jealousy both distinguishes people and makes them one: it is here that Erasmus places a passion both singular (possessing each member of the community) and collective (it possesses them all).

The paradoxes of Erasmus's gloss on Paul's Epistle to the Romans take us to the center of the problem of the relationship between Christian humanism and nationalism—and thus to a dilemma that structures Rabelais's *Gargantua*. Rabelais's text both satirizes Charles V, the hated Spanish enemy of the French king, and advocates new models of Christian spirituality associated with Erasmian humanism. This leads Rabelais simultaneously to endorse two ideologies—an ideology of French glory and an ideology of Christian universalism. Rabelais must take two positions at once—positions involving distinct and often contradictory sets of elements. Political satire, which is also political ideology, cannot function without the ontological categories of self and Other, which it translates into the moral categories of "good" and "evil."[12] In constructing Charles V as a mad tyrant, Rabelais's text inevitably sets up a binary opposition between Spanish imperialism ("bad") and French patriotism ("good"). Yet this transvaluation inevitably works against a model of Christian universality, for which, to appropriate Paul's phrase in Romans 10:12, "there is no distinction between French and Spanish."

The depiction of Picrochole reflects in miniature the ideological double bind of the text. Picrochole is presented as both inherently angry and only recently made angry. On the one hand, his name suggests that he is afflicted by an imbalance of the vital humors just as "essential" as the proverbial jealousy of the Jews in Erasmus's formulation. Because he is named Picrochole, "the coleric one," he is angry. Yet he is also depicted as an old friend of Gargantua's father Grandgousier, and one with whom Grandgousier has often stood in the

< *Nation and Utopia in the 1530s* >

past. Thus, his anger, or "fury" (for that much more powerful Renaissance word is also used to describe him), would seem to be something he can overcome by (as Grandgousier intimates) subjecting his will to God's grace (103). As both a permanently angry fellow and a temporary enemy, Picrochole fits the exigencies of Rabelais's ideological double bind. As recent enemy, he can, at least potentially, be brought back to the fold of a unified Christendom. As an "essentially" choleric madman he becomes invested with all of the tyrannical amorality required by Valois ideology in demonizing the Holy Roman Emperor. This paradox is neatly erased in the conclusion to the war, where Picrochole's men are reabsorbed into "the order of charity"—while the madman himself vanishes from the scene.

This double bind finds a parallel in discussions of political policy scattered through Erasmian advice literature. For example, in the *Complaint of Peace* Erasmus simultaneously attacks all Christian princes for their divisiveness and praises Francis I for his peacemaking activities. However, when Rabelais confronts these issues, what is a *rhetorical* problem for Erasmus becomes a problem of *literary form*. We may see this principally at the level of genre. The plot of invasion and conquest that occupies most of *Gargantua* draws upon epic topoi in which aggressive political and religious enemies are conquered and absorbed into new forms of community. Indeed, the topical presence of Charles V lends the war against Picrochole a political immediacy that was lacking in Pantagruel's allegorical battle with Anarche, and that becomes even more apparent in the prologue to Rabelais's third book, in which the narrator depicts his country's preparing for war. The topical references to Charles are frequent enough to suggest that, at one level, *Gargantua* is a French epic. It is, however, an epic of "self-defense" rather than of conquest. As such, the themes of French patriotism are articulated through the depiction of a territory in danger. And part of *Gargantua's* generic hybridity stems from the ways in which it draws consistently on clichés of epic literature, while appropriating the language of conquest for a project of national defense and Christian reconciliation.[13]

Epic action in *Gargantua* centers on the adventures of the fighting monk Frère Jean. Yet it is this same monkish figure who is most intimately connected with the other generic registers that structure the book. These are, principally, the colloquoy, exemplified most influentially during the period by Erasmus's *Convivium Religiosum* or "Godly Feast," and the conventions of utopian literature, of which

< *Nation and Utopia in the 1530s* >

Saint Thomas More's *Utopia* provides the pertinent literary example. Frère Jean is central to the deployment of both of these generic registers: the colloquoy tradition is recalled in the supper the monk shares with Gargantua and his men toward the end of the war, and the utopian tradition is echoed and transformed in the famous depiction of the Abbey of Theleme that ends the book. Whereas epic favors an ideology of conquest, the colloquoy promotes the inclusiveness of the Christian community, and utopian discourse provides a theology that is also a politics.[14] These generic registers—epic, colloquoy, and utopia—stand as markers of the tension between an ideology of difference (Franco-Spanish rivalry) and an ideology of in-difference (Christian inclusionism).

As I suggested in the analysis of *Pantagruel*, issues of identity in Rabelais are also issues of language. Scholars of Rabelais have tended to understand the contrast between "spiritual" or "allegorical" modes of reading, on the one hand, and "literalist" interpretations, on the other, as a topical contrast between a reformed, Evangelical Christianity, which Rabelais is supposed to champion, and formulaic, "traditional" Sorbonnard Catholicism, which he is assumed to decry. Yet here the issue of literalism, the world of the letter that splits people apart, is no less linked in Rabelais to issues of emerging political difference than it is to the theological themes that scholars have traditionally stressed. Indeed, Erasmus himself insists that the dangers of literalism are political as well as theological. In his *Education of the Christian Prince* he complains at length about the fascination that princes have for signing treaties, arguing that treaties often turn out to be disruptors of harmony instead of guarantors of peace. And he suggests that, in the last analysis, the maintenance of peace may be a question of reading:

> If some clause of a treaty has apparently not been observed, this must not be taken at once as evidence that the treaty as a whole is null and void . . . indeed the best course sometimes is to wink at something like this, since even an understanding between private citizens will not hold together for long if they take everything, as it were, too literally [si cuncta ad vivum, quod aiunt, exigant]. Do not immediately follow the course dictated by anger, but rather that suggested by the public interest.[15]

Erasmus's phrase "exigere ad vivum," which is here translated as "literally," means "to go to the essence of things."[16] The problem with selfish princes, he says, is that, in this most political of all acts of reading,

< Nation and Utopia in the 1530s >

they take the inessential as the essential, the letter of the law for its spirit.

For Erasmus, in fact, the question of language, of the letter and the spirit, is central to the relationship of political community to spiritual community. In the *Complaint of Peace* he stresses the way in which the most basic of all speech acts, the simple act of naming, may have political consequences. If Paul rebukes those who say "I am for Apollos, I am for Cephas, I am for Paul" as destroyers of the unity of Christ,

> Are we then to treat the common name of our country as a serious reason why one nation should be bent on exterminating another? Even that is not enough for some people, whose minds are avid for war; with perverted zeal they seek occasions for dissension, they tear France apart, and by mere words create divisions in areas not divided by seas, mountains, or genuine place-names. And just in case sharing a name may unite people in friendship, they make Germans out of the French.[17]

Language, for Erasmus, seems to be both a destroyer of Christian unity and a creator of national community. Here the spirituality of Christian readers turns back into the literalism of the "jealous" Jews. The power of the letter, of "the common name of our country," breaks peoples apart and brings them together in a different way. Because men and women take the names applied to them literally, as essential features of their identity, they may at any moment be brought to the point of war. By giving in to the spell of naming, they forget the true bond, beyond all language, that unites Christians—that bond that Paul evoked when he noted that in Christ there is "no distinction between Jew and Greek." As Erasmus goes on to lament, "Nowadays the Englishman generally hates the Frenchman, for no better reason than that he is French . . . Why do these ridiculous labels do more to separate us than the name of Christ, common to us all, can do to reconcile us?"[18] Just as the Jews in Paul's letter to the Romans live trapped in a world of the letter and of ethnic difference, so, in Erasmus's formulation, do his contemporaries live prey to names and to hatred. As Frenchman and Erasmian, Rabelais participates in both a world of "ridiculous labels" and a world unified by the name of Christ.

Rhetorical Performance and the Representation of Community

Rabelais's balancing of theological ideals and political topicality comes in the wake of the rise of modern political theory. The ques-

< *Nation and Utopia in the 1530s* >

tion of political difference, of what we would today call "foreign policy," was first examined systematically by humanist political philosophers in the second decade of the sixteenth century. Works such as Claude de Seyssel's *Monarchy of France* and Machiavelli's *Prince* shaped the emergence of modern political thought. For they brought the traditional Aristotelian and Platonic concerns with the ideal government and the perfect prince together with a focus on the government's relationship to other governments and peoples. Rabelais's mentor Erasmus, too, participates in this important body of work. In such texts as the *Education of the Christian Prince* mentioned earlier (written for the future Charles V), the *Complaint of Peace*, and the *Enchiridion*, Erasmus seeks to blend reflexions on contemporary politics with Christian homily.[19] These texts and authors formulate a language for thinking about terrestrial political power and the genesis of forms of authority distinct from (though often intertwined with) ecclesiastical institutions. They provide a rich reflection on how signs of identity are produced, circulated, and read among peoples. As we shall see, Rabelais appropriates the themes and topoi of humanist political thought in his own self-conscious linguistic play.[20]

Yet if humanist political thinking seeks to confront the realities of a Europe consisting of newly unified states, the topic of foreign policy is also a source of anxiety. For when political action involves dealings with foreigners, the task of offering counsel—so central to humanist writing—seems to run into difficulties. Thus, for example, Erasmus devotes a section in the *Education of the Christian Prince* to the negotiation of treaties. But his last words on the topic acknowledge the complexity of dealing with the Other. Erasmus urges the prince to learn all he can about other lands by study. Beyond this, he adds, "it may not be easy to lay down hard and fast rules."[21] Seyssel's language is similar: "if the practice here is hard, the theory, involving the enunciation of specific laws and doctrine as to how to manage relations with neighbors and foreigners, is harder, because the rules vary according as the princes, habits, desires, and affairs of the foreigners change and vary."[22] Whereas the political thinker can offer advice about how to organize a state made up of people who share a history and a culture, when it comes to dealing with diverse peoples, the language of advice literature falters. The encounter with difference—be it political or cultural—seems to mark the point at which advice reaches its limits, at which the transition from theory to practice is most fraught with difficulty.

< Nation and Utopia in the 1530s >

Seyssel notes in the *Monarchy of France* that the first point of foreign policy is to prevent your neighbors, "whatever friendship they
display towards you" from entering or crossing your territory.[23] This
warning bears on the beginnings of the Picrocholine war. In chapter
25 of *Gargantua*, we learn that a quarrel has erupted between two
groups of peasants from the Touraine: the shepherds belonging to
Grandgousier, Gargantua's father, who are guarding the grape har-
vest, and the bakers of "fouaces," a kind of cakelike bread, who belong
to the neighbor Picrochole, an old friend of Grandgousier. This
quarrel may be seen as an allegory of the disunity of Christendom itself. The grapes and the cakes represent the wine and bread of the
sacrament, and the fight between the grape-men and the cake-men
suggests a rending of the mystical body of Christ. By setting the quarrel at a crossroads, where Picrochole's men are passing through
Grandgousier's vineyards, Rabelais recalls Seyssel's warning. And the
long-standing friendship points to the difficulty of knowing who is
an enemy and who is a friend—who is "one of us," and who is not.

The theme of political difference becomes linked to the question
of language a moment later, in chapter 34. The war has begun, and as
Gargantua is preparing to engage with Picrochole's army, he sends
out his friend Gymnaste, along with a local scout Prelinguand, to
look over the territory ("descouvrir le pays" [132]). Their adventure
constitutes their first encounter with the enemy. It recalls classical
spying missions, such as the episode of Nisus and Euryalus in the
Aeneid. However, its central importance for our concerns involves the
way it constitutes an important rewriting of the episode of Panurge's
escape from the Turks, analysed in the previous chapter. There are
unmistakable echoes between the scenes, not least of which is the fact
that Picrochole's men are presented as dogs; they put out their
tongues "like greyhounds" (114) and run like hounds who have "stolen
a hen" (116)—recalling the "Turkish dogs" of the episode in *Pantagruel*.

The scene of Gymnaste's capture and escape unfolds as follows.
Gymnaste and his companion are riding across the countryside when
they meet a group of Picrochole's men, "pillaging and plundering
everything they could" (114). When the enemies spy Gargantua's two
scouts, they surround them. As he is taken captive Gymnaste cries,
"Sirs, I'm a poor devil. Have mercy on me, I pray you" (114)
["Messieurs, je suis pauvre diable; je vous requiers qu'ayez de moy
mercy" (132)]. He offers them wine, gives them money, offers to sell
his horse, and volunteers to become their cook. Tripet, the captain of

< *Nation and Utopia in the 1530s* >

the enemy troop, immediately picks up on Gymnaste's image, announcing mockingly that if he really is a "poor devil," he can't be a captive. He must "pass on" or "passer oultre," since devils come and go as they please. Tripet then remarks that devils are not usually so well mounted and orders Gymnaste to get down from his horse and carry him. His command literalizes a frequent oath in Rabelais, "let the Devil carry me away" ["que le Diable m'emporte"]. This, says the domineering Tripet, is what he likes: "I like the idea of being carried off by a devil like you" (114). However, the pun backfires against the bullying captain. For as soon as they hear the expression "poor devil" Tripet's men are struck with fear, thinking Gymnaste a real devil. They call to God in Greek, "Agios ho Theos" ["God is holy"], using the very invocation employed by Panurge when tied to the spit in Mytilene. And they tell Gymnaste to declare his allegiance: "If you are on God's side speak. If you're from the Other, be gone" (115) ["Si tu es de Dieu, sy parle! Si tu es de l'Aultre, sy t'en va!" (134)]. When Gymnaste fails to budge, they begin to take flight. Noticing their fear, Gymnaste leaps onto his horse and carries out a series of astonishing gymnastic tricks, crying all the time, "I rage, devils, I rage, I rage! Hold me Devils! Hold me! Hold me!" (116). At this, Tripet's men, certain that they are in the presence of a "starving devil," take flight. Gymnaste kills Tripet and escapes with the scout Prelinguand back to Gargantua's camp.

Gymnaste's cry for help, "Have mercy on me, I pray you," may be seen both as a distant echo of Panurge's requests for pity in thirteen languages when he meets Pantagruel, and of the Turks' extension of "natural pity" toward their prisoner when they meet him in the burning city. Indeed, Gymnaste's initial offer to Tripet and his men of a wine from "La Faye Montjau" sets in motion, in sixteenth-century pronunciation, a pun on "la foi," or "faith," and suggests that we are on the verge of a sacramental reaffirmation of Christian unity. However, even more striking is Gymnaste's naming of himself as "poor devil." Here, as in the Turks episode, an encounter between adversaries is marked by the deployment of a metaphor. Yet it is integrated into a somewhat different set of relations. This episode turns the earlier one inside out. It is almost as if Gymnaste has read *Pantagruel*, since he deploys metaphorical language as a strategy of self-preservation, and even volunteers to become Tripet's cook (as a hedge, one might think, against being cooked himself, like Panurge nearly was). Whereas in the story of Panurge's escape the metaphor applied to the

< *Nation and Utopia in the 1530s* >

Other ("Turks are dogs") was literalized to become a motivation for the narrative, we here see the process of literalization emerging from a superstitious misapprehension. Gymnaste doesn't apply metaphors to the Other, he applies them jokingly to himself. When these metaphors are taken literally they create confusion in the adversary. The issue is no longer, as it was in the encounter with the Turks, how the Other can be made to seem the same, but how the same is mistaken to be the Other. For there are no aliens or devils in this episode. There is, in fact, no cultural or religious difference whatsoever between Gymnaste and Tripet's men, just as there is no difference between Gargantua and Picrochole, and no difference between Francis I and Charles V. Because all are Christians—and neighbors—all should be able to live in peace. As Erasmus says in the *Complaint of Peace*, "The Pyrenees are the mountain barrier between the Spaniards and the French, but they do not destroy the communion of the church;" and in the *Education of the Christian Prince*, "There is a most binding and holy contract between all Christian princes, simply from the fact that they are Christians."[24]

The Erasmian discourse on community and alterity helps us read Gymnaste's joking self-nomination. Gymnaste's metaphorical description of himself as a "pauvre diable" functions quite differently from Panurge's use of figures in his description of the Turks. Panurge's language makes legible the unerasable difference between Christians and infidels. By contrast Gymnaste's joke is uttered within a context where his identity and helplessness *should* be clear to all. His quip seems designed not to define him as an alien, but to incite the mercy of Tripet and his men.

Tripet, the captain, joins in on Gymnaste's joke—extending it not to help him, but to dominate him. He wants to humiliate his enemy by treating him like a horse, by literalizing him into the symbol of his own knightly status. In the exchange between Tripet and Gymnaste, Gymnaste's phrase "I'm a poor devil" becomes the source of witty verbal sparring between the two men. And through that sparring Tripet behaves viciously, instead of charitably. Thus, on one level, the episode might be said to offer a moral message about charitable behavior toward captives (a question on which we will see Gargantua expatiate at length in a moment). As befits one whose name suggests "guts," Tripet seems invested in the fleshly world of violence and domination that is also, in *Pantagruel*, the province of Panurge.

Tripet's lack of charity is connected to his use of language. For when

< *Nation and Utopia in the 1530s* >

he appropriates Gymnaste's metaphorical expression, "I'm a poor devil," he connects it up to a proverb, "let the Devil carry me away." The simultaneous mention of this proverb with his stealing of Gymnaste's horse is what literalizes the diabolical metaphor and terrifies Tripet's men. Indeed, at the outset of the scene they had been gathered around Gymnaste, ready to share the "wine of Faith" with him in a moment of conviviality. Tripet's proverb breaks up this communal moment. His obsession with power turns metaphors back into literal threats.

As a consequence of Tripet's literalism, his army turns against it-self. The soldiers abandon their captain. This vision of the enemy in chaos, moreover, is an epic topos. From Virgil's depiction of the forces of Mark Antony at Actium on Aeneas's shield, to Tasso's depiction of the many-tongued Saracen defenders of Jerusalem who cannot understand each other's orders, epic presents the enemy as disorganized and multiple.[25] Rabelais will stress this point later in the war, when Picrochole's men run from Gargantua's better-organized and more prudent troops. What is striking here is that the division that makes Tripet's men abandon their captain is a *linguistic* division—but of a very particular kind. It is nothing more than a difference in how they perceive metaphor. Rabelais inscribes the conventional chaotic multiplicity of the epic Other into language. But instead of giving us an enemy who speaks a Babelic multiplicity of tongues like the "variae linguis" employed by Antony's unruly army in Virgil, Rabelais locates linguistic difference at the level of figuration itself.

Linguistic division is also social division. The episode opens up a split between different social strata according to how they respond to Gymnaste's joke. On the one hand the episode seems to offer a humanist admonition on the spiritual bonds between Christians. Yet the epic conventions and political ideology of the book produce a split between aristocrats who simply behave badly, and soldiers who live in the world of the letter, in a world of differences that can never be bridged. Indeed, the soldiers recall the relationship between literalism and otherness set forth in the Turks episode by exclaiming that Gymnaste must be from the devil, the "Other side," the very embodiment of difference, and the agent of the Letter.[26]

Gymnaste, in turn, makes linguistic misprision into a tool. He assumes, to his advantage, the identity that has been placed upon him by his captors. Instead of giving up his mount to Tripet, he demonstrates his dexterity by leaping about on the back of his horse. If metaphor is the application of an "improper" name to describe an ob-

< *Nation and Utopia in the 1530s* >

ject, Gymnaste performs that otherness. First, his gyrations and strange cries seem to offer proof to the frightened soldiers that he truly is what he says he is, an emissary from "the Other." Rather than calling on devils, like the "devilish" pasha of Mytilene in *Pantagruel*, he pretends to be one. As he leaps and spins around he provides a bodily parallel to the rhetorical deformation implied in the use of metaphor. He seems to change into dozens of shapes all at once. His dance on the back of his horse provides a kind of demonstration of the deformation of identity that is implied in naming oneself as what one is not. It offers proof to Tripet that Gymnaste can "passer oultre" whenever he wants, even as he tricks Tripet's men into believing that he is from"l'Aultre." Indeed, moving "beyond" and being "other"—the two phrases applied to Gymnaste by Tripet and his men respectively—seem to blend in his strange dance, as if the single letter distinguishing the French words "oultre" and "aultre" were somehow effaced. This is a strange literalism, to be sure.

The conjunction between physical gyration and rhetorical deformation is not accidental. It evokes a classical association of rhetoric with the body. From the time of Quintilian, rhetorical exercise and athletic exercise are associated; good rhetoric is conventionally described as a good body. The connection between language and body is made from the very beginning of *Gargantua*, when the inarticulate, slovenly young giant is humiliated in the face of his neighbor Eudémon, who exemplifies good manners, cleanliness, and eloquence. Moreover, the parallel between rhetoric and physical movement is made explicit by Quintilian, who suggests the importance of gymnastics as a way of training the gestures of the orator and preparing him for the "war" of the law court.[27] Gymnaste, whose name suggests both the humanist educational ideal of the gymnasium and physical exercise, here bridges the passage from language to action by turning rhetoric into a martial stratagem. As both rhetorician and gymnast, in both language and action, he spins and whirls to subdue his listeners.

The shifting relationships of language and body in the episode of Gymnaste's escape suggest that the relationship between an epic, national ideology and an ideology of Christian community might—here as in *Pantagruel*—be understood as an issue of figuration. The tension between an ideal of community and similarity and an ideal of conquest and difference is made legible at the point where language flips back and forth between the literal and the metaphorical. Yet, by the same token, Gymnaste's heroic escape might be seen as a kind of

< Nation and Utopia in the 1530s >

response to this same ideological double bind. Gymnaste's use of metaphor demonstrates how figural language can be used as a cover, as what Rabelais himself calls, in the neologism he coined to describe this very trick, a "stratageme" (137). Gymnaste's slipperiness, his manipulation of body and language to escape, hints at the close proximity between the illusions of rhetorical figuration and the tricks of military strategy. As such, it shows how the misprision that makes legible the splits within the Christian community subtend the epic triumph over the enemy. Rhetorical misprision becomes both the engine of political difference and, when projected into a register of political conquest, the epic solution to it. If the enemy is split along linguistic lines, one way to conquer him is to make the turns of language into turns of the body and outmaneuver him.

The Power of Speech

In *Gargantua*, then, language grounds community, be it saintly or secular. This is made clear in a whole sequence of episodes in which different images of community echo and replace each other. The first one comes in chapter 17, when the young Gargantua travels to Paris and steals the bells of Notre Dame as a prank. After the Parisians request their bells back, he pisses on them. Their response to the deluge is to swear on different saints: "By the belly of Saint Quentin! Virtue of God! By Saint Fiacre of Brye! Saint Treignant! I make a vow to Saint Thibaut!" ["Ventre Sainct Quenet! Vertus guoy! Par Sainct Fiacre de Brye! Sainct Treignant! Je fys veu à Sainct Thibaud..." (68)].[28] The scene of swearing constitutes the people of Paris as a community. The Parisians, we are told, are "made up of all nations and all sorts" (75). Yet at the moment they swear they recognize that they have been drenched, and "they began to swear and curse, some in a fury and others in sport" (74). Their swearing "in sport"—"par rys"—produces the pun that names the city—Paris. That pun and that name, we are told, replace an earlier name, Leucece, which means "White in Greek," and derived from the whiteness of the thighs of the local ladies. In this instance a community constituted through language replaces one defined according to a body. Indeed, the text insists on the relationship between swearing and community, for it goes on to tell us that the Parisians are twice named, first through the pun on "par rys," and then because of the swearing itself, which has earned them the name "Parrhesians from the Greek, in which language the word signifies bold of speech" (75).[29]

< *Nation and Utopia in the 1530s* >

This emphasis on the relationship between the speech act of the oath and communal identity is echoed later in the book, when a somewhat different community, the Abbey of Seuillé, is attacked by Picrochole. The attack is repulsed by the fighting monk Frère Jean d'Entommeures. As he kills the attackers who want to take over the abbey, the monk reduces them to swearing on various saints: "Some invoked St Barbara, others St George, others St Hands-off" (100)—the list goes on for a page. The scene recalls the proverb that a con-fused man "knows not which saint to swear by." And, sure enough, as the confused monks fearfully hide from the attack that very proverb is used to describe them. Here Picrochole's soldiers seem to know which saints to swear by, but their names become so many empty formulae bringing the victims no assistance. More important, their cries contrast with Frère Jean's own oath. As Frère Jean exhorts his men to battle, he does so to save the Abbey's wine, and in the name of the Eucharist: "by the body of God, follow me . . . on God's belly" (99)["le corps Dieu, sy me suibvez! . . . Ventre Dieu" (108)]. Frère Jean's invocation links the preservation of the community to the mys-teries of the Sacrament.[30] The echo of the earlier scene shows how the text replaces a legendary secular community—a Paris founded, first on women's white thighs and then on the urine of the giant—with a community founded on the body and blood of Christ. Yet the ecclesiastical body is itself seen to need renewal, and through the rep-etition of the oath, a formulaic Catholicism is subsequently displaced by a Christ-centered rhetoric of activism and courage.

Frère Jean is by no means an unambivalent figure. Indeed, his love of violence and his cross-shaped club make him look at times very much like those whom Erasmus attacks in his *Complaint of Peace* for carrying into battle "the cross as your standard," and "kill[ing] in the name of the cross one who was saved by it."[31] Rabelais's representa-tion of Frère Jean is marked by a troubling textual echo that further complicates the relationship between language and community. Af-ter he has defended the Abbey, Frère Jean joins Gargantua and his men for a banquet. During their colloquoy he mentions having given to a neighbor a fine greyhound that came into his possession. The anecdote provides yet another example of charitable behavior by turning the image of the dog, so closely allied to the flesh elsewhere in Rabelais, into a token of friendship and community. When the friar asks Gymnaste if he was wrong to have done so, Gymnaste replies, "Oh no, by all the devils you weren't!" (125). And Frère Jean answers

< *Nation and Utopia in the 1530s* >

the oath with a toast: "Here's a health to such devils ... Virtue of God ... By God's body" (125) ["Ainsi ... à ces diables, ce pendent qu'ilz durent! Vertus de Dieu! ... Le cor Dieu!" (150)]. The evocation of the devils who so terrified Picrochole's men, and the repetition of "God's body," the same phrase Frère Jean uttered as he liberated the Abbey, are surely not accidental. Ponocrates calls attention to them by asking, "What, do you swear, Friar John?" (125). And Frère Jean answers, "It's only to embellish my language ... It's Ciceronian" rhetorical colouring (125) ["Ce n'est que pour orner mon langaige. Ce sont couleurs de rhetorique Ciceroniane"(150)].

It is difficult to know precisely what Frère Jean means by "rhetorique Ciceroniane," or "Ciceronian rhetorical coloring." Certainly, the name of Cicero would have evoked for a sixteenth-century reader Erasmus's dialogue entitled *Ciceronianus*, in which the empty, inflated language of imitators of Cicero is mocked and contrasted with a fuller language rooted in the Gospels.[32] Frère Jean seems to be mocking his own earlier exhortation at the liberation of the Abbey. The repetition of the same powerful phrase, "the body of God," seems to point to the ways in which bits of language can have different functions and activate different forms of power in different contexts. In the first instance it is a rallying cry to bring together Christians in defense of the faith; in the second instance it is a party joke.

What is even more striking about Frère Jean's joke is that it serves as a kind of fulcrum for the definition of a new form of community, one that replaces both the "heroic" Paris and the "literalist" monastic community of the Abbey. Gargantua's friend Eudémon answers Frère Jean's remark with an exclamation, "Faith of a Christian" (125), that reminds us what is at issue in the episode. He then wonders why monks are thrown out of "all good companies" and cites Virgil's depiction of the political organization of the bees in his fourth Georgic. By citing Virgil, Eudémon raises the question of the relationship between theological communities and political communities. His perplexity is answered as the members of the group debate the uselessness of monks.

Gargantua points out that monks are hated because they are useless. When his father Grandgousier interjects that they pray on everyone's behalf, Gargantua notes that they mostly make noise with their bells, and that prayer belongs to everyone: "All true Christians, of all degrees, in all places and at all times, pray to God, and the Holy Spirit prays and intercedes for them, and God receives them into his

< *Nation and Utopia in the 1530s* >

grace" (126). He goes on to note that Frère Jean is wanted in all companies because he is a good companion and because he is always busy. Frère Jean concurs, adding that "I'm never idle" (126).[33]

Gargantua's depiction of an activist monk and of a Christian community unified by prayer repeats the homilies of Evangelical and Christian humanist thinkers, from Marguerite de Navarre to Erasmus. It breaks down distinctions between humans by projecting an interiorized spirituality, which now becomes the province of all, monk and layman, rich and poor, literate and illiterate (and to include the thuggish Frère Jean, one might add "semi-literate").[34] At the same time, the scene raises the question of how this new community can be grafted into the epic enterprise of defeating Picrochole—of an enterprise that looks at times very much like Francis I's various projects to defend and conquer lands to which he claimed ancestral rights. Frère Jean's status as both monk and soldier takes us back to the paradoxical double stance of the text, as both national epic and Christian colloquoy.

The Monk's Habit

Frère Jean seems to embody the combination of theological renewal and Gallican independence suggested by Francis I's special title "Roy très chrestien." These identifications are connoted by the fact that Frère Jean carries a staff in the shape of a cross and engraved with images of the fleur-de-lys. Since the fleur de lys images are almost erased, the inscription seems to suggest ancient, nearly forgotten, valor. The figure of the lily, associated with Christ, was appropriated by the Capetian line in the twelfth century and became a symbol of the privileged relationship between the French monarchy and the Church. As such, it may be seen to connote a type of "Frenchness" that Frère Jean wishes to evoke at a moment of political and theological crisis.[35]

Yet perhaps more important than the symbols of Frère Jean's heroism are his clothes—for virtually all of the scenes in which Frère Jean appears mention his clothing. The sartorial imagery, of course, recalls a well-known proverb, "The habit doesn't make the monk" ("L'habit ne fait pas le moine"). Moreover, the figure of the habit sets up an opposition between garment and body, between outside and inside, that recalls the "Prologue" to *Gargantua*, in which the text itself is compared with Socrates, whose ugly exterior conceals his wisdom. Frère Jean's frock is even described as "horrificque" (161), the same term

85

< *Nation and Utopia in the 1530s* >

used in the full title of the book (*La Vie très horrificque . . .*) and to evoke the "mysteries" ("mysteres horrificques" [8]), that the book proposes to reveal, from beneath its rough surface, about politics, religion, and domestic life. The parallel poses the question of how the hermeneutic paradigm of inside and outside is transformed once it is projected out of the liminal space of the "Prologue" and into the world of action through which new forms of community are defined.

Because of his heroism in battle Frère Jean is compared to Maugis, the fighting monk of the medieval epic *Les Quatre Fils Aymon* (The Four Sons of Aymon).[36] Both *Gargantua* and the *Quatre Fils* stress the importance of the fighting monk's garb. In the medieval text the monk changes clothes whenever he shifts from priest to warrior. Frère Jean's approach is somewhat different. When he takes control of the defense of the Abbey, his first action is sartorial. He sets down his "heavy habit" and picks up his staff. After the battle, he dines with Gargantua and enters his service, at which point the monk is dressed in armor by Gargantua's servants. This happens against his will: "he wanted no other protection but his frock over his stomach and the staff of his cross in his hand" (129). Frère Jean is willing to make do with his holy frock in place of armor. He soon dons the habit again and refuses thenceforth to remove it. He goes on to point out that anyone who runs in battle can be made brave by having the frock tied around his neck: "It carries a cure for cowardice in men" (129). Recalling again the curious parallel between men and dogs in Rabelais, he notes that this was once the case for a greyhound, which couldn't catch any rabbits—until he had a frock attached to his body.

Frère Jean's frock evokes a belief, current in late medieval culture, that the frock of a Franciscan monk could protect the dying soul from devils. The myth of the frock as spiritual shield is one of many evoked in the writings of humanists as signs of the corruption of the clergy. Erasmus mocks it in several of his colloquies and treatises.[37] Thus Frère Jean's dependence on his frock seems to signify a rejection of traditional heroism for renewed faith. Yet the ambivalence of such "magical" signs is stressed a moment later, when Gargantua and his men are caught in an ambush mounted by Tyravant, one of Picrochole's minions. This episode exactly echoes and reverses the scene of Gymnaste's escape seen earlier. There, Gargantua sent out Gymnaste as a scout to reconnoiter the country ("pour descouvrir le pays" [132]). Here Picrochole sends out a group of sixteen hundred men to do the same ("pour descouvrir le pays" [160]). However their garb doubles

< Nation and Utopia in the 1530s >

and parodies the very trappings that Frère Jean wears. For if he wears his frock, they come into battle covered with stoles, in case they should meet any devils. And, indeed, the monk's frock seems to do precisely what it is supposed to do, and what Picrochole's men hope their stoles will do. Frère Jean scares Picrochole's men by activating Gymnaste's pun about devilry, "Charge! Devils, charge!" (132). Only Tyravant refuses to run, and he charges Frère Jean with his lance in position, just like a medieval knight out of *Les Quatre Fils Aymon*. However, the lance does no damage, for as it hits the monk's frock it bends backward: "But when it met the horrific frock, its steel point buckled. It was like striking an anvil with a small candle" (132). Here the frock seems to be as miraculous as the legends say it is. It not only gives Frère Jean courage, it protects him. Yet, a moment later, Frère Jean is attacked again, this time by a whole group of enemies. They shower him with blows, yet he feels nothing "so tough was his skin" (133) ["tant il avoit la peau dure" (163)]. Frère Jean never says that his frock protects him, only that it gives him courage. And yet it does protect him, when it drives back the lance of Tyravant. Here, however, its protective function seems to be absorbed into his skin. It turns out that Frère Jean doesn't need armor, a stole, or even a frock. He's a tough guy just as he is.

The sequence of scenes in which Frère Jean appears takes us from one image of heroism to another, from medieval fighting monks like Maugis, who must change clothes every time they change functions, through the "horrific" frock, to an acknowledgment of the power of the body itself to withstand violence, "so tough was his skin." The sequence offers a reflection on the relationship between signs and things. As we shift from one episode to the other the figure of the cloak (a figure for figuration generally, in Rabelais as elsewhere) is, as it were, demystified. It goes from being both an object and a sign (as both shield and marker of status) to being a sign of power (it gives Frère Jean, the greyhound, and Picrochole's men all courage to do battle), to merely being a garment. More important, the progressive disappearance of all of Frère Jean's coverings effects a shift from an *externalized* version of epic virtue, in which the knight's heroism is signified by his armor, through a traditional Catholicism, in which the clergy is protected by its special garb, to a new, *internalized* Christianity.

This new figuration of body and community is motivated by Gargantua's convivial speech to his father and men about prayer, cited earlier. Here Gargantua echoes the discussion in Erasmus's *Enchirid-*

< *Nation and Utopia in the 1530s* >

ion, where, in the section entitled "The armour of the Christian militia," Erasmus insists on the importance of prayer: "We must prepare two weapons in particular against the seven tribes with whom we must do battle ... These two weapons are prayer and knowledge. Paul wishes us to be always armed, bidding us to pray without ceasing ... Prayer is the more effective of the two, since it is a conversation with God ..."[38] Frère Jean is able to do without his armor precisely because he is protected by a new, invisible armor—prayer. Here, again, we can see the shift from Rabelais's first book, *Pantagruel,* to the later *Gargantua.* In the first book, Pantagruel enters his battle against anarchy by offering a prayer to God. God responds with a sign, as a voice cries out, "Hoc fac et vinces" ["Do this and you shall win"] (262). In the ensuing battle, the emboldened hero defeats a werewolf, who is himself protected by a magical sword and an armor made up of anvils. Here, the anvil is evoked metaphorically to describe the "horrificque" frock, which gives way to an internalized "armor" that seems to protect the friar. In *Gargantua,* Christian virtue and divine will are no longer revealed—they are *performed.*

Yet, despite these doctrinal explanations, the depiction of Frère Jean's tough skin is troubling. For it makes the friar into a supernatural hero, a kind of Achilles, protected by precisely the type of armor that Erasmus says the Christian, protected by prayer, no longer needs. Frère Jean's tough skin is the equivalent of Gargantua's size; it saves him from danger. This curious insistence on the friar's skin evokes the ideological double bind mentioned earlier, in which the text must simultaneously project a model of French heroism and a model of Christian reconciliation. In order to depict Frère Jean's Christian exemplarity, his status as a man whose armor is prayer, Rabelais shows him bare of all protection. Yet, in order to depict the monk's courage, Rabelais gives him the skin of a tough guy who looks very much like the heroes of traditional epic. Indeed, to take a famous example, well known to Rabelais, it is one of the characteristics of Ariosto's Orlando that his skin is, like Frère Jean's, as hard as steel.[39] Frère Jean's body becomes the site at which the text's attempt to blend Christian spirituality and political heroism overlap. The mediating term that harmonizes those visions is the strange evocation of his "tough skin."

Just as Gymnaste's body makes legible a crisis of Christian community, a moment at which members of the same mystical or corporate body suddenly see each other as aliens, Frère Jean's body enacts

< *Nation and Utopia in the 1530s* >

the shift from traditional epic heroism toward a new, internalized Christianity that would heal that crisis. Yet, in order to *represent* that new ideal, Frère Jean's mortal body must take on attributes of the very epic ideology it seems to be denying. The monk's body is protected by prayer, yet it is epic in its toughness. The invisible forces that would heal the torn community of Europe cannot be represented outside the language that divides it. In the figure of the monk's "habit," which represents the entire hermeneutic model of "inside" and "outside" that dominates *Gargantua*, the crisis of Christian community that gives birth to French national identity is represented at both the level of genre and of the sign itself.

The Economics of Generosity

Humanist literature of counsel, which seeks to tame the violence of political life, must simultaneously criticize and persuade. It must show the princely reader that his vision of the world is skewed, and that rules of comportment, what Seyssel called "the order of charity," provide a model of action that is not only morally desirable, but politically expedient. The prince must be shown that moral action leads to political success, that, to use the language of Montaigne, the *honorable* way is also the *useful* one. Erasmus attempts this task in his *Education of the Christian Prince* by evoking a kind of economic model of foreign policy. Since war can only bring more war, he says, princes would be much wiser to pursue peace. For from peace springs peace: "civility invites civility, and fairness, fairness."[40] This language draws on the discussions of generosity in two of the most widely read moral treatises of classical philosophy, Cicero's *De Officiis* and Seneca's *De Beneficiis*. Erasmus echoes this same formulation in the exhortation that closes the *Complaint of Peace*, where he urges the princes of Europe to virtuous action with the claim that one good turn will produce another: "Now let generosity breed generosity, kind actions invite further kindness, and true royalty be measured by willingness to concede sovereignty."[41] It is no accident that this idea is expressed in an exhortation, since it describes a form of behavior that few princes are likely to take up. Indeed, even the movement of the phrase is telling, as it first blends a properly economic model of foreign policy (good deeds will produce more good deeds) with the language of generation and "breeding," before moving to an astonishing reformulation of the notion of sovereignty that is, in effect, the precondition for the first half of the sentence.

< *Nation and Utopia in the 1530s* >

Erasmus's attempt to blend the useful and the honorable provides the context for a reading of the politics of reconciliation in *Gargantua*. For after the defeat of Picrochole and his men, Gargantua deals with them in ways that recall, and often directly echo, discussions of political virtue in Erasmus. The main organ for reintegrating Picrochole's men into a new, humanist Christian community is the series of harangues to the vanquished after the defeat of Picrochole. First, Gargantua's father Grandgousier speaks to Picrochole's captain Toucquedillon, then Gargantua addresses the company of the captives. In the *Education of the Christian Prince* Erasmus distinguishes between the actions of "pagan princes," who, he says, are generous toward their own citizens but "merely just towards foreigners." "It is the mark of a Christian prince," he continues, "to consider no one a foreigner except those who are strangers to the sacraments of Christ, and to avoid provoking even them by doing them injury."[42] Grandgousier projects Erasmus's "us/them" dichotomy onto a temporal axis by pointing out that the age of heroism and revenge has given way to a new time of charity. He begins by noting that the great deeds of ancient heroes, "what the Saracens and Barbarians of old called deeds of prowess" (138) are now frowned upon and referred to as "robbery and wickedness." Imitation of ancient heroes is contrary to the teachings of the Gospel.[43] Throughout this passage, Rabelais follows Erasmus closely. In both the *Education of the Christian Prince* and the *Complaint of Peace* Erasmus quotes Plato, who had noted in the *Republic* that wars between Greeks were not wars, but sedition. Wars between Christians, adds Erasmus, are even more horrendous than wars among the Greeks: "Are men less than brothers when they are united in Christ?"[44] Grandgousier evokes the same Platonic passage, citing chapter and verse, when he admonishes Toucquedillon that he and Picrochole are really old friends, ("voisins et anciens amys"[171]). He goes on, "If by misfortune [war] should happen, says Plato, all moderation should be shown. However, if you do call it war, it is only skin-deep; it has not entered into the secret places of our hearts" (138)] ["si par male fortune [guerre] advenoit, [Platon] commande qu'on use de toute modestie. Si guerre la nommez, elle n'est que superficiaire, elle n'entre poinct au profond cabinet de nos cueurs" (171)]. Names, as his last sentence suggests, have nothing to do with a true community of the heart.

Grandgousier's language is echoed several pages later, when Gargantua addresses the vanquished. He begins by evoking a common-

< Nation and Utopia in the 1530s >

place from Pliny the Younger's *Panegyric of Trajan*, the most famous panegyric of antiquity and the model for Erasmus's own panegyric of Philip of Austria. In his praise of Trajan's modesty Pliny points out that emperors need not worry about their immortality, for "this is preserved not in portraits and statues but in virtue and good deeds."[45] Gargantua echoes this famous line to open his speech:

> Our fathers, grandfathers, and ancestors from time immemorial have been of such nature and disposition that as a memorial to the victories and triumphs they have won in the battles they have fought, they have preferred to erect monuments in the hearts of the vanquished by grace, than to raise trophies in the form of ar-chitecture in the lands they have conquered. (145)

> [Nos peres, ayeulx et ancestres de toute memoyre ont esté de ce sens et ceste nature que des batailles par eulx consommées ont, pour signe memorial des triumphes et victoires, plus voluntiers erigé trophées et monumens es cueurs des vaincuz par grace que, es terres par eulx conquestées, par architecture. (182)]

Gargantua contrasts monuments and the memory of the human heart. This contrast recalls Grandgousier's claim that ancient heroism has given way to a new type of merciful treatment of one's adversaries, but here locates that mercy in his own family, which is seen to have demonstated charity in the past. Indeed, the distinction set up here between dead stones and "the living memory of men" suggests Paul's claim that the law of Moses was written on tablets of stone (that is, here, monuments) whereas the new law is inscribed on the heart.[46] Yet what is striking about the passage is that it simultaneously sug-gests domination and reconciliation, thereby resolving the tension between the epic project of conquest and the Christian humanist thematics of charity. Rabelais's phrase for this resolution, "in hearts of the vanquished by grace" (145) ["es cueurs des vaincuz par grace" (182)], suggests both political domination and charitable reconcilia-tion. The term "grace" artfully underscores the complexity of the scene, since it is both theological and political, suggesting an infusion of both divine love and simple political clemency. I noted in the in-troductory chapter Richard Rorty's claim that communities may be imagined as "vocabularies," and that they change by finding new meanings in old words. Here, at a moment in which the violence of power politics conflicts with the moral imperative to reconstitute the Christian community, Rabelais seems to be manipulating both old

< *Nation and Utopia in the 1530s* >

words and new meanings, deploying a vocabulary that suggests both conquest and persuasion.

Gargantua offers three examples to illustrate why one should be charitable toward the conquered. First he speaks of how his ancestors behaved with gentleness ("mansuetude") towards the Bretons, after the battles of Saint Aubun du Cormier and Parthenay. He then notes the "good treatment" that they exercised toward the "barbarians of Spagnola" after they pillaged southwestern France. Finally, he notes at great length how his own father treated Alpharbal, the "King of Canary" with courtesy ("courtoisement, amiablement") after Alpharbal engaged in piracy in the islands off Brittony a number of years earlier.

These examples are not random. They all evoke the question of the border, of the frontiers along which France defines its difference from its neighbors. The first example recalls the battles that brought Brittany into France and ended one of the most difficult and complex struggles over French identity of the fifteenth century.[47] The second and third examples point directly to the great rivalry with Spain. Political topicality is expanded a bit later, as Gargantua laces his harangue with satirical references to Charles V, the "rex Catholicus." He refers to Charles's "ungenerous" treatment of his captive Francis following the Battle of Pavia and notes that his father, by contrast, was a generous victor toward Alpharbal. A bit later he alludes to the stiff ransom exacted by Charles for the freedom of Francis, saying that Grandgousier could well have behaved in a similar fashion. Rabelais's depiction of a defeated Picrochole who may stand in for Charles, and a victorious Gargantua/Francis expounding on the virtues of political justice, offers a fictional revenge on the hated Spanish king. However, since the harangue is also filled with clichés about treating one's neighbor humanely, the burden of the passage is to bring topical reference into harmony with the Erasmian dictum that virtuous action leads to political success. Indeed, paradoxically, Charles V is inscribed in this scene in two positions. He is both the victor and the victim. On the one hand, Gargantua perfectly inverts the roles defined in Francis's capture: the French ruler is here in command; the Picrochole/Charles figure is defeated and in flight, and his men are about to be "punished" by Gargantua's generosity—just as Alpharbal was punished by Grandgousier. But at the same time, the references to Francis's captivity implicitly recall Charles as a victor, evoking French humiliation after Pavia. Thus Francis/Gargantua will dis-

< *Nation and Utopia in the 1530s* >

pense generosity; in the process he will demonstrate why generosity is good politics. He will illustrate why good things might have come to Charles, had he behaved toward Francis like the true humanist prince he claimed to be. We have a scenario that is structurally analogous to the one imagined in Erasmus's closing injunction in the *Complaint of Peace*, cited above, in which he exhorts princes to "let generosity breed generosity, kind actions invite further kindness, and true royalty be measured by willingness to concede sovereignty." However, whereas Erasmus seems uncertain about how such an economy would work in actual practice, Rabelais's fiction resolves the situation by virtually placing both partners in the exchange on both sides of it at the same time. That the exchange is purely fantasy is underscored by the fact that Charles's humiliation of Francis is long past and that Picrochole himself is nowhere to be found, having fled at the end of the battle.

As noted earlier, these images recall classical discussions of generosity in Cicero and Seneca. They also evoke one of Rabelais's greatest contemporary models, Thomas More's *Utopia*, in which Utopian military triumphs are seen to lead to a system of tribute that places conquered nations in perpetual financial debt to the Utopians. The loosely veiled allegory of English life provided by More's text makes possible a strongly "nationalist" version of foreign affairs. Rabelais draws from More. However, he concerns himself, not with an ideal state, but with an ideal image of the relationship *between* states. Thus he must reconcile victor and vanquished in a manner that satisfies all.[48]

Having captured the "pirate" Alpharbal, Grandgousier sends him home laden with gifts and tokens of friendship. In response, Alpharbal assembles all of the princes of his kingdom and resolves to create an example of peaceful coexistence for all the world to see: "to show the world an example of gracious honour to match the example we had shown of honorable graciousness" (146) ["en façon que le monde y eust exemple, comme avoit jà en nous de gracieuseté honeste, aussi en eulx de honesteté gracieuse" (183)]. The chiasmatic structure of the formulation closely follows Erasmus and suggests an equivalence of power and generosity between former enemies. However, no sooner has Alpharbal made his pronouncement than he and his fellow princes engage in a series of activities that are strange indeed. They immediately begin showering Grandgousier and his subjects with gifts. They send ships laden with treasures from every house in the kingdom: "Whereupon it was unanimously decreed that an offer

< *Nation and Utopia in the 1530s* >

should be made to us of their entire lands, dominions, and kingdom, to be disposed of according to our discretion" (146) ["Là feut decreté par consentement unanime que l'on offreroit entierement leurs terres, dommaines et royaulme, à en faire selon nostre arbitre" (183)]. Grandgousier and his subjects refuse these lavish gifts, an act which only compels the vanquished to send more, to offer themselves as Grandgousier's subjects, and finally to pay Grandgousier a tribute that would increase yearly until the end of time. So great has this tribute become that Gargantua admits they will have to put an end to it soon.

Surely, this is a peace any ruler, even Charles V, would love to negotiate. Whereas the recently freed Francis had several times tried, unsuccessfully, to deceive Charles, to avoid paying the stiff ransom exacted for his freedom, here tribute flows unchecked. The passage offers an exaggerated demonstration of Erasmus's repeated admonitions that generosity and Christian charity are preferable to violence and domination in the conduct of international affairs. It even reifies Erasmus's claim that by giving away sovereignty one becomes more powerful, as generosity toward the vanquished here produces material wealth.

The tension between spirituality and materiality illustrated by this anecdote is inscribed in the very lexicon of Rabelais's description. To conclude his description of Alpharbal's grateful behavior, Gargantua explains that there is something in generosity itself that produces increase. This closing formulation bears close attention:

> Such is the nature of gratitude; for Time, which gnaws and fritters all things away, augments and increases benefits; because a good turn freely done to a man of reason grows continuously by noble thought and memory. (147)

> [C'est la nature de gratuité, car le temps, qui toutes choses ronge et diminue, augmente et accroist les bienfaictz, parce q'un bon tour liberalement faicte à l'homme de raison croist continuement par noble pensée et remembrance. (184)]

With its repeated conjunctions, "car," and "parce que," this is a complicated sentence, even for Rabelais. And its logic is particularly difficult to follow. It begins by suggesting that there is something inherent in "gratuité" that makes it grow. This virtue increases through time. Time destroys "all things"—except it doesn't seem to destroy "gratuité." I cite the French word, because it doesn't simply mean "gratitude,"

< *Nation and Utopia in the 1530s* >

as the translation suggests. In fact, it means both "gratitude," that is which is returned, and "generosity," that which is given. It suggests simultaneously both halves of the structure of exchange which is here being advanced. This equilibrium of victor and vanquished is, however, upset when we see, on a closer look, that it isn't "gratuité" at all that resists Time. It is the "good turn" done to a man of reason. That good turn is a sign of the "benefits," the "bienfaictz," which are in turn the signs of "gratuité." It is difficult, moreover, to see what exactly Gargantua means by "bienfaictz." The word seems to be a French translation of "beneficentia," the term used throughout the writings of Erasmus, Cicero, Seneca, and More to refer to good deeds done by princes to each other.[49] In fact, More uses the term in a passage which Rabelais may here have in mind, where he discusses the relationship between pleasure and property and notes that doing good to others is compensated by "the return of benefits" ("beneficiorum vicissitudine") as well as by the actual consciousness of the good deed. "Remembrance of the charity you have extended to those whom you have benefited" he goes on, "gives the mind a greater amount of pleasure than the bodily pleasure which you have forgone would have afforded."[50] Yet where More distinguishes clearly *between* material and spiritual rewards, and suggests that a single good deed is remembered, Rabelais complicates the situation by insisting on the repetition of tribute, which makes "bienfaitz" *both* material and spiritual, *both* money and satisfaction. Indeed, if the word "grace," discussed a moment ago, suggests both theological gift and political power, "bienfaictz" suggests both spiritual and material reward. What defies all-destroying Time may be either the initial, spiritual, gesture of generosity, or the lucrative payments that commemorate it—two very different, if not opposing, elements. Indeed, the only thing that gets bigger with time in this scenario is the amount of tribute paid by Alpharbal. And since the increase in appreciation can only be signified by an increase in tribute, that tribute is essential if Gargantua is to know that Alpharbal and his subjects are ever more appreciative of Grandgousier's generosity. As the end of the sentence shows, it is not the original gesture of generosity that produces benefits at all (as seems to be suggested by the opening of the phrase), but rather the sequence of previous payments of tribute, which grow "continuously." The responses to the original gesture of generosity, those things that were exchanged in response *to* it, become signs *of* it. The very thing that Gargantua doesn't want anymore—increased payments—is the

< *Nation and Utopia in the 1530s* >

only thing that can signify how generosity breeds generosity. This alone can show how "gracieuseté honeste" is being matched with "honesteté gracieuse." Generosity can only be represented through material exchange.

Here, as in the depiction of Frère Jean, moral action can only be made legible through the very materiality it rejects. The material and the spiritual are held in tension by the polysemy of such key terms as "bienfaictz" and "grace," even as the tension between them is then resolved by the temporal movement of the sentence. The tension in Rabelais's text between different models of community embeds itself in the word. Linguistic exorbitance, which I associated in the first chapter with figural distortion and posited as characteristic of the encounter between communities, here gets built into the technical vocabulary of political and moral reconciliation.

A no less complex shift of terms marks the description of Alpharbal's motivation. Unlike the Erasmian prince, who expects to get peace for peace and increase of sovereignty for the relinquishment of power, Alpharbal is a defeated prince, a renegade pirate—the ultimate outsider or Other. Moreover, he has been described as having behaved "furiously" ("furieusement"), the same word used to describe the mad Picrochole. But if Alpharbal is "furious," or out of his mind, why is he so willing to participate in the wonderful Erasmian economy of generosity and charity that structures the anecdote? His motivation is traced in Gargantua's description. Early on in the anecdote, when Alpharbal and his men first bring their gifts to Grandgousier and try to cede their lands to him, Gargantua's father is moved to tears: "my said father began pitifully to lament and to weep copious tears, when he considered the frank generosity and the simplicity of the Canarians" (146) ["mon dict pere commença lamenter de pitié et pleurer copieusement, considerant le franc vouloir et simplicité des Canarriens" (184)]. This is a strange description. A moment earlier the Canarians were pirates; now they are "simple" and possessed of "franc vouloir"—a phrase which is almost impossible to translate, meaning literally "free will," but suggesting as well something like "innocent desire." And a moment later they are described in yet another set of terms, when Gargantua explains that generosity breeds generosity if it is inspired by a "good turn" made to "a man of reason" ("un bon tour liberalement faict à l'homme de raison") and remembered "by noble thought and memory" (146) ("par noble pensée et remembrance" [187]).

Thus, as the anecdote proceeds, Alpharbal and his men turn from

< *Nation and Utopia in the 1530s* >

pirates and madmen into simpletons, then into men of reason. At first glance, the passage may seem to be suggesting that generosity toward one's furious enemies somehow "civilizes" them. Yet the concluding explanation, that generosity extended to "men of reason" resists Time, makes it clear that the vanquished must *already* be civilized if the economy defined here is to work in the first place. And the required metamorphosis from simpleton to man of reason takes place before our very eyes, as we read. That is, it is *Rabelais's own language*, the unfolding of Gargantua's narrative, that tames the furious Alpharbal and his men. They are reintegrated into the Christian order by the dazzling rhetorical energy of Rabelais's own text.

Alpharbal is a fantastic personage indeed. But without such a preposterous identity the economy of generosity that underscores the Erasmian moral lesson of the episode cannot function. In a sense, we are back where we began in the previous chapter, when we first considered the disruptive force of the Other in humanist notions of community. Yet here, the terms have been reversed. If my discussion of *Pantagruel* demonstrated the difficulty of extending charity to the non-Christian Other, here, we witness the alienation and subsequent reappropriation of Alpharbal. If charity is to be represented as a principle for structuring mutually beneficial political relationships, one party in the equation must be a defeated adversary whose burlesque simplicity makes him happy to turn over his possessions. In *Pantagruel* the very literalism of the Turkish Other impedes his integration into the "order of charity" (to recall again Seyssel's phrase). In *Gargantua*, the order of charity cannot be instituted without projecting a fictional Other who is then domesticated as the text unfolds. In order for Rabelais to reconcile the satire of Charles V and the doctrines of Erasmian humanism, he must produce a vanquished subject who lies outside the recognizable world altogether. The logic of his presentation requires the creation of Alpharbal, an enemy who is both bellicose and simple, both furious and reasonable, an Other whose name suggests both the first letter of the Greek alphabet and an Arabic potentate. This floating identity for the vanquished permits Gargantua to enunciate humanist political precepts while setting forth a fantasy that depicts Charles/Picrochole in defeat. If *Pantagruel* confronts the problem of appropriating the real, "historical" Other, *Gargantua* bases its model of charitable political action on an image of an enemy who is both in and out of Europe. He stands in for Charles V but is also a "pirate" from just beyond the horizon. He is much easier to appropriate than the

< Nation and Utopia in the 1530s >

Ottoman Turks because he is pure fantasy, recuperated by a "grace" that is both theological transformation and political mercy.

Through the metamorphic energy of his own description Rabelais links humanist ideology and political satire. For the ideology of humanism to offer a useful response to contemporary politics, it must produce a figure who can be both excluded from and included in the European ambit in the space of a few lines. Humanist ideology, with its blending of political advice and moral counsel, can only be illustrated through an outrageous form of representation which transforms characters before our very eyes. Here, as in the case of the bacon adorning Panurge's waist in the previous chapter, it is fiction making itself that saves humanist doctrine in the face of political difference.

Yet the fragility of such moments of harmony as the one seen here is suggested by Gargantua's final words to Picrochole's men. He offers them three months' pay and sends them home accompanied by six hundred armed men and eight thousand footsoldiers commanded by his squire Alexandre. The escort is provided not to police the newly vanquished enemies, but to protect them, "so that you shall not be molested by the peasants" (147) ["affin que par les païsans ne soyez oultragez" (185)]. This closing reference to marauding peasants casts an ironic light on the entire peacemaking project detailed in Gargantua's harangue. On the one hand, Gargantua preaches generosity; his kindness projects a fantasy of international peace. Yet, on the other hand, his own homeland seems to be anything but peaceful. Ideals of Christian harmony are still threatened by unrest, but no longer from an epic conflict between communities. Rather it is *social* unrest that remains to trouble the landscape. Here we see a distant echo of the depiction of social difference in language noted earlier in Gymnaste's escape from Tripet and his men. Yet now, instead of a joke about devils which motivates the actions of the "mob," we get a much darker image, a vision of a world in which imaginary "pirates" are tamed only to be threatened by yet another Other, the lower classes, which, as the history of peasant revolts during the period suggests, would not fit quite so easily as did the aristocratic Alpharbal into the economy of generosity. It is beautifully ironic that Gargantua's harangue should end with a reference to a group of peasants attacking men crossing their territory. For it was a similar scenario that sparked the Picrocholine war to begin with. The final mention of peasant unrest takes us back to the beginning of the conflict, and to Seyssel's admonition that the most dangerous moment in political life is when one nation's

< *Nation and Utopia in the 1530s* >

men cross the territory of another. The war with Picrochole begins at a crossroads. We last see his men in the same dangerous landscape.

Imperial Fantasies and the Language of Nationhood

The themes of body, language, and community that I have been tracing through *Gargantua* all converge in the famous description of the Abbey of Theleme that dominates the last chapters of the book. And, despite the generic contrast it marks with the Picrocholine war that precedes it, the story of the Abbey reflects the same ideological tensions between politics and spirituality that haunt the rest of the book, and that characterized France in the 1530s. For Theleme is both Church and court, both spiritual community and political collective. As the poem over the doorway to the Abbey notes, it welcomes gallant knights, lovely ladies, and Evangelical preachers. *Gargantua* is explicit about how different genders interact in the Abbey. It is less forthcoming about how knights commited to military heroism are able to get on with those who preach the Word. We never learn how those accustomed to dress in armor of steel give that armor over for the armor of prayer. Relations between the sexes may be easier to control than relations among the different social orders. Yet the harmony of Theleme seems to be based as much on social homogeneity, on the fact that all of its inhabitants are nobles, as it is on spiritual sympathy. Indeed, if, as the episode of Gymnaste's escape has shown us, one of the differences between nobles and commoners is that nobles (be they uncharitable like Tripet, or spiritual like Gymnaste) realize that metaphors are metaphors, whereas commoners live in the world of the letter, it may be no accident that everyone in Theleme is well born. If nobles are good readers, one way to represent a community of good readers is to represent a community of nobles.

My reading of Theleme will focus on how communal experience is represented. For, as Frère Jean's habit and Alpharbal's gratitude have taught us, the Christian humanist project of advancing new forms of virtuous action necessarily requires a mode of representation that would bypass both conventional Catholic iconography and traditional nobiliary clichés. Theleme is described as a place of the heart. "Enter, so that here one may found deep faith" (153) ["Entrez, qu'on fonde ici la foy profonde" (197)], says the inscription over the doorway in a phrase that suggests both an established faith and a faith that is always being renewed. The description of its inhabitants, however, is quite striking:

< *Nation and Utopia in the 1530s* >

Never were seen such worthy knights, so valiant, so nimble both on foot and horse; knights more vigorous, more agile, handier with all weapons than they were. Never were seen ladies so good-looking, so dainty, less tiresome, more skilled with the fingers and the needle, and in every free and honest womanly pursuit than they were. (159)

[Jamais ne feurent veuz chevaliers tant preux, tant gualans, tant dextres à pied et à cheval, plus vers, mieulx remuans, mielx mani-ans tous bastons, que là estoient, jamais ne feurent veus dames tant propres, tant mignonnes, moins fascheuses, plus doctes à la main, à l'agueille, à toute acte muliebre honneste et libere, que là es-toient" (204–5)].

The representation of inner virtue can only take place through the evocations of signs that connote that virtue. In the case of the Thelemites, those signs come from traditional aristocratic fiction. Thus, whereas Frère Jean carries a staff ("baston") in the form of a cross, these knights are adept at all weapons ("bastons"). Indeed, the description above recalls the conventional descriptions of courtly society that one finds in medieval romance, and that would later be satirized in Lafayette's *La Princesse de Clèves*.

Rabelais tells us that the Thelemites eat, drink, and rise when they please. They have only one rule, *"Fay ce que vouldras,"* "Do what you will,"

because people who are free, well-born, and easy in honest company have a natural spur and instinct which drives them to virtuous deeds and deflects them from vice; and this they called honour. When these same men are depressed and enslaved by vile constraint and subjection, they use this noble quality which once impelled them freely towards virtue, to throw off and break this yoke of servitude. For we always strive after things forbidden and covet what is denied us. (159)

[parce que gens liberes, bien nez, bien instruictz, conversans en compaignies honnestes, ont par nature un instinct et aguillon, qui tousjours les poulse à faitz vertueux et retire de vice, lequel ilz nommoient honneur. Iceulx, quand par vile subjection et con-trainct sont deprimez et asserviz detournent la noble affection, par laquelle à vertuz franchement tendoient à deposer et enfraindre ce joug de servitude; car nous entreprenons toujours choses de-fendues et convoitons ce que nous est denié. (204)]

< *Nation and Utopia in the 1530s* >

Scholars have long puzzled over the meaning of this famous passage, and of the images of human nature and community that it presents. A number of years ago Michael Screech tried to reconcile the "natural" goodness of the Thelemites with conventional Christian doctrine by alluding to the doctrine of "synderesis," whereby humans are seen to retain certain parts of human goodness not obliterated in the Fall. More recently, in an exemplary reconstruction of the theology of Theleme, Edwin Duval has linked the "spurs" that drive the Thelemites to do good to Erasmus's gloss on Paul's Second Letter to the Corinthians (3:17), who are told that wherever Christ's spirit is, there humans behave virtuously, prodded by a "secret spur." It is this spur that lends harmony to Theleme, argues Duval, and that defines it as "the Pauline Church imagined by Erasmus."[51]

However, the final moralizing tag, which links the Thelemites to a general dynamic of "human nature" (denoted by the "nous"), qualifies the initial description and brings us again to the question of how invisible spiritual renewal can be represented in language. For the spirit of Christ, with its "secret spurs," drives humans from the inside, as it were, pushing them to behave virtuously. Yet Rabelais is careful to point out that once humans are enslaved this drive toward virtue falls away. Indeed, if it *is* Christian liberty that is being depicted here, it seems fragile indeed. For the enslavement that threatens it is not the spiritual enslavement of the will, but the more trivial enslavement of institutions (either monastery or court), where one cannot "do what one likes." In other words, Christian liberty, which seems to come from the inside of the subject, cannot function unless it has a carefully defined external field for its exercise. Otherwise, it turns aside into something that looks more like political restiveness, and loses track of its goal of virtuous action. There can be no internal renewal without an external institution, no spirit without letter.

This curious flip-flop between spiritual interiority and collective organization is carried out through a rewriting of Saint Paul, which suggests that we are here in a world beyond conversion, a world in which "Greek" and "Jew" do not exist. Rabelais tells us that when humans are oppressed they naturally want to throw off the "yoke of servitude" that oppresses them. The image of the yoke echoes Grandgousier's earlier prayer that he will be able to bring Picrochole back under the "yoke" (102) of God's will. More authoritatively, the phrase comes from Paul's letter to the Galatians (5:1), in which the Apostle deals with precisely the issues of community that have concerned us

< *Nation and Utopia in the 1530s* >

here. Paul's concern is with those who have slipped from Christianity back toward other forms of behavior—with those who have given up their Christianity, or have tried to reconcile life in the new community of believers with their earlier lives and practices as Greeks and Jews. The "yoke of servitude" is the yoke they had seemed to discard, but have now put back on, forgetting that "in Christ Jesus neither circumcision nor uncircumcision is of any avail, but faith working through charity" (5:6). Rabelais, however, exactly reverses Saint Paul. For whereas Paul recommends throwing off the yoke of servitude, Rabelais uses the same metaphor to denote a restiveness that threatens the Abbey. Or, more precisely, Rabelais links the yoke to the forms of oppression which the very constitution of the Abbey forecloses. Rabelais turns Paul's spiritual image into a figure for intolerable oppression—presumably, the routine of the conventional monastery. He takes a figure productive of difference (Greeks and Jews) and uses it to describe the one thing that Theleme cannot tolerate. Strife, even the struggle to throw off the yoke of servitude, seems to be a threat to Theleme. Rabelais negates the negation of difference figured by the yoke image by proposing a community in which the yoke has already, from the outset, been thrown off.[52] Thus, when one Thelemite wants to dance, they all dance, "and thus, they most laudably rivalled one another" (159) ["en louable emulation" (204)]. Such cooperative emulation echoes Picrochole's repeated call to his men, "Let him that loves me follow" (113) ["Qui m'ayme, si me suyve" (131)], and Frère Jean's exhortation to defend the body of Christ, "all you who love wine: God's body, follow me" (99) ["vous aultres qui aymez le vin: le corps Dieu, sy me suibvez" (108)]. But it also recalls the relationship between Jew and Christian we saw set forth in the Vulgate version of Romans 11, discussed at the outset of this chapter, wherein Jews lose their ethnic particularity and join the universal community of Christians through a process of *aemulatio*, or emulation ("ad aemulandum provocem carnem meam," says Paul).[53] Yet to be in Theleme doesn't involve conversion; it involves never having lived in a world of difference, of Greek and Jew, Spaniard and Frenchman, to begin with.

The key mediating term in the yoking together of theology and political utopia here is the word "honneur," which is the word the Thelemites use to describe the spur to goodness. Honor, however, is primarily a courtly and political concept. In fact, honor and worldly virtue are precisely what the Christian is generally supposed to ignore. The term appears in the New Testament principally in I Peter,

< *Nation and Utopia in the 1530s* >

where Peter tells the believers, "Honor all men. Love the brother-hood. Fear God. Honor the emperor" (2:17).[54] Peter is concerned precisely with political expedience and the differences between communities, with how Christians are to get along with other peoples and not be persecuted. Certainly Rabelais seems elsewhere to understand "honor" as a collective phenomenon with political and chivalric resonances, since Gargantua urges his men into battle against Picrochole in chapter 43 with the claim that victory will bring them "honor." Moreover, the "enigma" that follows the description of Theleme depicts a world in which political chaos reigns because subjects will have forgotten their honor toward the powerful: "And even great men, come of noble line,/Will find themselves attacked by their own vassals;/Honour and reverence will lack their due/Order and sense of rank will be forgotten" (161) ["Mesme les grandz, de ce noble lieu saill-liz,/De leur subjectz se verront assailliz,/Et le debvoir d'honneur et reverence/Perdra pour lors tout ordre et difference" (206)].

Rabelais's claim that the Thelemites were driven by a spur toward the good, and that "they called it honor," suggests the difficult conjunction of courtly heroism with Christian piety that underpins Theleme. For it is unclear whether honorable aristocratic identity is here understood to be the same as Christian liberty, or whether the newly freed Christians (who, we recall from the inscription over the door, are here "founding" a new faith) are retrospectively glossing a term that has a very different history indeed. Rabelais's use of the ambiguous verb "nommer" (both to name and to call) in the phrase "lequel ilz nommoient honneur," and his use of the imperfect past tense (suggesting both habitual repeated actions and ongoing actions) only further complicates the situation. Here, as elsewhere, Rabelais's manipulation of the technical vocabulary of moral and political action ("grace," "bienfaictz,") seems deliberately aimed to hold in tension two distinct systems of comportment and value.[55]

Both the courtly tenor of its inhabitants and Rabelais's use of the image of the yoke suggest that Theleme can only be represented by displacing a series of tropes taken from the aristocratic rivalries and political struggles between "Greek" and "Jew" evoked in the Picrocholine war and the topical references to Charles V. The importance of this strategy for the representation of community in *Gargantua* is made even clearer when we consider one of the most striking characteristics of the description of Theleme. This is the attention paid to clothing. The obsession with sartorial detail seems to be a topos, as it

< *Nation and Utopia in the 1530s* >

were, of utopian representations, since More dwells on the same topic in his *Utopia*. As both a sign of social status and a form of protection, clothing provides a semiotic field where use value and exchange value converge. By manipulating clothing one can suggest different forms of labor and value. Yet throughout Rabelais, reflection on clothing is also reflection on language and meaning, on how signs signify. And signs, we know, signify through their difference from other signs. More's Utopians, who are the contrary of English aristocrats, dress like monks. The Thelemites, who are the contrary of Catholic priests, dress like aristocrats. Yet Rabelais is careful to point out that the splendid signs that signify Theleme are made possible by the labor of others. Not only is the Abbey equipped with a staff of craftsmen who work to provide it with all comforts, it is depicted as the beneficiary of an empire. The finery of the Thelemites is made possible by yearly deliveries of "supplies and material from the hands of lord Nausiclete, who rendered seven ships to them each year from the Perlas and Cannibal Islands, loaded with gold ingots, raw silk, pearls, and precious stones" (158) ["Iceulx estoient fourniz de matiere et estoffe par les mains du seigneur Nausiclete, lequel par chascun an leurs rendoit sept navires des iles de Perlas et Canibales, chargées de lingotz d'or, de soye crue, et perles et pierreries" (203)].

Nausiclete's regular delivery of wealth and raw materials recalls the earlier example of Alpharbal, whose gratitude toward the generosity of Grandgousier impelled him to provide a flood of tribute money and goods. Indeed, one might even posit that Rabelais's description of Alpharbal as a "furious" enemy who turns into a simple and honest victim willing to give up all his wealth looks very much like the image projected in European writing of the period of the New World "savage" who longs to turn over his riches to the European conqueror. The "simple" Canarians, who looked suspiciously like the European fantasy of New World natives in the Alpharbal anecdote, are here replaced by "Nausiclete," or "Famous-for-ships," an epithet applied by Homer to the Phaiakians. Nausiclete's name suggests that the sea-wise Phaiakians, who escorted Odysseus home from their own mini-utopia, have undergone a metamorphosis. For the fact that this wealth is "rendered" "from the hands" of Nausiclete and given "each year" indicates that we have here an instance of tribute payment that precisely recalls what we saw in the Alpharbal episode. The essential relationship between political violence and imperialist booty is emblematized in the very juxtaposition of the two islands. The "Canni-

< *Nation and Utopia in the 1530s* >

bal" island, with its connotations of viciousness and savagery, is carefully evoked with the island of "Perlas," whose very name seems to embody the wealth ("perles et pierreries") that Theleme requires.

A juxtaposition of the Theleme episode with the Alpharbal scene underscores the tension in Rabelais between the ideal of harmonious community and the language through which that ideal is represented in action.[56] In the scenes examined here, the representation of community seems to require a particularly troubling element which is simultaneously present and absent. In Gargantua's harangue, it was Alpharbal himself who was both located outside the ambit of European community and shown to be essential to the economy of humanist reconciliation. Here, where the issue is the establishment of a harmonious European collective, we learn that the struggle over property and goods—the very struggle that so viciously pitted Francis I against Charles V and, in slightly different terms, Picrochole against Gargantua—has been dissolved into a fantasy of tribute and endless wealth. The banishment of violence and alterity, from the scene of the book to a pair of far-off islands, makes it possible for the Canarians, who give money to Grandgousier by virtue of their free will or "franc vouloir" (184) to be replaced by the aristocratic Thelemites, whose "franc vouloir" (200) and "franc arbitre" (203) power a corporate body blending individual will and collective need. With the threat of alterity neutralized the Thelemites can find collective harmony in the benign dynamic of "emulation."

What is at issue here is not the theology of Theleme, which may indeed, as some scholars have argued, constitute some type of abstract model of a renewed Pauline Christian community. The point is that a new Christian community cannot be *represented* in action without the lexicon of mercantilism and empire. The signs that make Theleme different from other monasteries are the jewels and silk that come through Nausiclete's tribute. Without them, Theleme is not Theleme. And those riches can only be provided through an imperialist fantasy that recalls nothing so much as the ambitions of Francis I. Theleme's spiritual community can only be imagined if it is built upon French imperialism. The optimistic humanist dynamic of gratitude that marked the close of Gargantua's harangue to the conquered is here recalled in the image of islanders who provide riches to pious Christians. Moreover, the fact that the "Perlas" islands have a Spanish name, and that the "Cannibal islands" were a common term for those lands first discovered by Columbus, underscores the "na-

< *Nation and Utopia in the 1530s* >

tionalist" nature of this fantasy. Those Spanish lands here magically seem to have passed into French control. Or, even more fantastically, perhaps we are to understand their "tribute" as coming from an eventual defeat of Charles V by Francis I, and a subsequent "charitable" taming of the ferocious Hapsburg Emperor by the Valois monarch. It may be no accident that we are in Utopia here.[57]

Thus the Evangelical community of the spirit, the utopia of a world where there is no distinction between Greek and Jew and where all are one, can only be defined through a fantasy of French empire, in which Greek and Jew, Frenchman and Spaniard, are different indeed. The ideal community that Evangelical humanism proposes as the balm to a wounded Christian body can only be made legible through a set of signs that are produced out of a fantasy of French imperialism, out of the very world that Theleme replaces. Both the political struggles against Picrochole, and the anguished evocation of the persecution of the Reformers by the Sorbonne set forth in the "Enigma" that closes the text, lead to an image of harmonious community that requires the very difference it seeks to efface.

Thus the ideological conflicts that mark France in the 1530s are transmuted aesthetically in Rabelais's text through a dialectical process. International political rivalries are depicted by humanist political theory as a crisis of Christian brotherhood. In dialogue with humanist thought, Rabelais repairs the cracks in Christendom by offering ideal images of a redeemed community. Yet precisely because he is attempting to show that new community in action (rather than, say, offering a set of emblematic images or precepts, as Erasmus does), Rabelais bases his fiction on the very symbolic language that Christian renewal struggles to leave behind. This paradox constitutes the splendor and misery of humanist fiction in the 1530s. Rabelais provides a temporary resolution to the ideological pressures on his text through the rhetorical energy and formal resources of fictional narrative. In this relationship of language, politics, and theology, moreover, he exactly reverses the terms set up by his contemporary Machiavelli for understanding the relationship between political harmony and theological discourse. In a famous passage from his *Discourses on Livy* (1.2.13), Machiavelli recommends that secular governments deploy religious symbols and institutions as a kind of discourse of power to keep subjects in line. For Rabelais, by contrast, the signs of chivalric and epic literature are deployed to produce a fiction that would perform a regime of Christian liberty. And the fact

< *Nation and Utopia in the 1530s* >

that the tension between these two discourses structures the very rhetoric of Rabelais's text in a way that it doesn't structure Machiavelli's may have resonances that are both generic and ideological. At one level, it maybe a sign of the difference between fiction and political theory. Yet at another level it may point to the dilemma (and eventual failure) of French Evangelical thought itself, which sought to instill a new spirituality into political life without providing a new vocabulary and repertoire of images for representing political action.

If *Pantagruel* sets forth the limits of the Christian humanist ideal of charity in the face of *cultural* alterity, *Gargantua* probes the rhetoric of humanism under the pressure of *political* difference. And we may conclude this chapter by considering the interrelationship of the various images of collective identity set up in Theleme. To be sure, the French crown had long defined itself as blessed among the princes of Europe through the special unity of Church and the monarchy, and the particular authority enjoyed by the Gallican church as northern representative of the Pope. In Rabelais, however, we get a very different vision of politics and theology, a model that clearly reflects the emergence of a new national political identity that is beginning to split from Christian idealism. We are told that the Thelemites dress in different styles, reflecting the different countries of Europe; on Sundays, they dress like the French. These customs underscore the fact that Theleme is Christian, international, and Gallic. The nationality of the Thelemites is never defined, and comes, it seems, with the territory—or, perhaps, with the empire. In fact, it is difficult to know whether the imperial fantasy, mentioned a moment ago, exists as material support for Theleme, or whether Theleme exists as justification for the imperial fantasy. The tension between Frenchness and Christian universality here takes the form of the split between material culture (empire) and idealism (Theleme), between, on another level, letter and spirit. French identity is dissolved into the universality of Christian identity while nonetheless depending on the power of a French empire. Thus we may say that the inhabitants of Theleme are Christians by *design*, and French only by *chance*. However, they are aristocrats by *necessity*. For the mediating element tying Christian renewal to national empire is aristocratic virtue which lends Theleme its social homogeneity. In this world, only aristocrats can be *both* universal and French. For after all, it is aristocrats who wander the world like Nausiclete, exact and pay tribute, and define the terms of a virtue "which they called honor." In Rabelais these

< *Nation and Utopia in the 1530s* >

three identities—Christian, French, and aristocratic—float in a kind of suspended animation in the space of Theleme. In the next chapter, however, we shall see that the emergence of a newly powerful French state, with its attendant imperial rhetoric, requires a process of transformation whereby "Frenchness" begins to take precedence over Christian and aristocratic universalism.

By defining ideals of Christian harmony through a language based in the violence of worldly power Rabelais suggests the folly of reading *Gargantua* as either a strict political fable or a purely theological tract. His own language shows us how not to read his book. For if we ignore the text's many admonitions against violence and factionality, we choose to live in the world of Picrochole. By contrast, to reduce the book's complexity through a strictly theological reading would require a hermeneutic as wary of difference as Theleme itself. Instead, as I have argued, *Gargantua* demands to be read as textual performance aimed at mediating, through the magic of literary form, between two increasingly incompatible models of community which struggle for the identity of France in the 1530s. Indeed, the conflicted rhetoric that I have stressed in my reading of the book is evidence of the scope and honesty of Rabelais's imagination. Just as Shakespeare seems at once to criticize and embrace empire in *The Tempest*, or as Cervantes simultaneously condemns and offers a sympathetic vision of the Moors in *Don Quixote*, Rabelais both holds forth humanist idealism and acknowledges its limits. He shows a vision of peace where he knows that peace can only be shown through a language of violence. A less expansive vision would have produced propaganda. Instead, Rabelais draws on discourses that are heavily ideological (political theory, moral philosophy, theology) and reconfigures them to open the space of an emerging secular discourse that will come to be called literature. Moreover, the rigor of Rabelais's vision leads him to locate the limitations of humanist thought at the level of language itself, in the very material of his own trade, the cement that bonds community. His dramatization of the link between moral philosophy and political violence, between the philosophy of indifference and the world of difference, constantly extends to include and threaten the language of his own text, which balances precariously between violence and dogma. Almost by a miracle, it seems, *Gargantua* avoids toppling off to either side. France, in the decades following *Gargantua*, was not so fortunate.

Chapter Four

Narrative Form and National Space:
Textual Geography from the Heptaméron to
La Princesse de Clèves

Gaul is a whole, divided into three parts.
—CAESAR, *The Gallic War*

So far I have been writing mostly about problems of ideology. The previous two chapters were concerned principally with the ways in which the imagination of an ideal community of Christian believers is transformed by increasing pressure on the edges of community— be it pressure from without, in the form of cultural alterity, or pressure from within, in the form of political rivalry. In this chapter, however, I want to turn to a less abstract, conceptual problem. I want to consider the ways in which literary narrative constructs images of national space, marking out the how subjects move and act. "Each genre possesses its own space . . . and each space its own genre," writes Franco Moretti in a discussion of the relationship between the nineteenth-century novel and the nation-state.[1] However, we have seen so far that, in Renaissance France, neither genres nor spaces are stable and homogeneous. Just as the identity of community in Renaissance France is multiple, variegated, and motley, so are the texts that seek to construct or define that community marked by a struggle among different and often competing generic registers. Moretti and others have argued that the definition of the modern nation-state is intimately linked to the emergence of the novel, that nations may be understood as narratives or "narrations"—as symbolic forms unfolding in time, like stories. Yet the novel is but one kind of narrative, and, since my concern is with the pre-history of modern nationalism, it is important to account for the multiplicity of narrative forms that shape early modern culture. One must avoid, in considerations of nationhood, the temptation to collapse "narrative" (a mode of organizing events) into "novel" (a contingent, historically defined, literary genre). Indeed, the problems raised by the frequent association of

< *Narrative Form and National Space* >

novel and nation may be seen when one considers the relationship between the borders of nations and the limits of literature. Timothy Brennan notes, commenting on a passage of Bakhtin, that "It was the novel that historically accompanied the rise of nations by objectifying the 'one, yet many' of national life, and by mimicking the structure of the nation, a clearly bordered jumble of languages and styles. Socially, the novel joined the newspaper as the major vehicle of the national print media, helping to standardize language, encourage literacy, and remove mutual incomprehensibility."[2] Brennan's formulation finely articulates an important temporal paradox in the relationship between nationhood and novel. For it suggests that the novel at once "follows" the invention of the nation by "objectifying" and "mimicking" its features, even as it "precedes" it, by helping to produce the linguistic unity that makes nationhood possible. How is one to understand this complex dynamic?

In this chapter I will approach this problem by considering the interrelated variety of narrative forms that shape the pre-history of the novel, and the pre-history of the modern nation-state. I will trace the ways in which a set of influential narratives from sixteenth- and seventeenth-century France depict territory and the borders of territory. I shall begin with a brief look at yet another passage from Rabelais, before moving to more extended discussions of Marguerite de Navarre and Madame de Lafayette, two writers who, after Rabelais, were probably the most influential practitioners of fictional narrative prose during the early modern period in France. To be sure, the conjunction of narrative form and national space has an ideological dimension that is just as important here as it was in my earlier discussions of Christian humanism. Yet now the concern will be with *social* (rather than religious) identity, in particular with the crisis of aristocratic identity that accompanies the centralization of political power attendant on the rise of the modern state. As a way of measuring the ramifications for literature of a certain process of social upheaval, I will be tracing a set of generic transformations that take us from the world of epic, the canonical form for thinking about nationhood in classical culture, to the new world of the novel and the absolutist state. However, I shall show that the interplay of space, social identity, and narrative form in these texts results in a much more complex dynamic than anything suggested by such well-worn phrases as "epic to novel," or "the rise of the novel." Rather, I will show, it is precisely through their *mixing* of genres that such writers

< *Narrative Form and National Space* >

as Marguerite de Navarre and Lafayette attempt to confront the social transformations that accompany the emergence of modern nationhood. And, conversely, that very generic complexity constructs a
spatial regime that gives expression to the inclusive volume of the
nation-state.

The starting point for this analysis comes from the very last lines
of Virgil's *Aeneid*, the most influential narrative of "state building" ever
written. As Aeneas, the Trojan refugee and founder of Rome, struggles in single combat against the local hero Turnus to decide the fate
of Italy, Turnus loses his spear. In a fit of rage he picks up and hurls a
stone, "a giant stone and ancient [saxum ingens/...saxum an-
tiquum]." But the stone he hurls isn't just any stone. It has a specific
function: "a stone ... which haply lay upon the plain, set for a landmark to ward dispute from the fields." Unwittingly, the Italian hero
seeks to defend his homeland with the very material of territoriality.
In fact, by removing the stone from its place, Turnus destroys the
border between fields, thereby mimicking the very process of consolidation of peoples and territories which Aeneas's conquest of Rome
will bring about. To defend his homeland, he disfigures its topography. And it is surely no accident that the same image of the stone is
repeated a moment later as part of an epic simile used to describe Aeneas's final spear-thrust, which disables Turnus: "Never stone shot
from engine of siege roars so loud ... [murali concita numquam tor-
mento sic saxa fremunt]." The epic heroes demonstrate their
strength in a battle which reconfigures the landscape itself.[3]

The Measure of France

This striking epic connection between stones, heroism, and national
space is parodically rewritten in chapter 23 of Rabelais's *Pantagruel*.
Pantagruel travels from Paris to Honfleur to begin a war in defense of
his homeland of Utopia. During the journey, Pantagruel's friend Panurge explains to him why the territory of France is measured out in
leagues that are smaller than those of other countries. Citing as his authority a nonexistent text, the *Gestes des Roys de Canarre* (*Deeds of the
Kings of Canary*) by an imaginary monk called Marotus du Lac, Panurge relates that it was Pharamond, the legendary first king of
France, who originally marked out French territory. In olden days, he
reports, there was no difference between countries until Pharamond
separated them out ("Pharamond les distingua" [336]).[4] He did so by
selecting from among his people a hundred gallant young Parisians

< *Narrative Form and National Space* >

and a hundred beautiful young women from Picardy, pairing them off and sending them traveling across the landscape, willy-nilly. Wherever they engaged in sexual intercourse, Pharamond instructed the men, they were to erect a stone: "commanding them to go here and there, through diverse places, and every time they jumped on their wenches, they were to put a rock" (245) ["leur faisant commendement qu'ilz allassent en divers lieux par cy et par là, et, à tous les passaiges qu'ilz biscoteroyent leurs garses, que ilz missent une pierre" (336)]. The distance between the stones would mark a league. Early in the journey, not far from Paris, the men were fresh, and the urge came on them at the edge of every field they crossed. Later, however, they began to wear down. They were content with sex only once a day, and the space between the rocks increased accordingly. For this reason, concludes Panurge, the leagues in Brittany, Germany, and the Landes are longer than those in France. He adds that there are other proposed explanations, but that this is the one he believes. Pantagruel concurs.

In its selection of young, beautiful aristocrats, Pharamond's scheme recalls nothing so much as the pairing of knights and ladies which will occur later, in *Gargantua*, in the founding of the Abbey of Theleme. Here, however, the aim is nationalistic and topographic, rather than theological and communitarian. Pharamond's project asserts a connection between the country's political identity and its topographical difference from other countries. The unusual shortness of the league in France—a detail noted as well by Montaigne in his travel journal—is here associated with the founding of the nation itself. When they define the French league ("lieue") Pharamond and his subjects make France into a place ("lieu"). The command of the king results in the topographical definition of the nation which will then subordinate itself to that king. Topography and political authority mirror one another.

Yet the relationship of space to politics is mediated by the conventions of literary discourse. Panurge's obviously spurious authorities, the *Gestes des Roys de Canarre* and Marotus du Lac evoke the two major narrative traditions of medieval Europe—epic and romance. The epic or *chanson de geste* here gets displaced to the Canary Islands (conventionally the goal, rather than the origin of heroic quests). And the literary conventions of romance are evoked through the fictitious Marotus du Lac, who suggests a blending of Chrétien de Troyes's Lancelot du Lac and Rabelais's friend, the poet Clément Marot, whose edition of the *Roman de la Rose* was a Renaissance bestseller.

< *Narrative Form and National Space* >

Though these literary sources are phony, their presence is not arbitrary. For both of these traditions, the genre of epic (already seen in my discussion of Virgil) and the genre of romance, involve the motif of the quest. They narrate projects of exploration and conquest powered by desire. However, Rabelais evokes these conventions precisely in order to turn them upside down. The conventional quest narrative relies on the deployment of unsatisfied desire, on the deeds of a protagonist who must find and claim a prize. In Panurge's anecdote we have the exact inverse of narrative desire. Rather than sending his men chasing after elusive damsels, Pharamond sends the damsels and the men out together. He orders, not the deferral of desire, but the *satisfaction* of desire, *jouissance* itself. In place of a quest, we get a parody of the notion that people should go forth and multiply.

Pharamond's ambitious project, like the fantasies of so many monarchs in the Renaissance, imagines a perfect unification of literature, political power, and land management. On one level, the coupling of boys from Paris and girls from Picardy suggests a kind of emblematic unification of Paris and the countryside—those two spaces which French political culture has always had such trouble imagining together. Pharamond's plan calls for the inscription of signs on the land. It envisions the fixing of a series of marks that will make France legible. A stone is to be erected for each erection.

But it is not these erected rocks that make France France. Rather, France becomes France *between* the rocks, through their differential relationship to each other. Only by moving from sign to sign does one find out what France is: "between these rocks," Pharamond might say, parodying Christ, "I found this nation." And this same differential slide from sign to sign feeds perfectly into a consideration of literature, since it mimics the movement of narrative itself. Just as narrative, like language, slides from event to event, body to body, so, in Pharamond's initial project, France would take shape between the marches. Indeed, Pharamond's plan both mimics narrative and aims to control its vagaries. The deferral of sexual satisfaction conventionally represented in the quest narrative would be replaced by the repeated gratification of sexual desire. From this repetition would come a powerful monarch, a unified country, and happy subjects.

Such, however, is not to be. Pharamond's ideal is disrupted by the very pleasure it promotes. Panurge is careful to point out that when the rate of lovemaking falls from several times a day, at the edge of every field, to only once a day ("quelque meschante et paillarde foys le

< *Narrative Form and National Space* >

jour" [336]), it is against the will of the women, who remain strong and lusty. The repeated intercourse that would mark out a series of uniform leagues is disrupted by the limits of male potency. These limits, moreover, lend Pharamond's project a political outcome unimagined at the outset. As befits a king whose name suggests both "pharaoh" and "world" ("monde"), Pharamond's initial command to go forth and fornicate is implicitly imperialist. It aims at marking out the entire world in the same manner, at making everything into French territory, with Paris as its center.[5] It prefigures the imperialist rage of that other great topographic maniac in Rabelais, Picrochole, whose harangue in *Gargantua*, chapter 33, projects an even more terrifying vision of world conquest. Yet the outcome of Pharamond's project is a parody of the welding of narrative to empire. For as soon as the men begin to wear down, the uniform space between stones begins to grow, and the couples begin tracing out leagues that are no longer French. Sexual difference produces both topographic and narrative chaos. Yet it simultaneously produces the space of the nation. When the men begin to weaken, France ends. The breakdown of the male French sex drive produces the limits and unity of France itself. Through these fragile male bodies, the world is separated into different national units. Sex several times a day produces France; once a day measures out the neighboring lands. Together with a nation of leagues, we get a league of nations.

Thus Pharamond initially sends his subjects out as part of a scheme that establishes French sovereignty through a revision of the traditional quest narratives so important in the epic and romance traditions. The result, however, is neither endless desire nor endless France. Indeed, if the narrative traditions of epic and romance feature characters endowed with limitless strength, this story takes us from a fantasy of unlimited male sexual potency to a burlesque of that fantasy. Panurge's tale injects into a fantasy of power and repetition the weight of mortality, of the body, of time and history. In contrast to the Virgilian depiction of superhuman strength destroying the borders of territory, it suggests that the emergence of France as France, as a space different from other nations, goes hand in hand with the emergence of new forms of representation that register the weight of time and contingency on bodies and nations. The shift from a stateless, unmarked world of fields and forests to a world of political and topographical difference parallels the fall from a world of omnipotent epic heroes into a world in which potency comes only once a day.

< *Narrative Form and National Space* >

Within Rabelais's own text this reflection on the particularity of France comes at a moment of generic mixture or crossing. Not only do the vague references to romance and epic set up an implicit contrast between Rabelais's strange generic hybrid text and more codified traditions, but the very placement of Panurge's anecdote within the larger structure of *Pantagruel* makes the connection between national homogeneity and generic heterogeneity explicit. The tale comes just as the hero is leaving his youthful follies and taking up the serious tasks of kingship. In literary terms the text moves from echoes of late medieval traditions of farce (student life, misogynistic humor, jokes about lawyers) to the burlesque epic quest that Pantagruel must pursue in defense of Utopia. The shift to maturity and epic purpose is underscored both by Rabelais's playful spelling of Honfleur as "Hommefleur" ("flower of manhood") and by a series of allusions soon after to the fourth book of the *Aeneid*, in which Aeneas leaves Dido (whose very first words to the Trojans, it should be recalled, justify her defense of her borders).[6] Panurge's anecdote about the link between territory and narrative desire is itself a passage to a new land and a new narrative: the France of Pharamond and of Pantagruel's youth gives way to the Utopia of the final chapters. To mark the shift, the ersatz romance and epic sources for Panurge's tale give way to the burlesque epic of *Pantagruel* itself, in which sexual dalliances are renounced in the name of political duty, but where the outsized epic force of the hero is constantly tempered by an awareness of the limitations of human capacity.

Romance and the Aristocracy

In order to explore the larger political and ideological importance of the intertwining of narrative, desire, and topography suggested by Panurge's fable, I would like now to look in some detail at the major collection of short narratives from Renaissance France. This is Marguerite de Navarre's *Heptaméron*, presumably written in the 1540s, but only published in 1559, a decade after her death. I want to focus principally on the longest and most complex narrative in the *Heptaméron*, the tenth story of the first day. This is the story of the love of Amadour and Floride—a story of great literary and historical importance, since it is often considered the prototype for the first "modern" French novel, Madame de Lafayette's *La Princesse de Clèves* (1678), of which more will be said a bit later. De Navarre's story tells of the obsession of a young noble, Amadour, with a young woman of high

< *Narrative Form and National Space* >

rank, Floride. It recounts how Amadour follows Floride as a "serviteur," or courtly admirer, over many years, how he marries her lady-in-waiting Aventurade in order to gain proximity to her, even as Floride is married off to a man she does not love. It tells how she chastely acknowledges Amadour's love until he attempts to rape her, and how, when she resists him and eventually mutilates her own face with a stone to drive him away, they eventually part, he to die heroically in battle and she to bury her husband and enter a convent.

The question of borders and territories is central to this tale, since it unfolds in Catalonia, on the border between France and Spain. Unlike most of the tales in the collection, this one is removed from the present of the France of Marguerite's brother, Francis I, and located in a past moment of Spanish history (presumably at the end of the fifteenth century). This "exotic" setting allows Marguerite to paint a background to the main action that is filled with border wars and territorial conflicts around the imaginary line that distinguishes France from Spain. Yet the thematic evocation of borders and political boundaries in the story's setting is counterbalanced by another element, namely, the genre of romance, which informs the plot of the story and supplies many of its motifs. The deployment of the romance tradition offsets the thematic concern with boundaries. For the wandering romance hero is, almost by definition, a crosser and transgresser of boundaries. The words and deeds of the romance hero are typically emblematic not of a *national* entity, but of a set of values relating to a particular *social group*—the aristocracy.[7] From its medieval "origins" romance, as a genre of aristocratic education and socialization, projects a fantasy image of the unity of the aristocracy as an "international" class. Shifts in the genre of romance in turn register the steps in the history of the social group. By the sixteenth century, this history was in the midst of a great transformation. At the time of Marguerite de Navarre, the universalism that had traditionally characterized the aristocracy was beginning to be threatened by developing forms of centralized political power—and this occurred nowhere more rapidly than in France. In the face of this new threat to the internationalism of the aristocratic subject, romance began to take on a new function. Always a form whose fantastic elements are threatened by a disenchanting realism, romance began to take on the formidable ideological task of reaffirming, through wish fulfillment, an ideal of disappearing aristocratic independence. The easy slippage of the romance hero from country to country, a figure of the interna-

< *Narrative Form and National Space* >

tionalism once enjoyed by an aristocracy without borders, became transmuted into the theme of travel. That internationalism is reflected ironically in the figure of Astolfo, who in Ariosto's *Orlando Furioso* circumnavigates the globe on a winged horse. Its more pathetic form may be Don Quixote's desire "to sally forth through the four parts of the world in quest of adventures on behalf of the oppressed."[8]

The mobility characteristic of the romance hero is stressed in the representation of Amadour, the male protagonist of Marguerite's tale.[9] He is defined by movement. As the very first paragraph of the story notes, he is so heroic that when peace breaks out at home he goes off to seek out war abroad ("aux lieux estranges" [56]).[10] Moreover, his combination of martial virtue and mobility produces a kind of universalism that I have been suggesting underpins fantasies of aristocratic identity. Amadour transcends differences between warring parties: whenever he fights he is loved and respected by both friends and enemies, "où il estoit aymé d'amys et d'ennemys" (56). He is admired not only in Spain, but in France and Italy. This heroic universality extends to his ethnic identity as well; we are told that, though born into a rich and honorable family in Toledo, he seemed more a Catalan than a Castillian for having frequented the border region ["et avoit tellement hanté ceste frontiere, à cause des guerres, qu'il sembloit mieulx Cathelan que Castillan, combien qu'il fust natif d'auprès de Tollete, d'une maison riche et honnorable" (56)].

The type of the military hero respected by his enemies is, of course, common in literature since Homer, and, indeed, Amadour is referred to at one point as the Achilles of "all Spains" ("Achilles de toutes les Espaignes" [68]). However, midway through the story the relationship between Amadour's geographical mobility and his social identity is thematized. Like the Spain of Marguerite's day—though unlike the actual Spain of the fifteenth-century setting—the Spain of the story is disrupted by constant border wars with its neighbor to the north. Encouraged by this recurring sign of Christian disunity, the King of Tunis decides to attack Spain—a project with clear parallels to the Turkish threat that terrified sixteenth-century Europe. In the ensuing battle Amadour is captured and falls into the hands of a Turk named Dorlin, ["gouverneur du Roy de Thunis" (68)], who keeps him as a servant for two years. Word gets around that the Tunisian king plans to torture Amadour unless he renounces his faith ("renoncer sa foy"[70]) and converts to Islam. This threat of forced conversion provides the moment at which Amadour's status as a kind

< *Narrative Form and National Space* >

of international aristocrat emerges; he negotiates his release from Dorlin by giving his word of honor that he will pay a ransom once he is back in Spain. Dorlin releases him without even informing his king: "And thus, without speaking of it to the King, his master let him go on faith" (138) ["Et ainsi, sans en parler au Roi, le laissa son maître aller sur sa foy" (70)].

The repetition of the word "foy," which describes both religion and the gentleman's word of honor, sets up a contrast between religious identity and social identity. The role of chivalric "foy" in saving Amadour's religious "foy" (as well as his skin) defines him as a member of an international aristocratic network. Again, as I discussed in chapter 1, there is moment at which the vocabulary of community is split against itself, to be manipulated by an opportunist word-master like Amadour. More of this linguistic splitting will be seen later. Here, chivalric faith turns the master Dorlin into a gentleman first and a Moslem second. It overcomes the bonds and boundaries of religion itself. The romance trope of chivalric friendship across religious lines (used with great effectiveness by Marguerite's contemporary Ariosto) is here reduced to a strategy in an economic exchange.

Amadour's geographical wandering, his status as a kind of international aristocrat, is paralleled in the more circumscribed sphere of his social relations. Amadour's virtue is so accomplished, his transgression of boundaries so easy, that he has no trouble penetrating the household of Floride's mother, the Countess of Arande. However, here his behavior is characterized not by the affirmation of class universalism, but rather by a kind of malleability suggesting duplicity. He is compared to the countess's son ("fut traicté comme son propre filz" [61]), to a saint or an angel ("l'on se fyoit en luy de toutes choses comme un sainct ou ung ange" [61]), and even, in a remarkable moment, to a woman ("print telle hardiesse et privaulté en la maison . . . que l'on ne se gardoit de luy non plus que d'une femme"[60]). The faintly parodic dimension of these similes suggests that the social and political landscape of the story is somehow at odds with the literary topography of romance upon which it draws so heavily. In the increasingly constrained court society that was already beginning to dominate France in the time of the Valois monarchy, the wandering of the romance hero doesn't quite fit. When inserted into the reduced space of the manor house or country château heroic universalism begins to look like mere slipperiness. To move at ease through the domestic space of the house the hero must take on multiple identi-

< *Narrative Form and National Space* >

ties—identities that may even end up effeminizing him, as suggested both by the comparison of Amadour to a woman and by the later cliché of the courtier as fop or dandy.

Thus the figure of Amadour offers an image of the perfect aristocrat whose manners and virtue carry him across all boundaries and through all doors. He is the ideal exemplar of the international aristocracy that ran the nascent states of Europe. Indeed, he is introduced as that one young man in a thousand perfectly suited to take over the state ("on l'eust jugé entre mil digne de gouverner une chose publicque"[55]). Moreover, his relationship to Floride is mediated by an exteriority and a lack of psychological motivation that suggest conventions of romance more than the scheming lovers and merchants of the novella tradition. Both characters are described, in their initial appearance, with a series of words evoking an over-determined courtly code of behavior and value. Amadour is first introduced from the outside, through the eyes, as it were, of the court. He is presented as he is observed, as a young man possessing such grace and good sense that one would judge him ("l'on l'eust jugé"[55]) the one in a thousand worthy of governing the polis. So strong is the link, in this context, between chivalric qualities and reputation, that Amadour himself is figured as a kind of tournament field on which various moral or psychic qualities compete for the "honor" of being first: "If his beauty was exquisite, his language followed so closely that one knew not which one to bestow honor on, whether it be grace, beauty, or eloquence" ["si la beauté estoit tant exquise, la parolle la suyvoit de si près que l'on ne sçavoit à qui donner l'honneur, ou à la grace ou à la beauté, ou au bien parler" (56)].[11] This description both asserts the absolutely superficial nature of Amadour's identity—he is created by the "judgment" of others—and the fundamental ambiguity that lies at the center of his being. He is so great that the gaze of the "one" or "on" speaking for courtly opinion is unable to identify the nature of his excellence. The description of Amadour underscores a paradox of models of sociability based upon external measure; that is, that the perfect accomplishment of external comeliness results in a disintegration of interiority.

Yet what is most important here is the conjunction between this valuing of reputation and the heavily coded language of courtly virtue that describes it. For that same language is echoed a few lines later in the description of Floride, who is first seen through the eyes of Amadour: "Never, he thought to himself, as he contemplated her

< *Narrative Form and National Space* >

grace and beauty, had he beheld so fair and noble a creature. If only she might look with favour upon him, that alone would give him more happiness than anything any other woman in the world could ever give him" (123) ["Et . . . en regardant la beauté et bonne grace de . . . Floride, qui, pour l'heure, n'avoit que douze ans, se pensa en luy-mesmes que c'estoit bien la plus honneste personne qu'il avoit jamais veue, et que, s'il povoit avoir sa bonne grace, il en seroit plus satisfaict que de tous les biens et plaisirs qu'il pourroit avoir d'une autre" (56)].[12] Thus both Floride and Amadour are described in similar terms: "beauté," "honneur" (or "honneteté," in the case of Floride, though her "honneur" is affirmed elsewhere), and "grace." The repetition of these key terms, which appear again and again throughout the story, suggests the extent to which Amadour and Floride are, like the protagonists of many a romance, exact doubles.[13] The one characteristic Amadour seems to possess that Floride does not is "le bien parler"—control of language—that gift that serves him well not only when he seeks freedom from the Turks, but when he seeks entry to Floride's room. It is also a faculty that leads to a fundamental crisis in the story.

What keeps these romance twins apart is economics and social hierarchy. Though noble, Amadour is without a large fortune. And the difference in social standing between him and Floride is sufficient to prevent them from marrying. The impossibility of legal union provides the occasion for an elaborate and lengthy process of amorous servitude. Much of the story is taken up with describing the elaborate rituals of fidelity and confidence played out between the two protagonists. In good romance fashion Amadour marries a lady-in-waiting to Floride named Aventurade, who permits him access to his beloved. Through a series of barely perceptible signs known only to lover and lady—including at one point absolute silence and separation—desire flows back and forth between the two friends. In a classic economy of courtly service, looks, words, and sighs are sent, received, and returned, with each year of devotion by Amadour increasing his value in the eyes of Floride, and each year of Floride's chastity increasing her worth in the mind of Amadour. Through his respect for the "honneur" of Floride and his desire for what is called her "bonne grace," he is led, as predicted at the outset, away from the more mundane temptations of "biens" and "plaisirs." A process of education and service is undertaken that recalls such late medieval romances as Antoine de la Sale's *Petit Jehan de Saintré*, which Marguerite

< Narrative Form and National Space >

would have known well. The combination of a socially prescribed amorous servitude with the errancy of the young knightly protagonist produces a potentially endless narrative of desire and heroism.[14] The story unfolds, as it were, between the extremes of the wide world, through which Amadour wanders at will, and the circumscribed house of Floride's mother. Its terrain is both boundless and absolutely local. Notably absent here is the space between the house and the world, the space of the nation—despite the many border wars and territorial struggles that are raging in the background.[15]

Rape, Politics, and the End of Romance

However, both the wandering of the hero Amadour and his service to Floride come to an abrupt end two-thirds of the way through the tale. Upon Amadour's release from captivity in Tunis, he and Floride are joyfully reunited, and the narrator tells us that Floride is finally, after many years, on the verge of accepting Amadour as her lover. Yet it is at this moment that the story suddenly shifts tonality. Without warning, Amadour is summoned by the king, who dispatches him on "some affair of importance" (139) ("quelque affaire d'importance" [71]). This summons has dire consequences. When she hears that her husband is to be sent away, Amadour's wife Aventurade collapses in a swoon and falls down a staircase, injuring herself fatally. This conjunction of events—the claim of the king on his person and the subsequent death of his wife—places Amadour in a desperate situation, since they remove all possible pretexts for ever again seeing Floride. Amadour decides to force the issue. He tries to rape the woman he has "served" as courtly admirer for seven years.[16]

The crucial event in this story is generally understood to be the horrendous rape attempt, which has attracted much critical attention as a kind of emblem of the absolute primacy of gender difference in structuring the world of the *Heptaméron*. To be sure, the social problem of rape was of major importance in early modern society. To deny that this scene reflects on the violence against women that characterized court society would be to ignore an important dimension of the story, and of the *Heptaméron* more generally.[17] Yet a close look at the plot of the story suggests that to read the rape separately from the king's summoning of Amadour is also to neglect an important political dimension to the story, which in turn informs the way gender is defined more generally. Not only does the king's summoning of Amadour suddenly shift the plot line of the story away from the dy-

< *Narrative Form and National Space* >

namics of courtship, but it marks the point at which both romance and aristocratic identity itself are placed in question. The king's enlistment of Amadour for "an affair of importance" is an anachronism. It is a textual moment at odds with the rest of the story, a topos out of place. For it marks the incursion of sixteenth-century political life into the timeless world of romance. The hero of romance is conventionally his own man. His service usually consists of doing what comes naturally—slaying monsters and fighting Saracens. Seen against the romance background of the tale, the "affaire d'importance" evoked here connotes the more immediate political world of the sixteenth century, in which nobles are enlisted as envoys or ambassadors by kings whose political destinies are imminently at risk in ways unknown to the benevolent Charlemagnes and Arthurs of the romance tradition. When the king summons Amadour the text speaks from its own Renaissance context and breaks the illusion of quaintness suggested by the "medieval" setting. Furthermore, Amadour's gift of "bien parler," which in medieval romance is conventionally taken as a mode for channelling male desire into courtly conduct, is now turned to the purposes of international politics.[18]

The importance of this moment of summoning becomes clear when we notice its resemblance to the other royal gesture in the story, the plan by the king of Tunis to force Amadour to renounce his faith and become a "good Turk" ("le randre bon Turc" [70]). That command could, no less than the death of Aventurade, have irrevocable consequences, since conversion implies circumcision. Yet Amadour escapes this forced conversion by pledging his faith or "foy" to his noble master. In the case of the command from the king of Spain, however, Amadour cannot escape. And the result of the crisis produced by this command is that, in place of the fever of seduction and the "service" he has paid to Floride, Amadour wants immediate domination over her body. The command of the king, which enlists the actions of his subject, is translated into the violent touch of the subject as he attempts to rape his lady.

The king's claim on Amadour comes into focus when seen in light of the situation of the French aristocracy in the early decades of the sixteenth century. The increasing emphasis on political centralization under Francis I had the effect of beginning to shift power away from the traditional aristocracy and into the hands of a single ruler. As Machiavelli noted in his *Ritratto di cose di Francia*, previous French rulers had constantly been forced to fight against provincial barons

< *Narrative Form and National Space* >

("privati baroni") whose own interests and power had kept the country fragmented. Under Francis, however, the country was for the first time united and powerful, with the good land all in the hands of the king. Brittany, Guienne, Bourbon and Burgundy had become, as Machiavelli put it, "subject and very obsequious" to the king of France.[19] This contrast between aristocratic household and centralized politics informs Marguerite's story. Throughout the tale it is made very clear that Amadour comes and goes as he pleases. His concern is for the honor of himself and his country, but he seems to have no duty, in any modern sense of the word, toward that country. Rather, political action is defined according to clan. When the Christians and Moors meet in the battle that brings about Amadour's death, the Christian knights beg the king to let them participate, which he does, according to their houses. When Amadour is captured by the Moors, the text says that some lament for the honor of the country ("l'honneur du pays" [68]), while Floride describes the loss as a loss for the house ("grande perte pour toute leur maison" [68]).[20]

The intertwining of international aristocratic heroism and emerging national consciousness that I have been tracing here is central to understanding the impact of Valois politics on French identity. One may see it as well, and perhaps even more clearly, in the life of Bayard, the great hero of Marignano and the contemporary French figure whose exploits most clearly recall those of Amadour. In his hagiographic *La vie du preulx Chevalier Bayard* (1525), the Lyonnais humanist Symphorien Champier recounts how Bayard was captured by a vassal of the Emperor Maximilian. The Emperor, realizing that he had in his hands the greatest knight in Christendom, offered to pay Bayard's ransom if, in return, he would serve the Empire. When the French king Louis XI got wind of this situation, he hurried to pay Bayard's ransom himself. Unlike Amadour, who ransoms himself, Bayard has to be rescued to preserve his allegiance. The French king must step in to keep this "French subject," whose battle cry, Champier assures us, was "France! France!," from defecting to a rival prince.[21]

No less striking is one of the last episodes in Champier's biography, describing Bayard's relations with the young Francis I. In his camp outside the gates of Milan, Francis decides to make his captains into knights to reward them for their service. Since one must be a knight to make knights, the king must first undergo the ritual himself. He asks to be knighted by Bayard, who, like Amadour, is famous the world over ("in many countries and provinces," as Francis puts it). Ba-

< *Narrative Form and National Space* >

yard hesitates, claiming that Francis has been knighted by God and needs no earthly sanction. But Francis insists and orders Bayard, as one of his subjects, to go through with the ceremony: "do my will and commandment, if you want to be among my good servants and subjects" ["faictes mon vouloir et commandement, si voulés estre du nombre de mes bons serviteurs et subjectz"]. In this beautifully ironic moment, the prince of the nascent modern state must use his authority as prince to bring about completion of a ceremony that will make himself and his men members of the international "order of chivalry."[22]

Whether or not the actual fabric of political life during the period may be reduced to a tension between centralization and aristocratic autonomy (still an issue of debate among historians), it is nonetheless true that writers during the period consistently register anxiety about the diminishing role of aristocratic heroism. Thus, for example, such otherwise different writers as Blaise de Monluc and Pierre de Bourdeille Brantôme lament the rise of the new practice of selling letters of nobility, which works to create a *noblesse de robe* indebted to royal authority. State service, instead of martial prowess, thus becomes the criterion for social advancement. Indeed, Brantôme complained that the whole debacle of Francis's foreign policy could be traced to the fact that his diplomatic corps tended to be staffed by men of the robe, instead men of the sword—that is, to translate into the terms I have been using here, by diplomats and bureaucrats, instead of romance heroes. The more subtle Machiavelli realized that the venality of offices not only displaced the central role of the traditional aristocracy, but redefined aristocratic family customs. Property, including high government posts, had traditionally passed to first-born sons. The venality of offices, however, made it possible for second sons, like Amadour, to find success by purchasing offices ("comperare uno stato"). To do so, however, they had first to gain fame through military exploits. The new system thus both strengthened the French military (which, notes Machiavelli, had improved in recent decades) and deflected sibling infighting traditional among the aristocracy into state service. For Machiavelli, whose admiration for the centralizing strategies of the French state make him one of its greatest apologists, romance heroism becomes the first step toward a career serving the prince.[23] As a second son whose military exploits prepare the way for an enlistment in the king's service, Amadour's career perfectly illustrates the political transition explicated by Machiavelli.

Thus the incursive claim of the king on the wandering Amadour

< *Narrative Form and National Space* >

may be seen as a symptom of a crisis of aristocratic identity, of an emerging tension between "internationalism" and "nationalism." Yet what is at issue here is not merely the historical shift to a new political order theorized by Machiavelli. For my purposes, no less crucial is what this shift means for the literary genres that conventionally articulate the threatened model of identity. When the king summons Amadour on an "affair of importance," the free-flowing circulation of desire and aristocratic male bodies that characterizes romance is suddenly channelled by an overarching authority. In an instant, Amadour becomes the subject of a state.[24] The general tension that the story registers between a topical interest in borders and limitations, on the one hand, and, on the other hand, a discourse of romance suggesting an aristocracy without borders, is concentrated in this moment.

The incursion of the king and the attempted rape cannot be separated. In fact, they make each other legible. It is the call of the king that brings about the crisis in the story, that puts an end to the narrative structure of romance upon which courtly love relies. That arresting of the logic of romance makes it possible to strip courtly love of its veneer of gentility and suggest that, in this context, at least, seduction without a romance plot to sweeten it is nothing but rape. Conversely, however, just as the king's *political* claim on Amadour puts an end to romance, halting the narratives through which aristocratic fantasies of mobility articulate themselves, so is the rape attempt, for all of its horror, the necessary *literary* response to the king's summons. For the rape marks the point at which the structure of romance that has informed the story till now is replaced by another literary genre. That other genre is the novella, which relies not upon endless wandering and courtship, but upon sudden reversals of fortune and tests of moral character in a domestic space. The rape attempt turns romance into novella. It shifts attention away from the perfect heroism of the knight Amadour and onto the lady Floride's attempt to preserve her chastity. Female integrity, rather than male martial prowess, becomes the focus of the story.

The crisis point in the narrative, then, marks a tension between diverse perspectives on the identity of the aristocracy, which in turn makes visible a conflict between competing literary genres. Amadour's perfect romance heroism is precisely what leads the king to choose him for the "affair of importance." That calling, however, produces a moral crisis that disrupts the romance idyll by questioning

< *Narrative Form and National Space* >

its sexual politics. The king's summons stops the *plot* of romance, while the rape demystifies its *ideology* by clouding the heretofore idealized representation of Amadour as hero. Amadour drives romance perfection to the point at which it turns on itself, in a dialectical fillip, to question its own representation in narrative. Moreover, the staging of the relationship between gender and violence that is the rape attempt mediates the relationship between politics and literature. For at the very same moment that it demystifies romance, the rape attempt dramatizes the exemplary excellence of the lady Floride, whose protection of her chastity becomes the *new* demonstration of virtue—a demonstration associated with the genre of the novella.[25]

The two types of virtue exemplified here, male romance heroism and female chastity, are set in contrast at the close of the story, when the storytellers in the frame tale debate whether Amadour's virtue is more laudable than Floride's. Yet, once again, this debate works to underscore the sense that the problem of gender relations is also a problem of narrative genre. Both Floride and Amadour are defined by members of the group of storytellers as exemplary. Geburon, a male member of the group, using a language that prefigures Don Quixote's later descriptions of Amadis, claims that Amadour "was the most noble and valiant knight that ever lived"(154) ["estoit ung aussy honneste et vertueulx chevalier qu'il en soit poinct" (84)]. The female narrator of the tale, whose name is Parlamente, holds Floride up as an example for the way she defends her virtue. However, at the same moment that she praises Floride's virtue, Parlamente cautions the ladies in the group to avoid her naïveté toward men. For it was excessive naïveté, she says, that resulted in her "cruelty" (that is, her flirting with Amadour), and in her excessive despair when she realized Amadour's true character. This warning about Floride's naïveté is important. For it shows the impossibility of reconciling romance heroism and exemplary chastity within the increasingly limited world of a courtly society. Romance heroism, when it is arrested by political authority, reveals the violence it has kept hidden. The virtuous defense of chastity against that violence makes Floride the heroine not of a romance, but of a novella. Moreover, from the perspective of the novella, that is, from the viewpoint of a post-romance consciousness, Floride's love for Amadour is read as naïveté, as the enchantment of one who doesn't see how deceitful men can be. In short, these two types of virtue and these two literary genres cannot inhabit the same world. The logic of character and the logic of narrative cannot go to-

< *Narrative Form and National Space* >

gether. Men cannot be perfect heroes unless they have naïve heroines; and women cannot show virtue unless threatened by unheroic men. Yet, by the same token, romance provides the necessary ground or semiotic atmosphere for the tale, since it is the romance décor that lends Floride's self-defense its heroic proportions: her idealized virtue and long suffering lend her a dignity not usually accorded female protagonists of the more bourgeois genre of the novella.

The fact that the storytellers understand conflicting genres as if they were contrasting moral or psychological dispositions suggests that gender roles in the *Heptaméron* have little to do with any type of essential notion of "maleness" and "femaleness" and everything to do with the location of the subject in a particular position—a position defined by the conjunction of a narrative and a social space. In the story of Amadour and Floride, both the romance fantasy world of an international aristocracy and the narratives through which that world is represented suddenly find themselves broken up, fragmented, by the eruption of a new proto-national centralized political regime. This process of fragmentation, furthermore, may also be seen on the level of the courtly lexicon itself. For the violence visited by Amadour on the body of Floride occasions the return of the coded language of courtly love, displayed in the initial presentation of the two characters. Now, however, that language is stripped of its gentility. If Floride and Amadour are initially described, on the first page of the story, in terms of their "honneur" and "honnettée," we learn that Amadour's attack on Floride is in search of "that which a lady's honor protects" (140) ["ce que l'honneur des dames défend" (72)], a euphemism that has nothing to do with genteel excellence and everything to do with feminine corporeity. This linguistic difference is stressed when Floride confronts Amadour: " 'And what,' she replied, 'has become of the honour you preached about so often?' 'Ah! my Lady,' he said, 'no one in the world could possibly hold your honour as dear as I do! Before you were married I was able to overcome the desires of my heart so successfully that you knew nothing at all of my feelings' " (141) ["Et où est l'honneur, dit Floride, que tant de fois m'avez prêché?"—"Ah, madame, dit Amadour, il n'est possible de plus aimer pour votre honneur que je fais, car avant que fussiez mariée, j'ai su si bien vaincre mon coeur que vous n'avez su connaître ma volonté" (73)]. Honor for Floride is virtue and chastity, whereas for Amadour it connotes reputation. A bit later, still other key terms in the courtly vocabulary are redefined in similar ways. The word "grace," which is

< *Narrative Form and National Space* >

used countless times throughout the story to describe Amadour's desire for Floride (he seeks to "avoir sa bonne grace"), appears again, when Amadour returns several years later and tries once more to assault Floride. After disfiguring her face with a stone, Floride tries to call him off: "I plead with you and ask for grace [mercy]. Just let me live in peace! Let me live the life of honour and virtue to which, as you yourself once urged me, I have committed myself" (148) ["je vous fais ma plainte et demande grace, à fin que vous me laissez vivre en paix et en l'honnêté que selon votre conseil j'ai délibéré de garder" (79)]. The word "grace" appears here almost as a parody of its earlier self—now suggesting neither sexual favor nor courtly esteem but simple pity. And as for the "beauté" that was so central to the initial descriptions of the two young people, it has now given way to disfiguration. As Amadour's lust sets his handsome face afire ("rouge comme feu" [78]), Floride's despair drives her to maim herself with a stone. Her reproach that Amadour tested her will "in the days when I was young, and when my beauty was at its most fresh" (147) ["du temps de ma jeunesse et de ma plus grande beauté,"] whereas now she is older and ugly ("en l'âge et grande laideur où je suis" [78]) suggests that the descriptive symmetry that linked the two characters when they were first presented has now been thrown off balance. Indeed, the sense that the rape brings about a breaking of the spell of romance is underscored by the fact that, even as Floride dramatically disfigures herself by cutting her face with a stone, she also points out to Amadour that she has aged, and so long since lost her beauty. The lack of preparation for this admission in the text suggests that by falling into the world of the novella, we have somehow fallen into time, into the moment at which history takes over from romance timelessness.[26]

These exchanges make explicit what the text has kept implicit until now—that the same words mean different things to different genders. The courtly vocabulary that defines this community is now turned against itself. Sexual difference is now thematized, for the first time in the *Heptaméron*, as a problem of the word.[27] Each of the key terms used to describe the main characters of the story on their first appearance—"honneur," "grace," and "beauté"—is fractured and demystified at the moment of the rape attempt. The coded language of courtly love and romance fiction is stripped bare of its gentility and revealed to be a mask that promotes class solidarity by obscuring sexual difference. The story questions the ideologies of aristocratic hero-

< *Narrative Form and National Space* >

ism through a critique of the narrative conventions that promote it. The eruption of an emerging national consciousness, represented by the king's claim on Amadour, is displaced into a discourse on gender. Borders between states seem to take on increasing importance at the moment that the borders between men and women are first violated and then reconfigured in linguistic terms.

Within this newly fragmented world, the "universal" aristocratic subject Amadour has no place. And if Marguerite's text replaces the diachrony of Amadour's "quest" with a more "spatial" model of experience organized according to opposing political and sexual identities, it is only fitting that his death should raise yet again the question of how the linguistic sign embodies opposing perspectives—and of how social identity and gender identity relate. As the tale ends, Amadour fights the Moors again. Having courageously rescued, in the heat of the fray, the bodies of the Count of Arande (Floride's relative) and the Duc of Cardonne (her husband), Amadour finds himself surrounded by enemies:

> and he, who no more wanted to be taken than he had been able to take his beloved, nor to break his faith with God than he had broken his faith to her, knowing that, if he were brought before the King of Granada, he would die a cruel death or renounce Christianity, decided not to give either the glory of his death or his capture to his enemies; so, kissing the cross on his sword, and offering body and soul to God, gave himself such a blow that he needed no help.[28]

> [et luy, qui ne vouloit non plus estre pris qu'il n'avoit sceu prendre s'amye, ne faulser sa foy envers Dieu, qu'il n'avoit faulsée envers elle, sçachant que, s'il estoit mené au Roy de Grenade, il mourroit cruellement ou renonceroit la chrestienté, delibera ne donner la gloire ne de sa mort ne de sa prinse à ses ennemys; et, en baisant la croix de son espée, rendant corps et ame à Dieu, s'en donna ung tel coup, qu'il ne luy en fallut poinct de secours. (82)]

Whereas earlier Amadour's chivalric "faith" had taken precedence over his religious "faith," he himself now recasts that notion in light of his own breaking of "faith" toward Floride. For the first time Amadour brings his experience as a lover and his experience as a knight together, using one to learn from the other. Moreover, the relationship between political subjectivity and sexual violence suggested in the conjunction of the king's summons with the rape at-

< *Narrative Form and National Space* >

tempt is now underscored by Amadour's recognition that his being "taken" by the Saracens—with all of the fear of circumcision and rape that that might imply in the sixteenth century—would somehow answer back to his attempt to "take" Floride. The character's retrospective reconsideration of his own experience provokes a final gesture that redefines him as a "chivalric" subject—though now his "universalism" takes the form of martyrdom. It is no accident that this moment of self-consciousness comes at the end of the story, since Amadour's actions have demonstrated the incompatibility of romance heroism and the world of the novella. If the novella, as some critics have argued, finds its origins in the medieval tradition of the moral exemplum or saint's life, Amadour here comes as close to that tradition as possible while remaining in the world of romance. For here romance wandering veers off into hagiography.[29]

Novella and Nation

To understand the implications of the overlapping of questions of gender, genre, and politics set forth in the story of Amadour and Floride, we may turn now to the book's prologue. The *Heptaméron* opens in disputed territory. On the first page we are introduced to a group of aristocrats who have come to take the waters at the spa of Cauterets, in the Pyrenees. Cauterets lies in Marguerite's own kingdom of Navarre, which itself lies on the border between the two most bitter enemies in sixteenth-century Europe—the Spain of Charles V, and the France of Marguerite's brother, Francis I. Thus, the very location of the text in Navarre could not have failed to evoke, for sixteenth-century readers, the vexed question of the political and geographical identity of France itself; for Navarre was one of the several spots on the edges of "France" that seemed unable to stay "French." The small multilingual kingdom was a major pawn in territorial disputes between Charles and Francis, and changed hands a number of times over the course of the century.[30] Yet into this unstable background Marguerite inserts an irenic scene, as she depicts a group of international aristocrats, "many people, from both France and Spain" (60), who have come to bathe in peace. The book opens by setting a scene of international harmony in a contested area.

Into this tableau of tranquil vacationers comes the catastrophe that will occasion the stories to follow. After three weeks of soaking, when the previously unwell visitors realize that they are now capable of going home, there breaks forth a series of rainstorms, "with such

< *Narrative Form and National Space* >

extraordinary force you would have thought that God had quite forgotten that once He had promised to Noah never again to destroy
the world by water" (60) ["les pluyes si merveilleuses et si grandes,
qu'il sembloit que Dieu eut oblyé la promesse qu'il avoit faicte à Noé
de ne destruire plus le monde par eaue" (1)]. The marvelous rains replace the marvelous waters of the spa and suggest a need for a spiritual cleansing of humanity. Yet, here again, the politics of this allegorical moment are worth noting. When the opening scene of
international harmony is obliterated by the deluge, the consolidation
of nations results. The flood may be a symbol of universal wrath, but
here it is a mechanism for producing the map of Europe. For, as soon
as the rains come, the visitors to the spa, "many people, from both
France and Spain," split immediately into two groups divided along
national lines. The Spaniards get home, "as best they can" ("le mieulx
qu'il leur fut possible" [1]), and the French take refuge in an abbey to
tell stories.

A comparison of this moment of division with the opening description suggests that what is at issue, here as in the story of
Amadour and Floride, is the tension between emerging national
states and fantasies of aristocratic universalism. For it is indeed one of
the historical clichés of the aristocracy that it meets at watering holes
like Cauterets, Baden Baden, or Abano. The scene set at the opening
of the text evokes the world of an international aristocracy whose
family connections and intermarriages construct a web of influence
transcending national boundaries and language—this world, however, is destroyed by the storm. And that fragmentation makes possible the *Heptaméron* itself. For the splitting into nations coincides
with the moment at which this text finds its project, at which the
French bathers, trapped in the mountains by flood waters, decide to
tell stories until they are rescued. Bathing with the enemy is all well
and good, but a novella collection seems to require the consolidation
of a national group. And it may be no accident, in this context, that
the place of storytelling is described as a *locus amoenus*, a beautiful fertile space recalling the topos of France as a garden.[31]

The consolidation of group identity and the affirmation of
Frenchness are underscored again at the end of the prologue, where it
becomes clear that the forced retirement of the group will result in a
token of courtly and political esteem. It is revealed that the idea of
writing a new collection of tales modeled on Boccaccio's *Decameron*
has in fact been proposed by Marguerite herself, to a group of men

< *Narrative Form and National Space* >

and ladies of the French court.[32] When the court became preoccupied by "the important affairs which have since occupied the king" (68) ("les grands affaires survenuz au Roy depuis" [9]), the project had to be scrapped. As an antidote to such "affairs" (which recall nothing so much as the "affair" on which Amadour was called away from Floride) and as a gesture of reverence, the storytellers now decide that they will collect the stories they tell and present them to Francis and his circle when they return from their forced isolation. The *Heptaméron* itself will reaffirm the unity of the Valois court. The book in our hands will be the material sign of political unity. If romance heroism and aristocratic wandering are questioned *within* the *Heptaméron*, the consolidation of a new national group is furthered *by* the *Heptaméron*.[33]

The correspondence between the return from alpine exile and the assertion of the text's political role points yet again to the way in which literary genre and political identity are constantly intertwined in this text. The very evocation of Giovanni Boccaccio's *Decameron* underscores the differences in focus between the two works: Boccaccio's fourteenth-century collection of tales is set in plague ridden Florence. Marguerite's book opens with the flood—an image of universal divine punishment. Yet the transition from cosmic disaster to political reconfiguration enacted by the prologue underscores yet again how this text appropriates tradition and turns it toward the imagination of a new, national community. As the prologue moves from an allegory of human catastrophe to a portrait of a much more circumscribed court society it parallels the shift from romance and novella.[34] This shift in genre suggests that the members of that society are to understand their conflicts in moral, rather than cosmic, terms. Indeed, it is Marguerite's very moralism that imprints the novella genre with her particular stamp and turns this most bourgeois and international of forms into the most nationally inflected story collection in European literary history. The long French tradition of appropriating foreign cultural goods may be said to begin here, with Marguerite's marshalling of the international genre of the novella for national ends.

As sister to the king, Marguerite would have looked with favor on the processes of political centralization that I am positing as an essential, if muted, force in her text. And the presence of this force imposes upon us a reconsideration of one of the most obvious features of the *Heptaméron*—the feature that has, in fact, been instrumental in its re-

< *Narrative Form and National Space* >

cent rising fortunes among literary scholars. This, of course, is the importance it accords debates about gender roles. Like its prototype, Boccaccio's *Decameron*, the *Heptaméron* features a group of young people who tell stories. Unlike the *Decameron*, however, it has them follow each story with a long debate about the relative virtues and vices of the men and women in the stories and the general question of the relations between genders. Seen against the background of the Floride/Amadour story, however, the deployment of the novella form itself—of the form that makes possible this discourse on gender—may be seen as a response to the failure of romance ideals of aristocratic universalism. Marguerite's appropriation of the traditionally mercantile or bourgeois novella form offers the stage both for the demonstration of new forms of *courtly* (as contrasted with *knightly*) virtue, and for a discussion of what that virtue might be. I have tried here to locate that discourse on gender within a larger political realignment, as a way of suggesting why it should become as necessary and as important as it does. The gender debates emerge as a form of discourse that *gives voice* to a new alignment, because it is aimed at an aristocracy whose identity is suddenly in question. And through the various forms of this emerging conversation, the terms for a critique of the patriarchal power that structures romance can for the first time be formulated in a systematic, almost encyclopedic, form.[35]

Thus the cultural work of the *Heptaméron* in the emergence of the French state under Francis I involves the displacement of narrative traditions that conventionally transgress territorial boundaries. The impact of an emerging political realignment is expressed through the depiction of the impossible relationship between romance and community, while the relationship between emerging political space and emerging literary culture is mediated through the representation of gender relations. Indeed, the connection between an emerging national community and debate on gender was stressed as well by Marguerite's contemporaries. The proto-feminist pamphleteer François de Billon, whose book *Le fort inexpugnable de l'honneur du sexe feminin* [*The Impregnable Fortress of the Honor of the Female Sex*] of 1555 was an important document in the mid-century "querelle des femmes," links the French attitude toward women to the political strength of France itself. He distinguishes the French from the Italians by the relative freedom the French accord to women. Because the Italians keep women locked up and silent, he argues, their women are the objects of excessive fits of jealousy among men. This jealousy leads to

< *Narrative Form and National Space* >

vendetta ("vengeance sur ses propres parentz et voisins") ["vengence against their own relatives and neighbors"], which has in turn produced a divided and servile Italy. France, by contrast, is unified and strong. Thus, for Billon, dialogue among men and women of the type that forms the frame of the *Heptaméron* is vital to French identity and to the political triumph of France.[36] The achievement of Marguerite's text is that it explores questions of identity and community, not merely in polemical terms (though it does that too), but in terms of literary form. Marguerite's exploration of gender roles inscribes politics into the text on the level of genre, in the shift from romance to novella. By divulging the sexual violence that underpins fantasies of martial virtue, Marguerite's text points up the anachronistic status of romance ideals in an increasingly circumscribed court society.

Evangelical Reverie

The political and courtly themes and forms whose interplay I have been exploring in this chapter do not, of course, exhaust the complexity of the *Heptaméron*. No less important is Marguerite's insistence on religious concerns—the mystical piety for which she was famous among her contemporaries. The emptying out of the self in the presence of the divine is not only a prescription offered at the end of many of the tales in the *Heptaméron*, but a motif that helps to structure most of Marguerite's drama, and to provide the themes of her lyric poetry. This mysticism, linked to her engagement with Christian humanism, and the so-called "Evangélique" group around Cardinal Briçonnet, proposes, to be sure, a model of selfhood that is universal in a way quite different from the social ideals I have associated with the aristocracy. At a moment when the princes of Europe were at each other's throats, a model of identity based on the recognition of universal imperfection, in which everyone is an exemplar of vice or virtue, must have seemed attractive. The moralistic temper of many of Marguerite's stories underscores the ways in which the form of the novella feeds her evangelical ideology. The universal subject of late medieval aristocratic society, it seems, would be replaced by the universal subject of a renewed Christianity. Yet as I have shown in both this chapter and the preceding one, the Christian humanist dream of a renewed Christianity is consistently interrupted, in literary representation, by the contingency of emerging national identity. The tension between these identities inscribes itself in literature at the level of

< *Narrative Form and National Space* >

form, as an overlapping of different generic conventions. Multifaceted texts like the *Heptaméron* and Rabelais's *Gargantua* manipulate their own generic promiscuity to mediate the relationship between distinct figures of community. The ultimate paradox of the *Heptaméron* may be that the representation of new political, gender, and religious identities comes in a text that simultaneously emphasizes individual responsibility and promotes group identity.

Yet even in some of Marguerite's most mystical writings, when politics seems far indeed from the center of concern, the old ideologies of aristocratic heroism continue to appear. No better example of this can be found than in Marguerite's last major work, the long visionary poem entitled "Les Prisons." "Les Prisons" recounts the spiritual history of a male character named simply "Amy," who writes to his female friend "Amye" and tells her his experiences. He recounts in Book 1 how he lived in the prison of his desire for her, but was eventually freed from it. Thinking himself finally at liberty, he emerges into the wide world in Book 2, but he is led astray by his desire for power and riches. Having been alerted by a friendly hermit that his pursuits are in vain, he realizes that his love of the worldly is simply another prison. In Book 3 he turns to learning, and gives himself over to the study of books of all kinds, until he is enlightened by the voice of God and finds true freedom.

At the beginning of Book 2, as Amy leaves the prison of erotic desire to go out into the world, he sees, for the first time, the beauty of the things around him. He admires the heavens and the sun, the fields and forests. At the sight of wild beasts he feels the excitement of the hunt. This passage is filled with references to the loveliness of the world, and to the greatness of the Almighty who made it. It ends with a moving evocation of the power of the sea, as it turns in its basin like a great mountain: "O what power has this hand which presses/Such a great body into such a limited space;/This is no other power than the power of God" ["O quel povoir a ceste main qui serre/Ung si grand corps en un limitté lieu!/Autre elle n'a sinon celluy de Dieu"].[37] This brief vision ends with a song praising the physical world. It is a moment that seems out of phase with the poem's larger message of *contemptus mundi*. A vision of a kind of aristocratic utopia leads to a humble recognition of the power of God and the place of man under His dominion. Here, for a moment, the type of deception that leads Amy to prize other things (women, riches, books) above God seems to be absent. And as he turns from this

< *Narrative Form and National Space* >

beautiful and humbling vision of the sea, Amy is overtaken by a curious reverie, unique in this immense poem:

> Seeing this, I thought of the journeys
> Of the heroes, filled with great courage,
> And I wanted to do as they had done,
> To win the renown of the virtuous man.

> Voyant cecy, je pensay aux voyaiges
> Qu'ont fait les preuz, rempliz de haulx courages,
> Et desiray de faire ainsy comme eulx
> Pour acquerir le bruyt des vertueux.

From his vision of the sea Amy recalls the tales of great heroes, who have won for themselves reputations of virtue. This lovely reverie is the romance moment in "Les Prisons." It offers an image of heroism and virtue untainted by social violence and characterised by humility before God. It projects an ethos that is heavily Christian, but connected to terrestrial heroism, instead of the mystical transport that elsewhere informs the poem. It is located here, as the character prepares to enter the world of men, to function as a kind of template or ideal image of what he hopes to achieve among them. This ideal will of course be destroyed, for he immediately succumbs to temptation, and the irony of the passage lies in the fact that an image of freedom and solitary wandering is evoked as a preface to a journey through cities. Yet the appearance of the reverie here suggests just how difficult it is to efface romance ideals from aristocratic literary forms. Briefly, in an allegorical landscape free of the contingencies of desire and politics that mark the tale of Amador and Floride, the old romance fantasy of wandering and heroism can return. Though the rest of the poem may trace out the lamentable consequences of the hero's misplaced ambitions, it never quite repudiates this moment of fantasy. In a poem that preaches renunciation of earthly desire, the desire for power and renown is figured as romance, as an image of heroism and freedom without borders. If, in the *Heptaméron*, the moralistic fictions of the novella form stand in tension with romance ideals, here, in an analogous opposition, the Evangelical/mystical ideal of an effacement of the self finds its opposite in romance heroism. Moreover, the dangerous attraction of this fictional form—for both aristocratic courtiers and mystics—may suggest why the moment of reverie stands apart from the sections around it. It is never broken by any external event in the plot of the poem, but is suddenly

< *Narrative Form and National Space* >

relinquished, as if by the will of the author, rather than of the character. In a sudden break with the momentum of the preceding lines, Amy simply turns away from the shore and walks into the city: "I left there the sea and its ships/To go and see cities and castles" ["Je lessay là la mer et ses bateaux,/Pour aller veoir et villes et chasteaux"].

Lafayette and the Nationality of the Novel

I have suggested that Marguerite's displacement of romance ideals by new forms of moral enquiry embodied in the novella form may be seen as a fictional response to a massive political realignment that began—and began to be perceived—in the early years of the sixteenth century in France. The rise of court society, with its new rituals of centralized power and control, redefined the rituals of aristocratic life in increasingly restricted circumstances. The *Heptaméron* may be seen as a mediating or transitional text in that process of centralization, not only because it operates a kind of cultural import-export business that turns foreign or international material into a source of reflection for the French court, but also through its very form. In the tension between the frame and the stories the text maintains a distance between the representation of political and sexual violence, on the one hand, and the interpretation of its consequences, on the other. Yet, the debates following the stories attempt to apply those stories to contemporary life, thereby gesturing toward later forms in which the integration of anecdote and plot will be fuller.

Breaks between observer and actor, storyteller and character, are of course frequent in early novels, many of which include intercalated tales that interrupt the main flow of the narrative. It is only in that text usually described as the first "modern" French novel, Madame de Lafayette's *La Princesse de Clèves* (1678), that one finds a full-blown instance of a novelistic world turned completely in on itself, in which actors and commentators all belong to the same tiny social and political context. If the connection is indeed to be made between nationhood and the novel (to evoke again the language I used at the outset of this chapter) one way to do it would be to explore the ways in which the formal integration of the novel, as a genre that can appropriate other generic traditions and turn them to its own purposes, may be related to the type of geopolitical themes explored in the *Heptaméron*. In other words, how does the closing off of the world of the novel parallel or echo the closing off of France itself? Are there ways in which the thematics of nationhood may be seen as the effect of literary representation, and vice versa?

< *Narrative Form and National Space* >

Lafayette's novel is a historical novel in that it recounts events at the court of Henry II immediately before and after his death in 1559, more than a century distant from the world of the author—and exactly contemporaneous with the first publication of the *Heptaméron*. If Lafayette gives us one of the first instances of a unified social world in the novel (in contrast to such earlier experiments in France as Scarron's *Roman Comique*, in which intercalated tales constantly break any narrative movement), she also inscribes into the form of the book an ironic split between past and present, between the present of composition and the past of the events narrated. This split is registered, not as a narrative device (as a tension between the present of telling and the past of the story, for instance), but, again, in generic terms. Because the text is a history it draws heavily on the genres of history writing, and most especially on the genre of the portrait or courtly sketch of a well-known figure. It is in this genre that Mme de Lafayette made her literary debut, and it is the convention of the portrait that structures the famously difficult opening pages of the book.[38]

Yet if the conventions of the portrait present a form of narration that is detached from the actions depicted, those actions are themselves steeped in the courtly clichés seen in the writings of Marguerite de Navarre. Indeed, the gallantry and heroism that Lafayette celebrates and critiques in the court of Henry II are the products of a mid-sixteenth-century fascination with the same courtly romance I analyzed in the *Heptaméron*. Henry's tragic death in a tournament is an event born of the anachronistic custom of sixteenth-century monarchs playing at being romance heroes. This romance consciousness is registered in Lafayette's novel, in the invitation that Henry issues to the tournament that will be his last: "It was announced throughout the whole kingdom that a tournament would be opened in the city of Paris on the fifteenth day of June by his Very Christian Majesty . . . ready to meet all comers . . . French or foreign" (47) ["L'on fit publier, par tout le royaume, qu'en la ville de Paris le pas était ouvert, au quinzième juin, par sa Majesté Très Chrétienne . . . pour être tenu contre tous venans . . . tant français qu'étrangers" (304)].[39] This type of generalized challenge parodies the language of romances like Garcí Montalvo's *Amadís of Gaul*, the most famous romance of the late sixteenth century. It sounds like a speech from the mouth of Don Quixote. Yet what is particularly striking is that Lafayette's own deadpan citation of the cliché seems contaminated by it. The text of the invitation proper

< *Narrative Form and National Space* >

begins, presumably, in the passage above, with the literary cliché of "in the city of Paris." Yet Lafayette precedes the text of the proclamation with the statement that it was spread "throughout the whole kingdom," a phrase which turns France into a fairyland of gentle kings and wandering knights, "tant français qu'étrangers." Indeed, the description of the country as "kingdom" contrasts with Lafayette's statement, at the crisis moment of the novel's political intrigue, that Henry II's decision to break one more lance—the lance that kills him—was a decision that brought on "the misfortune of the State" (81) ["le malheur de l'Etat" (355)]. The contrast between a chivalric "kingdom" in which the king challenges all comers by posting handbills in every town square (a detail one can assume to be pure romance in this context) and the more modern term "Etat" suggests the tension within the novel between romance cliché and novelistic observation. And the appearance of "royaume" underscores the ways in which Lafayette's own deadpan historical style is infected with the language of the romance culture on which it casts so critical an eye. This stylistic contamination, coming as it does at the supreme moment of chivalric self-delusion in the novel—just before the gallant atmosphere of the Valois court comes crashing down—suggests the difficulty aristocratic literary discourse faces in defining a critical position from which to judge its own rituals. Because of its very setting, Lafayette's book is already contaminated by the themes and obsessions of a court that lives—and dies—through the fictions of romance.

Lafayette herself would seem to have rejected any relationship between her novel and the tradition of romance traced in the *Heptaméron*. In a letter about the novel, written partly to deny authorship of it, Lafayette praised it precisely because it had nothing to do with the conventions of romance: "There is nothing novelistic/romance-like, and there is nothing exaggerated in it. Thus it is not a romance/novel: it is, indeed, a set of memoirs." ["Il n'y a rien de romanesque et de grimpé; aussi n'est-ce pas un roman : c'est proprement des mémoires"].[40] For Lafayette it is exaggeration that seems to characterize the tradition of romance (which here bleeds into the "novelistic" or "merely fictional"—all suggested in the period by the term "romanesque"). In this regard, as a way of tracing the veiled presence of the topoi already seen in Marguerite, one might consider how the novel frames images that are perceived to be exaggerated or untrue.

The tension between true and untrue representation is thematized early on in the novel, just as the Princess is beginning to fall in

< *Narrative Form and National Space* >

love with her admirer, the Duke of Nemours. News has been circulating that Nemours is involved in a possible dalliance with Elizabeth of England. When a portrait of Elizabeth is passed around at court, the Princess (though she has never seen Elizabeth) cannot stop herself from remarking that she found it overly flattering ("elle ne put s'empêcher de dire qu'il était flatté" [299]). She is corrected by Mme la Dauphine (that is, by Mary Stuart), who replies that, in fact, this is not the case. Elizabeth is every bit as beautiful and spirited as she appears to be in the portrait. Indeed, it appears that Elizabeth is a kind of model for the women of the court, since, adds the unhappy Mary, "all my life she has been held up to me as an example" (43) ["on me l'a proposée toute ma vie pour exemple" (299)]. Since the novel ends with the claim that the Princess herself, having rejected Nemours and retired from the world, offers an example, one might see Elizabeth as the counterexample to the Princess. She is that figure who tests the veracity of the portrait—both as literary genre and visual representation. If, as Lafayette says, there is nothing exaggerated in the novel, Elizabeth would seem to represent the threat of a reality that is too good to be true, that seemingly must be exaggerated, but cannot be. She is everything she seems to be, and her perfection poses a threat both to the self-image of the somewhat insecure Mme la Dauphine and to the passion of the Princess.[41]

Marguerite de Navarre is mentioned in the novel in the context of Nemours's dalliance with Elizabeth. Since Marguerite is the only author mentioned in Lafayette's book, her mention suggests a literary filiation between the two writers. What is striking about Marguerite's appearance, however, is that it highlights not issues of literature, but questions of religion and foreign affairs. For she is explicitly associated with the rise of Protestantism, with the great crisis of community that divided Europe and humiliated France in the late sixteenth century. Marguerite makes her appearance in the same scene in which the Princess speculates on the truthfulness of Elizabeth's portrait. As she asserts the excellence of the English queen, Mme la Dauphine tells the story of Elizabeth's mother, Anne Boleyn. Though not born in France, she points out, Anne spent much time there. She came when the sister of Henry VII married Louis XII. When Louis died, Anne stayed on, and began to frequent the circle of "Madame Marguerite, the king's sister, the Duchess of Alençon, since then Queen of Navarre, whose stories you have seen" (43) ["Mme Marguerite, soeur du roi, duchesse d'Alençon, et depuis reine

< *Narrative Form and National Space* >

de Navarre, dont vous avez vu les contes" (299)]. In the proximity of Marguerite, Ann took on the "stain" of the new religion ("les teintures de la religion nouvelle"). Upon her return to England, she set her sights upon Henry VIII, began to frequent his company, and spoke to him about Protestantism: "She began to instill into the King of England the principles of Lutheranism, and persuaded the late king [i.e. Francis I] to urge at Rome Henry's divorce" (43) ["Elle commença à donner au roi d'Angleterre des impressions de la religion de Luther et engagea le feu roi à favoriser à Rome le divorce de Henri" (300)]. The rest, one might say, is history.

But it is a very strange history indeed. For in this fascinating passage Lafayette virtually traces the onset of Protestantism in England and the great schism between Henry VIII and Rome to the influence of Marguerite de Navarre. Far from bringing about the universal renovation of the Christian community that she intended, Marguerite, in Lafayette's version, has helped to split Europe in two: "Henry declared himself the head of the Church, and carried all England into the unhappy change of religion in which you now see it" (44) ["Henri . . . se déclara chef de la religion et entraîna l'Angleterre dans le malheureux changement où vous la voyez" (300)]. A feminine literary tradition, a literary filiation between Marguerite and Lafayette, is articulated at the same moment as the breakup of Catholic Europe—all of which suggests, yet again, that narratives and spaces don't always coincide.[42]

To be sure, this evocation of the "errors" of England in the midst of a narrative that hints at a Franco/English marriage would have resonated strongly for seventeenth-century French readers. They would have remembered the troubled union of Charles I and Henriette Marie, the sister of Louis XIII, whose presence at the Stuart court was often seen by English Protestants as a "Catholic" influence no less dangerous than the Protestant contagion described by Mary Stuart in her tale of Ann Boleyn. Indeed, the Nemours/Elizabeth union would aim to heal this split within the Christian community even before the Stuarts came to power. The union of the gallant hero and the new English queen would build an alliance between England and France, between Protestant and Catholic. The marriage would undo the negative consequences of the new ideas spread about by Marguerite. In this context, it is worth examining the representation of this alliance more closely.

Nemours, whose very name seems to recall and negate (ne+

< *Narrative Form and National Space* >

amours) the heroic faithfulness of Marguerite de Navarre's protagonist Amadour, spends the first third of the novel engaged in international intrigue. As the novel opens we are given a description of the relations between the three great unified powers that battled for domination in Western Europe throughout the first sixty years of the century—France, England, and Spain. It is revealed that Charles V has finally been tamed by the French at the battle of Metz and that he and Henry II are about to make peace. The king is on the border ("sur la frontière" [246]), in Artois, negotiating the peace of Cateau-Cambresis, which would put a temporary end to hostilities between France and Spain. The seal on the treaty was to be the marriage of Elizabeth of France with Charles's son Philip. At this moment, however, there is a shift of power in England, as the death of Mary Tudor brings the ascension of Elizabeth to the throne. When the king sends an ambassador to congratulate Elizabeth, the legate brings back surprising news. He reports that the reputation of the Duke of Nemours has taken hold in the heart of the new English queen, who might be disposed to consider a proposal of marriage.

The characters' various responses to this possibility replay, on a more abstract level, the tension between romance wandering and royal power already seen in the *Heptaméron*. Nemours's reaction suggests the aristocrat's investment in his own independence. When the king first proposes "this great fortune" (7) to him, he deflects the idea by joking. He then points out the risk of such a "fantastic enterprise," namely that he would be seen as vainglorious to seek the hand of so great a princess. A bit later, in another conversation with the king, he reveals his fear that failure will make him look like a fool in front of all of Europe: "He said that the whole of Europe would blame his imprudence if he were to presume to go to England as a claimant for the queen's hand without being assured of success" (36) ["Il dit que toute l'Europe condamnerait son imprudence s'il hasardait d'aller en Angleterre comme un prétendu mari de la reine sans être assuré du succès" (290)]. Nemours's hesitation evokes once more the image of Europe as a club of aristocrats who move easily across borders. Like Marguerite's Amadour, who wanders the world in search of adventure, Nemours travels fluidly from country to country, from court to court. Unlike Amadour, however, it is not his sword that is in demand, but his grace and gallantry, which is so great that "all eyes followed him whenever he appeared" (5) ["on ne pouvait regarder que lui dans tous les lieux où il paraissait" (243)]. Manners have taken

< *Narrative Form and National Space* >

over from arms; the new courtly hero is as slippery and in demand as the old one, but his wandering is amorous, not martial. Earlier wandering heroes risk their bodies; Nemours risks his reputation.

For the king, the marriage with Elizabeth has nothing to do with social reputation. It involves an important question of foreign policy. The death of Mary Tudor, the text tells us, brought "great obstacles to peace." A marriage with Elizabeth would constitute a union of France and England that might counterbalance the power of Spain. Nemours agrees to consider the marriage only when commanded by the king, "under the advice and in behalf of your Majesty" (7) ["par le conseil et pour le service de Votre Majesté" (246)]. Like Nemours, the king wants negotiations with Elizabeth conducted in secret. However, this is not to save Nemours's reputation, but because he knows that political success requires secrecy. His ambassador, M. de Randan, advises Nemours to travel to England as a kind of tourist, and, in effect, to spy out the situation. Later, the king suggests the importance of this marriage to the state by averring that, if Nemours won't go to England himself, the matter may have to be arranged like the Dauphin's, and that Nemours may have to be married by proxy, through the mediation of ambassadors (37; 291).

Elizabeth's passion is presented quite differently. The story of Elizabeth's interest in Nemours is taken from an episode in Brantôme's *Dames Galantes*, a collection of tales and gossip about sixteenth-century court life first published in the 1660s. In Brantôme's version, Elizabeth's interest is described as an expression of a general characteristic of women to love those who are known to be gallant. She is one example among many, and Brantôme's chronology differs from Lafayette's. He depicts Elizabeth first falling for Henry II and expressing a desire to come and visit him in France, "for, she said, my temperament is to love valiant people" ["car disoit-elle, mon humeur est d'aymer les gens vaillants"]. After Henry's death, having heard about the virtues of Nemours, she asks for more information about him from a passing French diplomat sent by Francis II to Scotland. The diplomat, "knowing as much about love as arms" ["qui s'entendoit en amours aussi bien qu'en armes"], sings Nemours's praises and recognizes the spark of love in Elizabeth's attitude.[43] In Lafayette, by contrast, Elizabeth's passion is uniquely for Nemours, arises from her own knowledge of the French court, and appears at the moment she becomes queen. Lafayette thus sets up a coincidence between Elizabeth's coming to power and her coming to love.

< *Narrative Form and National Space* >

Elizabeth acts out of desire and attraction, out of her interest in the beauty and elegance of Nemours. In this she contrasts with her namesake, Elizabeth of France, whose arranged marriage with the next king of Spain indicates the norm by which women in the aristocratic world are married off for political alliance. Indeed, the contrast is stressed by the fact that the arrangements for the marriage between Elizabeth and Philip are interrupted by the news of Elizabeth's interest in Nemours. Elizabeth of England seems to represent an ideal of female power and desire. She marks the modern alternative to Marguerite's Floride and the foreign alternative to the Princess of Clèves. In a newly defined world of constituted national states, the admiring lover is now made the object of desire, preceded by a reputation no less flattering than the queen's portrait. Elizabeth has been freed from the submission to custom that oppresses both Floride and the Princess. As a foreign woman she can ascend to power (something forbidden in France by Salic law). She thus becomes a kind of Amazon queen led by her own desire— not unlike the heroines of D'Urfé's *Astrée* or Madeleine de Scudéry's *Artamène*, the two greatest prose romances of the century. She stands as an emblem of the freedom that the Princess can never have.

How the French Novel Became French

Elizabeth's marriage to Nemours, were it to come to pass, would also have implications for the genre of Lafayette's text. For it would bring with it a set of conventions which Lafayette explicitly rejects in her famous letter cited earlier. These are, of course, the conventions of romance. Such a marriage would write out in history a romance courtship between the exemplary Nemours (the most dashing figure at the French court) and a foreign queen. Hence, the proposed dalliance between Nemours and Elizabeth might be seen as the romance alternative, as the plotline that the novel must repress or control. The centrifugal energy represented by romance in Marguerite de Navarre is here channelled by the king's command for Nemours to court the English queen. Should the alliance come off, romance, female desire, and international peace would be working hand in hand. Through the device of the attraction of Elizabeth for Nemours, Lafayette goes Marguerite one better. Romance and political authority now work, not at odds, but in harmony. The desire that Floride must keep hidden and that the Princess only reveals fleetingly makes possible a new romance world of heroism and international alliances powered, as Nemours puts it at one point, "by love."[44]

< *Narrative Form and National Space* >

However, neither the marriage nor the romance narrative of courtship ever comes to pass. By exercising her free choice, Elizabeth has raised the possibility of a political union that would heal a Europe torn by the "unhappy change" that has come over England. Yet in order to effect that union, Henry must rein in the flighty Nemours. The centralized power that was a mere phantom in the *Heptaméron* is here represented in the form of a monarch who cannot control his own aristocrats. Henry can call upon Nemours for state service in the same way the king called upon Amadour in the story by Marguerite de Navarre, but, unlike Amadour, Nemours is not compelled to obey. Yet throughout the early sections of the novel the relationship between king, subject, and foreign queen in what soon comes to be called the "Affaire d'Angleterre" (shades of Marguerite's "affaire d'importance," which separated Amadour and Floride!) is constantly held out as a possibility. In the opening pages, it is set in direct contrast with the unfolding passion of Nemours for the Princess of Clèves. Lafayette stresses this contrast through careful juxtaposition. The Princess first makes her appearance at court in the very paragraph following Nemours's initial decision to open communication with Elizabeth. One woman pursues Nemours, the other resists him. One is distant, the other is near. One is well known, the other is unknown upon her arrival at court. One is English, the other is French.

Yet the romance is not to be. If Amadour gives up romance to follow the summons of his king and slip into the world of the novella, Nemours simply defers his proposed trip to England and, in the interim, falls for the Princess. This failure of romance is paralleled by the Duke de Guise's heroic vow, upon realizing, after a tennis match with Nemours (that parody of a knightly tournament), that he has not won the Princess's heart, to mount a crusade to recapture Rhodes (48; 307). Yet neither Guise nor Nemours ever leaves France. And Nemours's new passion puts an end to the international intrigues that subtend the first third of the novel. When he gives up his quest for Elizabeth, Nemours turns the action of the novel back toward France. That gesture has both political and literary implications. Politically, it means that the possibility of a union with England, between Catholic and Protestant, is closed off. The long-standing antagonism between France and England will continue throughout the wars of religion that break out after the action of the novel has ended. Elizabeth will remain a virgin, and England will take its own national identity partly from the symbolism of her independence. In literary terms, it means

< *Narrative Form and National Space* >

that the idealized English heroine—every bit as perfect as her portrait suggests—is now shunted aside for the very imperfect heroines
of the French court. And these ladies are the protagonists of the
emerging literary form that will be come to be called the novel.

It is worth pointing out, to underscore the topographics of this
text, the way in which Lafayette stresses the "Frenchness" of the
Princess of Clèves. She is first introduced as a mysterious beauty who
appears suddenly at court ("Il parut alors une beauté à la cour"
[247]). A sentence later she is identified in terms of money and origin: "Of the same family as the Vidame of Chartres, she was one of
the greatest heiresses of France" (7) ["Elle était de la même maison
que la vidame de Chartres et une des plus grandes héritières de
France" (247)]. A paragraph further on, her fortune is mentioned
again, as an available one: "This heiress was, then, one of the greatest
matches in France" (77) ["Cette héritière était alors un des grands
partis qu'il y eut en France" (247)]. In a text where characters are often (confusingly) referred to as "this princess" or "this prince," the
Princess is introduced as "this heiress." This description is striking,
since at no point in the novel is any interest shown in her inheritance.
Thus, in contrast to the fragile Elizabeth, whose right to the English
throne is described as "insecure"(7), the Princess seems to represent
the strength of the traditional French aristocracy. Indeed, given the
aristocratic context of the novel, in which money, as cash, is of no importance, what the Princess brings to her mate is land. She effectively
brings with her chunks of France itself. And when the Duke of
Nemours falls in love with her, he turns his back on international romance to locate the remaining action of the novel in the land with
which she is so strongly associated.

In an insightful discussion of the sexual politics underlying the
emergence of the novel in France, Joan DeJean traces the birth of the
female author to the closing volume of Madeleine de Scudéry's prose
romance *Artamène*, in which the poet Sappho establishes a "feminine"
space within which she can write every day. My reading of Lafayette
suggests that Scudéry's ability to define a female authorial space is as
much a question of genre as it is of gender. Or, more precisely, it is located at the crossing of genre and gender. If Scudéry's Sappho is able
to write, this is because she does so, not in France, but in the land of
the Sauromates, to which she has effortlessly repaired after an encounter with a "stranger" who wanders into Mytilene. The establishment of the feminine space can occur easily within romance, because

< *Narrative Form and National Space* >

romance has a particular relationship to travel, to territory, and to the marking out of territory. It will be the task of the novel to try to locate that space in France. And to do so involves a complicated negotiation between competing literary forms.[45]

Thus, the introduction of the Princess into the world of the novel transforms French literary geography. It turns the narrative away from international politics, from the intrigue with England that opens the scene, to focus on the dalliances of the French aristocracy. This shift, moreover, powers a move away from a narrative model of romance, toward the territory of the novel. For it is what makes possible the emergence of the so-called "adultery plot," that critics have seen as paradigmatic for the development of French fiction after *La Princesse de Clèves*. In a world broken up by international boundaries, adultery plots cannot traverse those boundaries, lest they bring about international crises. If they do, they give us the *Iliad*. The emergence of the novel requires a homogenous political space, free from the scandals of international relations. In other words, if the French novel, the novel of adultery, is to emerge as a genre, it must be entirely French. And the imposition of that French space on the world of fiction entails the sweeping aside of the world of romance, with its wandering heroes, foreign Amazon queens, and endless dalliances. *La Princesse de Clèves* dramatizes the closing off of romance in its representation of the alliance between Nemours and Elizabeth as a possibility that can never be realized. The consciousness of a new world of national states is no longer represented through gestures of royal authority as it was in the *Heptaméron*. Indeed, in this text Nemours loves the Princess by disobeying the king, who, it should be noted, is responsible for their meeting in the first place. Rather, the sense of the uniqueness of French identity emerges through the space of the novel, which limits aristocratic fiction to love intrigues among French aristocrats. Frenchness finds expression, not through the imposition of political authority, but *through literature itself*, through a narrative form that turns away from internationalism to center itself and the passion it narrates in France.[46]

Tony Tanner notes in his study *Adultery in the Novel* that desire has a spatial dimension, that it is connected "to environment (which includes objects, food, clothes, architecture, money, as well as less tangible operative factors)."[47] My contention in this chapter has been that desire is also geographical, and that the articulation of desire in narrative, from Rabelais's lusty couples measuring out the French

< *Narrative Form and National Space* >

league, through the wanderings of Amadour, to the private passions of the Princess of Clèves, is intimately intertwined with the mapping of narrative onto territory. Indeed, before novelistic desire can be connected to such things as "food, clothes, architecture [and] money," it must first be centered in a politically homogeneous space. The emergence of the new narrative form that seventeenth-century France understood as the novel occurred via a complex process through which narrative desire had to be mapped onto a national territory imagined as unified and distinct from other nations. That process of mapping, moreover, involved the displacement of both rival narrative forms, such as romance, and rival geographical formations, such as the aristocratic utopias imagined by romance. In its immobility, moreover, this fictional tradition distinguishes itself from the more free-floating tradition of the picaresque, in which low-born heroes swindle their way from country to country.

The relationship of territory to narrative in early modern France is mediated through a double movement that simultaneously recognizes the limitations of French power (suggested first in Rabelais's gallants, who were unable to perform more than once a day) and turns that recognition into the basis for a strategy of importation and appropriation (as Marguerite makes the foreign material of the novella tradition the basis for the constitution of a uniquely French community). Both of these movements are distantly echoed in *La Princesse de Clèves*, where the two principal characters are introduced through their relationships with foreign spaces. The great aristocratic hero Nemours first appears in the book as part of a plan to link France and England. The Princess first appears in a space no less foreign, both ethnically and socially. She is first glimpsed by the Prince of Clèves in the house of an Italian jewelry merchant, who is the only non-aristocrat in the entire book: "This man had come from Florence with the queen, and had grown so rich by his business that his house seemed that of some great nobleman rather than of a merchant" (8) ["Cette homme était venu de Florence avec la reine, et s'était tellement enrichi dans son trafic que sa maison paraissait plutôt celle d'un grand seigneur que d'un marchand" (248)]. The Princess of Clèves enters the world of the novel through a space associated with those Italian merchants who brought the Renaissance to France. And while it's obvious that the precious stones or "pierreries" (248) that she goes there to view have no direct filiation to the stones that mark out France in Rabelais, the attraction that they exert parallels the at-

< *Narrative Form and National Space* >

traction exerted by the Princess on all who see her. They thus figure metonymically the way in which Lafayette's novel defines France as a space shaped, not by sexual pleasure, but by narrative desire.

The French penchant for cultural importation, seen earlier in Marguerite's appropriation of the novella tradition, is here distantly echoed in the presentation of the Princess. Through her metonymic relationship to these Italian jewels she is made Other, or even exotic, and prefigures the exotic heroines of such later French novels as Sand's *Indiana* and Merimée's *Carmen*. And yet, as noted earlier, she is completely, essentially French. In this paradox she illustrates the ambiguous nature of the imagined community that is the space of France in the novel. As the magnet holding Nemours in France, the Princess may be seen as a figure for the entire centralization of political power at Versailles. Louis XIV's fixing of the aristocracy at court is paralleled in the way Nemours can't seem to give up his attraction to the Princess to pursue greater glory abroad. Nemours, who is the real-life Jacques de Savoye, is, after all, only bound to the court by his allegiance to the crown—an allegiance that persisted through the wars of religion and led Brantôme, in his "portrait," to call Nemours a "bon Français" (in contrast to his cousin, who became attached to the King of Spain and became a "bon Espagnol").[48] Nemours's fiefdom lies, in fact, on the French-Italian border, just as the Duke of Clèves's fiefdom lies in territory that is today Germany. The erotic desire that keeps Nemours and Clèves attached to the Princess may be seen as a figure for the political submission of the French aristocracy more generally—that submission first signaled in literature when Amadour is summoned by his king. In this regard, it may not be by accident that, as has often been noted, the Princess is the only figure in this novel who is completely fictitious and not based on a real-life personage. The Princess stands as the imaginary center of France, as the embodiment of a centralized power that is a fiction (constructed through ceremony and ritual), but a fiction powerful enough to keep wandering aristocrats at home. She resolves within herself the contradictions of French absolutism, which pays lip service to a vestigial medieval system of nobiliary allegiances while emptying that same system of practical importance. By fixing Nemours's wandering eye in France, on a French object of desire, the Princess makes possible the geographical congruence of novel, state, and nation.

Chapter Five

Representing France at Mid-Century:
Du Bellay and the Lyric Invention
of National Character

*Thus one volume of Propertius and eight ounces of snuff may have
the same exchange-value, despite the dissimilar
use-values of snuff and elegies.*
—MARX, *Contribution to a Critique of Political Economy*

This chapter and the next will to some extent shift the terms of my
analysis. So far, I have been concerned with how a certain number of
works of narrative literature represent community. My focus has been
on how narrative texts are marked by diverse generic conventions,
and on how the interplay of those conventions responds to different
ideological struggles involving the definition of French nationhood.
Now I turn to lyric poetry, to the form of literary representation
most directly concerned with individual subjectivity and the relationship between the subject and language. Yet central to the discussion
will be the *national* dimension of this relationship—how lyric poetry
is related to the rise of a national language, and how a lyric subject
may be defined as being specifically French.

The conjunction of these concerns in the work of Joachim Du
Bellay came at a crucial moment in French literary history. For the
literary generation that came of age in the middle years of the sixteenth century, after the death of Francis I, the question of what, precisely, constituted French identity became an issue of immediate relevance, as religious factionalism and aristocratic rivalry began to drive
France toward civil war. Yet even for a poet who remained securely
within one religious camp, as did the Catholic Du Bellay, the cultural
politics that shaped Frenchness were marked by a convergence of diverse and seemingly contradictory factors. On the one hand, Du Bellay and his friends in the so-called Pléiade (the major literary coterie
of the second half of the century), advocated an explicitly nationalist
and even imperial cultural politics, aimed at promoting the French
vernacular through the appropriation of classical and Italian literary
forms. They associated themselves with the pomp of the Valois court

< *Representing France at Mid-Century* >

under Henry II, and sought to shine within a courtly context they saw as defining a glorious future for all of France. Yet at the very moment that the members of the Pléiade sought to define a new French culture, they struggled against a general anxiety that French identity had been overwhelmed or expropriated by Italian influence over both language and literature—and this nowhere more than at court. Du Bellay lived these tensions in the very shape of his career, as he wrote his most influential poetry while living as a functionary of the French embassy in Rome. In his *Regrets*, Du Bellay reflects on his relationship to France, and on his position as an expatriate. The early part of the collection recounts his unhappiness in Italy, his dismay at the decadence of Papal Rome, and his longing to go home to France. The later parts tell of his return and subsequent disillusionment at the corruption he finds at the French court. He thus defines the image of the court poet who longs to return to the seat of power, and who must negotiate the complicated networks of influence and exchange that define coterie culture. As such, he may be seen, not only as a representative figure for the paradoxes of French culture at a particular moment of national definition, but as a prototype of the European court poet struggling with new forms of cultural authority and new strategies of authorship. Indeed, the questions raised by Du Bellay's lyric about the relationship of the subject to language, community, and poetic form are replayed throughout the period by poets in a variety of national traditions, from Ben Jonson to Francisco Quevedo.

The relationship between language and community is central to much of Du Bellay's work. He reflects, toward the end of his famous treatise on French poetry and language, the *Deffence et Illustration de la Langue Françoyse* (1549), on the relationship between the national vernacular and poetic immortality. He claims that the act of writing in a "foreign" but widely known language like Latin may make the poet's name known in more places ("en plus de lieux") than the name of the poet who writes in French.[1] However, the mere fact of being in so many places at once may also turn that name into smoke, which dissipates as it expands, and eventually fades away into the air ("peu à peu s'évanouit parmi le grand espace de l'air"). By contrast, the writer who writes excellently in his own vernacular is more limited, but because his language is based in a single place ("comme ayant son siège de demeure certaine"), it will last much longer ("de plus longue durée"). By locating himself, or finding a "seat" (the same term that Montaigne will later use to describe his own position), the poet

< *Representing France at Mid-Century* >

achieves immortality. By remaining in a national linguistic space, by limiting oneself *spatially*, one transcends one's limitations *temporally*. In order to be for all time, one must be fixed.

It would be difficult to find a clearer example of the way the literary emphasis on a new "national" community (prefigured in both Rabelais and Marguerite de Navarre), begins to displace the "universal" culture of Latinity in the mid-sixteenth century. However, the new national culture is also an anxious culture, both about its authority, and about its relationship to the France it represents. And as is often the case in the *Deffence*, it is unclear whether Du Bellay's praise of France and the French language is descriptive or prophetic, whether it celebrates the strength of French culture, or expresses its weakness. His praise of France concludes with a celebration of French virtue, which, he says, sets France apart from other lands. But he then veers into a series of troubling questions: "Why are we then such admirers of others? Why are we so unjust to ourselves? Why do we go begging for the languages of others, as if we were ashamed to use our own?" ["Pourquoi donc sommes-nous si grands admirateurs d'autrui? Pourquoi sommes-nous tant iniques à nous-même? Pourquoi mendions-nous les langues étrangères comme si nous avions honte d'user de la nôtre?"].[2] The wavering between confident pronouncements of national triumph and anguished browbeating suggests the complications that arise when language becomes the single mark of national identity, when the vernacular is pressed into service to define the relationship between culture and politics. Du Bellay constantly evokes the heroic past of France and claims that contemporary poetry can make that past congruent with the imperialist fantasies of the Valois dynasty. In order to do so, however, it must seize and appropriate resources from abroad—a gesture that seems to undermine the very national self-identity that Du Bellay is seeking to promote.

This tension between an elegiac praise of France and anxiety directed toward a rival Other (in this case, the Italians) marks all of Du Bellay's work. And it is a central feature of his most important lyric collection, the *Regrets*. In this chapter I shall argue that Du Bellay's canonical formulations of Frenchness are closely linked to his social identity as a petty aristocrat. Caught between traditional aristocratic landedness and a new court society, Du Bellay sought his fortune by travelling to Rome in the service of his cousin, Jean Du Bellay, the French legate to the Holy See. This journey, occasioned by worldly ambition, produced a crisis in poetic authority. In response to this

< *Representing France at Mid-Century* >

crisis, Du Bellay articulates a number of discordant positions, often linked to disparate strains of thought, in which various forms of Frenchness lend authority to his poetic persona. In other words, Frenchness functions as a mediating term that brings a crisis of aristocratic identity into harmony with the experience of alterity. The typical French national subject incarnated so famously by Du Bellay—nostalgic, unpretentious, amicable, straight-talking—is produced out of social and poetic crisis. Frenchness is poetic, not natural.

Du Bellay defines these diverse positions, through his manipulation of the sonnet form itself. He deploys a variety of different sonnet types and poetic postures, principally the pose of the longing Petrarchan lover and the satirical commentator on Roman life. Together these permit him to position himself as a liminal figure who is neither altogether in France nor altogether in Rome. The juxtaposition of these diverse and even mutually exclusive positions through the sonnet collection makes possible the construction of a national character in lyric.

The Economics of Poetry

The rise of vernacular literature and the definition of the national language are phenomena that scholars have conventionally located at the origins of modern nationalism. As Benedict Anderson has shown, the moment of the Renaissance is precisely that moment at which the nascent capitalism of the printing trade is beginning to construct "print-languages" that, in Anderson's fine formulation, lie "below Latin and above the spoken vernaculars." These print-languages create "the possibility of a new form of imagined community, which in its basic morphology set the stage for the modern nation."[3] Du Bellay and his contemporaries stand at a crucial moment in the process described by Anderson. They have, for the most part, made the choice to write in French and to seek to define and promote the vernacular. However, they do not yet have a clear sense of what type of nation that vernacular might define. They have the language, but haven't yet grasped the way to "set the stage for the modern nation." Therefore, they must invent a France for which they can speak.

The complex motivations underpinning various considerations of the language question suggest, moreover, that the relationship between nation and language may be more complex than the encounter between the capitalist energies of the printing trade and the "fatal diversity of human language" Anderson privileges.[4] For most of the dis-

< *Representing France at Mid-Century* >

cussions of language and nation by Du Bellay's contemporaries focus, not on the printing trade, but on the relationship between the nation and the court, which is frequently seen to have been invaded by Italians. For many writers, the center of France is seen to have been taken over by foreigners. Thus, even as print capitalism creates a unified print-language, that language is placed under pressure by the ethnic complexity of the court society which will come to dominate Europe in the seventeenth century.[5] How, then, is one to define France? For some writers about the French vernacular, such as Du Bellay's friend Jacques Peletier du Mans, the French language is coextensive with the political domination of the king. Peletier recommends, in his "Art Poétique," that the poet should use all words spoken by French subjects, no matter in what dialect. For it is political power itself that connects language to territory: "All these words are French, because they come from the country of the King" ["Tout est Français, puis qu'ils sont du pays du Roy"].[6] And yet, in a country still marked by strong regional identity and a powerful provincial nobility, the very notion of the "pays du Roy" was a point of contention. The Lyonnais humanist Barthélemy Aneau, whose pamphlet, the "Quintil Horatien," criticized the *Deffence et Illustration*, attacked Du Bellay's use of the term "patrie" to describe France by saying that, "whoever has a *pays* has no need of a *patrie*" ["qui a pays n'a que faire de patrie"]. Aneau goes on to praise the distinguished Greek origin of the term "pays" over the transparently Italianate "patrie." Writing from the prosperous mercantile space of Lyon, Aneau sees Du Bellay as a representative of the court, which is viewed as an exclusive institution rather than as the seat of an all-embracing monarchy. And his own vocabulary suggests uncertainty about the unity and identity of France itself in the face of an emerging "statist" vision. The term "pays" suggests, as it still does today, everything from "country" to "village," and Aneau wavers between this vocabulary of regionalism and an equally idealized universalism, as he shifts from the praise of "pays" to an evocation of "the community of men" ["la communauté des hommes"], which he contrasts with the "elitism" he discerns in Du Bellay's project.[7]

Even more interesting in this regard is Aneau's conclusion that "patrie" is a kind of foreign agent, having recently entered France along with other "Italian corruptions" ("venu en France nouvellement avec les autres corruptions italiques"). He notes that "ancient" poets (presumably earlier French poets) rejected the word "patrie" as an ex-

< *Representing France at Mid-Century* >

ample of bad Latin: "which name the ancients refused to use, fearing a skinning of Latin" ["duquel nom n'ont voulu user les anciens, craignans l'escorcherie du latin"]. Instead they contented themselves with what was "their own, and good" ("se contentant de leur propre et bon").[8] Anxiety toward court society takes the form of hostility toward Italy. The impact of Italian culture on the French vernacular (especially under the influence of Catherine de' Medici) becomes a cipher for addressing larger anxieties about the relationship of the court to other forms of social organization. Here, the processes of political centralization discussed in the last chapter produce an anxiety against the cultural Other who seems to be infecting the court—the very center of France.[9]

Probably the most virulent anti-Italian of the writers on the language question was the Protestant printer Henri Estienne. His *Précellence du langage françois*, of 1579, attacks the court for its Italianate style, arguing that the real "heart" of France corresponds to the spots where the most "naïve" and "pure" French is spoken: "As regards language I can call the heart of France those places where its naturalness and purity are best conserved" ["en cas du langage je puis appeler le cueur de la France les lieux où sa nayfveté et pureté est le mieux conservée"].[10] Language is here a synecdoche of France. Pure language means pure France. In the preface to his *Deux dialogues du nouveau langage francoys italianizé* of a year earlier, Estienne makes his claim about language and character even more specific. He observes that the only place one can still find French well spoken is "partly among certain families which remain faithful to the ancient traditions, and partly in the Parliament of Paris, though there, too, the contagion of incorrect pronunciation has penetrated."[11] Italian influence is depicted as a kind of plague on France, with only a few old French families and members of the traditionalist judiciary holding out.

Moreover, the linguistic destabilization brought on by Italian influence is matched by hints of disruptive social mobility. For Estienne goes on to locate the origin of linguistic contagion in Francis I's wars in the Piedmont. Young men came back from these battles, he says, with the trace of Italian in their pronunciation. Italian affectation thus became the marker of having served the King in battle—the linguistic equivalent of the soldier's scar. However, because words, unlike scars, are not attached to actual bodies, it is easy to counterfeit such signs of distinction, and Italianate pronunciation was soon adopted by men who had never been at war at all. French was thus

< *Representing France at Mid-Century* >

"infected" (and the parallel with syphilis, that other import from the Italian wars, is probably not accidental), by a kind of counterfeit heroism, by language that circulates like phony money and creates a simulacrum or illusion of royal service.

The centralization of political power, as I noted in the previous chapter, had by now made royal service, rather than noble birth, the grounds for advancement. This makes possible a curious reversal. The mark of otherness, Italian affectation in one's speech, becomes the sign of having served the king. Estienne laments this falsification of one's war record as a corruption of French identity itself. Ten years later, the Protestant soldier François de La Noue would link the terms *pays*, *patrie*, and *nation*, as communities that shape the duty of the subject. La Noue laments that, while the French nation ("la nation françoise") has always had a good reputation for military valor, now the French spend their time fighting abroad instead of remaining at home. The duty of the French soldier, he says, is to show affection to his "patrie" and to leave children to his "pays."[12]

What is important here is the way in which Estienne, like Aneau and many other writers on the topic, seeks to attach French to the soil of France, and to find "Frenchness" in the relationship of language and land.[13] It is in contrast to these writers that one can see the originality of Du Bellay, for whom the vitality of French lies, not in its purity, but in its capacity to appropriate other cultures. The *Deffence* promotes precisely the type of cultural transmission and cross-fertilization that nativists like Estienne and Aneau seem to fear. If French poets wish to create a new imperial French poetics, argues Du Bellay, they must pillage the cultures of the Greeks, Latins, and Italians.

To be sure, there are local politics behind this import-export model of culture. Du Bellay aims at seizing literary authority from a previous generation of poets and writers: the generation of Clément Marot, which favored such traditional French forms as the rondeau and the ballade. In the *Deffence*, Du Bellay denigrates this native French tradition by lamenting that many contemporary poets think they are accomplished if they imitate and resemble Antoine Heroët or Marot. Such practice, he says, is useless, since it profits nothing: "I admonish you . . . not to imitate willy-nilly . . . the most famous [French] authors, as do most of our French poets, a thing which is as vicious as it is profitless, since it is nothing (o great liberality!) but giving back to French what already belonged to it" ["Je t'admoneste donc . . . de non imiter à pied levé . . . les plus fameux auteurs d'icelle, ainsi que font or-

< *Representing France at Mid-Century* >

dinairement la plupart de nos poètes français, chose certe autant vicieuse, comme de nul profit à notre vulgaire: vue que ce n'est autre chose (ô grande libéralité) sinon lui donner ce qui était à lui"].[14] It is too bad, he goes on to note, that French is not as "rich" in native examples of excellent poetry as are the Latin and Greek traditions.

I shall return, at the close of this chapter, to the issue of the relationship between literature and territory. For now, what is striking is the way Du Bellay defines the relationship between language, literature, and the national collective in terms of investment and economics. Whereas writers such as Aneau and Estienne link language to particular places, institutions, or groups, Du Bellay sets forth linguistic practice as a kind of economy. The problem with mimicking French poets, he says, is that such imitation brings nothing new to French and those who speak it. It doesn't enrich the language. It is a weak investment, whereas the imitation of models from abroad produces "profit." This kind of economic imagery can be seen throughout Du Bellay's work. For example, in a long poem written to Charles IX in the late 1560s on the "Four Estates of France," the poet exhorts the king to remember the contributions of the people ("le peuple nourricier"), upon which the rest of the commonwealth depends. For it is they, he says, who keep the land fertile, and the lives of kings comfortable ("Sans luy des Roys seroit la vie miserable,/Sans luy la terre mere infertile seroit"). And he goes on, somewhat surprisingly, to extend this praise of the people to trade: "Through [the people] we trade with foreigners,/From whom we receive, for drink and food,/Riches and gold, with which your France abounds,/Being, as it is, a fertile cornucopia of all goods" ["Par luy nous trafiquons avec l'estranger,/Duquel nous recevons, pour le boire & manger,/Les richesses & l'or, dont vostre France abonde,/Comme estant de tous biens une Corne feconde"].[15]

The image of the cornucopia, which is often seen as a figure for textuality in Renaissance French literature, here undergoes a metamorphosis.[16] When the image is deployed to describe national productivity it involves a relationship of identity and difference. On the one hand, the passage lauds the natural fecundity of the French countryside, worked by peasants, which produces "drink and food." Yet the peasants are praised for the way they are involved in a process of economic exchange, which brings the riches that ornament the kingdom. The text suggests that the "drink and food" that the French countryside produces are somehow not enough. If France is truly to

< *Representing France at Mid-Century* >

be rich it must be adorned by gold, and that gold must also be seen as somehow intrinsically French. The cornucopian image, in fact, bears the burden of inscribing the surplus value produced by trade back into the soil of France, as a kind of second order native wealth. The passage seems uncertain whether France is to be defined in its own native terms, or in terms of a series of exchanges with other nations.[17]

These concerns turn up again in the *Regrets*. The *Regrets* were written during and shortly after Du Bellay's so-called "exile" in Rome, in the service of his cousin Jean Du Bellay. In discussing Du Bellay's depiction of his exile, scholars have tended to focus their attention on Du Bellay's several literary masks, on the ways he compares himself to both Odysseus and the Ovid of the *Tristia*. Yet this emphasis on an "epic" or an "elegiac" Du Bellay runs the risk of failing to account for the ways in which he manipulates the resources of the sonnet collection. I shall argue that Du Bellay's depictions of his own poetry are intimately involved with images of exchange, and issues of value. For the vocabulary of exchange, profit and loss, and money, already seen in the *Deffence*, recurs on virtually every page of the *Regrets*. However, whereas the *Deffence* speaks confidently of cultural plunder, the *Regrets* speak only of loss and bad business. The economic and fiscal images in the *Regrets* are too numerous to list: Du Bellay bemoans the time he must spend worrying about the accounts of his cousin Jean's houshold (sonnet #15); he deplores his lack of cash (sonnet #61); he laments that his tears are not worth more (sonnet #52); he complains that he has invested badly in the trip to Italy (sonnet #44); he notes that he has "exchanged" one language for another and one climate for another (sonnet #10); he envies the man who never cedes to the "miserable concern for acquisition" ["le miserable soing d'acquerir d'avantage"] (sonnet #38), and so on. And in virtually every one of these instances, unprofitable exchange is linked to the failure of Du Bellay's own ambitions. Thus, in the thirty-third sonnet of the collection, he bitterly regrets his decision to leave home in search of success. His original hope, he notes, was to learn, to master the disciplines of medicine, mathematics, and philosophy. This led him to "exchange France for Italy" ("Quand je changeay la France au sejour d'Italie"). Unfortunately, he admits, knowledge has not led to advancement, and he has come so far only to be enriched with misfortune: "Je suis venu si loin/Pour m'enrichir d'ennuy, de vieillesse, et de soin,/Et perdre en voyageant le meilleur de mon aage." And he goes on to compare himself to the sailor who sets to sea in search of riches, but re-

< *Representing France at Mid-Century* >

turns bearing only herring: "Ainsi le marinier souvent pour tout tresor/Rapporte des harencs en lieu de lingots d'or,/aiant fait, comme moy, un malheureux voyage."[18] Instead of the treasures of the Americas, Du Bellay gets fish.

To understand the stakes of Du Bellay's depiction of poetry as a token of exchange, one might contrast it with an example from the preceding poetic generation—Clément Marot's "Petite épître au roy." Addressed to Francis I, the poem deploys a series of equivocal rhyme words, all of which contain some version of the word "rhyme" ("rimailleurs" rhymes with "rime ailleurs;" "rimassez" with "rime assez," and so on). It begins with the poet's noting that while writing rhyme he often "enrhymes" himself ("je m'enrime," a pun on "je m'enrhume," "to catch a cold"—and yet another linking of language and body). The poem goes on to claim that the poet lives in hunger and poverty ("Mon pauvre corps ne serait nourri mois,/Ne demi-jour"), and entreats the king to respond with help. A gift from the king, it concludes, would mean that one day people might recall that Marot garnered the "goods" ("biens") that can be had from poetry: "Afin qu'on die, en prose, ou en rimant: 'Ce rimailleur, qui s'allait enrimant,/Tant rimassa, rima et rimonna,/Qu'il a connu quel bien par rime on a'" ["So that one will say, in prose, or rhyme: 'This rhymster rhymed,/Rhymicized and rhymated so well,/That he knew what goods one can get from rhyme'"]. The joking equivocal rhyme of the last two lines underscores the identification of poetry with property, as "rhyming" ("rimonna") exactly echoes possession of property ("par rime on a").[19] As both Ullrich Langer and François Cornilliat have noted in recent finely nuanced readings of this poem, it simultaneously evokes the structures of economic exchange that define culture in early Renaissance France and breaks with those traditions. It inscribes itself in a structure of exchange, yet also acknowledges that the king's response to it may be purely arbitrary, since he is depicted as a poet with adequate supplies of both money and rhymes ("Des biens avez et de la rime assez"). Yet what is important for our concerns is the way in which the poem's claim on its reader is linked to the technical manipulation of the resources of French.[20] The interest of the poem resides in the ever-thicker layering on of multiple strata of semantic content. For though the king may already be a poet, he is no poet like Marot, and his own rhymes have nothing of the semantic richness of this lyric, in which surplus meaning aims to produce surplus value. That is, it is the poem's virtuosity that makes it worthy of exchange with a king who already has rhymes of his own.

< *Representing France at Mid-Century* >

Yet the type of courtly economy in which Marot worked had itself become problematic for members of Du Bellay's generation, which was active in the period after the flowering of the first Valois court. Pierre de Ronsard, Du Bellay, and their cohorts were for the most part members of the provincial petty nobility. As the first generation of poets after Francis I, they found themselves caught between the martial ideals embodied in that prince, and the growing bureaucracy of an emerging court society. Norbert Elias has noted the importance of a money economy for this new social system. He points out that the invention of the letter of exchange in the fifteenth century made it increasingly easy for the king to control his aristocratic subjects through the disbursement of funds, and "the king who owns and distributes land gradually becomes a king who owns and distributes money."[21]

In France, this new money economy is mirrored by a system of privileges, centered on the court, in which professional advancement and cultural eminence are related. Achievement in poetry, oratory, and philosophy leads to fame, which helps to secure pensions, patronage, high office, and other forms of worldly success. It is in this system that petty nobles like the members of the Pléiade pursue their careers. They are the sons, in J. H. M. Salmon's words, of "petty country seigneurs, whose dreams had evaporated in Italy and who saw office for their sons as the only means of recouping the family fortunes."[22] Most of these sons studied law, with the intention of seeking careers in royal service. However, they found themselves in direct competition with a well-educated bourgeoisie come to prominence under Francis and Henry. Less qualified than many of their competitors for salaried posts, they soon found that advancement at court depended upon patronage and favor, which required an endless struggle with intrigue and hierarchy. Caught between an emerging meritocracy for which they were unprepared, and a traditional aristocratic order in which they had low standing at best, these poets privileged an image of the poet as simultaneously hard-working and inspired, as both competent to excel in a competitive world, and "naturally" above others—a kind of aristocrat of the spirit.[23] In this context, the exchange value of poetry might be linked to the way in which it both provides evidence of technical mastery (the result of labor), and bears various forms of cultural material only available to an educated elite. The poem thus becomes a medium of a cultural import business, the raw materials for which are a set of literary forms and conventions drawn from classical and Italian literature. No

< *Representing France at Mid-Century* >

longer able to win fame in the fields of Italy, the aristocrats of the Pléiade sought to bring classical culture to France as a way of increasing their own symbolic capital. Thus, whereas a poet like Marot, from the generation preceding Du Bellay, could speak of the economics of literature, however paradoxically, as trading poetry for money, Du Bellay operates within a much more complex and mediated system of exchange. Marot's bid for power relies on his own presence at the king's side. Indeed, at one point, in his "Enfer," he even speaks of having been given, literally, by the King to his sister, Marguerite de Navarre.[24] His very body was a token of exchange among members of the political elite. By contrast, Du Bellay's struggle for cultural power is hampered by his very absence from court, and by the fact that he must reconstruct his poetic authority through a collection of sonnets, most of which are addressed to absent friends.

The Place of Poetry

The attempts to define the relationship between language and territory seen in Aneau and Estienne, and in our opening citation from Du Bellay's *Deffence*, are also important for a reading of the *Regrets*. Du Bellay depicts himself as stuck in space, limited by the absolute contingency of his geographical position in Rome. There is something peculiarly modern about this sense of space, for it breaks with an entire tradition of courtly love poetry, in which poets send their songs and imaginations flying through space to dwell with their ladies. Indeed, Du Bellay's insistence on the power of place sets him apart from, say, his friend Olivier de Magny, who was in Rome at the same time, and whose *Soupirs* are often seen as a companion volume to the *Regrets*. Magny's love sonnets use the poet's expatriation to Rome as the occasion for swearing that his passion for his lady is no less intense than it was in France. Even if, on occasion, Magny seems to change ladies, Rome is always the backdrop for expressions of renewed desire and devotion that transcend time and space. Desire in Magny is everywhere the same.[25] By contrast, Du Bellay is hemmed in. And his awareness of his literal spatial removal from the French court is a central feature of his poetic persona.

As an impoverished aristocrat, Du Bellay is the perfect heir to Marguerite de Navarre's aristocratic hero Amadour, discussed in the previous chapter. However, when Du Bellay is called away on an "affair of importance" he goes, not as a knight of romance, but as a bureaucrat, and ends up spending years in misery in a foreign court. In-

< *Representing France at Mid-Century* >

deed, the problem here seems to be that, just as court society has become increasingly complex, so has foreign service. The political economy of international relations (permanent ambassadorial legations, negotiations with political rivals, and similar signs of the emergence of a community of nation-states) makes the type of heroism seen in the *Heptaméron* obsolete. Du Bellay registers this paradox in his very lexicon through play on the various meanings of the word "service," which denotes by turns the poet's service to his prince, his subjection to his muse, his muse's subjection to his will, and the "use value" of poetry itself. As he says in the dedicatory poem to the *Regrets*, "Quelqu'un dira, 'A quoy *servent* ces plaintes?' " ["Someone will say, 'what are these complaints for?' "] (my emphasis)—a question that sets up an extended meditation on the value of poetry in the pursuit of public recognition.

Du Bellay registers his absence from court as a threat to poetic power. As he notes in the seventh sonnet of the *Regrets*, geographical displacement to Italy makes him a forgotten poet. So long as the court read his writing ("ce pendant que la cour mes oeuvrages lisoit") and he enjoyed the patronage of Marguerite, the sister of Henry II, he was inspired by poetic furor ("une fureur d'esprit au ciel me conduisoit"), and was able to write easily. Now, however, far from court, he has lost his source of inspiration and has fallen silent ("Ores je suis muet"). He concludes by noting that "honor nourishes the arts" ["l'honneur nourrit les arts"] and that the Muse requires an audience, "the theater of the people and the favor of Kings" ["la Muse demande/Le theatre du peuple, et la faveur des Roys"].

This expression of poetic infertility comes early on in the *Regrets*. It is pursued through a whole series of sonnets that set the stage for the drama of exile that follows. The themes of absence and muteness just evoked are developed a moment later, when, in the eighth sonnet, Du Bellay addresses himself to Ronsard, on the first of several such occasions in the collection. This is a key sonnet for understanding how Du Bellay's poetics constitute a response to his distance from court:

Ne t'esbahis Ronsard, la moitié de mon ame,
Si de ton Dubellay France ne lit plus rien,
Et si aveques l'air du ciel Italien
Il n'a humé l'ardeur qui l'Italie enflamme.

Le sainct rayon qui part des beaux yeux de ta dame,
Et la saincte faveur de ton Prince et du mien,

< *Representing France at Mid-Century* >

Cela (Ronsard) cela, cela merite bien
De t'eschauffer le coeur d'une si vive flamme.

Mais moy, qui suis absent des raiz de mon Soleil,
Comment puis-je sentir eschauffement pareil
A celuy qui est pres de sa flamme divine?

Les costaux soleillez de pampre sont couvers,
Mais des Hyperborez les eternelz hyvers
Ne portent que le froid, la neige, et la bruine.

[Do not be surprised, Ronsard, other half of my soul,
If France reads no more of your Du Bellay,
And if, with the air of the Italian heavens
He has not breathed in the ardor that inflames Italy.

The holy ray that leaves the eyes of your lady,
And the holy favor of your Prince and mine,
That (Ronsard), that, that is truly worth
Heating up one's heart with such a lively flame.

But I, who am absent from the rays of my Sun,
How can I feel the same heat/As he who is near his divine flame?
The sunny hillsides are covered with vines
But the eternal Hyperborean winters
bring only cold, snow, and drizzle].

The poem opens with an evocation of Ronsard as the "other half of my soul," a neo-Platonic cliché that seems to suggest a communion across distance. However, it immediately slips into a meditation on the link between geographical position and poetic inspiration. The connection between place and poetry is embodied in the word "ardeur," in line four, which suggests both poetic furor (alluded to with the same term in preceding poems) and inspiration intrinsic in the Italian climate. The earthly ardor of Italy (which Magny, by the way, celebrates as a "divine fire") leaves this poet cold.[26] Because he is far from the French court, he cannot write as he did before. The second stanza then expands the analysis of the conditions of poetry by considering the relationship between the poet and the object, erotic or political, that "inspires" him to write. Ronsard is depicted as inspired by both the presence of his lady and the presence of his prince—presumably the sources of both his love poetry and his circumstantial epideictic (though Du Bellay may as well have had in mind Ronsard's work on his epic, the *Franciade*). Yet there is also a

< *Representing France at Mid-Century* >

kind of leveling out of the status of ladies and princes as sources of inspiration which is suggested by the echo of the lady's "sainct rayon" in the prince's "saincte faveur." The impossibility, a few lines later, of knowing whether "mon Soleil" refers to a lady or a prince underscores the fact that the power of these entities over the poet's inspiration is less visceral or spiritual than it is locational. Both may function as reasons to write so long as the poet is near them. Indeed, the claim, a few lines later, that both lady and prince "merit" being written about underscores the sense that they are, as much as anything, convenient topics, mediated through an economy of favor. The notion is further stressed by the stumbling repetition of "cela," which one might translate as something like "all that stuff."

The poem thus explores what it means to live in space. It argues that geographical distance severs the relationship between subject and object in lyric. In this it undermines an entire lyric tradition of poetic praise, from the troubadour Jaufré Rudel to Petrarch, whose example Du Bellay's use of the sonnet form inevitably recalls. For as all readers of Petrarch know, absence makes the heart grow fonder. Du Bellay evokes the Petrarchan language of desire, yet he depicts the poetic self in terms of a courtly career pursued through the traffic in praise.[27] The overlapping of these two codes (poetry as longing, poetry as career) leads to the curious way in which the poem depicts agency. Agency seems to reside both inside the poet and outside of him. He is inspired from the outside by an object, yet the "si vive flamme" that concludes the first tercet may be either the object of the poet's contemplation (a synonym, as it were, of the holy ray of the lady's eyes), or the consequence of that object's power over the poet (poetic inspiration). The ambiguity is underscored by the verb "t'eschauffer," which suggests at once that the poet is "heated up" from the outside, and that he "heats himself up."

This sense of a floating agency, of a poetic impulse that cannot be located, may be what makes the final tercet so arresting. For here the subject disappears. We shift suddenly into an impersonal contrast between two climates. The poem has up to now relied on an oppositional logic of geographical presence and absence, of France versus Italy. The final tercet, however, gives us a contrast of "sunny hillsides" (either the hillsides of Italy or France, it makes no difference), and the psychological state of "eternal Hyperborean winters." The contrast between France and Italy is replaced by a contrast between the outside of the poet and the inside; there is a shift from "real" geogra-

< *Representing France at Mid-Century* >

phy into an allegorical or emblematic space. Indeed, in their failure to reach the type of dialectical resolution conventionally associated with the sonnet form, the closing lines recall the emblematic logic of a text such as Maurice Scève's *Délie*, wherein psychological trauma is repeatedly distilled into conceptual paradox.[28] In a note to this poem Michael Screech has pointed out that the phrase "des Hyperborez les eternelz hyvers" may echo the "Solus Hyperboreas glacies" of Virgil's fourth Georgic (v. 517).[29] That Latin phrase describes the wandering of the poet Orpheus after his loss of Eurydice and just before his demise at the hands of the Maenads. At issue here is the very power of poetry itself, and the sonnet dramatizes the plight of the court poet when circumstance removes him from the cultural economy through which he defines himself.

It is interesting that Du Bellay addresses the poem, not to his patrons in France, but to his friend Ronsard. This custom of addressing poems to friends is, of course, frequent in sixteenth-century French poetry, and an especially important (though little studied) dimension of the work of the Pléiade.[30] Indeed, the virtual ubiquity of the gesture distinguishes French Renaissance lyric from contemporaneous lyric developments in other countries. However, given Du Bellay's insistence on a rhetoric of exchange, and his obsession with geographical location, the epistolary gesture becomes central to the poetics of the *Regrets* in a way that it is not in the works of other poets such as Ronsard, Antoine Baïf, and Etienne Jodelle. For Du Bellay, the call to friendship, to the "other self" that is the friend (recalling again the language of the eighth sonnet of the *Regrets*), has the function of producing a mediating space within which the poet may define his authority. Unable to communicate with the court, and unable to claim that he speaks for the "nation" (as he does in the *Deffence*), Du Bellay constructs an imaginary community of friends who read and appreciate his work. For the poet exiled from court, the literary coterie emerges as the space within which poetic discourse is authorized. Since the coterie is engaged in redefining French poetics, by speaking *to* his friends, Du Bellay can see himself as speaking *for* France.

The fragmented character of the lyric collection, coupled with the resources for textual diffusion supplied by the new technique of printing, makes possible the evocation and invocation of a group experience that contrasts with the strategies available to other literary genres for constructing community. Thus, by contrast, Ariosto famously evokes his friends waiting for him on the quay as he com-

< *Representing France at Mid-Century* >

pletes the long journey of his *Orlando Furioso*. For Ariosto, writing and community seem to be antithetical, and he returns to society only at the end of his poem. Because he writes lyric, Du Bellay can turn to his friends at every moment of his book, giving the impression that, though they follow different paths, all are witnesses to his literary project. These turns to the coterie place the reader both in and out of the literary group. The reader is witness, like Ronsard and his friends, to Du Bellay's suffering, while, of course, not being included in the group because she or he is not named. Such complex positioning of the reader (which parallels Du Bellay's own location of himself between France and Italy) is a rhetorical strategy that will be repeated countless times in the rhetoric of later French avant-garde movements. Yet whereas later movements define their collective identity and authority through such genres as the manifesto, the published correspondence, or the preface, Du Bellay here deploys the resources of the lyric collection to construct the image of the first French avant-garde.[31]

When Ronsard praises the king, says Du Bellay in sonnet #16, he "honors" himself, "by honoring the man who honors the honor/Which you give him with your learned song" ["Chantant l'heur de Henry . . . /Tu t'honores toymesme, et celuy qui honore/L'honneur que tu luy fais par ta docte chanson"]. In this version of epideictic, the exchange of poems for honor produces a kind of surplus value. That value stems, however, not only from the exchange, but from the praise's object: the king has a magical power, and so to praise the king is to gain honor. Because Du Bellay is far from court, however, he is far from the royal body that exudes such power, and so can only exchange poems with other poets. Yet therein lies a risk. When the body of the king or the lady is absent, poetry becomes a set of exchanges among writers writing about each other. In this context, language is cut loose from the material surface of the desired object to which it refers, and from which it takes its authority. We seem to be witness to what Pierre Bourdieu has described as the emergence of literature as an autonomous "field," in which words are exchanged for words, and "the producers within it produce first and foremost for other producers."[32] Words of praise are dislodged from their attachments to bodies and acts, and become so many circulating signs—as empty as the words of those young men who have never served the king, yet affect Italian pronunciation. Du Bellay's lyrics are caught in a no-man's land, between the obsession with the royal body that grounds so much courtly

< *Representing France at Mid-Century* >

literature of both the sixteenth and the seventeenth centuries, on the one hand, and a truly "public sphere" in which literature speaks for and to a specific social or national group, on the other. The image of poetry seen in Marot, where poetic language is connected to the direct exchange of goods for praise, and where language seems to adhere to the poet's very body, here gives way to a world in which texts are exchanged for other texts. In sonnet #152, the *Regrets* register both the resources and the risks of this moment, when poets build their identities upon their relationships to other poets:

Si mes escripts (Ronsard) sont semez de ton loz,
Et si le mien encore tu ne dedaignes dire,
D'estre enclos en mes vers ton honneur ne desire,
Et par là je ne cherche en tes vers estre encloz.

Laissons donc je te pry laissons causer ces sotz,
Ces petitz gallandz, qui ne sachant que dire,
Disent, voyant Ronsard, et Bellay s'entr'escrire,
Que ce sont deux muletz, qui se grattent le doz.

Nos louanges (Ronsard) ne font tort à personne:
Et quelle loy defend que l'un à l'autre on donne,
Si les amis entre eulx des presens se font bien?

On peut comme l'argent trafiquer la louange,
Et les louanges sont comme lettres de change,
Dont le change et le port (Ronsard) ne couste rien.

[If my writings (Ronsard) are sown with your praise,
And if you do not disdain to praise me,
Your honor has no desire to be enclosed in my verses,
And, by the same token, I do not seek to be enclosed in your verses.

I beg you, let us let those idiots chatter,
Those little gallants who know not what to say,
Saying, when they see Ronsard and Bellay write each other,
That we are two mules who scratch each other's backs.

Our praises, Ronsard, do no ill to anyone:
And what law prohibits us from giving them to each other,
If gifts are given among friends?
One can traffic praise, just as one trafficks silver,
And praises are like letters of exchange,
Which cost nothing (Ronsard) to carry or cash.]

< *Representing France at Mid-Century* >

This poem registers the anxiety that afflicts a poetry produced only for other "producers." So long as praise circulates around royal bodies, it is acceptable. When it becomes the mere circulation of texts about other texts, it becomes the object of ridicule. To defend himself from the charge of poetic vacuity, Du Bellay evokes a convenient enemy, the "petitz gallandz" of the sixth line, whose calumny is the inverse of praise, a purely destructive use of language.

It is the public dimension of the mutual praise among poets that seems most to threaten the integrity of poetry. Du Bellay depicts himself and his friend in the gaze of rivals. The two poets are seen as both writing to each other and actually "writing each other," "s'en-tre'scrire"—a curious verb that underscores the power of writing to shape both its subject and its object. The image of the mules scratching each other's backs is mentioned by Erasmus, who uses it to admonish those who praise each other in a kind of mutual admiration society.[33] Du Bellay responds to this cliché of bodies pleasing bodies by evoking an idealized exchange, a kind of aristocratic gift economy in which friends give each other presents. Yet the shift from the third to the fourth stanzas is striking. For he immediately discards the image of the poem as gift, as if it were inadequate, and likens poetry to money. He evokes the letter of exchange, a relatively recent development in the world of international finance. The letter of exchange provides the perfect metaphor for an exchange of poems, since both exchanges are free. Du Bellay is cutting close to the quick, here, to the very terms through which courtly poets define themselves. His evocation of the "traffic of praise" that poets deploy, in fact, echoes one of Ronsard's most famous poems, the "Ode to Henry II" that opens his vastly influential first book of *Odes*. There Ronsard depicts himself ironically as a merchant who exchanges verses for other valuables, "Trafiquant mes vers... Troque pour troq'" ["Trafficking my verses... Barter for barter"].[34]

Du Bellay turns this moment of praise against itself by describing a free exchange between friends. Yet this final image, which emerges to figure the friendly circulation of poems, effectively shifts attention away from the referential status of the object of praise—the concern of the poem up to now—and onto the circulation of language itself. Poetry among friends is licit not because of what it says, but because it circulates freely. It has no exchange value beyond its own movement. Indeed, one might put even a bit more pressure on this passage and note that the "letter of exchange," which emerges as the figure for

< *Representing France at Mid-Century* >

a perfect economy, doesn't completely fit the use to which it is here put. The whole point of the letter of exchange is that it is exchanged for money, that it frees merchants from carrying large sums of gold. As Fernand Braudel writes, "the taker [of the letter] would [then] be repaid at another market, three months later, according to the rate of exchange at the time."[35] The exchange of letters for each other, without the mediation of money—the image used by Du Bellay—is a kind of "second order" economic activity, removed from the material exchange of money for goods. Du Bellay's evocation of it suggests both the hybrid nature of the poetic coterie (simultaneously an aristocratic confraternity and a quasi-professional guild) and the difficulty of finding a language to celebrate poetry written for other poets, without the mediation of royal bodies to praise.

Sonnet #152 might be seen as an extreme moment in Du Bellay's exploration of the economics of poetry. In response to his distance from court, he constructs an exchange of texts with friends. The exchange of praise among poets shifts us away from a courtly setting, in which poems are exchanged over the body of a lady or a prince, toward a world of purely paper money, as it were, in which the phenomenon of "producers" who write for other "producers" becomes both the basis for constructing a literary coterie, and the source of anxiety about the value of poetry itself.

The Consolation of Form

In the fifty-fifth sonnet of the *Regrets*, Du Bellay complains that, whereas before he went to Italy he longed for knowledge and pleasure, now he only finds that he has become richer in sorrow ("m'en-richir d'ennuys"), like the mariner who sets out in search of gold, but only finds herring. He writes: "Du lut et du pinceau j'ebateray ma vie,/De l'escrime et du bal. Je discourois ainsi,/Et me vantois en moy d'apprendre tout cecy,/Quand je changeay la France au sejour d'Italie" ["With the lute and the paint brush I'll frolic,/With fencing and dancing. Thus did I talk,/And bragged about learning these things,/When I exchanged France for Italy"]. The image of "exchanging" one country for another evokes the three hundred and eighth poem of Petrarch's *Canzoniere*, "Quella per cui con Sorga ò cangiato Arno" ["She for whom I have exchanged the Sorgue for the Arno"], in which the poet praises Laura, the lady who has led him to forsake a life of politics and action for one of retirement.[36] He notes that he has often tried to praise her so that other people will understand his

< *Representing France at Mid-Century* >

actions, but that his poetry has always fallen short. For Petrarch the "exchange" of one landscape for another is evidence of his devotion to Laura—an object beyond his reach. Du Bellay turns that desire back on himself and defines it in temporal terms as disappointment, as thwarted desire for worldly success, for an object that never should have been sought to begin with. This gesture of transmuting longing into professional disappointment is central to Du Bellay's self-representation. Certainly, he is one of the first French poets to define his *poetic* self through the narrative of the *professional* career.

Still, what is most remarkable here is the way in which the depiction of unsatisfied desire in the *Regrets* consistently draws upon the language of Petrarchan longing. Like Thomas Wyatt, Du Bellay appropriates the language of Petrarchism as a psychological vocabulary which he then applies to scenarios that are not those of Petrarch or his followers. And his understanding of the relationship between desire and selfhood is the reverse of Petrarch's. Petrarch uses erotic humiliation as a pretext to poetic glory. The more miserable he is as a lover, the more he praises Laura, and the more he gains immortality. In the *Regrets* Du Bellay uses the language of erotic longing to explore professional disappointment.[37] In this lies at least one aspect of Du Bellay's modernity—that fame comes through a poetry so insistent on the failure of the quest for fame. This failure is given psychological authority through a vocabulary borrowed from the Petrarchan tradition. Thus, for example, in the poem addressed to the diplomat d'Avanson that opens the *Regrets*, Du Bellay tells how he was struck by a "sweet arrow," ("le doulx traict"). This recalls the hackneyed scene of Petrarchan *innamoramento*, in which the poet is struck by the lady's beauty (usually through the eyes, though sometimes in the heart or, as in the case of Ronsard, in the flank) and becomes the prisoner of her image. Here, however, Du Bellay claims that the arrow is lodged in his imagination, and that it comes from his Muse ("la Muse m'a laissé/Cest aiguillon dedans la fantaisie"). This turns the classic longing for erotic fulfillment into a longing for poetry itself. Whereas in Petrarch the poet's desire for the lady Laura, when expressed in language, becomes the mark of his glory, for Du Bellay, poetry is both the object of longing and the solution to longing. It is what has struck him in the imagination with its arrow, and what he uses to express his unhappiness; as he says in sonnet #11, "song alone can enchant my sorrows" ("le seul chant peult mes ennuys enchanter"). And yet, because song only brings glory when it has been sanctioned by

< *Representing France at Mid-Century* >

the court from which Du Bellay is absent, his songs are always lacking, his professional ambitions are always thwarted, and he is always in a position of weakness.

One can see the importance of this self-portrait of abjection for the larger context of the debates around French identity with which I began this chapter in one of the most famous poems in all of French literature, the ninth sonnet of the *Regrets*:

France mere des arts, des armes, et des loix,
Tu m'as nourry long temps du laict de ta mamelle:
Ores, comme un aigneau qui sa nourrice appelle,
Je remplis de ton nom les antres et les bois.

Si tu m'as pour enfant advoué quelquefois,
Que ne me respons-tu maintenant, ô cruelle?
France, France respons à ma triste querelle:
Mais nul, sinon Echo, ne respond à ma voix.

Entre les loups cruels j'erre parmy la plaine,
Je sens venir l'hyver, de qui la froide haleine
D'une tremblante horreur fait herisser ma peau.

Las, tes autres aigneaux n'ont faute de pasture,
Ils ne craignent le loup, le vent, ny la froidure:
Si ne suis-je pourtant le pire du troppeau.

[France, mother of arts, of arms, and of laws,
You have nourished me for a long time with the milk of your breast:
Now, like a lamb who calls his nurse,
I fill caves and woods with your name.

If you once recognized me as your child,
Why do you not answer me, cruel one?
France, France answer my sad complaint:
But none, except Echo, answers my voice.

Among cruel wolves, I wander on the plain,
I feel the winter come on, whose cold breath
Makes my flesh crawl with trembling horror.

Alas, your other lambs do not lack for pasture,
They never fear the wolf, the wind, or the cold:
And yet I am not the worst of the flock.]

This poem constitutes an answer, of sorts, to the sonnet that precedes it, the eighth sonnet, addressed to Ronsard, and discussed

171

< *Representing France at Mid-Century* >

above. That sonnet, I suggested, was concerned with the impact of space on the poet. This poem responds by turning literal space into literary landscape. The opening line of the poem quotes a Latin poem by Petrarch, "Ad Italiam," which in turn is based on the passages praising Italy at the beginning of Virgil's second Georgic.[38] Petrarch's poem is set on the top of the Alps, with the poet looking down at the Italian countryside below, and was occasioned by his return to Italy from France. In citing Petrarch's description of the peninsula as "land praised for arms, and laws, home of the sacred Muses" ["armorum legumque eadem veneranda sacrarum Pyeridumque domus"], Du Bellay enacts his own translation of empire northward.[39] At the same time, he sets himself up as the anti-Petrarch, as the figure who cannot return home.

The gesture of addressing the nation takes on different forms in different poets. Both Virgil and Petrarch call to Italy with the salutary "Salve," and then describe the country in minute detail, by sliding metonymically from ocean, to mountain, to history.[40] There is no lack of poems evoking France among Du Bellay's fellow French poets. The two great predecessor "exile" poets are Charles d'Orléans and Marot. Charles's many poems written during his imprisonment in England tend to define France as the place of his lady love. For Marot, writing from exile in Ferrara, the noun "France" refers collectively to a group of courtiers and judges, some of whom have betrayed him.[41] Among Du Bellay's contemporaries poems "about" and "to" France conventionally speak through allegory. Thus, for example, Ronsard writes an ode in which "The Nymph of France" speaks. And Du Bellay himself praises the poets of France by evoking the different rivers with which each is associated. All of these poets depict the country through a *representation* of some type of figure that stands for the whole.[42] The power of the sonnet cited above stems from the way it seems to call the country into existence as a whole, and to place the poet in a direct relationship with the entity it has invoked. That incantatory force, no doubt, may be traced to Du Bellay's own position as exile. Because Du Bellay's fellow poets are in France, they must speak *for* France, through allegory. Since Virgil and Petrarch are already in Italy, they can describe it. Because he is outside France, Du Bellay can speak *to* it, and try to move it through language, in the same way that, in his *Antiquitez de Rome*, he tries to open a dialogue with the ghosts of ancient Rome. Here, however, the dialogue is spatial, not temporal; it involves persuasion, not magic; it is Orphic, not

< *Representing France at Mid-Century* >

necromantic. Du Bellay can call France into being because he is in Italy. He can invent it because he is not in it.[43]

The incantatory power of Du Bellay's poem often blinds readers to the way it traces out a set of complex rhetorical shifts between subject and object, between poet and "France." The sonnet opens with an evocation of France as mother, an image that follows Petrarch and Virgil. However, where Virgil hails the country as "mother of the earth's fruits" ("salve, magna parens frugum") and Petrarch as his own mother ("Salve, pulcra parens"), Du Bellay connects the image of maternity to the more abstract list of institutions that define collective French experience, "arts, arms, and laws."[44] This depersonalization of maternity is then violently contrasted with the image of the second line, in which the poet enters the text as a nursing babe. A second reference to the poet, as lamb ("comme un aigneau"), complicates the maternal image by turning the country into a nursing ewe, introduced through the functional, mediating term of "nourrice," which could be applied to both women and sheep. The oblique "comme un aigneau" then gives way in the second quatrain to a parallel construction, "pour enfant," which reaffirms the filial relationship between country and poet. The stanza sets up a tension between abstract institutions such as war and law, and the concrete person of the poet. However, by providing no narrative to connect the different elements, it asks us to wonder how these seemingly distinct entities can all be "children" of the same "mother."

Throughout both of the first two stanzas the elementary and alimentary relationship of mother and nursing child is offset by the fact that what is being described is a relationship of two voices. The poet's agency is linked to his language, to the fact that he fills the woods with his laments. Those laments ask only for an answer. On one level, perhaps, the juxtaposition between a thematics of voice and a thematics of alimentation activates an elaborate play on the old notion—a cliché at least since Dante—that men imbibe their native language with their mothers' milk. Here both nourishment and dialogue have ceased, and the poet is turned into a kind of Narcissus figure, who is only answered by Echo. The Narcissus reference underscores the fact that we are in a literary landscape here. That landscape is, however, not Ovidian (Ovid's Narcissus never leaves poolside) but a blending of pastoral cliché with the Petrarchan solitude evoked in Petrarch's famous lyric "solo e pensoso."[45] For the image of the poet lost in the woods like a lamb recalls the emblem of the wandering Pe-

< *Representing France at Mid-Century* >

trarchan poet, who fills the woods with the name of his lady. This point is underscored by the reference to France in the fifth line as "cruelle" (a conventional term used to address the Petrarchan lady), and by the fourth line, "Je remplis de ton nom les antres et les bois." The pairing of the words "antres" and "bois" ("caves" and "woods") occurs literally hundreds of times in early modern French poetry, and seems to be a kind of coded sign for Petrarchan solitude. Indeed, as Du Bellay himself says in a long poem to his friend Olivier de Magny on the perfections of his lady, when he was in love, he spent his days wandering the countryside speaking of love and hearing only the echoes of the caves and woods: "Il me sembloit qu'antres et bois/ Piteux respondoient à ma voix" ["It seemed to me that caverns and woods/Answered back, with pity, to my voice"].[46] Du Bellay appropriates the language of this pastoral tradition refracted through the Petrarchan lyric to describe the subject's desire for the object that is France. At the same time, he turns that object into pure voice, mere Echo. He has called it into being, but it is empty.

The subsequent movement of the sonnet, however, shifts yet again the terms of the relationship between poet and country. No sooner have we left the second quatrain, than we suddenly learn that the poet is not in the woods after all, as we have just been told, but on the plains, among the wolves. This places us in yet another literary landscape. The image of the threatened sheep, fearful of the wolf and of winter, recalls the world of Virgilian pastoral, and, specifically, the fearful vulnerability that haunts the shepherd Meliboeus at the close of Virgil's first eclogue. Indeed, as Marie-Madeleine Fontaine has shown, the closing lines seem to echo several passages from Marot's eclogues, and thus place us, both textually and generically, in the Virgilian landscape that is one of the fundamental loci of French Renaissance poetry, beginning with Marot's famous translation of the first eclogue, published in the 1520s.[47] Here, however, the speaker is not a shepherd, fearfully driven into exile, as he is in Virgil, but just one of the sheep. And the poem ends with the poet comparing himself to the "other lambs," who, presumably, receive protection. Yet this final call makes evident what the forward movement of the poem tends to obscure. This is that while the conceit of the poet as lamb unifies the two halves of the poem, as we move from one landscape to another, the metaphorical status of France undergoes a mutation. For if France is a ewe in the first half of the poem, it cannot be a ewe in the second half, since a ewe is powerless to protect a frightened lamb

< *Representing France at Mid-Century* >

against a pack of wolves. Rather, the only one in this pastoral scenario who can protect the poet in the second half of the poem is the shepherd. The end of the sonnet, then, invokes, not a nourishing mother, but a powerful protector—a royal shepherd no less powerful than the Octavian of Virgil's first eclogue. As the poem unfolds, the metaphor used to describe its addressee changes. France is first invoked as mother and then as shepherd.

Whereas the preceding sonnet, #8, had ended on an impasse, with a contrast between the literal geography of Italy or France and the timeless metaphorical Hyperborean winter in the poet's soul, here both subject and object, inside and outside, are expressed through figures. Yet the deployment of these figures is particularly complex. The poet remains a sheep, while the poem slips from one figure to another to describe France. The subject is allegorized, represented through a single sustained metaphor, whereas the object is described with two different metaphors, between which we move as we read our way from octave to sestet.

This slide from metaphor to metaphor has interesting implications. The figure of the ruler as shepherd recalls a tradition of satire on the papacy (running from Dante, through Petrarch's most famous patriotic poem "Italia mia," to Ariosto) in which the Pope is criticized for being a bad shepherd and letting his flock stray into danger.[48] Du Bellay's poem recalls this tradition, but binds it to a cliché of royal propaganda. It was Homer who, in the second book of the *Iliad*, referred to Agamemnon as the "shepherd of his people."[49] Virgil developed the image by making Octavian the protector of Tityrus in his first eclogue.

This epithet was dear to the members of the Pléiade. In his poem on the four estates of France, Du Bellay recalls the image for Francis II, and Ronsard refers to it in the opening of the *Franciade*.[50] Thus, when set against Du Bellay's Italian poetic models, the veiled deployment of the shepherd figure enacts a shift from papal politics to the politics of emerging national identity (and the powerful secular leader missing from fragmented Italy). Moreover, on the level of national ideology itself, the sidestep from France as mother to France as protecting shepherd reflects the tension discussed at the outset of this chapter between a figure of France as *nation* (that is, as tradition, custom, collective identity) and a figure of France as embodied in a powerful *monarch*, surrounded by a centralized court society. The shift in lyric landscape, from Petrarchan solitude to Virgilian pas-

< *Representing France at Mid-Century* >

toral, makes it possible for Du Bellay's call to "France" to be paradoxically at once and successively a call to both "versions" of France, to a collective myth of nourishment and a single protective figure.

No less important here is the way in which the rhetoric of the sonnet responds to the crisis of poetic selfhood evinced in the poem that precedes it. For one thing, the pairing of ewe and shepherd recalls, if obliquely, the juxtaposition of lady and prince as pretexts for poetry in sonnet #8. What is more, if the earlier poem registers the weight of space, of the contingency of distance, on the poet, the second poem transforms topography into tropology. Unable to alter the *literal* landscape that separates him from France, the poet alters the *literary* landscape in which he sets himself by exchanging one cliché for another, by shifting from Petrarchan woods to Virgilian field. This replacement turns the poet's call into a different call, and France into a different France.

There is here a parallel with the tension described in my first chapter between Clément Marot's depiction of the paternal space of the court and the maternal space of an idealized garden in Cahors. However, whereas Marot defined the gendered tension between the feminized image of local culture and the paternalism of royal patronage as a well-nigh unbridgeable gap between the literal and the figural, between a real garden and a metaphorical "garden of letters," Du Bellay subtly resolves the tension between them by a slippage from figure to figure that shifts the poet's isolation into a purely allegorical realm. No longer at issue is the physical, literal distance between Rome and France that weighs so heavily on him in sonnet #8; the focus here is the unwillingness of France to answer his call. France is now both an object of desire and an object of praise, and the poet's call to his country creates the effect of a poetic "interiority" defined by longing. The slippage between two different versions of France turns Du Bellay into a poet who suffers for *both* nation and king. His plea for protection is, in the context of the figure of the "king as shepherd," a plea for patronage. Yet coming on the heels of the Petrarchan call to the "cruel" lady France, the desire for protection takes on the tonalities of a deep psychological expression of homesickness and bitterness. Through the rhetorical slippage that generates a "unified" image of France, a plea for patronage and poetic favor blends with nostalgia. No longer able to fight for France, like the heroes of romance, Du Bellay longs for it, and suffers for it in "honneste servitude" (sonnet #27, v. 9).[51] If sonnet #8 ends with an emblematic impasse, in which

< *Representing France at Mid-Century* >

outside and inside, landscape and psyche, stand in tension, the ninth sonnet enacts a transformation of ideological conflict into psychological affect. In order to resolve the tension between diverse "versions" of France, it produces an image of a poetic self defined by abjection.

It is Du Bellay's appropriation of Petrarchan clichés that provides the vocabulary through which the anguish of exile is articulated. Within the larger structure of the *Regrets*, that anguish is modulated through a complex manipulation of the form of the sonnet. As the collection presents Du Bellay's unhappiness in Rome, his desire to return to France, his repulsion at the excesses of the Roman court, and his later disillusionment at the French court, it features a variety of formal variations on the sonnet. And it is here, in the manipulation of the sonnet form (which now stands in for the more abstract notion of genre deployed in previous chapters), that the drama of Du Bellay's location of himself as French is played out.

In many of the poems of the *Regrets*, the language of exile is tightly bound up with the structure of the sonnet itself. The formal conventions of the sonnet work through a logic of outside and inside: the poet describes the "normal" world of nature or society and either contrasts himself with it, or compares himself to it in such a way as to suggest his uniqueness. This logic falls easily across the territory of the fourteen-line poem, which conveniently breaks into two semantic units, of eight and six lines. Thus, just as in a typical formulaic sonnet the Petrarchan lover praises his lady in the two quatrains of his sonnet ("your eyes are like suns"), and then turns to consider his woeful state in the two tercets ("but I am miserable"), so does Du Bellay, in, for example, the forty-third sonnet of the *Regrets*, speak of his long service to the king, before turning to a friend in the ninth line with, "Voilà ce que je suis. Et toutefois, Vineus ..." ["This is what I am. And yet, Vineus ..."] and then launching into a personal lament and concluding, with acerbic irony, that he takes consolation from the fact that he deserves better than he gets. The turn at the center of the poem thus sets up the familiar dialectical movement among incompatible elements—outside and inside, community and self, fortune and ambition, law and desire.[52]

Du Bellay's mastery of this structure, distilled through his manipulation of Petrarchan clichés of desire and longing, works to create the effect of a solitary lyric subject, at odds with the world around him. On one level, this literary persona is also a social type. For Petrarch, lyric desire was morally and theologically dangerous, with the

< *Representing France at Mid-Century* >

poetic persona's endless desire for Laura placing him at odds with "normal" society. Yet by the mid-sixteenth century, Petrarchan poetic identity has become a badge of aristocratic individuality. In the face of political centralization and a socially aggressive bourgeoisie, the suffering Petrarchan lover emblematizes, as Mary Thomas Crane has put it, "a privatized, individual self which was fully present and authoritative without humanist education, and which sought to preserve, in a private sphere, aspects of feudal ideology that were disappearing in society at large."[53] For Ronsard, this involves the endless play with social rank in the relationship of poet and lady which one sees in his various sonnet cycles. For Du Bellay, it may be seen most obviously in his insistence that poetry is the product of aristocratic leisure—and in his laments that such leisure has been given over to "service." The "And yet . . ." that opens the second half of Du Bellay's forty-third sonnet recalls dozens of depictions of Petrarchan lovers who have given up liberty for love, but recasts the scene as the drama of the aristocrat who has given up autonomy for royal service. However, that appropriation of Petrarchan language is only made possible by the severing seen earlier, in sonnet #8, of the conventional lyric relationship between subject and object, between the exiled lover and the "sainct rayon" of the lady's eyes. Distance from France permits Du Bellay to recast Petrarchan servitude and desire in political terms, as the characteristics of the aristocrat on diplomatic mission.

Yet no less important in the *Regrets*, and no less present, are those sonnets in which the division between octave and sestet is, as it were, muted. In these poems, the poet sets up a series of statements, only to turn, in a closing point, to make a bitter joke that reflects upon what has just been said. Thus, in sonnet #105, for example, he speaks for thirteen lines about one of the absurdities of the papal court, the fact that the Pope's boyfriend has been raised to a cardinalship, before concluding sarcastically that such "miracles" only happen in Rome. Even more revealing in this regard is sonnet #79, which consists of a thirteen-line list of things the poet doesn't write about. Each line is divided easily in two, beginning with the anaphora "Je n'escris point . . ." and concluding with an explanation of why the poet doesn't write on a certain topic. Thus, "Je n'escris point d'amour, n'estant point amoureux,/Je n'escris de beauté, n'ayant belle maistresse" ["I don't write about love, not being in love/I don't write about beauty, having no beautiful mistress"], and so on. The poem projects onto the level of the single line the tension between inside and outside which the

< *Representing France at Mid-Century* >

traditional sonnet form often deploys through the split between octave and sestet. Each item in the list offers a justification for the poem we are reading by providing concrete details about the poet's situation ("I have no mistress, I'm far from my Prince, I have no money," etc.) The final line, however, overturns this "fact-based" description with a condemnation of the ignorance of the members of the papal court: "Je n'escris de sçavoir, entre les gens d'eglise" ["I don't write in a learned way, being among Church people"].

The poem is like a machine for producing satire. The pattern set up by the first thirteen lines prepares the way for a "factual statement" in the last hemistich of the poem, which would describe the poet's failure to write by virtue of a logic of opposition: I don't write about X because there is no X here. However, the final evocation of the poet's companions, "Church people," when contrasted to the assertion that "I don't write about learning," establishes a tacit identification of the papal court with ignorance. What appears to be a simple factual description is in fact a powerful moral condemnation of the corruption and ignorance of the Papal See. That condemnation brings with it, moreover, an assertion of the poet's own authority and superiority to those around him, despite the fact that he is consistently described through negation.[54]

These satirical poems, of which there are dozens in the *Regrets*, tend to function formally like epigrams. Instead of deploying the octave/sestet logic of the traditional Petrarchan love sonnet, they divide semantically into units of 12 + 2, or 13 + 1. And this epigrammatic voice presents a model for inscribing the poetic subject in the form of the sonnet that differs from what was seen above in the discussion of the Petrarchan lyric. Whereas the Petrarchan lyric subject is in a position of lack, of misery and abjection, the subject of the epigrammatic sonnet is in a position of power—even when, as in the sonnet just discussed, he expressly chooses *not* to deal with a certain subject. The deployment of the sonnet as "epigram," with its characteristic satirical *pointe*, produces a cagey lyric subject, who, like a card sharp, conceals his power even as he sings of his misery (no money, no lady, no prince), only to spring it on the reader at the last minute. The form of the poem itself sets in motion a kind of textual power, through which the subject judges or demystifies court society.

It is difficult to say where Du Bellay picked up this gesture of distorting the sonnet form away from its Petrarchan incarnations. A hunt for sources would engage one in the same type of commuting

< *Representing France at Mid-Century* >

between France and Italy that Du Bellay's poetry thematizes. To be sure, there had been in France for a number of years a vogue of the epigram, since Marot's translations of Martial's *Epigrams* and the lyrics of Mellin de Saint-Gelais. However, Du Bellay could just as easily have been influenced by Francesco Berni, or by the tradition of the Roman pasquinade, with its satirical deployment of the sonnet form to mock figures of authority. The exact provenance of this technique is not the point here. What is important is that it signals a breakdown in the hegemony of the Petrarchan love sonnet. This formal flexibility, in turn, permits Du Bellay to inscribe himself into the sonnet in a variety of postures. The emergence of social satire in the sonnet involves pressing the oppositional logic of Petrarchan lyric to its extreme, and turning it to social ends, as part of a satire against power and pretense. Moreover, it projects that oppositional logic into the context of collective social experience. The "me versus the world" rhetoric of the solitary amorous sufferer becomes an "us versus them" language of satire and parody: a lyric form which had become identified in early sixteenth-century French cultural life with a particular form of aristocratic inwardness and solitary suffering assumes, in the tradition of the pasquinade or the epigram, a popular voice.[55]

For his part, Du Bellay appropriates the lyric logic of the satirical sonnet for a discourse that is based, not in class antagonism ("low" culture versus "high" culture), but in national difference (France versus Italy). And whereas the Petrarchan moments in the collection paint him as a solitary aristocrat, the satirical or epigrammatic voice relies for its power precisely upon the presence of a community. For satire requires the acknowledgment of a group of shared values, which the object of satire is corrupting. In order for Du Bellay to satirize the Roman court, his French readers must share in the values that the papacy is perverting. They must share the same cultural space as the Romans, so that they can see how corrupt they are. In this sense, then, the satirical postures of the *Regrets* reveal Du Bellay to be no stranger at all in Rome. He and his readers know Rome all too well because, like Gargantua and Picrochole, they are all Christians and Rome is their spiritual home. Thus one can say that by blending two postures of the *Regrets*—Petrarchan solitary and outraged satirist—Du Bellay locates himself at the juncture of two communities. His satire of Rome is a satire for Christian subjects, who "know" what the papacy is supposed to represent. Yet by blending satire of an ecclesiastical community with a longing for France, he

< Representing France at Mid-Century >

propels his moral outrage and authority into the imaginative space of "Frenchness." If writers such as Estienne and Aneau had expressed French anxiety toward Italy by trying to locate spots on the French map that would be free of "contagion," Du Bellay's authority to speak as a Frenchman emerges from the complex positioning of his lyric persona in language, at the juncture of Petrarchan sonnet and satirical epigram.

It is important to underscore that the various voices and lyric forms I have been describing are dialectically related. For it is precisely the satirical impulse of the collection that redeems the abject aristocrat, who longs for France as Petrarch longs for Laura. The satirical sonnets lend the nostalgic sonnets their moral power. They turn the solitary poet into a subject whose concerns are communal and ethical, instead of merely personal and neurotic. At the same time, however, the nostalgic voice, with its longing for a France that cannot hear his call, lends urgency and relevance to the satirical impulse of the collection. In the process, it shifts the terms by which communal identity is articulated. It turns a satire of the *spiritual* home of the Catholic into a longing for the *nation*. The moral alternative to the ruin of Christendom becomes an idealized vision of France.[56] In other words, if the poet is not abject and desperate for France, his observations about the corruption of the Roman court are mere curiosities. Conversely, if his homesickness is not connected to a larger social vision, it remains private misery. Petrarchan desire authorizes satire as moral philosophy; satire transmutes Petrarchan individualism into patriotism. It may be no accident, in this context, that sonnet #123, which evokes the treaty of Vaucelles (signed by Henry II and Charles V in 1556) and begins the transition to the cycle of return to France, is one of the few moments in the collection in which Du Bellay uses the first person plural pronoun "nous" to refer to the French. Collective identity is thematized when personal and collective destiny are shared, at the moment of transition from one location to another.

The Language of Flowers

In the dedicatory poem to the ambassador d'Avanson that opens the *Regrets*, Du Bellay figures the authority and role of the diplomat in terms of garments, of covering the body. He notes that d'Avanson is famous for the honor he has shown toward "the long robe" of the intellectual, toward "counsel and writing" (v. 96). For this reason, Du

< *Representing France at Mid-Century* >

Bellay goes on, the king has chosen to place on d'Avanson's back his own grandeur, which is now to be worn abroad ("Sur vostre doz deschargea sa grandeur,/Pour la porter en estrange province" [v.99–100]). The ambassador dons responsibility like a piece of clothing. The figure of the robe offers a kind of metonymic extension of the king's talismanic body, a rhetorical device for describing the invisible power invested in the diplomat. Du Bellay turns this figure against itself when he applies the same image of the garment to his own situation. In following the Muse, he says, he has taken poverty "upon his back" ("sur mon doz" [v.42]). D'Avanson dresses in power; Du Bellay dresses in powerlessness.

The description of political or poetic agency through the image of the garment links the issue of the poet's position in a given community to yet another of the major preoccupations of the *Regrets*. This is the concern for ornament—be it corporeal or linguistic. In sonnet #38 Du Bellay declares: "O qu'heureux est celuy qui peult passer son aage,/Entre pareils à soy! et qui sans fiction,/Sans crainte, sans envie, et sans ambition/Regne paisiblement en son pauvre mesnage" ["O happy is he who can spend his life,/Among those like himself! and who without fiction,/Without fear, without envy, and without ambition/Reigns peacefully in his poor household"]. To live with one's fellows is to live without "fiction." This assertion, of course, expresses a cliché that is both anti-aulic and anti-Italian, as both the court and Italy are seen to be sites of "feigning" and "disguise." Indeed, the very next sonnet complains that "Je n'ayme la feintise, et me fault deguiser" ["I hate feigning, and yet have to disguise myself"]. However the praise of a life "without fiction" is no less connected to the terms of writing itself, as Du Bellay repeatedly describes the poetry of the *Regrets* as "simple," and "without artifice." The association of social homogeneity, of living "among those like oneself" (which recalls the association of friendship, charity, and similitude in Erasmus, seen in chapter 2), raises the issue of how "simplicity" (be it poetic or psychological) relates to the experience of alterity which informs Du Bellay's sense of himself in Rome.

Du Bellay opens the *Regrets* by saying, in the very first sonnet, that, while others may write about nature or the cosmos, he will write only of what he sees before him. In other words, the type of poetry he will write, satirical poetry, is determined by the *place* itself, by the contingencies of Italian life: "suivant *de ce lieu* les accidents divers,/Soit de bien, soit de mal, j'escris à l'adventure" ["following the diverse acci-

< *Representing France at Mid-Century* >

dents *of this place*/For better or worse, I write willy-nilly"] (emphasis mine). Location determines subject matter. The accidents of Roman life affect the poet, who shifts quickly from happiness to melancholy. This mutability determines the nature of the poetry to be written—a poetry without artifice: "Je me plains à mes vers, si j'ay quelque regret,/Je me ris avec eulx, je leur dy mon secret,/Comme estans de mon coeur les plus seurs secretaires./Aussi ne veulx-je tant les peigner et friser,/Et de plus braves noms ne les veulx desguiser,/Que de papiers journaulx, ou bien de commentaires" ["I complain to my verses if I have a regret/I laugh with them, I tell them my secret,/As they are the surest secretaries of my heart./Thus I don't want to comb or curl them so much/And don't want to disguise them with braver names/Than that of journal or commentary"].

The trope of simplicity, initially applied to the poet's response to the occasion and the place of writing, is, however, soon applied to the poet himself. In contrast to the affected and artificial Roman courtiers among whom he spends his days, Du Bellay describes himself as a simple man who writes simple verse. In a poem to his friend Vineus, he asks for sympathy for his pain, "en ces vers sans artifice peinte,/Comme sans artifice est ma simplicité" (sonnet #47) ["in these verses painted without artifice,/Just as my simplicity is without artifice"]. The parallel lends authority to the rhetoric of the collection, linking the man to his poems and producing the impression of Du Bellay as a "sincere poet." Yet this impression is, at the very least, inexact. For the entire point of the "simple style," he has told us, is that it is flexible and can be easily changed, "according to the accidents of this place." And changeable it is. The uniqueness of the *Regrets* among sixteenth-century French poetic collections may be traced to the remarkable variety of tone and subject matter they explore. By contrast, Du Bellay's psychological or moral "simplicity" implies a kind of constancy, a refusal to change in the face of the capriciousness of courtly fashion. In other words, what seems to be a parallel at the level of poetic vocabulary, is in fact a conceptual chiasmus. The notion of "simplicity" holds within itself both moral constancy and rhetorical inconstancy. This paradox permits the poetic self to resist the type of psychic fragmentation that might seem initially to accompany a poetry written "according to the accidents of this place" and makes it possible for some type of unity or self-identity to emerge out of multiplicity.

I have shown in my readings of Rabelais and Marguerite de

< *Representing France at Mid-Century* >

Navarre that the experience of alterity, the encounter with an alien culture or nation, leads to a kind of breakdown of figuration, to moments at which the vocabulary shared by a given community reaches its limits. At the borderline between cultures, states, and classes, one comes across phantasmic objects or actions—Panurge's bacon, Frère Jean's frock, Alpharbal's gratitude, Amadour's heroism—that seem both to defy the logic of representation and function as mediations between communities and genres. Du Bellay's "simplicity" seems to serve a similar function. For even as the association of poetic simplicity and psychological or moral simplicity is imperfect, and seems to be an effect of the poet's own enunciation, it is also the link that binds his experience in Italy to his identity as a Frenchman, his satirical voice to his Petrarchan longing. Indeed, there is ideological content to Du Bellay's simplicity. His depiction of himself as a "simple" man activates a long-held cliché of French national definition which sees the French (through a pun on the adjective "français") as "frank," "honest," "straightforward." The overlapping of these two conflicting impulses in the trope of "simplicity" authorizes Du Bellay as the embodiment of "Frenchness." His recoiling from the experience of alterity in Italy produces a poetry posited on "simplicity" and lack of artifice. At the same time the deployment of the cliché of the French as "simple" lends his poetic simplicity positive content, making it the demonstration *in language* of national character. In other words, the parallel set up between "simple man" and "simple poem" yokes together two distinct forms of experience, both of which are necessary for the creation of "French" character. The complexity of this construction may be seen in the fact that it is impossible to determine which form of simplicity comes first. Neither seems to be able to stand alone as the origin of the other. If the simplicity of the poetry is the product of the simple man, arising somehow from his deepest self, why does Du Bellay claim that this set of poetry (in contrast to all of his other collections) is determined by the place ("suivant de ce lieu les accidents divers") in which it is written? Conversely, if one presumes that the image of the simple Du Bellay is itself the product of the simple verse which he composes, this would mean, preposterously, that the text precedes the man, that Du Bellay's moral simplicity is the mere shadow of his own verse. However one understands the causality of this relationship, it is clear that Du Bellay's French simplicity works to graft poetic authority onto national character. The poetic persona of the *Regrets* cannot be French unless that Frenchness is inscribed

< *Representing France at Mid-Century* >

into the very language of his text. And, most amazingly, that language takes its character from the place that is Rome.

The delicate link between simplicity and Frenchness set up in the Roman sonnets is thrown into crisis upon Du Bellay's return to France. The last sections of the *Regrets* trace Du Bellay's geographical trajectory from Rome to Paris. Sonnets #133 through 138 evoke moments on Du Bellay's journey homeward. Then, in sonnet #139, he begins his depiction of the French court, and of his disappointments there:

> Si tu veuls vivre en court (Dilliers) souvienne-toy,
> De t'accoster tousjours des mignons de ton maistre,
> Si tu n'es favori, faire semblant de l'estre,
> Et de t'accomoder aux passetemps du Roy.
>
> Souvienne-toy encor' de ne prester ta foy
> Au parler d'un chacun, mais sur tout sois adextre
> A t'aider de la gauche autant que de la dextre,
> Et par les moeurs d'autruy à tes moeurs donne loy.
>
> N'avance rien du tien (Dilliers) que ton service,
> Ne monstre que tu sois trop ennemy du vice,
> Et sois souvent encor' muet, aveugle, et sourd.
>
> Ne fay que pour autruy importun on te nomme.
> Faisant ce que je dy, tu seras galland homme:
> T'en souvienne (Dilliers) si tu veuls vivre en court.
>
> [If you want to live at court (Dilliers) remember,
> Always to frequent the favorites of your master,
> If you're not a favorite, pretend to be,
> And to conform to the pastimes of the King.
>
> And always remember never to believe
> The talk of just anyone, but, especially, be adroit
> At finding help on both the left hand and the right,
> And let the habits of others regulate your own.
>
> Never give anything of yourself (Dilliers) but your service,
> Or show that you are too much the enemy of vice,
> And be often mute, blind, and deaf.
>
> Never let yourself be called importunate on the part of others.
> Doing these things, you will be a gallant man:
> Remember (Dilliers) if you want to live at court.]

< *Representing France at Mid-Century* >

This poem takes the form of a piece of advice to a friend, and opens a sequence of "counsel poems," in which the poet laments the corruption of the French court by explaining to others how to survive in it. It unfolds through a series of stanzas, each of which is opened by an admonition: "souvienne-toy," "souvienne-toy encor'," "n'avance rien du tien," and "ne fay que pour autruy." Yet this sequential logic, which unrolls easily across the four stanzas of the sonnet, is upset by another formal convention upon which the poem draws. This is the tradition of the rondeau, which is evoked by the repetition of the first hemistich, "Si tu veuls vivre en court," in the last hemistich. This formal nod toward the rondeau is no accident. The rondeau is the most occasional of lyric forms, perfectly adapted to the exchanges of wit characteristic of court life. In the *Deffence*, it is one of the native French poetic forms that Du Bellay explicitly rejects, as he militates for a set of new forms such as the sonnet and the ode, which would lend French poetry classical dignity and permanence. It might also be seen to connote the presence of Marot, one of the two or three most accomplished practitioners of this form and the representative of a French tradition which the Pléiade's cultural project is seeking to displace. Indeed, when one recalls that the form of the rondeau turns in a kind of circle and is said to "come home" or "rentrer" when the last line emerges to echo the first, one might even hazard that the poem ironically dramatizes, in its very form, Du Bellay's own experience of "coming home" to France.

The use of the rondeau form sets up a tension between the expository logic of "advice literature," and the ironic wit of satire. Yet here that satire turns back against Du Bellay's own voice. I noted earlier that many of Du Bellay's "epigrammatic" or satirical sonnets feature a moment at which the poet claims a kind of implicit authority, as he demystifies the pretentions of the court. Here, the repetition of the first line at the end of the poem ironically points back to the opening, and to the admonition, in stanza two, not to pay attention to "just anyone"—a warning that raises questions about the authority of the very poem we are reading. Moreover, the poem makes no pretensions to power over the situation it describes. When Du Bellay returns to Paris, his satire loses its authority either to render its object ridiculous, or to change it. For though Du Bellay is here mocking the pretentions of the French court, the poem does not assume that it has rendered the court unattractive. The very repetition of the final line suggests that, despite everything, Dilliers may still want to live at that court.

< *Representing France at Mid-Century* >

This "rondeau" to Dilliers suggests both a crisis of selfhood, and a questioning of the power of the sonnet form to satirize courtly fashion. In the Roman sonnets, Du Bellay enjoyed a distance from convention through his imaginary identity as an Other, a stranger. Here, that distance is eclipsed, as the poem quite literally recommends the effacement of autonomy. Du Bellay advises Dilliers to define himself according to the words and deeds of others—a theme that will become central through the sections of the *Regrets* that depict the French court. One should "faire semblant" to be a favorite, we are told, and take on the mores of others. In this context, all that remains of the self is the economic token of "service"—the same term that Du Bellay used repeatedly to justify his expatriation in Rome—though now expressly distanced from the self that offers it. Economic logic takes over the body itself, and the courtier is advised to remain "mute, blind, and deaf" as a way of increasing his value.

This undermining of the authority of both form and persona suggests Du Bellay's difficulty, upon returning to France, in finding a location or position from which to speak. When he went to Italy, Du Bellay tells us in the early sonnets, he left a cultural economy in which he was successful, protected, and read. In response to the loss of that world, he constructs a complex posture of exclusion and inclusion, of longing and bitterness, which locates him geographically outside of France and morally outside of Italy. On the space created by that dynamic of exclusion, he imposes a lyric subjectivity that is simultaneously superior to the Italians and longing for France, that simultaneously rejects the Other and imagines a community to which the poet can belong. Upon return to France, however, this posture is thrown off balance. Court life requires an effacement of the negativity through which Du Bellay defined himself while in Italy. Mimesis, imitation of courtly fashion, replaces alterity.

The difficulty of finding a place from which to speak is thematized in a sonnet #154, to Baïf, one of a series of poems to different friends that opens the section located in the French court. Here Du Bellay echoes his earlier claim, made in sonnet #32, that he had "exchanged" France for Italy, by ironically counselling Baïf to "exchange" Parnassus for Paris: "Su tu m'en crois (Baïf) tu changeras Parnasse/Au palais de Paris" ["If you believe me (Baïf) you'll exchange Parnassus/For the Palace of Paris"]. He links the theme of geographical displacement to the theme of economics by ironically encouraging his friend to give up poetry for things of profit. The economic vocabulary of the Ro-

< Representing France at Mid-Century >

man sonnets returns, as the Muses are called "chattering Sisters . . . with only green laurels for a treasure" ["ces babillardes Soeurs . . . /Qui pour tout leur tresor n'ont que des lauriers verds"]. However, what is striking here is that the opposition which structured the earlier sections of the collection—the opposition between Rome and France—has now turned into an opposition between geography and myth, between a real space (the space of the court) and a metaphor for poetic inspiration (Parnassus). Here, as in sonnet #9, figure displaces geography.

The ironic advice Du Bellay gives Baïf is a temporary rhetorical solution to a much larger problem involving the poet's position in court society. This is the problem the poet addresses in the final poems in the collection, in his praise of Marguerite de Valois, the sister of the king. These final sonnets stand in symmetrical relation with the opening sonnets, echoing and redeeming the expressions of fragility and impotence that mark them. The poet's claim in sonnet #3 that he has lost the "ardeur" that once inspired him is now recalled in sonnet #180, where he points out to his friend Jodelle that he feels no "divine ardeur" when writing about any topic except Marguerite. In contrast to the "trafiqueurs d'honneurs" (sonnet #183) (which recall his own earlier anxiety about being a "trafiqueur de louanges," or "trafficker in praise"), he notes that he is happy to pronounce only the name of Marguerite. It is she alone who gives him language: "[le subject] . . . produit naïvement en moy/Ce que par art contraint les autres y font naistre" ["(the topic) . . . produces naturally in me/That which others give birth to through the constraints of art"] (sonnet #180). The talismanic power of the object produces a superfluity that annuls the economy of lack expressed throughout the preceding 180 or so sonnets: "en loüant (Gournay) si loüable subject,/Le loz que je m'acquiers, m'est trop grand' recompense" (sonnet #182) ["in praising (Gournay) such a praiseworthy subject,/The praise that I receive, is too great a recompense"]. Proximity to the object of praise reinstates the old epideictic code, which exile in Rome had threatened.

Readers of Du Bellay have often been bothered by the unabashed flattery of the final sonnets, which seem to contradict Du Bellay's "sincerity" and hatred of artifice. However, as Oscar Wilde reminds us, only bad poetry is always sincere. Indeed, the turn to Marguerite is less a psychological gesture than a rhetorical solution to a series of problems that have plagued the poet's search for a new articulation of poetic value.[57] The frustration with Italy had been expressed as a distaste for ornament and disguise, as a hatred of the courtier who sports his "masque d'hypocrite" and his "beau semblant" (sonnet #73). As sonnet #128, the final sonnet in the section of the book dedicated to the Italian experience, puts it, "Icy de mille fards la trahison se desguise" ["Here treason disguises itself in a thousand ways"]. Du Bellay's bewilderment at the French court stems from the fact that it is no less a place of ostentation than was Rome. He links sumptuary excess to linguistic excess in sonnets #182 and #183, when he attacks those who manipulate rhetorical tropes by "exchanging" the "colors of rhetoric" and the "flowers of rhetoric" one for another to disguise reality and produce a kind of surplus value of praise: "Je ne suis pas de ceulx qui robent la louange . . . /changeant la noire à la blanche couleur" ["I'm not one of those who dress up praise . . . /exchanging black for white"] (sonnet #182); "Qui pourroit . . . se contenir de rire/Voyant un corbeau peint de diverses couleurs,/Un pourceau couronné de roses et de fleurs" ["Who could keep from laughing/Seeing a crow painted in many colors/A pig crowned with roses and flowers"] (sonnet #183). These evocations of the time-honored images to describe rhetorical tropes (colors, flowers) are set in contrast to the personage of Marguerite, who grounds rhetoric and lends language authenticity. For Marguerite is, of course, herself a pearl and a flower, "ceste belle fleur" (sonnet #185), "de notre siecle et la perle, et la fleur" (sonnet #180) ["this beautiful flower"; "the pearl and flower of our century"]. Whereas other poets deploy the flowers of rhetoric to praise nothing, Du Bellay deploys the flowers of rhetoric to praise a flower. Marguerite, in other words, is both the ornament and the thing, both the trope and the object of praise. Du Bellay has no need of rhetorical ornamentation. As he says, echoing his earlier description of himself as a simple Frenchman, "Je ne veulx deguiser ma simple poësie/Sous le masque emprunté d'une fable moisie" (sonnet #188) ["I don't want to disguise my simple poetry/Beneath the borrowed mask of a moldy fable"]. Because Marguerite embodies both sign and referent, by speaking about her, Du Bellay claims to transcend the split between empty ornament and "the thing itself."

Within the structure of the *Regrets*, praise of Marguerite de Valois recalls the nostalgic evocation of the French court in sonnet #7, where she is depicted as having praised Du Bellay beyond his merit. The recall of one moment by the other, of one flower by the other, suggests that nothing has changed between the initial experience of

< *Representing France at Mid-Century* >

success at court and the return from Rome. However, whereas the earlier poem had evoked the court as a theater of praise, now the question of where the poet is to locate himself remains, as in the poem to Baïf cited above, a problem. Marguerite is depicted as Du Bellay's mediator, and the love of virtue is his guide, his "new swan," a "cygne nouveau" (sonnet #189)—or, perhaps, one might say, a "signe nouveau"—that leads him towards the "grand espace vide" (sonnet #189) of the heavens. Whereas earlier poems had suggested the pressure placed on writing by geographical distance from France, and then by the proximity of the French court, now Du Bellay seems to aspire to a place beyond Italy, beyond France, possibly beyond language itself. However it is unclear what this means, precisely, for a poet who is as concerned as Du Bellay is with his location. It may only be accidental that the "grand espace vide" ["great empty space"] aspired to in the last poems echoes the "grand espace de l'air" ["great space of air"] which, in our opening citation from the *Deffence*, Du Bellay had seen as the sad destination of those who fail to find a secure place from which to write. Certainly, such a place seems to elude him on his return to France, despite his evocation of the unique flower Marguerite. It remains, perhaps, an open question whether the final sonnets signal transcendance or mere evaporation.[58]

Ronsard, Epic, and the Economics of Culture

I have argued that Du Bellay's invention of French nationhood in the *Regrets* is linked both to his paradoxical positioning of himself as a liminal figure, between France and Italy, and to his manipulation of the resources of the lyric collection. Du Bellay's contemporaries, writers such as Aneau and Estienne, confront the "Italian question" by linking language to land. Du Bellay, by contrast, understands poetry and national identity in terms of an imagery of investment, of "enriching" France by importing cultural goods from abroad. The *Regrets* offer his meditation on a set of poetic investments gone bad. The collection traces a series of moments in which a crisis of social identity (the petty aristocrat forced to seek his fortune abroad) is figured as a crisis of poetic authority. In response to the abjection of exile, the poet strikes a variety of poses that draw for authority on his status as Frenchman. In the face of alterity, various forms of "Frenchness" emerge, which have subsequently become clichés of the discourse of French nationalism. In other words, a crisis of *social* identity provides the occasion for the construction of a *national* character. Yet that

< *Representing France at Mid-Century* >

character, as the final sonnets suggest, remains curiously rootless, despite its famous nostalgic evocations of Anjou and the French countryside. Indeed, the subsequent success of Du Bellay's achievement
may stem from the fact that his poetic persona never finds its proper
place after the return from Rome, that his "simplicity" remains linguistic and moral, and thus available to all subsequent readers. When
he constructs a "national" poetic persona out of a set of disparate responses to the otherness of Rome, Du Bellay imagines, not a France
made up of aristocrats, as had Marguerite de Navarre, but an aristocracy of Frenchmen.[59]

Du Bellay invents a poetic persona caught between the nostalgia
for a France which he cannot own, and the artifices of a courtly world
in which he cannot be at rest. In this regard he embodies a set of paradoxes faced by a whole host of European lyric poets working in the
shadow of the great court cultures that arise in the late Renaissance.
And in this context it is worth considering, if only briefly, the contrast between Du Bellay's invention of France and the much more
ambitious projects of his friend Ronsard. For one of the ironies of the
relationship between these two poets is that, whereas Du Bellay has
been picked up by subsequent cultural history as the embodiment of
a certain notion of Frenchness, and as the figure of the nostalgic
Frenchman, it was Ronsard who made the literary construction of
French identity his life's work, principally through the writing of his
unfinished epic, the *Franciade*, which aimed to define French nationhood once and for all in the way that Virgil's *Aeneid* had supposedly
done for Rome. Yet whereas Du Bellay's representation of French
identity is constructed precisely out of the experience of alterity, and
through the blending of diverse generic registers and formal structures, Ronsard's work never confronts the alterity of the non-French
with the directness seen in the other writers addressed in this book.
Nor does Ronserd experiment with the kind of generic variegation
seen elsewhere. Ronsard does not invent new genres; he resuscitates
old ones.

It is, of course, the argument of this book that these two facts are
not unrelated, that the generic promiscuity that shapes such writers
as Rabelais, Marguerite, and Du Bellay is precisely related to their attempt to represent the alterity of the non-French. For Ronsard, by
contrast, the courtly circle which Du Bellay both desires and deplores
in the *Regrets* shapes and mediates his rare attempts to represent national diversity. This may be seen most clearly in the second of the

< *Representing France at Mid-Century* >

four books he completed for the *Franciade*. There we see the hero, Francus, heir to the blood and virtue of defeated Troy, wash up on the shores of Crete. He is met by Dicée, the king of the Cretans, who greets him and his men with the same language we have seen uttered throughout this book at the moment of the encounter with alterity:

> "Where are you from (he said), from what place,
> What are your names, and what is your race?
> What fortune, or what faithless sea
> Has betrayed you? Guests answer me.
> For to look at you (though you are filled with misery)
> You are not bad, nor the sons of bad fathers
>
> [D'où estes-vous (dit-il) de quelle place,
> Quels sont vos noms, et quelle est vostre race?
> Quelle fortune, ou quelle mer sans foy
> Vous a trahis? hostes respondez moy.
> Car à vous voir (bien que pleins de misères)
> N'estes mauvais, ny fils de mauvais pères"].[60]

Whereas Pantagruel's first encounter with Panurge, discussed at the outset of my second chapter, was filled with a kind of wonder and confusion at the presence of a figure both miserable and noble, here that tension (possibly suggested by the term "hostes," which could mean either "guest" or "enemy") is immediately deflated in Dicée's somewhat flat acknowledgement that the strangers don't look "bad," or like the sons of "bad fathers." If this sounds more like the language of domestic comedy than heroic epic, it may be because Dicée has already been warned in a dream that a new son-in-law is on his way to Crete. Indeed, the very next book of the poem descends into a kind of family intrigue, as Dicée's two daughters compete for the hand of the handsome stranger through a variety of enchantments, love letters, and deceptions. For Ronsard, the foreigner is already a neighbor, as national poetry becomes courtly intrigue. The alterity of the stranger is neutralized from the outset by the poem's context and ideology, which never leave the world of the court. In this regard, the *Franciade* already points toward such later national narratives as d'Urfé's *Astrée*, the early seventeenth-century pastoral romance in which strangers come and go, enter and leave, without ever threatening the integrity of the fictional world. As d'Urfé locates his text in the closed world of the fictional Gauls and his familial domain of

< *Representing France at Mid-Century* >

Forez, so Ronsard's Francus is insulated from the non-French by the poet's investment in the world of the Valois court.

At one level, Ronsard's epic failure may be linked to the fact that political conditions in late sixteenth-century France were unfavorable for the production of national epic. Du Bellay considers the Italians as a cultural and moral Other, not as a political rival. Yet epic is always about politics. The epic projects of such contemporaries as Spenser, Camoëns, Ercilla, and even Tasso rely upon a rhetoric of conquest, of an aggressivity toward an Other who could be subsumed into a newly imagined community—whether national or religious. In France, however, the difficulty in defining such a community placed in question the very possibility of epic. The emerging political crisis of the wars of religion made all but impossible the imagination of a national community that could be unified within a single narrative. Thus Ronsard's epic can only be the epic of the French crown. Yet it cannot be merely the epic of the French crown, since the powerful centralization of French political culture under Francis I had already rendered too limiting the type of dynastic, local epic one finds in Ariosto and Tasso. And an epic of national conquest on the model of the *Aeneid* would inevitably evoke comparisons with struggles between Catholics and Protestants, and turn, against itself, into a religious epic of the type seen much later, at the turn of the century, in d'Aubigné's *Les Tragiques*. In other words, the political topography of France during the period between Francis I and Henry IV provides no more of a place for the epic imagination than it does for Du Bellay's restless poetic persona.

Yet Ronsard's failure to engage the experience of alterity in the *Franciade* may also be linked to the fact that, by the later years of the century, alterity and community are already beginning to define themselves in terms that would take the problem of nationhood far beyond the scope of courtly intrigue. Thus, in a posthumously published preface to the *Franciade*, Ronsard offers a meditation on the relationship between literary language and political community that recalls the texts by Du Bellay, Aneau, and Estienne with which I began this chapter. He notes that French is spoken in many different forms in many different regions and asserts that the poet should take advantage of all of them. At the same time, he acknowledges that one form of French enjoys special status. This is the language of the court, or what he calls "le Courtisan." Courtly language is the most beautiful of all, he says, since it takes its beauty from the beauty of the prince himself. Yet it cannot stand alone:

< *Representing France at Mid-Century* >

it cannot be perfect without the help of the others: for each garden has its own flower and all nations have dealings with each other: as, in our harbors and ports, merchandise sought from so far away in America is hawked everywhere . . . All provinces, however barren, support the more fertile ones, just as the smallest members of the body support the more noble ones.[61]

To describe the power of new vernaculars, Ronsard evokes the traditional image of France as a garden. Yet the passage just cited uses the garden image twice, in slightly different ways. Ronsard's claim that every nation has its own flower implies equality among nations or provinces, a kind of feudal model in which principalities coexist in loose confederation. By contrast, the second image presents a clear hierarchy, in which weaker regions support stronger ones. The political struggles of late sixteenth-century France over the relationship between center and periphery, between centralized power and regional autonomy, are figured in these two images. The traditional image of France as garden seems on the edge of disintegration.

In contrast to this figural multivalence, Ronsard deploys a somewhat different vocabulary to describe the contacts between nations. It is mercantilism, evoked through the image of goods from the New World, that here seems to unify states. New World imports ("hawked everywhere" ["qui se debite par tout"]) symbolize contacts among nations. They also produce language: Ronsard's verb "se debiter" means both to sell and to deliver a discourse. Then, as now, American goods are hawked all over France, and France is already caught up in a series of encounters with alterity that redraw the terms of nationhood. American imports are both other and everywhere. They both make legible the edges of France and hold it together in a way that a common language cannot yet do. This mercantilist imagery, of course, places us in the context of New World exploration, and the encounter with the Other that is America. A consideration of the impact of this new type of otherness on French identity and French writing will be the focus of the last chapter of this book.

Chapter Six

History, Alterity, and the European Subject
in Montaigne's Essais

Three degrees of latitude disrupt an entire system of justice.
What is truth on this side of the Pyrenees
is error beyond them.
—PASCAL, *Pensées*

In the previous chapter, I argued that Du Bellay's definition of the re-lationship between his lyric poetry and his French identity involves a complex game of approximation and removal, as the poet is both in-side and outside of France. This is a game that involves both texts and countries, depending on both the manipulation of the form of the sonnet and the location of the poet in relationship to the French court. By the later years of the sixteenth century, however, the clear antinomies that Du Bellay manipulates—court and province, Italy and France, disguise and sincerity—had themselves undergone a metamorphosis. The chaos brought on by the wars between Protes-tant and Catholic in the years following the death of Henry II broke France into a group of zones crisscrossed by marauding private armies. Political and social structures were thrown into upheaval. As the Protestant soldier and moralist François de La Noue noted in 1584, "half of the nobility has been killed, along with legions of sol-diers, the population is reduced everywhere, the finances of the state are drained and debts multiply, military discipline has been over-thrown, piety is in retreat, individual behavior is out of control, jus-tice is corrupt, men are divided, and everything is for sale."[1] His co-religionist, the poet Agrippa d'Aubigné, broadens the vision of chaos to include the very topography of the nation, as he claims that every city is now a fortified border town: "The only places of repose are abroad,/And the cities in the center of the country are frontier cities."[2] Center and periphery have been reversed. No place is safe.

In such a context, where the very space of the country has been turned inside out, how can community be imagined and represented? From where is the writer to derive his authority? And how might lit-

< *History, Alterity, and the European Subject* >

erary discourse participate in the process of defining the relationship of self and collectivity? These are the topics that will guide my reading of Montaigne's *Essais* (1580–1595). I will argue that Montaigne's definition of himself and his literary project involves precisely the type of encounter with alterity that I have explored in the preceding chapters of this book. However, for Montaigne, the alterity that places pressure on literary representation is heavily mediated. It is the alterity of the New World, which Montaigne knows only second-hand, through his reading. Montaigne uses the problem of representing New World alterity as a kind of mirror against which to define and structure his own status as a subject who is at once French and European. In the process, he marks out the terms of the literary genre that he bequeaths to modernity—the personal essay.

Montaigne rarely reflects on the question of the edges of France, and seems to have little interest in imagery of frontiers and border transgressions. Instead, his depictions of France involve the traditional discourse of the humors, which posits an essential link between nations, climates, and individuals. In this tradition, the Spanish are choleric because of their hot climate, and the Germans are phlegmatic because of their cold one. The French, as is often pointed out by French writers, are perfectly balanced, because of the temperate climate of France. Of course, these are very old notions, predating the Greek medical thought of Galen. But in the late sixteenth century, perhaps under the pressure of the emergence of new unified states, there came a new reflection on how nations differed from each other, and the "physiology" of peoples achieved new currency. Jean Bodin's *Method for the Easy Comprehension of History* (1566) and Huarte de San Juan's vastly popular *Examination of Spirits* (*Examen de ingenios*) (1575) had used it in central ways to describe the variety of nations and peoples. Montaigne evokes it at a number of points in the *Essais*. It informs his general vision of France as a living organism, rather than as a space circumscribed by borders. He uses this imagery to lend a social and political connotation to his own reflections on illness, corporeity, and decay.

The Frames of Reading

The link between body and body politic is stressed at the beginning of the twenty-third chapter of the second book of the *Essais*, the short text entitled "Of Evil Means Employed to a Good End" ["Des mauvais moyens employez à bonne fin"]. Nature, says Montaigne in

< *History, Alterity, and the European Subject* >

the opening passages of that essay, has marvelously established the link between history and biography, between the lives and health of states and the lives and health of persons: "kingdoms and republics are born, flourish, and wither with age, as we do" (516a) ["les royaumes, les republiques naissent, fleurissent et fanissent de vieillesse, comme nous" (663a)].[3] And this link between bodies and communities, here articulated through the implicit metaphorical claim that both of them "flower" like plants, takes on a moral and ethical dimension a moment later, when Montaigne considers whether the strategies used for curing sick bodies may be used to cure sick states as well. He notes that both bodies and states often require purging, and that many states have healed themselves of political unrest by sending unruly citizens abroad. In fact, such a bleeding lies at the origins of France, he goes on to note, since the incursion of the Franks into France and their subsequent conquest of the Gauls was the result of their being driven from Germany. France itself, in other words, exists as a cure for the ills of Germany. The Romans, moreover, built their colonial policy on a system of sending the "least necessary" people into newly conquered lands, thereby turning a physiological necessity into a political strategy.

This policy is the "evil means" occasioning the title of the essay—and Montaigne notes that many of his contemporaries propose employing such means in France, by using a foreign war to purge the country of its excess humors. The idea seems to have been a topos of late sixteenth-century political rhetoric, and is noted as well by La Noue. In his *Discours Politiques et Militaires*, written at the same time as the *Essais*, La Noue claims that, while the French nation has long been noted for its valor, the current habit of Frenchmen to go to fight abroad will ultimately merely feed the chaos of the civil wars, since soldiers will return from foreign engagements having forgotten how to live normal lives without violence. Moreover, La Noue adds, France is already so weak that it can stand no more hemorrhaging, even of "bad humors."[4] Montaigne rejects the "evil means" on moral reasons, arguing that the French should solve their problems instead of exporting them: "But I do not believe that God would favor so unjust an enterprise as to injure and pick a quarrel with others for our own convenience" (518b). Curiously, his altruistic concern is not for those French people who would die abroad in such an enterprise, but for the Other, the neighboring state which would suffer needlessly for "us."

< *History, Alterity, and the European Subject* >

However, just as he seems to have passed judgment on the ethics of this political strategy, Montaigne reopens the question of means and ends. With an adversative "however," or "toutefois," he turns back on his own position. He notes that the weakness of the French condition is such that the French are often pushed toward the use of bad means for a good end. He then offers a series of examples of peoples who have been "cured" through bad means. Lycurgus, "the most virtuous and perfect legislator who ever was" (518b), forcibly inebriated the captive Elotes to show his Spartan subjects the dangers of drink, and the Romans used gladiators to demonstrate martial virtue and heroism. The gladiatorial games are the primary example of this spectacular "education"; and there follows a group of citations from Prudentius and others, with commentary by Montaigne, on the use of gladiators to teach virtue and courage. However, the description of this new ritual seems to reverse the argument again, as we learn that the violence of the games tends to take over the very populace it is intended to serve. For if the gladiatorial games begin with foreign prisoners being slaughtered for the edification of the Romans, the Romans themselves soon become involved as well: "Senators, and knights, and even women" lend themselves to the games as combatants. The frame that separates game from spectator, moral drama from audience, dissolves as everyone becomes a potential gladiator.

What is most important here is the way in which the shift at the center of the essay provides a contrast between two forms of representation. The opening passages see the community as a metaphorical body to which the language of medicine can be figuratively applied. By contrast, the second half, which is concerned with the soul of the nation, turns to the language of spectacle. The first set of images is rejected on ethical grounds. The second is never condemned completely, but simply shown to be ineffective. The emphasis on spectacle suggests that the relationship between ethics and politics in the *Essais* involves an act of reading. It concerns the ways in which citizens read and interpret the deeds of others, drawing moral lessons from them. However, the political use of such strategies is undermined by the fact that when they are put into practice, the distance between audience and actor seems to dissolve. In both ancient Rome and Renaissance France the frames of reading have become eroded, just as the edges of community seem to have been eroded, in d'Aubigné's terms, every city is now a border town. Indeed, the essay ends with the weary remark that not even the excesses of the gladia-

< *History, Alterity, and the European Subject* >

torial games strike Montaigne as strange, since every day he sees foreigners who sell their bodies to die in a war in which they have no personal interest. The theme of death abroad and the theme of mercenary conflict come together in the last sentence. The gladiatorial games seem to be right outside Montaigne's front door.[5]

The problematic relationship between cultural or social alterity and literary representation that Montaigne underscores here is central, as well, to modern considerations of the essay. In the opening chapter of his *Notes to Literature*, the great meditation entitled "The Essay as Form," Theodor Adorno describes the procedures of the essay in terms that recall the issues of alterity and strangeness explored in this book. For Adorno, the essay is itself a kind of encounter with foreignness: "The way the essay appropriates concepts can best be compared to the behavior of someone in a foreign country who is forced to speak its language instead of piecing it together out of its elements according to rules learned in school."[6] At each turn, suggests Adorno, the essay proceeds like the foreigner, combining elements in new ways, viewing words and images from diverse perspectives. And that mode of exploration is carried out, for Adorno, not on exotic ground, but on material that is all too familiar. Adorno points out how the essay takes as its concern the historically mediated object, what he calls the "artefact." The essay, he notes, seizes on the fragment of discourse, the cliché, the disembodied citation, the ruin. Its force lies in the way it takes that seemingly well-known scrap of cultural debris and defamiliarizes it by reading it against the illusion of totality.

Two features of this description help set the stage for my discussion in this chapter. The first is Montaigne's considerations of the New World, which thematize precisely the question of newness that Adorno discounts. To be sure, for Adorno, who is working against a German philosophical tradition obsessed with achieving unmediated access to either nature or Being, the important thing about the essay is its recognition that all representation is mediation, and that there is no free encounter with "nature" itself. However, Montaigne's essays underscore the ways in which mediation itself has a history, as the alterity of new worlds shapes the very understanding of what might constitute an "artefact." The second point of interest in Adorno's discussion involves the way in which he seems to lend a kind of agency to the essay form itself, as if it "did" certain things. I have made similar arguments about literary form throughout this book, suggesting

< *History, Alterity, and the European Subject* >

that genre engages with ideology in ways that go beyond the limitations of authorial intention. However, such emphasis on the power of form is only possible at a moment in which the genre itself has become an "artefact," a mediated object, with its own conventions of authorial presence and sanction, embedded in a particular literary field. For Montaigne, however, the authority of the essayist to ruminate on the ruins of history is by no means a given, and must be fixed in language as he defines his relationship to the material he judges. My aim in what follows will be to consider at least one aspect of the emergence of the symbolic form that we call the essay, to trace the ways in which its own mediating strategies come forth for the first time.

The notion of history as a kind of spectacle, which is set forth in "Of Evil Means Employed to a Good End," reappears more explicitly in two essays from the third book: "Of the Useful and the Honorable" (essay 1) and "Of Coaches" (essay 6). Here, I will argue, it constitutes a kind of response to the breakdown of frames of reading just analyzed. "Of the Useful and the Honorable" opens with a meditation on the moral dilemmas posed by the political chaos that has overcome France during the wars of religion. Both the public and the private constructions of society, says Montaigne, are weak and wracked with vice. However, those very vices are what make us human. Whoever would remove such vices from us, he concludes, would take something essential from our beings. At the center of this reflection Montaigne inserts two lines of Latin: "Suave, mari magno, turbantibus aequora a ventis,/E terra magnum alterius spectare laborem" (768b) ["Pleasant it is, when on the great sea the winds trouble the waters, to gaze from the shore upon another's tribulation" (600b)]. The lines come from the opening of the second book of Lucretius's *De rerum natura*, in which the Latin poet offers a whole list of situations in which one may take pleasure, not from the misfortunes of others, but from knowledge of one's own safety.

The Lucretian passage was a commonplace for describing the perilous position of the sage in the face of uncertainty. Its presence here recalls the theme of spectatorship adumbrated in "Of Evil Means Employed to a Good End." It suggests that the essayist's authority to comment on the catastrophes of his day depends on his ability to place himself on the "shore." A further, more attenuated, appearance of the image of the shipwreck, in "Of Coaches," develops this notion further. For in the final pages of that essay, Montaigne condemns Spanish atrocities in the New World, and notes with some glee that

< *History, Alterity, and the European Subject* >

Spanish plunder has for the most part been lost in storms at sea, or consumed in internecine warfare: "God deservedly allowed this great plunder to be swallowed up by the sea in transit, or by the intestine wars in which they devoured one another; and most buried on the spot without any profit from their victory" (697b).[7] Here the essayist seems to take positive pleasure in the suffering of others, attributing the loss of Spanish gold to God's vengeance, and transmitting the image of cannibalism, so famously discussed in his essay on Brazil, "Of Cannibals," to the Spaniards themselves. Particularly striking (though impossible to translate into English) is the fact that the "plus part," the greater part of that which was buried on the site of plunder, may refer either to the Spaniards or the gold, as if the two had merged. "Of Coaches" embeds the image of the shipwreck, not in philosophical allegory, but in contemporary history.

"Of Coaches," on which I want to concentrate in detail here, brings together the themes of wealth, spectatorship, and political power. It opens with a consideration of Montaigne's taste in modes of transportation, then turning to consider various forms of ancient magnificence and pomp, such as the classical triumph and the gladiatorial game just seen in "Of Evil Means Employed to a Good End." However, the tenor of Montaigne's treatment of these phenomena has shifted since that earlier essay. His interest is now less in how they may or may not educate the viewer than in how they were used by ancient princes to demonstrate their liberality and define their relationship to their subjects. In other words, focus has moved from the context of the community and how it may be cured of its ills, to how representation is used as a form of propaganda. Yet even as Montaigne acknowledges that public spectacle may be more a strategy of domination than a form of education, he also notes that it is an imperfect strategy. For the problem with such forms of representation seems to be that their impact on their viewers cannot be predicted. Montaigne suggests that such demonstrations of wealth, instead of pleasing subjects, may seem wasteful: "It seems to the subjects, spectators of these triumphs, that they are given a display of their own riches, and entertained at their own expense" (688b). Thus, as one moves from the second book of the *Essais* to the third, public spectacle shifts its function. No longer a pedagogical tool aimed at welding community together, it has now become a phenomenon around which social unrest may crystallize. Moreover, Montaigne's concern has now become the specific strategies employed by princes at a time

< *History, Alterity, and the European Subject* >

of communal crisis. Political disarray is depicted as a problem of reading, and a fragmented community is one that has lost the capacity to read the signs intended to instruct and impress it. My claim will be that the encounter with the New World serves the function of helping Montaigne to redefine a place from which to read and speak about collective experience.

Ancient Tales, Modern Fragments: Narrative and the Essay

Montaigne's skepticism about the ability of communities to guide themselves by reading the past is developed throughout "Of Coaches." Near the center of that essay, he pauses to consider the limits of human knowledge. Human reason, he says, is "weak in every direction. It embraces little and sees little, short in both extent of time and extent of matter" (693b). As an example of how little humans know, Montaigne considers history. He cites Horace and Lucretius to the effect that the Trojan War, generally thought to be a unique event, was itself only one in a series of many such actions. Historians have simply forgotten the others.[8] Montaigne comments that we are ignorant of a hundred times more than we know about the exemplary deeds of the past and the great civilizations of the world.[9] He suggests that human knowledge of the past is arbitrary—that events get remembered and celebrated largely by chance. Indeed, many of the greatest achievements of the contemporary world may simply be repetitions of accomplishments long forgotten.

The *Essais*, of course, are full of such gloomy pronouncements on the value of history. However, in this case, the examples that Montaigne adduces are particularly significant: "We exclaim at the miracle of the invention of our artillery, of our printing; other men in another corner of the world, in China, enjoyed these a thousand years earlier" (693b).

The pairing of the printing press and artillery recalls a cliché of Renaissance culture. It was common in the sixteenth century to point to three marvelous inventions that seemed unique to modernity and thus marked a break with the past. These inventions were the printing press, gunpowder, and the nautical compass. As one might expect, Montaigne calls to mind this commonplace only to scorn those who would praise modernity. He grumbles that the novelty of these miracles is no novelty at all, but merely proof of human weakness. What is striking, however, is that Montaigne only mentions two of the three famous inventions that are conventionally grouped together. He makes no note of the compass. Yet the compass is clearly

< *History, Alterity, and the European Subject* >

present, since a few sentences later Montaigne twice cites Lucretius, the same author whose shipwreck allegory opens the third book. The second of the citations sings the praises of new developments in navigation. This shadowy allusion to the compass occurs at the exact center of the essay, at the very moment that the text turns to consider the New World. The compass thus poses a problem for Montaigne. Since it truly *is* a new invention it is the evidence that questions his own questioning of the greatness of his age. Its hidden presence functions as a kind of crossroads where diachronic binaries (ancients versus moderns) intersect with synchronic binaries (Europeans versus Americans).[10]

Montaigne's first citation of Lucretius comes from book two of Lucretius's poem, in which he discusses the movement of nature: "Jamque adeo affecta est aetas, affectaque tellus" (886b) ["The age is broken down, and broken down is the earth" (693b)]. The second is from Lucretius's fifth book: "Verum, ut opinor, habet novitatem summa, recensque/Natura est mundi, neque pridem exordia coepit:/Quare etiam quaedam nunc artes expoliuntur/Nunc etiam augescunt, nunc addita navigiis sunt/Multa" (886b) ["The world, I think, is very young and new, and it is not long since its beginning. Even now some arts are being perfected, some are developing; even today many improvements have been made in the arts of navigation" (693b)].[11] The two citations from Lucretius appear next to each other and seem to offer conflicting versions of the progress of the world. In one history is the history of decay; the other shows a positive movement from primitive technology to more sophisticated inventions.

The two citations from Lucretius thus raise the question of whether history is a process of triumph or one of decline.[12] The issue was often addressed by Montaigne's contemporaries. For example, in his *Method for the Easy Comprehension of History* (1566), Jean Bodin ponders this question and concludes, on the evidence of the same topos, that neither in morality nor in technical knowledge do the ancients surpass the moderns; history is not a process of decline.[13] Thus Montaigne's citations of Lucretius, coming on the heels of his denunciation of historical truth, suggest that what is at issue in his considerations of the New World is the appropriation of new material from abroad and the inscription of that material into conventional literary form. How can one know what the meaning of history is? What does the presence of American alterity suggest for an understanding of history?

< *History, Alterity, and the European Subject* >

To be sure, these considerations were not peculiar to Montaigne in the late sixteenth century. In fact, a number of his contemporaries were concerned precisely with redefining the nature of historical understanding in the light of both the influx of new knowledge from the New World and the extremism of the French wars of religion. Thus, for example, in the opening pages of Etienne Pasquier's *Recherches de la France*, which dates from the 1560s, Pasquier states that traditional forms of history writing are a hindrance to the historian in search of the truth. He notes that since all princes are constantly on stage to provide examples of virtue for their people, and since the people constantly seek to learn everything they can about their princes, princes are driven to hire historiographers who will paint their deeds in the best light possible. D'Aubigné makes a similar claim in the preface to his highly partisan *Tragiques*, as a way of justifying an epic recasting of history in light of the persecution of the Protestants. For both of these writers, then, historical narrative is but the site of exaggeration and misunderstanding. To avoid this type of rhetorical distortion, writes Pasquier, he has chosen to investigate the history, not of French kings, but of France itself.[14]

By choosing to write about the Gauls, those people who were already in France at its origins, Pasquier avoids having to produce a *narrative* of the translation of empire and of national conquest and origin. In this refusal of history as narrative he deflects the tradition of "epic" history practiced most illustriously by his predecessor Jean Lemaire de Belges, whose *Illustrations de Gaule et Singularitez de Troye* (1512) sought to link the French to the Trojans. The refusal of heroic epic history makes it possible for Pasquier to define a new vision of French nationhood and invent a new object of study, France. Similar revisions of historical method were developed by certain of the most influential of Pasquier's contemporaries: Jean Bodin's *Method for the Easy Comprehension of History* proposed to offer a system for distinguishing historical truth from historical error. In slightly different terms, La Popelinière's *Idée de l'histoire accomplie* (1599) offered a new, demythologized or "proto-Enlightenment" approach to the past. The flight from rhetorical history offers a literary counter to the crisis of French political life itself, caught, as it was, between the rhetorical distortions of warring factions. The accompanying emphasis on a new examination of the veracity of sources leads to an extension of the historian's gaze beyond the limits of historical tradition, to include the recently encountered New World. Together, these develop-

< *History, Alterity, and the European Subject* >

ments might be linked to the ideology of the so-called "politiques" group, the moderate French intellectuals, including Montaigne and Pasquier, who sought a political, rather than a religious, solution to France's political troubles. By shifting the historian's gaze away from the "heroism" of dynastic history, these writers carry out nothing less than a reimagination of France and of its relationship to world history. By yoking a discussion of public spectacle as political rhetoric to a consideration of the epistemological and moral problems raised by the conquest of Mexico, "Of Coaches," like "Of Cannibals" before it (though in different terms) suggests that the French wars of religion and the New World encounter both pose similar questions about the relationship between history and representation.[15]

Montaigne's relationship to new developments in the philosophy of history is particularly complex. Even as his skepticism toward historical authority mirrors that of such writers as Bodin and Pasquier, his own allegiances are to a traditional aristocratic morality, which draws much of its energy from the the heroic history that his contemporaries are questioning. His text is thus caught between a revisionary attitude toward antiquity and a nostalgia for what appears to be vanishing classical virtue.

These paradoxes inform the treatment of the New World in "Of Coaches." Indeed, they may be seen in the relationship between the character of the Americans and their achievements. In "Of Cannibals" Montaigne had described Brazil as "very pleasant and temperate" (153a), blessed with an endless supply of fish, fowl and fruits. This paradisical space, which corresponds to the "simple" character of the Brazilians, gives way in "Of Coaches" to a somewhat different use of the garden topos, which turns it into a sign of collective character. The first of these comes at the outset of the essay, where Montaigne speaks with admiration of the Emperor Probius, who erected an entire forest ("une grande forest ombrageuse" [883b]) in the gladiatorial arena and allowed the people to enjoy themselves there at will. The garden becomes the sign of an excess that the essayist both admires and condemns. The wandering of the people in the artificial forest figures the overflowing of the "frame" of the gladiatorial games that he had lamented in "Of Evil Means Employed to a Good End." This ambiguous figure of ancient liberality is then recalled, a bit later, in the praise of Montezuma's garden, "in which all the trees, the fruits, and all the herbs were excellently fashioned in gold and so arranged as they might be in an ordinary garden" (693b).

< *History, Alterity, and the European Subject* >

As one moves from one essay to the other, the metaphor of the garden is displaced, first into a sign of princely excess, and then into a kind of reification of the notion of the golden age. This new garden, moreover, which one might see as a distant relative of the "garden of letters" of Francis I commended by Marot in my first chapter, hints at the paradoxical nature of the Americans. We are told that in their virtue and morality, they were praiseworthy but doomed: "But as for devoutness, observance of the laws, goodness, liberality, loyalty, and frankness, it served us well not to have as much as they: by their advantage in this they lost, sold, and betrayed themselves" (694b). The Americans function as the Turks do in the discourse of Erasmus; they are ideals of virtue which may be held up to the Europeans as models. Yet their very virtue condemns them precisely because they have too much of it. They are like the Europeans, except more so. Indeed, when one considers that the last term in the list of qualities Montaigne evokes is "frankness," or "franchise," one might even posit that they are an extreme or overdone version of the "simple" French evoked by Du Bellay. Unlike the Gauls in the encounter with Alexander the Great discussed at the outset of this book, however, their frankness kills them in its excess. They are "too French" to survive the shock of the encounter with Europe. They are both too European and not European enough. Having not yet learned its "A, B, C," their garden of letters is illiterate.

It is, of course, fitting that the veiled mention of the compass should occur in a discussion of the limits of human knowledge. For it was the New World encounter that demonstrated with shocking power the limitations of European understanding. The paradox of the compass is thus that the voyages it makes possible reveal to Europeans their cultural limitations, even as the transformation it effects in navigation shows them their technological power. By placing the Lucretian references at the hinge point of the essay, between a consideration of public spectacle and a discussion of the New World, Montaigne raises a series of questions about how the New World material relates to the politics of representation already addressed in "Of Evil Means Employed to a Good End." Indeed, the tension between the two Lucretian citations, between an ascending movement of "progess" and a slide into decay, suggests that the problem of America is a problem of *narrative*, of how to set new models of culture and identity into histories that would bring them into phase with a European understanding of the past. Throughout "Of Coaches," the

< *History, Alterity, and the European Subject* >

spectacular or theatrical model of representation evoked by the ancient triumph is constantly played off of a concern for the relationship between events and narratives. Adorno's depiction of the essay as a "stranger" stresses the way its rhetoric depends on the manipulation of mediated cultural artifacts. Yet here Montaigne confronts the very problem of mediation itself, of how one civilization produces the structures through which the alterity of another civilization might be understood.

The sense of the New World as a historical, rather than a natural, object, informs Montaigne's shifting description of America, which seems to enact the very collapse it describes. He begins by declaring, "Our world has just discovered another world . . . no less great, full, and well-limbed than itself, yet so new and so infantile that it is still being taught its A B C" (693b). A moment later, however, this present infancy is already a past event: "It was an infant world" (693b). And at the end of the essay he will reveal that, in fact, this young world is very old, and living at the end of history.

"Of Cannibals" ends somewhat comically, as the essayist tries to communicate with a Brazilian captive who has been brought to France and paraded before the king as a kind of modern copy of a classical triumph. By the time of "Of Coaches," however, Montaigne has read of Spanish atrocities in the New World, and he is quick to express his disapproval. His condemnation of the Spanish not only implies a moral judgment, but links their vices to the whole question of novelty. For as he laments the outrages visited upon native populations, Montaigne remarks that they are unexampled. Never before, he says, have human beings so destroyed each other: "So many cities razed, so many nations exterminated . . . for the traffic in pearls and pepper! Base and mechanical victories! Never did ambition, never did public enmities, drive men against one another to such horrible hostilities and such miserable calamities" (695b). Thus the moral consequences of the encounter with the New World mark a break with the past no less important than that signaled by the nautical compass and the "discovery" of America itself. Yet no sooner has this novelty been acknowledged than it is counterbalanced by the description of the virtue of the Aztecs and the Incas. Their virtue rivals the virtue of the ancients, reestablishing a link with the past: "As for boldness and courage, as for firmness, constancy, resoluteness against pains and hunger and death, I would not fear to oppose the examples I could find among them to the most famous ancient examples that we have

< History, Alterity, and the European Subject >

in the memories of our world on this side of the ocean" (694b). The paradox of the New World, in other words, is that the site of geographical novelty is the site of moral traditionalism. Yet here again, this praise of virtue is tinged with a sense of lateness and loss. For these peoples only reveal their classical heroism through their vain struggle against the Spaniards. In order for New World natives to practice classical virtue, their civilization, like that of Troy, must be destroyed.[16]

The context of Montaigne's juxtaposition of fragments from Lucretius converts the Roman poet's cosmological reflection into a commentary on history, and on the way in which narrative captures the unfolding of events. By using Lucretius to suggest an impasse of narrative understanding Montaigne lends authority to his own skeptical suspension of judgment. Indeed, he follows his citations with the remark that, just as Lucretius is wrong to assume that the world is young, so may he and his contemporaries be wrong to assume that it is old. By citing conflicting images from the De rerum natura Montaigne makes Lucretius into a kind of Pyrrhonist, a skeptic who shares his own uncertainty about the movement of history. This suspension of judgment is both reversed and reaffirmed a moment later—again in terms that suggest a disruption of narrative:

> If we are right to infer the end of our world, and that poet is right about the youth of his own age, this other world would be coming into the light when ours is leaving it. The universe will fall into paralysis; one member will be crippled, the other in full vigor. (693b)

Whereas a moment ago both Montaigne and Lucretius were probably wrong, they now both may be right. Yet here Montaigne goes Lucretius one better. For the idea that the death of one thing brings about the birth of another is a central tenet of Lucretius's cosmology—one that was frequently echoed by Montaigne's contemporaries in their reflections on history. Yet by adding the notion of paralysis, Montaigne turns an image of change into one of stasis.[17]

The Lucretian references gloss the suppressed presence of the nautical compass, suggesting that it marks a point of resistance, the site at which the novelty of the New World disrupts the discourse of history. If the writing of history is a practice that turns past events into signs, the nautical compass and the great encounter it facilitates here disclose the limitations of traditional political history. The oth-

< History, Alterity, and the European Subject >

erness of America thus inscribes itself in Montaigne's text as a breakdown of narrative. And the breakdown of narrative implies a crisis in the positioning of the interpreter, and in the moral categories through which material is organized. As Hayden White has noted, narrative closure implies the establishment of a position from which the writer or reader can make sense of what has come before. This positioning, moreover, involves a moral stance, in that it leads to an act of judgment.[18] The Hellenistic historian Polybius had given voice to a cliché of imperialist historiography when he claimed that under Rome "history becomes an organic whole; the affairs of Italy and of Africa are connected with those of Asia and of Greece, and all events bear a relationship and contribute to a single end."[19] This dream of a unified history, however, is precisely what the American encounter places in question.

Thus, just as "Of Evil Means Employed to a Good End" used the figure of the gladiatorial game to raise the issue of where the sage is to place himself in society, that is, *in space*, if he is to judge the events around him, "Of Coaches" touches on the problem of the essayist's location *in time* by posing the problem of how a narrative may be constructed that would make the experience of New World alterity comprehensible. The earlier essay suggested that political violence overflows the frames erected to make it legible. "Of Coaches" underscores the difficulty of fitting the Other into sanctioned forms of narrative experience. It may not be accidental, in this context, that the first half of "Of Coaches" is concerned with the tradition of the Roman triumph, since the triumph—as both civic ritual and allegory—implies a kind of narrative without time, in which moral or political messages are articulated as spectacle.

Of course, this is not the first time in this book that an encounter with the Other has led to a kind of crisis of representation like the one suggested in Montaigne's citations of Lucretius. And, certainly, Montaigne knows that such revisions of historical knowledge are nothing new. In an addition made to the last version of the text he evokes Solon's journey to the Priests of Saïs in Plato's *Timaeus*. Plato's presentation of the tale deepens the complexity of Montaigne's concern with the relationship of events, historical authority, and narrative truth. In Plato's text Critias tells Socrates how Solon journeyed to Egypt to learn of the most "ancient famous action of the Athenians." This action, heretofore unknown to the descendants of those who committed it, turns out to be the Athenians' defense of the

Mediterranean against invasion from the people of Atlantis. Yet as he is told this story Solon is mocked by the Egyptian priests, who claim that the Greeks are ignorant of their past: "You Hellenes are never anything but children, and there is not an old man among you."[20] Even the wise Greeks seem not to know their own history. Though it thought itself old, the Greek world, too, was an "infant world."

The Atlantean invasion of Europe both reverses the European invasion of the New World and prefigures the Trojan War. Socrates remarks slyly (paralleling Montaigne's concerns with historical truth) that the story might even be true, and not just legend. If Pasquier hinted that historians' interest in the legendary ancient origins of national states may be mere propaganda, and Bodin aimed to replace national history with a larger vision of world history, Montaigne's skepticism toward the relationship of events and narratives seems to echo their revisionary approaches.[21] However, by citing Plato, Montaigne goes further and subverts the very notion of a national origin. History becomes a kind of infinite regress. The Greeks seem old to the moderns, but they are children to the Egyptians, who go on to point out their foolishness in believing that there has been only one great flood. World historical encounters are many; all history is relative. The arbitrariness of the connections between events recalls again the chance encounters between Lucretian atoms as they brush each other to make up the universe. The narrative of *translatio imperii* is scattered; Troy may just be an isolated incident. Everything and nothing is exemplary.[22]

Montaigne and His Doubles: Identity and the Rhetoric of the Essay

The contradictions revealed by Montaigne's citation of classical texts suggest the uncertainty plaguing any attempt to interpret the present, to fix the meaning of events that do not, as Polybius said, "contribute to a single end." And yet, as Polybius's own language suggests, interpretation itself implies an ending, a point from which sequences and deeds can be read. Montaigne's admiration of Aztec and Incan virtue implies its pastness. Thus one should not be surprised to find, in the last pages of the essay, a reflection on endings, and on that most final of endings, apocalypse: "The people of the kingdom of Mexico were somewhat more civilized and skilled in the arts than the others. Thus they judged, as we do, that the universe was near its end, and they took as a sign of this the desolation that we brought upon them" (698b).

< *History, Alterity, and the European Subject* >

The ending described here suddenly recuperates the disparate moments of history, marshaling them into a coherent story. The fragmentation of events in time gives way to an apocalyptic moment of unification, to a resolution of the tension between event and narrative.[23] Moreover, the alterity of the Aztecs vanishes; they understand history "as we do." The Americans' perspective merges with the Europeans' perspective as all "judge" the cosmos together. Both groups exercise the faculty of judgment. This is perfect history indeed.

However, this new community of readers is a mere chimera. For even as Montaigne here *seems* to unify diverse cultural perspectives in a gloomy narrative ending, he opens a perspective from which the impossibility of assimilating Aztecs and Europeans within the same story becomes evident. For this description marks a spot at which fragmentation in time gives way to fragmentation in space. Like the Europeans, the Aztecs live in history, read signs, and see that the end is at hand. Yet the Aztecs' experience of this ending is obviously unlike Montaigne's. For Montaigne the end is metaphorical, its structures a melancholy model of history that sees time as a long slow fall into disorder, into a moral weakness that Bodin playfully compares at one point to the debilitated body of an aging historian.[24] For the Aztecs, however, the arrival of the Spaniards is not only the sign of a fall—it *is* the fall, in a collapse as catastrophic as the fall of Troy. The tension between two distinct cultures is the tension between an *imaginative understanding* of the end (Montaigne) and a *literal experience* of the end (the Aztecs and the Incas). Though Montaigne's rhetoric seems to aim to unify human history in a single story, it only does so by blurring the distinction between literal and figural. This brings me back, as in previous discussions of Rabelais, Marot, Marguerite de Navarre, and Du Bellay, to the question of figuration, and to the way figural language sutures and splits the relationships between communities. Montaigne's thematic concern with how events are interpreted from diverse perspectives here works to underscore the difference between American and European experience. The attempt to reclaim a narrative unity for history leads to a fragmentation at the level of figuration.

This breakdown of figuration and narrative, moreover, raises the issue of the essayist's own authority and "placement" in discourse. For a similar set of paradoxes informs Montaigne's own placement in the essay, defining his status as judge and as witness (if only secondhand, through reading) of the confrontation between Spanish conquerors

< *History, Alterity, and the European Subject* >

and New World natives. For one thing, Montaigne's interpretation of the end is itself "after" the interpretation given by the Aztecs. It looks back on their prediction of doom as true, making it an episode in the tale of Spanish conquest. But an even more important difference in perspective is opened in the famous final paragraph where, as if to stress the literalness of the fall of New World glory, a kind of emblem of collapse can be seen. "Let us fall back to our coaches" (698b), says Montaigne, recalling the title of the essay. And he points out how the last Inca king was borne aloft on the shoulders of his men:

> That last king of Peru, the day that he was taken, was carried thus on shafts of gold, seated in a chair of gold, in the midst of his army. As many of these carriers as they killed to make him fall—for they wanted to take him alive—so many others vied to take the place of the dead ones, so that they could never bring him down, however great a slaughter they made of those people, until a horseman seized him around the body and pulled him to the ground. (698–99b)

The figure of the falling Atahualpa functions both temporally and spatially. Temporally, it signals the end of indigenous empires in the New World; spatially, it figures the relationship of conqueror and conquered. Yet this emblematic moment echoes another passage, at the very opening of the essay, in which Montaigne describes his own preference in modes of transportation: "I cannot long endure . . . either coach, or litter, or boat, and I hate any other transportation than horseback, both in town and in the country" (687b). Thus the essay is framed by two images of horsemen. The parallel between them sets up a momentary identification between the essayist as *chevalier* (horseman) and the Spaniard mounted on one of the *chevaux* (horses) that so terrified the people of the New World. Indeed, on one level there is a kind of essential link between Montaigne and this Spanish horseman. The essayist's very body refuses to travel except by horse. He seems to be a knight, a horseman, to his very core.

Yet no sooner is that link established than it is broken. For that same body also prevents the essayist from ever reaching the New World. He takes pains to point out that travel on boats makes him ill: "By that slight jolt given by the oars, stealing the vessel from under us, I somehow feel my head and stomach troubled, as I cannot bear a shaky seat under me"(687b). Thus the facticity of the body both associates Montaigne with the ravishers of the New World and saves him from being one of their company. Because he is a horseman,

< *History, Alterity, and the European Subject* >

Montaigne is identified with the man who pulls down the Inca emperor; he is part of the "we" that includes the Spanish colonialists. Yet the fact that he cannot travel by sea separates him, roots him in Gascony, and makes possible his imaginative identification and sympathy with the very victims of the Spanish invaders. He is essentially a *chevalier*, and essentially a European.

But the complex role of Montaigne the horseman is also connected to his implicit depiction of himself as French. In "Of Vanity" (3.9) Montaigne considers the importance of travel for philosophical reflection and discusses his relationship to his homeland. His sense of himself as a Frenchman, he says, stems from his love of Paris, nothing more, and he repeats Socrates's claim to be a citizen of the world. Indeed, Montaigne seems to be setting himself directly against the galenic tradition of linking temperament to climate when he claims that, "I am scarcely infatuated with the sweetness of my native air," and "Change of air and climate has no effect on me; all skies are alike to me" (743–44b). Yet this universalist vision encounters its limits when the essayist admits that he cannot travel by sea. The idealistic universalism of Socratic humanism is bounded by the material consideration of how one gets from one place to another.

Montaigne's evocation of the "essence" of the body is not without its own ideological shading. For the essayist's identification of himself and the Spanish horseman comes in the midst of a text that consistently attacks Spanish imperialism. And it is in these attacks, perhaps more than in Montaigne's famous depictions of his farm in Gascony, that one might begin to understand Montaigne's Frenchness. For, however morally laudable Montaigne's attacks on Spanish imperialism may seem to us today, they conform neatly to the emergence of a new nationalism, which sought to define French identity in strictly secular, that is, political, terms. For writers such as Pasquier, this involved returning to the Gallic origins of France. For others, it involved distancing French Catholicism and the French crown from the potential political domination of Spain (represented by the ultra-Catholic Guise family), and promoting a sense of the French nation as a political entity. Montaigne's glee at the shipwreck of Spanish gold may thus be read either as moral outrage or as French *ressentiment* over the failure of France's own colonial efforts in South America. The two readings, moreover, are linked, since the French/Spanish rivalry provides the frame for Montaigne's insistent meditations on historical lateness and the fall of empires in the New World. Only after the fail-

< *History, Alterity, and the European Subject* >

ure of France's own imperial projects in South America can a Frenchman speak as a moralizing European about Spanish conquest.

The figure of the horseman evoked at the two edges of "Of Coaches" both identifies Montaigne with a group and affirms his difference from that group. It figures the paradox that connects Montaigne's French identity to his European identity. And it marks the contrast between the *Essais* and the other texts studied in this book. Rabelais articulates the difference between Christians and Turks in principally moral or ethical terms, Marguerite de Navarre explores the emergence of an image of French community in terms of geography, and Du Bellay deploys the clichés of Petrarchan longing and satire to define a particular image of national character. For Montaigne, the relationship of individual to group takes the form of a split between the French moralist, trapped in a body that cannot sail, and the Spanish horseman, who destroys American civilizations. As an aristocrat, a *chevalier*, Montaigne is implicated in the Spanish expedition to America. As a queasy landlubber, he remains rooted in Europe. Collective identity here involves, not symbols like Panurge's bacon, ethical qualities like Amadour's ambiguous heroism, or national characteristics like Du Bellay's simplicity, but the relationship between location and body. And when that body is symbolically located in discourse, at one end of his essay, it makes possible Montaigne's moral judgments on the Spanish imperialism that unfold at the other end. By framing the essay with his own self-description Montaigne produces a frame for speaking about community in moral terms. If, as Henri Lefebvre has noted, the late Renaissance is marked by a "metaphorization" of space, through which the contingencies of different localities are collected under larger rubrics that help to organize them, one might posit that Montaigne's corporeal contingency becomes a metaphorical source of his literary authority.[25] Montaigne's Frenchness remains implicit in this essay, but it powerfully reinforces his judgment of the Spaniards. Whereas Montaigne speaks at length of the value of travel, and reflects at length on his journey to Rome elsewhere in the *Essais*, here his rootedness is a necessary feature of his literary and moral authority. Humanist universalism is both limited by and produced out of the location of the essayist in France.

The distinction Montaigne draws between the Spanish invaders and the Mexican and Incan natives sets up an opposition between the European subject and the American Other that looks familiar to stu-

< *History, Alterity, and the European Subject* >

dents of cross-cultural encounters. However, his self-representation as a horseman suggests that this paradigm is more complicated than it might first appear. For it seems clear that the Other who here haunts this Gascon nobleman, whose mother was a Jew of Spanish origin, may well be the Spaniard who destroys the Americas in the name of profit. Neither Spaniard nor American, but linked culturally to the one and sympathetically to the other, Montaigne can only speak with authority about the New World from his implicit position in France. His depiction of the encounter between European and Mexican in the final pages of the essay is marked by an attempt to locate himself and his reader, both geographically and morally. The staging of the encounter seeks to define in language a location from which to harmonize Montaigne's conscience, which recoils at Spanish atrocity, with his consciousness of himself as part of the "nous" who exploits the Americas. He can do this only by being both French and European.[26]

The Language of Europe

Central to Montaigne's location of himself and his reader is the question of language—both the language of dialogue and the language of the essay. "Of Cannibals," ends with an arresting image. After having ruminated at some length on the problems that plague European attempts to understand the peoples of the New World, Montaigne suddenly reveals that he has himself spoken with them: "Three of these men were at Rouen, at the time of the late Charles IX . . . I had a very long talk with one of them" (158a). Yet unfortunately this "long talk" turns out to be long not because it involves any type of true dialogue, but because both sides have to labor to make themselves understood. Montaigne reports that the interpreter mediating between him and his American interlocutor hindered the exchange of ideas by his stupidity—"par sa bestise" (212a). The dialogue seems to have been little more than a source of frustration.[27]

This comical scene of failed communication finds its analogue in "Of Coaches," when Montaigne paraphrases a passage from Lopez de Gómara's *Historia general de las Indias*. Montaigne describes a group of Spaniards landing on the coast of Mexico. The invaders ask the inhabitants for food and gold and tell them that they must become subjects of the Catholic King of Spain. The Mexicans offer the strangers the provisions they request, but state that they have neither use for gold nor desire to change their king or their religion. After

< *History, Alterity, and the European Subject* >

having paraphrased the discourse of the natives, Montaigne declares admiringly, "There we have an example of the babbling of this infancy" (696b). And he goes on to note approvingly that, in this case, the Spaniards, though finding none of the treasure they sought, chose not to ravage the spot on which they had landed. The elegant "babbling" of the natives seems here to be an example of effective persuasive rhetoric. Indeed, it is even more successful than the Gauls' mysterious response to Alexander the Great, analyzed in my first chapter, in that it sends the invader away. However, this moment of success, of natives driving off European invaders with nothing but their language, is fragile. For Montaigne's very mention of the "infancy" of the New World echoes his earlier statement that America "was an infant world," and suggests his sharp awareness that the noble rhetoric of the Mexicans, with its expression of proud independence, was, in the broader context, completely unsuccessful in persuading the Spanish to mind their own business and return to Europe. Indeed, one might even say that Montaigne's shiver of admiration at the speech is the very consequence of his knowledge of the Aztecs' sad destiny—for once their civilization has been destroyed, they cease to be a threat to Europe. They can then become an object of mourning and thus of aesthetic pleasure.

If the persuasive rhetoric practiced by the Mexicans in this scene is generally doomed to failure, it is in a different type of language—the language of the essay itself—that the tension between Old World and New World must be harmonized. Though the theme of Montaigne's own language is not raised explicitly in "Of Coaches," the essay is fascinated by the relationship between language, text, and cultural difference. For one thing, the split between Montaigne's identification as a horseman and his location in France parallels, on the level of the essayist's project of self-portraiture, the general rhetorical strategy of the essay, which plays constantly on the tension between letter and figure, between the *literal* consequences of events in America and their *metaphorical* equivalents. Montaigne is literally a horseman, but imaginatively allied with the Americans. In a more obviously self-referential context, the structure of the text seems to mirror the themes it treats. Thus, for example, the famous image of the falling Atahualpa comes at the end of Montaigne's essay—what in French is called its "fall," or "chute."[28] No less striking is the fact that it is not only the Atlantic Ocean that separates the images of the two horsemen: since they stand at opposite ends of "Of Coaches," it is lit-

< *History, Alterity, and the European Subject* >

erally Montaigne's text that keeps them apart. The essay itself stands between the image of the sedentary philosopher in Gascony and the cruel *conquistador* who brought down Atahualpa. Text mimics geography. Moreover, the final image of the fall of Atahualpa is introduced with the phrase, "Let us fall back to our coaches" (698b) ["Retombons à nos coches" (894b)], an exhortation that replaces both the collapse of the Incan empire and Montaigne's own aversion to four-wheeled vehicles with a purely textual voyage, a fall into the geography of the imagination.

Issues of figurality and perspectivism inform Montaigne's analysis of the cause of Spanish conquest. Montaigne points out that the reason why the vicious and outnumbered Spaniards were able to conquer the virtuous and heroic Aztecs was that they had an unfair advantage: they were deceitful.

Montaigne identifies two factors for the defeat of Mexico: Spanish ruse and Aztec astonishment. However, in his recreation of the encounter there is no mention of any ruse on the part of Cortez and his men. We are simply told that the Aztecs were astonished at the appearance of Spanish horses, at the noise of their cannon, at the sight of men in beards with strange religious customs. In this version the morally corrupt Spanish defeat their heroic adversaries by virtue of their very being, of their alterity itself. Or, more exactly, it is their alterity that is a ruse. The Spanish conquer the Aztecs by simply being themselves, by demonstrating their cannons and riding their horses and practicing their religion and wearing their beards. When he asserts that the Spaniards win simply by their alterity, Montaigne denies them any claim to heroism. They are deceitful like the Greeks invading Troy, but they lack Greek sagacity or courage; they ride real horses instead of building wooden ones. Traditional aristocratic virtue now surfaces among the Aztecs, whose perspective Montaigne here constructs for the reader. By thus locating classical virtue, however, Montaigne affirms the absolute difference between New World and Old World. If gladiatorial games cannot cure nations because they tend to overflow the frames constructed for them and infect the very people they aim to serve, true heroism may be seen in a world safely framed apart from the space of Europe.[29]

Again, it seems impossible to assimilate the geographical and cultural novelty of America without sacrificing the historical continuity between antiquity and modernity. In this case traditional heroism can be located only by asserting such an absolute difference between

< History, Alterity, and the European Subject >

groups that mere alterity becomes a ruse. We are here at the opposite extreme from the depiction of Rabelais's Gymnaste, who, in chapter 3, produced alterity where none existed by describing himself as a "devil." Here, mere being is strategy. It is no accident, moreover, that this difference emerges around the image of the horse. The horse appears countless times in Montaigne's text as a figure for transport and transportation, for displacement, translation, diplomacy, and a host of other border-crossing functions. The violent reality of cross-cultural encounters becomes legible in the fact that that same horse image, so easily deployed in a European context, is seen to strike terror into the members of another culture. It is terror that recalls the context of the bacon tied around the waist of Panurge by the Turks. Yet whereas the bacon functioned as the mark of cultural difference by virtue of its curious status *between* the figural and the literal, between impossible representation and ideological necessity, here the horse has a double function by virtue of its very being. As *thing*, rather than trope, it both defines the essayist and terrifies those he most admires.[30]

No less striking is that the reader sees the encounter from the perspective of the New World natives, who are so astonished by the strangeness of the Spanish that they are defeated by them. This reversal, moreover, marks the point at which the figural power of language assumes a mediating function between Old World and New World. Montaigne opens his description of an encounter between Spaniards and Aztecs by lamenting that Europe has subdued the New World not with virtue but with vice: "We have neither won it over by our justice and goodness, nor subjugated it by our magnanimity" (693b). This uniquely European lament is, however, undercut by Montaigne's subsequent description of the relations between the Spaniards and the Americans. It consists of a single sentence that must be cited at length:

> For as regards the men who subjugated them, let them take away the ruses and tricks that they used to deceive them and the natural astonishment of those nations at seeing the unexpected arrival of bearded men, different in language, religion, shape and countenance, from a part of the world so remote, where they had never imagined there was any sort of human habitation, mounted on great unknown monsters, opposed to men who had never seen not only a horse, but any sort of animal trained to carry and endure a man or any other burden; men equipped with a hard and shiny

< *History, Alterity, and the European Subject* >

skin and a sharp and glittering weapon . . . add to this the lightning and thunder of our cannon and harquebuses capable of disturbing Caesar himself . . . recount to the conquerors this disparity, I say, and you take from them the whole basis of so many
victories. (694b)[31]

This glorious sentence is marked, not only by grammatical incongruities, but by a strange series of shifts in the positions of reader and
speaker. The distinction between "we," the Europeans and "they," the
Americans is displaced at the opening of the passage into "the men
who subjugated" (that is, the Spanish) and "those nations" (the echo
of the introductory claim that "we have subjugated them" underscores the shift). Montaigne and his reader are now "outside" of the
encounter, located, presumably, as "French," observing the atrocities
of the Spanish. Yet a moment later Montaigne adds in the perspective of the Americans with the statement that the Spaniards arrived
from "a part of the world so remote" (as opposed to, say, a phrase like
"so far from them"). The Spaniard ("different in language") is now the
stranger. This perspectival rhetorical strategy then becomes an issue
of figuration in the description of the Spaniards, whose mounts are
first described by Montaigne as "great unknown monsters" (that is, as
they *appear* to the Americans) before being identified as horses (that
is, as they are *known* to Europeans). Similarly, but more pointedly,
Spanish armor and arms are simply evoked as "a hard and shiny skin
and a sharp and glittering weapon"—their European names are never
given. And finally, the description of the noise made by Spanish guns
("the lightning and thunder of our cannon and harquebuses capable
of disturbing Caesar himself") suggests two distinct viewpoints. The
phrase is a cliché, a metaphor for describing the noise made by
firearms. But only Europeans know that it is a metaphor. Indeed, the
curious effectiveness of gunpowder in Spanish conquest lay in the
fact that the Aztecs could not identify the noise it made. They took it
to be supernatural racket.[32]

Each of the previous chapters has noted the ways that the edges of
communities are marked by a kind of linguistic violence, a point of
crossing between the figural and the literal in language. Montaigne's
depiction of the American experience of European invasion recalls
those earlier moments, and links the violence of figuration to a shift
in genre. Those passages in "Of Coaches" that draw on conventions
of historical narrative, such as the depiction of the apocalyptic end of

< *History, Alterity, and the European Subject* >

the Incas, also assert the break between America and Europe as a break between metaphorical understanding of the fall of civilizations and the literally experienced fall of the king. The eclipse of historical narrative is also the affirmation of cultural difference. Through the deployment of figural language, the essay stages the death of history as a genre, to replace it with the language of the essay. The emblem of this breakdown in language might be the horse itself, which signifies cultural difference by suggesting both the absolute alterity of the Spaniards to the Americans, and the universality of Montaigne's chivalric identity. And yet—and this is the crux—in the passage just cited, a play with figuration works to mediate the split between civilizations. Through the perspectivism of his prose style Montaigne seeks imaginatively to bridge the literal split between New World and Old World, between native actor and European reader. By moving between literal description and figural evocation Montaigne places the reader *both* in the position of the Spaniard and in the imagined position of the New World native, in the place of the one who knows that gunpowder is gunpowder *and* of the one who thinks it is thunder. Through its play with metaphor Montaigne's prose commutes between opposing perspectives on the encounter, locating author and reader first among the (not yet) conquered and then in the company of the conquerors.[33] And this perspectival strategy is integral to the form of the essay. Even as "Of Coaches" draws upon clichés of historical narrative, only to disclose their inadequacy, it shifts to a rhetoric that holds in tension a variety of perspectives. This strategy is particularly powerful in "Of Coaches," given the theme of cross-cultural encounters that informs the essay. For the thematic concern of the essay makes the essay form's conventional strategy of juxtaposing different fragments of text into a dramatic recasting of the confrontation between cultures. Conversely, the cross-cultural confrontation that forms the ostensible topic of the essay might be seen as a giant world-historical dramatization of its form. Yet what seeks to resolve these oppositions is rhetoric itself. The standoff between Mexican and Spaniard depicted in Montaigne's paraphrase of Lopez de Gómara is here sublimated into an imaginary recreation that shows the European reader how the familiar world of horses and guns looks to another culture.

Certainly, this type of perspectivism is not restricted to the discourse of the essay.[34] But what is unique to the essay, and what sets Montaigne's consideration of these issues apart from those of the

< *History, Alterity, and the European Subject* >

writers discussed in my earlier chapters, is the complex interplay between the mediatory strategy of the text and the problematic location of the subject. The essay's play with the metaphorical and literal levels of language works against the contrasting positions suggested in the two images of the horsemen. Here again, the contrast with "Of Cannibals" is instructive. That earlier chapter relied for its authority about America on the introduction of a (probably) fictitious sailor, or "man," who is described as having lived in Brazil before coming to stay at Montaigne's castle. In "Of Coaches" the device of the mediating character disappears. It gives way, first of all, to the tension between the essayist and his Spanish double. That tension is then "resolved" provisionally by the dual perspective set up by the sentence I have just explicated.

In this improvisational play with figure, Montaigne breaks with the strategies seen in earlier writers. Rabelais diffuses the threat to community by difference through the construction of a phantasmic object (the bacon that hangs from Panurge's waist) that is both figure and body, both trope and thing. Erasmus tries to mend community by preaching a politics of the spirit, as over the world of the letter. Du Bellay seeks a flight from figuration altogether in his privileging of a simplicity, a world "without fictions," that would link French identity and poetry in the face of Italian culture. Montaigne, by contrast, uses tropes, not to save the integrity of the European community, but to affirm the absolute difference between communities, between American and European. He shows his reader how something as common as a horse might be a monster to someone from another culture. That representation of cultural difference then makes possible the acknowledgment that European political action is at odds with Europe's own moral principles. Through the fictional identification with the Other, Europe is shown to be at odds with itself.[35]

It is important to note the way in which the rhetoric of the scene of Spanish conquest extends to implicate the reader. At the end of his description of the American vision of the Spaniards, Montaigne turns to thematize his own process of recasting the encounter by appealing to a "you" who is to pass judgment. The sentence takes us, in its very unfolding, from politics back to language. It begins with a wish for the Spaniards to consider a different version of the terrible events under consideration: "let [the Spaniards] take away the ruses and tricks they used to deceive [the Aztecs]." It passes through an acknowledgment that the technology of the Spaniards is also that of all

< *History, Alterity, and the European Subject* >

Europeans ("our cannon and harquebuses"). It ends with an injunction to the reader to speak, to utter a word that will compel moral judgment: "recount to the conquerors this disparity, I say, and you take from them the whole basis of so many victories" ["contez, dis-je, aux conquerans cette disparité, vous leur ostez toute l'occasion de tant de victoires"]. In fact, the English translation, which speaks of taking away the "basis" of victory, is much weaker than the French. The original claims that without ruse the "occasion," that is, the moment of ripeness for effective political action, is gone. Thus the very possibility of Spanish victory is eclipsed.

Through the reader's response the essay maps out a reaction to the fall of Mexico. The apostrophic turn to the "vous" who reads is rare in Montaigne generally and occurs nowhere else in "Of Coaches." It enjoins the reader to move from an imaginary reconsideration of the past, through the viewpoint of the American, toward a retelling of the episode. That retelling, moreover, is a depicted as a speech act, as a piece of language that does something. It is a "recounting" ("conter") that is also a "taking away" ("oster") in that it will remove all arrogance from the Spaniards. With its imperative "contez, dis-je," the sentence transforms the reader into an imaginary messenger commanded to bear the urgent word of one horseman, the sedentary philosopher, to the ear of the fellow European, the Spanish *conquistador*. By ordering us imaginatively to "tell" the Spaniards the truth about their conquests, the essay seeks to send its language through our very bodies. Yet that act of transmission, which can only happen among Europeans (that is, horsemen) is also what distinguishes Montaigne from his Spanish double. The cultural bond that makes it possible for Montaigne to communicate his anger to the reader (they are all Europeans) is fractured by the fact that the Spaniard has obviously not understood the experience of the American that Montaigne's own rhetoric recreates.

Montaigne's authority in "Of Coaches" is linked to his location of himself, both literally, in France, and discursively, at either ends of his essay. This self-location in turn gives him the control of the play between figural and literal language that makes possible the moral judgments which inform the powerful final pages. Through this strategy, moreover, the essay offers an alternative to the various solutions to political disarray set forth in "Of Evil Means Employed to a Good End." Whereas the Spaniards wage war on other peoples, and the Romans seek to educate their populace through triumphs and gladi-

< *History, Alterity, and the European Subject* >

atorial games, Montaigne's text projects a reader who becomes a messenger, whose own body carries a condemnation of the very types of atrocities that Montaigne sees outside his door every day. In this regard, one might say that it is the essay itself that offers the modern alternative to the gladiatorial theater. The essay, through its very form, defines a model of self-education, as Europe watches itself in war and judges the consequences of its own thirst for power and wealth.

The essay's play with figuration is intimately linked to its persuasive rhetoric. Because it holds in tension two contradictory cultural experiences, it eschews the type of rhetorical energy one finds in such reports from the scene of the atrocity as Las Casas's treatise on the destruction of the Indies, where figural language is used to great dramatic effect, to describe the Spanish, for example, as "ravening beasts."[36] Because Las Casas's report actually aims to persuade those in power to act, its strategies of figuration remain within the circumscribed ambit of European moral philosophy. Montaigne, by contrast, deploys figures to evoke the *experience* of the American. Las Casas's report could only be written by a Spaniard. Montaigne's essay, whose authority depends upon a distance from both America and Spain, could only be written by a non-Spaniard. Indeed, because of his location in France, that is, neither in Spain nor in America, Montaigne can project himself in both directions. Through that projection he turns a fiction of alterity into a moral judgment. Yet even as his location in France makes such a judgment possible, it makes it clear that his claim that he can "remove" all glory from Spanish conquests with a piece of discourse is just one more fiction. If his reconstruction of the American vision of the invading Spaniards shows the power of the essay form, his claim that his text can demystify Spanish glory reveals its limitations. For it only offers hope of a Pyrrhic victory, which can change European attitudes, rather than the actual fate of New World natives.

The end of the essay thus commutes between three points: an experience of the perspective of the conquered Other, the sedentary essayist, and a *conquistador*. In the reader's passage as messenger between these points, Montaigne maps out the generic borders of the essay as form. Neither the ethnographic study, which pretends to put "us" in "their shoes;" nor the historical narrative; which assimilates "them" into "our" narrative; nor the advice treatise, which aims to offer fixed ethical rules for comportment, the essay abuts these rival genres. It seeks to appropriate the strengths of these other forms—

< *History, Alterity, and the European Subject* >

the imaginative transformation of experience in ethnography, the hermeneutic impulse of history writing, and the high seriousness of moral philosophy—while using them against each other.[37]

I have argued that "Of Coaches," and with it the new discourse of the personal essay, work through a tension between the literal placement of the essayist's body in France and his imaginary projection into the world of the Other. This tension may be seen as a response to the difficulty of understanding New World alterity in narrative terms, and as a necessary hedge against the political fanaticism of the French wars of religion. "Of Coaches" enacts the transformation of history into essay, suggesting how the essay form emerges as a response to a particular moment of crisis in historical understanding. Whereas the tension between antiquity and modernity so consistently evoked in this essay leads to an impasse, to a juxtaposition of conflicting versions of the movement of history, the introduction of the New World material leads to an attempt to subsume difference and multiple perspectives into the web of writing itself. That web of writing, however, is marked by the tension between a mediatory rhetoric, on the one hand, and the multiple poses of the subject—a tension that might be seen as the originary split or rupture that marks the emergence of the essay genre. This is not to say, of course, that the form of the essay is somehow "essentially" linked to the discovery of the New World. Certainly, the displacement of history writing by essay seen here is replayed throughout Montaigne's text with dizzying variety and complexity, as many different discursive traditions are split and reconfigured. Nonetheless, as in the case of the other writers studied in this book, these issues of generic rupture are articulated most powerfully at the edges of community.

Cartesian Weather

Montaigne's explicit commutation between diverse points underscores, to return to Adorno's description of the essay form, the mediated nature of the matter of the essay. Even as it figuratively evokes the "experience" of the American, Montaigne's text acknowledges that the alterity it represents is only an alterity to the conquered Americans. From the perspective of the European, there are no threatening Turks here, only legends about New World grandeur. And if, in Rabelais, the alterity of the alien culture seemed to invade the very language of Christendom, here it is language, metaphor itself, that mediates the cross-cultural encounter for the European reader. If the

< History, Alterity, and the European Subject >

Essais make any claim at all to an unmediated depiction of experience, it is in the space between mediations, in the ways mediated objects such as citations and topoi intertwine and jostle for position to offer a vision of the nuances of the author's mind at work. At the same time, however, it is Montaigne's acceptance of mediation that makes possible his own political moderation. Because he dwells in a world of mediated artifacts, he is shielded from the breathless enthusiasm of the political fanatic, be he Protestant or Catholic, who claims to possess Truth and speak for a "true" France. The pseudo-encounter with alterity is precisely what makes it possible for Montaigne to identify, provisionally, with the Other. Self-conscious acceptance of mediation makes possible ideals of cultural dialogue and tolerance—even if those ideals are tinged with Adornoesque melancholy at the ruin of civilizations.

In this context it may be useful, as a contrast with what has gone before, to close this chapter with a brief glance at a somewhat different philosophical genre—the treatise—and a somewhat different image of wandering and marginality. I have in mind the foundational text of much of seventeenth-century French culture, Descartes's *Discourse on Method*. Descartes opens his treatise by recalling the language of Montaigne's essay on education, "Of the Education of Children" (1.26). In that essay Montaigne urges the young student to study people around him, so as to learn from what he calls "the book of the world" (116a). He cites Socrates's claim that he is a citizen of the world, and of no country. "He, whose imagination was fuller and more extensive, embraced the universe as his city, and distributed his knowledge, his company, and his affections to all mankind, unlike us who look only at what is underfoot" (116a). The irony here, of course, is that Socrates never leaves Athens. His identification with the Other is purely in the realm of conversation and imagination. Descartes, by contrast, "literalizes" the notion of "knowing the world" by converting it into a kind of rootlessness. In the opening passages of the *Discourse on Method*, he describes himself as a kind of seaworthy Montaigne, or a latter-day version of Marguerite de Navarre's Amadour. If Montaigne is rooted in France, Descartes wanders the landscape of Europe "to see courts and armies" ("à voyager, à voir des cours et des armées"). And whereas Montaigne advocates a familiarity with the world as a way of encountering variety, so that one would not think one's own customs the only customs, Descartes is interested in something much more powerful. He wants to meet people in

< *History, Alterity, and the European Subject* >

situations that are more dramatic and immediate than those encountered by the scholar in his study ("dans son cabinet"). These are situations where the body itself is on line, where the wrong judgment will immediately be felt, as a kind of punishment: "For it seemed to me that I could find much more truth in the calculations that each man makes about affairs that are important to him, and where consequences would punish him soon thereafter should he judge badly."[38] For Descartes, one learns from others through their painful mistakes. The body of the Other becomes the surface on which Descartes reads his lessons.

Yet it is this immediacy that Descartes rejects. The threat to selfhood by the catastrophe of the Other's "punishment" is inadequate to Descartes's desire to define Truth. And if Montaigne's moral authority is linked to his location in France, Descartes's construction of a new, modern, philosophical subjectivity is contingent on contingency itself, on his being absolutely still. Finding himself in Germany during the winter of 1619–20, en route to rejoin the army, he tells us, he is driven by bad weather to stop his wandering. It is there that he enters his famous stove, and embarks on the philosophical project of the *Discourse on Method*. Descartes is mobile, but is stopped in Germany by the weather. He, too, dwells on the border, even as he will later remove himself to Amsterdam. But his response to this moment of contingency is to mistrust the body which Montaigne uses as a source of knowledge. He produces a new form of rationality that is everywhere and nowhere, shared by all as "common sense." In the process, he absents himself from both the literary territory and the communal space explored by the other writers discussed in this book. Descartes abandons the space of collectivity explored by Rabelais, Marguerite de Navarre, Du Bellay, and Montaigne, to define a new place for language and consciousness, free of the anxiety produced by the presence of cultural or political alterity. And whereas Montaigne's expansive vision is based on a blending of corporeity and imagination, contingency and movement, Descartes's invention of modern philosophical subjectivity involves a kind of conversion from movement, a turning from the dramas of the body which he comes so famously to mistrust. In contrast to both Montaigne and Du Bellay, who carefully locate themselves in the imaginary space of France and build their identities through careful meditations on their own bodily existence, Descartes reveals that his project can be carried out anywhere. All he needs is bad weather.[39]

Conclusion

Pauline's Dream

> It is evident that an exclusive attachment to the world of the mind
> was easier when there were no nations to love.
> —JULIEN BENDA, *La trahison des clercs*

In his great treatise on the forms of the state, *Les six livres de la
république*, Montaigne's contemporary Jean Bodin notes that the natural alacrity of the French makes them excellent servants of such less
energetic peoples as the Spanish. Hence, he remarks, so many
Frenchmen have crossed the border into Spain that Spain is now
nearly overrun by the French ("l'Espagne n'est quasi peuplée que de
Français"), and an invasion of that country would have to deal with
the disruptive presence of people who seem at once French and
Spanish.[1] The border between France and Spain, it turns out, is
hardly a border at all. I have argued that Bodin's anxiety about the
border and edge of France is a trope of Renaissance French literature.
In contrast to the centripetal cultural politics of England and Spain,
literary nationhood in Renaissance France is characterized by a constant preoccupation with the alien, and with the definition of French
community in the presence of the Other. The development of new
literary forms comes through a repeated moment of negotiation under the pressure of alterity, when the Other appears to be the same,
and the same may turn out to be the Other. Authors such as Rabelais
and Marguerite de Navarre confront cultural and political multiplicity in moral terms, seeking to define new forms of community in new
forms of narrative. For Du Bellay and Montaigne, crises of French
identity are registered as crises of literary authority, and the two writers inscribe themselves into their texts in ways that both register and
respond to alien influence. At the edges of community texts measure
the violence that underpins political change. Literature confronts the
vulnerability of France by reflecting on the limits of genre and language, and on the violence that marks both text and body.

< *Pauline's Dream* >

The itinerary of this book has included both a set of theoretical problems involving the relationship between language and collective identity, and a historical reflection on the embeddedness of influential forms of literary representation in particular ideological contexts. I have sought to trace a loose trajectory of the relationship between the emergence of secular literary culture and the great communal crises of the sixteenth century. I have also tried to sketch a kind of "anatomy" (to use a Renaissance term) of the interplay of literary genres. Although this book has moved in a loose chronology, it makes no claim to offer a comprehensive historical narrative. Still, culture and politics do have their histories. And perhaps the strongest argument that one might make for the specific relationship between community and literary form that I have been advancing lies in the fact that in the century immediately following the period considered here, virtually all of the genres I have studied fell into relative oblivion in France. The temporary resolution of political crisis under the ascendant Bourbon monarchy, the theory and practice of the absolutist state, and the emergence of neo-classicism in aesthetic theory resulted in the displacement of the big, generically promiscuous texts studied here from the center of literary production in a way not seen in other European literatures of the period. Such open forms as the personal essay, the novella collection, and the Rabelaisian novel move to the margins of the French canon. Moreover, the literary history of France during this period is remarkable for the fact that none of the major authors I have studied ever ascended to the type of "national" canonical status already beginning to be enjoyed by Shakespeare in England, Petrarch and Dante in Italy, or Cervantes in Spain. Perhaps, one might speculate, once France gets a nation-state and an academy, the type of literary canonicity and embodiment of national identity sought by a figure like Ronsard is no longer needed. Institutions take over from authors.

Anxiety about the edges of France, too, begins to take on different configurations after the period studied here. The virulent anti-Spanish sentiment reflected in both Rabelais and Montaigne reached a fever pitch in the last years of the wars of religion and became a cornerstone of the cultural politics of Henry IV. Yet after his death, the Regent Maria de' Medici made reconciliation with Spain a centerpiece of her foreign policy. And in 1617, the Spanish doctor Carlos García could write in his reconciliatory treatise *La Antipatía de Franceses y Espanoles* that France and Spain were the origins of all other na-

< Pauline's Dream >

tions, and, as such, despite their complementary temperaments, were destined to live in harmony.[2] This is not to claim, of course, that the French somehow felt less "threatened" in the seventeenth century (as if such an assertion were even something one could prove), only that the literary theme of the border is transmuted, and the figure of the alien is metamorphosed into such ridiculous types as the bumbling hot-tempered Spaniards and exotic Turks of the comedies of Corneille and Molière.

Some fifty years after the death of Montaigne, Cardinal Richelieu noted in his *Testament Politique* that the French nation may be defined by two contradictory characteristics. It is energetic and valiant, but it is impatient and "light" (that is, flighty). Thus, when they are in battle, the French are eager to attack, but they cannot sustain a long campaign. These characteristics, Richelieu notes, are not mere historical accidents, linked to the minority of Louis XIII. They are constitutive of "this boiling and impetuous nation" ("une nation si bouillante et si impétueuse").[3] Such a mixture of elements may seem to bode ill for the future of France, however, asserts Richelieu, it can be rendered solid and secure if it is under the hand of a powerful leader who is not afraid to punish excesses, and if foreigners are mixed in with French soldiers to offset their defects. This project of tempering and controlling French character, of course, becomes a central project of absolutism. And to consider the cultural figurations that the new regime develops, I want to turn, very briefly, in closing, to one of the first major "border encounters" in seventeenth-century French literature, Pierre Corneille's first "Christian tragedy," *Polyeucte*, written in the 1540s.

The play unfolds in the last years of the Roman Empire, and is set in Melitene, the capital of Armenia. There, the Roman governor Félix has married his daughter Pauline off to a local chieftain Polyeucte ("ici le chef de la noblesse"), as a way of pacifying the populace and promoting his own ambitions in the imperial bureaucracy.[4] Polyeucte, however, has been touched by the spirit of Christianity, and longs to be martyred. The situation is complicated when Pauline's former lover, Sévère, once believed to have been lost at battle but now a highly placed Roman official, comes to Armenia. As Polyeucte declares his Christian beliefs, Sévère is placed in the position of killing his beloved's husband unless he abjures. As Sévère hesitates, it is the politically ambitious Félix, Pauline's father, who steps in and martyrs his son-in-law. However, the martyrdom has unex-

< *Pauline's Dream* >

pected consequences, as Pauline suddenly converts and Sévère reveals that he has long been curious about the Christians and, in a gesture of magnanimity, decides to allow them to practice their beliefs without persecution.

Martyrdom and magnanimity; the two phenomena perfectly express Richelieu's own politics of political rigidity and religious tolerance. They emerge as central topoi through which early seventeenth-century French culture mediates the types of violence and rhetorical excess that authors such as Rabelais and Montaigne encounter on the edges of community. Through martyrdom, Polyeucte is absorbed into a unified community with much greater ease than what we saw in Rabelais's depiction of the stubbornly literal Turks, or Marguerite de Navarre's tale of the wandering Amadour. And Sévère's gesture of magnanimity requires less rhetorical energy to embrace the conquered than does Gargantua's charitable acceptance of Alpharbal, Du Bellay's depiction of himself as French, or Montaigne's complex location of himself in the essay. Yet what Corneille's seemingly happy ending disguises is that Polyeucte's martyrdom is also the effacement of local identity, of the stubborn community that threatens the edges of the Empire. Polyeucte dies as a Christian and is forgiven as a Roman subject. What disappears is his Armenian identity, his status as leader of a restless tribe of subjects no more at ease with Roman domination than were the Gauls in *Astérix*. When Polyeucte becomes a Christian martyr he dies, not for Armenia, which is living under Roman occupation, but for a religious creed whose universality will transcend the limits of local community.

What is most striking about *Polyeucte*, however, is that the question of cultural difference is thematized through a reflection on the truth of fiction itself. For we learn as the play opens that Pauline is haunted by a dream she has had, in which, as her lover Sévère looks on in triumph, her husband Polyeucte is killed by the hand of her father and a band of Christians. This is more or less the plot of the play that is to unfold before us. Yet there is much anxiety in the early scenes over whether the dream should be believed. Polyeucte's friend Néarque associates the horrifying vision of the dream with Pauline's gender, dismissing it as the "dream of a woman" ("les songes d'une femme" [v.1]). A moment later, Stratonice, Pauline's confidant, connects the power of the warning to the fact of cultural difference. Pauline is terrified by her dream because she is a Roman, she says, and Romans take dreams seriously, whereas Armenians do not: "Our

< *Pauline's Dream* >

two nations/Do not share the same ideas on this question;/A dream among us is seen to be ridiculous,/It leaves neither hope, nor fear, nor scrupule,/But in Rome it has authority/as the faithful mirror of fate" ["Nos deux nations/N'ont pas sur ce sujet mêmes impressions;/Un songe en notre esprit passe pour ridicule,/Il ne nous laisse espoir, ni crainte, ni scrupule,/Mais il passe dans Rome avec autorité/Pour fidèle miroir de la fatalité"] (v. 151–56).

Here, on the edges of the Empire, the truth of the dream—which might stand allegorically for the truth of literature itself—is up for grabs. The difference between Romans and Armenians, between the French and the non-French, may lie in whether or not they believe fictions. For Pauline, the dream is a vision of political strife and murder that, when played out in reality, becomes a mechanism for reconciliation and community. And the function of literature in the border town of Corneille's Melitene (as in Rabelais's Mytilene) may be to mediate between truth and fiction, identity and alterity, in the production of community. In the ambivalent image of the dream that haunts Pauline but brings her into a unified Christian empire, Corneille's play looks back toward the violence and excess of sixteenth-century nationhood, even as it advances an image of political reconciliation rooted in the magnanimity of the ruler. Not unlike the Turks or the pirate Alpharbal in Rabelais, the wandering Amadour in Marguerite de Navarre, the feigning Italians of Du Bellay, or the doomed Americans in Montaigne, Pauline's vision of her husband's dead body leads to the imagination of new forms of collectivity. From the historical perspective of this moment of reconciliation, the collective struggles that devastated Renaissance France seem little more than a dream, as Corneille sketches out a vision of community that both commemorates the eclipse of the nation and gestures toward the emergence of the modern state.

Notes

CHAPTER ONE

1. Strabo, *Geography*, 7, 3, 8, in *The Geography of Strabo*, trans. Horace Leonard Jones (London: Heinemann, 1924), 3: 203.

2. Pietro Crinito, *De Honesta Disciplina*, ed. Carlo Angeleri (Rome: Fratelli Bocca Editori, 1955), 135. My translation.

3. Etienne Pasquier, *Les recherches de la France*, ed. Marie-Madeleine Fragonard and François Roudaut (Paris: Champion, 1996), 1: 259. My translation.

4. For general background on Pasquier's work see George Huppert, *The Idea of Perfect History* (Urbana: University of Illinois Press, 1970). On the innovative quality of his interest in the Gauls, see Corrado Vivanti, "Les Recherches de la France d'Etienne Pasquier: L'invention des Gaulois," *Les Lieux de Mémoire*, ed. Pierre Nora (Paris: Gallimard, 1986), Part II, 1: 216–45. On the ideological context of Pasquier's project see Vivanti's book, *Lotta politica e pace religiosa in Francia fra Cinque e Seicento* (Turin: Einaudi, 1974).

5. For a succinct account of treatments of "otherness" in anthropological writing see John A. Armstrong, *Nations before Nationalism* (Chapel Hill: University of North Carolina Press, 1982). Throughout this study I will use the capitalized form "Other" to designate the figure or figures who occupy a particular position of strangeness or exclusion in depictions of collective identity. The term has become overused and somewhat ugly, but it is the most convenient solution available for speaking about these issues.

6. Colette Beaune, *The Birth of an Ideology: Myths and Symbols of Nation in Late-Medieval France*, trans. Susan Ross Huston (Berkeley: University of California Press, 1991), 310.

7. These passages are from the "Complaint of Peace," and may be found in the *Collected Works of Erasmus*, vol. 27, ed. A. H. T. Levi (Toronto: University of Toronto Press, 1986), 306.

8. See Le Roy Ladurie's *The Royal French State, 1460–1610*, trans. Juliet Vale (London: Blackwell, 1994), 243.

9. On the influence of the French example in the history of the nation-state, see Mark Greengrass's introduction to his *Conquest and Coalescence: The Shaping of the State in Early Modern Europe* (London: Edward Arnold, 1991), 13. Armstrong, too, stresses the uniqueness of France as the paradigm of nationhood in the "pre-nationalist" period. See Armstrong's *Nations before Nationalism*, chapter 8. On the vexed history of the "borders" of France, see Peter Sahlins, *Boundaries: The Making of France and Spain in the Pyrenees* (Berkeley: University of California Press, 1989).

10. Hugh Seton-Watson, *Nations and States* (London: Methuen, 1977), 20. Michel de Certeau uses slightly different but related terms when he notes that one of the chief effects of the political and religious upheavals of the

early modern period was that an understanding of the subject as a primarily theological entity began to be replaced by an image of the subject as a primarily political entity. This process began, perhaps, with the first fissures in Catholic unity brought about by the schismatic sects of the late fifteenth century and concluded, in France at least, with Louis XIV's razing of the Abbey of Port-Royal in 1711. As Certeau writes, "Because of its fragmentation into coexisting and mutually warring churches, the values once invested in the Church appear directed toward political or national unity. A defrocked Church favors the structure over the message, and geographical unity over all forms of 'catholicity.' Thus the nation is born." I quote from *The Writing of History*, trans. Tom Conley (New York: Columbia University Press, 1992), 127. On the complex history of religious ferment at the close of the Middle Ages, see Augustin Renaudet's authoritative *Préréforme et humanisme* (1916; Paris: Librairie d'Argences, 1953). For a suggestive treatment of the theoretical problems raised by these crises, see Donald R. Kelley, *The Beginning of Ideology* (Cambridge: Cambridge University Press, 1981).

11. See Benedict Anderson, *Imagined Communities: Reflections on the Origin and Spread of Nationalism* (London: Verso, 1983), and E. J. Hobsbawm, *Nations and Nationalism since 1780: Programme, Myth, Reality* (Cambridge: Cambridge University Press, 1990).

12. The Renan phrase is from his famous lecture, "Qu'est-ce qu'une nation," which I have consulted in *Nationalism*, ed. John Hutchinson and Anthony D. Smith (Oxford: Oxford University Press, 1994). For a somewhat different approach to Renaissance culture as the subject for a "pre-history" of many of the cultural structures that make up modernity, see Terence Cave's stimulating recent collection of essays, *Pré-histoires: Textes troublés au seuil de la modernité* (Geneva: Droz, 1999), which I read as I was completing this book.

13. Richard Rorty, *Contingency, Irony, and Solidarity* (Cambridge: Cambridge University Press, 1989), 48.

14. For an account of this split in the vocabulary of community see John Agnew and Stuart Corbridge, *Mastering Space: Hegemony, Territory and International Political Economy* (London: Routledge, 1995), 85. The authors go on to discuss the ways in which such major political theorists as Machiavelli and Guicciardini struggle to reconcile the tension between the emerging homogeneous space of the state and the complex networks of alliances that define feudal society.

15. Luigi Alamanni, *Versi e Prose*, ed. Pietro Raffaelli (Florence: Le Monnier, 1859), 2: 212. Seyssel's discussion of institutions may be found in chapters 13 to 18 of his *Monarchie de France*. I have drawn upon the analysis of Seyssel provided by Donald R. Kelley's introduction to J. H. Hexter's translation of Seyssel's text, *The Monarchy of France* (New Haven: Yale University Press, 1981).

16. For a good discussion of the stakes of these tendencies, see Sahlins's introduction to *Boundaries*. More generally, see Ernest Gellner, *Nations and Nationalism* (Oxford: Blackwell, 1983).

17. Etienne Balibar, "The Nation Form: History and Ideology," in Etienne Balibar and Immanuel Wallerstein, *Race, Nation, Class: Ambiguous Identities* (London: Verso, 1991), 88.

18. Henri Lefebvre, *The Production of Space*, trans. Donald Nicholson-Smith (1974; Oxford: Blackwell, 1991), 282.

19. Clément Marot, *Oeuvres poétiques*, ed. Gérard Defaux (Paris: Garnier, 1993), 2: 30, vv. 368–71. My translation.

20. Marot describes Cahors as a place "Où le Soleil non trop excessif est;/Parquoy la terre avec honneur s'y vest/De mille fruicts, de mainct fleur & plante" ["Where the sun is not too excessive;/Since the land is dressed with honor/By a thousand fruits, many flowers and plants"] (vv. 379–81). A moment later, he laments that his father has brought him "pour venir querre icy/Mille malheurs, auxquelz ma destinée/M'avoit submis" ["to come here seeking/A thousand miseries, to which my Destiny/Subjected me"] (vv. 395–96). My translation.

21. Beaune, *Birth of an Ideology*, 294.

22. Robert Gaguin, *Epistolae et Orationes*, ed. Louis Thuasne (Paris: Bouillon, 1903), 191. Later in the sixteenth century Jean Bodin's *Method for the Easy Comprehension of History* would explore the connection between climate and character at great length.

23. In an unpublished paper titled " 'No Sinister Nor No Awkward Claim': *Henry V*," Patricia A. Parker of Stanford University shows how the borders of France and the distinction between what is "French" and what is "English" are extremely fluid in Shakespeare. She notes in particular that Burgundy, who here helps to join the two countries, is elsewhere in the history plays responsible for splitting them apart. I would add that Shakespeare's concern for the differences between France and England extends to the way he manipulates the discourse of climate and temperament when he stresses throughout *Henry V* that the English overcome their naturally phlegmatic temperaments when they spring into action to defeat the French. Political heroism, which defines national identity, is at odds with the discourse of climates, which also (though differently) defines national identity. I would like to thank Professor Parker for sharing her work with me.

24. One thinks here of Geoffroy Tory's treatise on French script and orthography, the *Champ Fleury*, as well as of the popular late-fifteenth-century lyric collection, the *Jardin de Plaisance*. For historical reflections on the garden as a site of cultural and ideological contestation see Terry Comito, *The Idea of the Garden in the Renaissance* (New Brunswick, N.J.: Rutgers University Press, 1978), chapter 3. On the post-Renaissance history of the French garden as a tool of political absolutism see Chandra Mukerji, *Territorial Ambitions and the Gardens of Versailles* (Cambridge: Cambridge University Press, 1997), and Allen S. Weiss, *Mirrors of Infinity* (Princeton: Princeton Architectural Press, 1995). For a more lyrical but authoritative consideration of similar issues, see Denise Le Dantec and Jean-Pierre Le Dantec's 1987 *Reading the French Garden*, in the elegant translation by Jessica Levine (Cambridge: M.I.T. Press, 1990).

25. Tacitus's use of the figure would seem to be the most authoritative classical locus. In the penultimate section (#42) of his "Dialogue," Maternus notes that the great rhetoricians of old flourished in a time of political chaos, when the state "produced beyond all question a more vigorous eloquence, just as an untilled field yields certain herbage in special plenty." I quote from *The Complete Works of Tacitus*, ed. Moses Hadas, trans. Alfred John Church and William Jackson Brodribb (New York: Modern Library, 1942), 768.

26. Salel's poem is called "De la misère et inconstance de la vie humaine," and

may be found in his *Oeuvres poétiques complètes*, ed. Howard H. Kalwies (Geneva: Droz, 1987), 139–56.

27. See Champier's *Hortus Gallicus, pro Gallis in Gallia scriptus* (Lyon: Trechsel, 1533), 5.

28. Here is the original: "N'ayant dix ans en France fuz mené:/Là où depuis me suis tant pourmené,/Que j'oubliay ma langue maternelle,/Et grossement apprins la paternelle,/Langue Françoyse es grands Courts estimée" (vv. 399–403).

29. "Language Françoyse . . . /Laquelle en fin quelcque peu s'est limée,/Suyvant le Roy Françoys premier du nom" (v. 404–5).

30. See Bhabha's introduction to his edited collection, *Nation and Narration* (London: Routledge, 1990). On the hybrid nature of the sign see V. N. Volosinov, *Marxism and the Philosophy of Language*, trans. Ladislav Matejka and I. R. Titunik (Cambridge, Mass.: Harvard University Press, 1986), chapter 2. On the changes in the social situation of the poet between the generation of Jean Marot and the generation of Clément Marot, see Henri Weber, *La création poétique au XVIe siècle en France* (Paris: Nizet, 1955), 63–68. On the dynamics of praise in Marot's poetry more generally, see Ullrich Langer, *Vertu du discours, discours de la vertu: littérature et philosophie morale au XVIe siecle en France* (Geneva: Droz, 1999), 35–48.

31. Benedict Anderson, *Imagined Communities*, 45–48. See, as well, Liah Greenfield, *Nationalism: Five Roads to Modernity* (Cambridge, Mass.: Harvard University Press, 1992), 98–100.

32. Joachim Du Bellay, *La Deffence et Illustration de la Langue Françoyse* (1549), ed. Henri Chamard (Paris: Didier, 1948), 54. My translation.

33. "Nous ne vomissons pas notz paroles de l'estommac, comme les yvroingnes: nous ne les etranglons pas de la gorge, comme les grenoilles: nous ne les decoupons pas dedans le palat, comme les oyzeaux: nous ne les siflons pas des levres, comme les serpens. Si en telles manieres de parler gist la douceur des Langues, je confesse que la nostre est rude & mal sonnante. Mais aussi avons nous cest avantaige de ne tordre point la bouche en cent mile sortes, comme les singes." I cite Chamard's edition of the *Deffence*, 55.

34. Barthélemy Aneau, "Le Quintil Horacien" (1550), in *Traités de poétique et de rhétorique de la Renaissance*, ed. Francis Goyet (Paris: Livre de Poche, 1990), 203. My translation.

35. Chamard's commentary to this passage notes as well that the sweetness of their language is the only positive value that the French are seen to possess in the present. See page 54 of his edition.

36. François Rabelais, *Oeuvres complètes*, ed. Pierre Jourda (Paris: Garnier, 1962), 1: 244. The English is from J. M. Cohen's Penguin Classics version, *The Histories of Gargantua and Pantagruel* (Harmondsworth, 1955), 184. I have slightly modified Cohen's translation to conform more closely to the original.

37. Rabelais, *Histories of Gargantua and Pantagruel*, 184; *Oeuvres complètes*, 264.

38. For a good reading of the scene in the context of the language question, see Raymond C. La Charité, "Reflexion-divertissement et intertextualité: Rabelais et l'écolier limousin," in *Textes et intertextes: Etudes sur le XVIe siècle pour Alfred Glauser*, ed. Floyd Gray and Marcel Tetel (Paris: Nizet, 1979), 93–103.

39. For a quite different analysis that aims to link the scene to debates over the status, not of French, but of Latin, thereby reading it as a humanist satire on

the professors of the Sorbonne, see Gérard Defaux's notes to his coedited edition of *Pantagruel*, in *François Rabelais: Les Cinq Livres* (Paris: Livre de Poche, 1994), 330. I am arguing, by contrast, that the juxtaposition of the reference to French in the title of the chapter and the references to Latin in its text place us in a kind of "no-man's land" between languages. I would link the theme of linguistic and geographical displacement in the episode to something like the processes of "deterritorialization" and "reterritorialization" Deleuze and Guattari have argued accompany the emergence of the modern state. See their *Anti-Oedipus*, trans. Robert Hurley, Mark Seem, and Helen R. Lane (Minneapolis: University of Minnesota Press, 1983), 192–223. Tom Conley has analyzed the relationships among the geographical displacements in this scene in the context of the Renaissance discourse of cartography in *The Self-Made Map: Cartographic Writing in Early Modern France* (Minneapolis: University of Minnesota Press, 1996), 145.

40. See Gilles Deleuze and Félix Guattari, *Kafka: Toward a Minor Literature*, trans. Dana Polan (Minneapolis: University of Minnesota Press, 1986), chapter 3. Franco Moretti offers some useful insights on the relationship between rhetorical troping and geographical borders. See "Of Space and Style," in his *Atlas of the European Novel 1800–1900* (London: Verso, 1998), 40–47. For excellent analyses of the relationship between linguistic distortion and linguistic theory in the Renaissance, see Terence Cave, *The Cornucopian Text: Problems of Writing in the French Renaissance* (Oxford: Clarendon, 1978), as well as Michel Jeanneret, *Le défi des signes* (Orléans: Paradigme, 1994), and, for a specific case study, François Rigolot *Les langages de Rabelais* (Geneva: Droz, 2d edition, 1996). These critics, however, tend to see linguistic distortions and transformations as inherent to language itself, or to "the text." My project is to uncover the historical and political stakes of linguistic practice.

41. Without wishing to ignore the differences among a set of otherwise diverse thinkers, one could, in this context, evoke such notions as Nietzsche's concept of truth as an "army of metaphors," Kenneth Burke's study of the figural shifts in early Christian discourse (in his *Rhetoric of Religion*), Roland Barthes's idea of cultural "myth" as naturalized ideology, and Paul de Man's description of ideology as the confusion of linguistic with natural reality. For a critical account of ideology as literalized trope see Terry Eagleton, *Ideology* (London: Verso, 1991), chapter 7.

42. See Jameson's influential discussion of genre in *The Political Unconscious: Narrative as a Socially Symbolic Act* (Ithaca: Cornell University Press, 1981), chapter 2. But see also Franco Moretti's analysis of genre and rhetoric in *Signs Taken for Wonders: Essays in the Sociology of Literary Forms* (London: Verso, 1983), chapter 1. On the relationship between generic limitation and social violence in the Renaissance, one may also consult Stephen Greenblatt, "Murdering Peasants: Status, Genre, and the Representation of Rebellion," in his *Learning to Curse: Essays in Early Modern Culture* (New York: Routledge, 1990), 99–130. For an insightful study of literature and moral philosophy in the Renaissance that focuses on the rhetoric of praise, while occasionally touching on the formal questions that interest me, see Ullrich Langer, *Vertu du discours, discours de la vertu*.

43. On the spatial and temporal modes projected by different narrative genres see M. M. Bakhtin's several essays on the prehistory of the novel collected in

The Dialogic Imagination: Four Essays, ed. Michael Holquist, trans. Caryl Emerson and Michael Holquist (Austin: University of Texas Press, 1981).

44. On the relationship of epic to imperialist ideology, see David Quint, *Epic and Empire: Politics and Generic Form from Virgil to Milton* (Princeton: Princeton University Press, 1993). The most concise formulation of the relationship between epic form and the crises of community that mark the Renaissance may be found in Robert M. Durling, "The Epic Ideal," in *The Old World: Discovery and Rebirth*, ed. David Daiches and Anthony Thorlby (London: Aldus Books, 1974), 105–46.

45. René Goscinny, *Asterix the Gaul*, illustrated by Albert Uderzo, trans. Anthea Bell and Derek Hockridge (London: Hodder and Stoughton, 1969), 4.

CHAPTER TWO

1. Saint Augustine, "Faith, Hope, and Charity," in *Fathers of the Church*, trans. Bernard Peebles (New York: Fathers of the Church, Inc., 1947), 2: 470.

2. "Caritatem Paulus vocat aedificare proximum, omnes eiusdem corporis membra ducere, omnes unum in Christo putare, de fraternis commodis perinde ut de tuis in domino gaudere, incommodis mederi veluti propriis . . . in summa omnes opes tuas . . . ad hoc referre, ut quamplurimis prosis in Christo." The English is from the *Enchiridion*, in *Collected Works of Erasmus*, vol. 66, trans. Charles Fantazzi (Toronto: University of Toronto Press, 1988), 79. The Latin is from Erasmus von Rotterdam, *Enchiridion*, in *Ausgewählte Schriften*, vol. 1, ed. Werner Welzig (Darmstadt: Wissenschaftliche Buchgesellschaft, 1968), 224.

3. See Lefèvre's guide to reading the Bible, or "Breve instruction pour deuement lire l'escriture saincte" (1529?), in Eugene F. Rice, Jr., ed. *The Prefatory Epistles of Jacques Lefèvre d'Etaples* (New York: Columbia University Press, 1972), 502–17. I have cited p. 508: "Foy faict Jesuchrist nostre; charité nous fait à nostre prochain."

4. Symphorien Champier, "L'ordre de chevalerie," (1510), cited from Paul Allut, *Etude biographique et bibliographique sur Symphorien Champier* (Lyon, 1859), 310. My translation. On the relationship between the mission of the French crown and doctrines of charity see Liah Greenfield, *Nationalism: Five Roads to Modernity* (Cambridge: Harvard University Press, 1992), 97. Charity, of course, is one of the things that Machiavelli specifically advises the modern prince to ignore, if necessary, in order to seize and maintain power. See *The Prince*, chapter 18.

5. François Rabelais, *Oeuvres complètes*, ed. Pierre Jourda (Paris: Garnier, 1962), 1: 263. The English version is by J. M. Cohen, from *The Histories of Gargantua and Pantagruel* (Harmondsworth: Penguin, 1955), 196. All references will be to these editions and page numbers will be indicated in the text. For the sake of clarity I note here that the story of Pantagruel's father, Gargantua, was published in 1534, two years after the publication of *Pantagruel*. Many modern editors place *Gargantua* as the "first book" in the Rabelais *oeuvre*. However, since I am tracing shifts in Rabelais's responses to emerging political crises, I shall consider these works in the order in which they were published.

6. Panurge's *panourgos* embraces a semantic field that suggests everything from political prudence to handiness to moral duplicity. For discussions of the relationship between the semantic slipperiness of the name and the moral sta-

tus of the character, see Jerome Schwartz, *Irony and Ideology in Rabelais: Structures of Subversion* (Cambridge: Cambridge University Press, 1990), 27–29; François Rigolot, *Poétique et onomastique: L'exemple de la renaissance* (Geneva: Droz, 1977), 103; Edwin M. Duval, *The Design of Rabelais's "Pantagruel"* (New Haven: Yale University Press, 1991), 82–83; Raymond C. La Charité, *Re-creation, Reflection, and Recreation: Perspectives on Rabelais's "Pantagruel"* (Lexington, Ky.: French Forum, 1980), 85–87; and Ludwig Schrader, *Panurge und Hermes* (Bonn: Romanisches Seminar der Universität Bonn, 1958), 80–84.

7. For discussions of the moral implications of this encounter, see Gérard Defaux, "Au coeur du *Pantagruel*: Les deux chapitres IX de l'édition Nourry," *Kentucky Romance Quarterly* 21 (1974): 59–96; Schwartz, *Irony and Ideology*, 27–30; Duval, *Design of Rabelais's "Pantagruel*," chapter 4; and Ullrich Langer, "Charity and the Singular: The Object of Love in Rabelais," in *Nominalism*, ed. H. Keiper et al. (Atlanta: Rodopi, 1997), 1–10. Terence Cave has discussed Panurge's polyglottism in the context of developing French national identity in "Panurge, Pathelin, and Other Polyglots," in *Lapidary Inscriptions: Renaissance Essays for Donald A. Stone, Jr.*, ed. Barbara C. Bowen and Jerry C. Nash (Lexington, Ky.: French Forum, 1991), 171–82. Tom Conley examines the relationships between the episode and the encounter with the Limousin student in his book *The Self-Made Map: Cartographic Writing in Early Modern France* (Minneapolis: University of Minnesota Press, 1996), 145–48. Biblical citations quote the Revised Standard Edition. I have used the *New Oxford Annotated Bible*, ed. Herbert G. May and Bruce Metzger (New York: Oxford University Press, 1977).

8. Luke 10: 30–37. Conley, too, notes the importance of the Samaritan fable in *Self-Made Map*, 147.

9. Erasmus, *Enchiridion*, in *Ausgewählte Schriften*, vol. 1: 270. The English is from Erasmus, *Enchiridion*, in *Collected Works*, vol. 66: 93. Denys Hay gives a good account of the stress placed on the universal mission of Christianity at the onset of the Renaissance in his book *Europe: The Emergence of an Idea* (Edinburgh: University of Edinburgh Press, 1957), chapter 2. On the relationship between community and interpretation in Rabelais see David Quint, *Origin and Originality in Renaissance Literature* (New Haven: Yale University Press, 1983), chapter 6.

10. For a good account of the importance of Febvre's work in Rabelais studies, see Natalie Davis's essay "Rabelais among the Censors (1940s–1540s)," *Representations* 32 (1990): 1–32. Febvre's discussion of the relationship of Erasmus and Rabelais occupies chapter 8 of his book. For a cogent discussion of the stakes of reading Rabelais in the humanist tradition see Terence Cave's essay "Reading Rabelais: Variations on the Rock of Virtue," in *Literary Theory/Renaissance Texts*, ed. Patricia Parker and David Quint (Baltimore: Johns Hopkins University Press, 1986), 78–95.

11. Erasmus, *De ratione studii*, in *Collected Works of Erasmus*, vol. 24, trans. Brian McGregor, ed. Craig R. Thompson (Toronto: University of Toronto Press, 1978), 683.

12. On the relationship between the practical aims of humanist rhetoric and problems of judgment see Victoria Kahn, *Rhetoric, Prudence, and Skepticism in the Renaissance* (Ithaca: Cornell University Press, 1985). On the rhetorical paradoxes underlying the Erasmian hermeneutic see Terence Cave, *The Cor-*

nucopian Text: Problems of Writing in the French Renaissance (Oxford: Clarendon, 1979) 78–124. On the ideological and literary implications of the Renaissance attempt to appropriate specifically ancient models as images of action see Timothy Hampton, *Writing from History: The Rhetoric of Exemplarity in Renaissance Literature* (Ithaca: Cornell University Press, 1990).

13.   I cite Margaret Mann Phillips's translation of the *Adages, I,i,l to I,v,100*, in *Collected Works of Erasmus*, vol. 31, ed. R. A. B. Mynors (Toronto: University of Toronto Press, 1982), 30. For discussions of Erasmian notions of politics see Margaret Mann Phillips's *Erasmus and the Northern Renaissance* (London: Hodder and Stoughton, 1949), chapter 4; and James D. Tracy, *The Politics of Erasmus* (Toronto: University of Toronto Press, 1978). On the question of the political constitution of the Christian community see Otto Schottenloher, "Erasmus und die Respublica Christiana," *Historische Zeitschrift* 210, no. 2 (1970): 295–323. On Erasmus's difficulties in representing this community, see Hampton, *Writing from History*, chapter 2.

14.   "Summum autem amorem summae similitudinis esse comitem." *De Ratione Studii*, 686; the Latin is from Jean-Claude Margolin's edition, *Opera omnia* (Amsterdam: North-Holland, 1969–83), I (part 2): 141. For an extended discussion of the relationship between similitude and friendship, see Erasmus's interpretation of Virgil's second eclogue on pp. 141–43.

15.   Clément Marot, "Epistre à son amy Lyon," in *Oeuvres poétiques*, ed. Gérard Defaux (Paris: Garnier, 1993), 1: 92. Similarly, the prologue to Marguerite de Navarre's *Heptaméron* features a scene in which a desperate nobleman is helped by a passing shepherd who recognizes his misery "better from seeing him, than from his words" ["entendoit myeulx sa necessité tant en le voiant que en escoutant sa parolle"]. See the edition of Michel François (Paris: Garnier, 1967), 5. My translation.

16.   For a brief summary of Luther's changing attitude toward a Turkish war see Robert C. Schultz's introduction to his and Charles M. Jacobs's translation of the *On the War against the Turks*, in *Luther's Works*, vol. 46, ed. Jaroslav Pelikan and Helmut T. Lehmann, (Philadelphia: Fortress Press, 1967), 157–59; as well as Heinrich Bornkamm, *Luther's World of Thought*, trans. Martin H. Bertram (St. Louis: Concordia, 1958), 16–18. For background on the literary implications of changing Renaissance attitudes toward the Turks see C. A. Patrides, " 'The Blody and Cruell Turke': The Background of a Renaissance Commonplace," *Studies in the Renaissance* 10, no. 1 (1963): 126–35. For a discussion of the French attitude in the period, though with special attention to the later sixteenth century, see Michael J. Heath, *Crusading Commonplaces: La Noue, Lucinge and Rhetoric against the Turks* (Geneva: Droz, 1986).

17.   On the attempts of humanists in particular to deal with the Turkish threat see Heath, *Crusading Commonplaces*, chapter 1, as well as Robert P. Adams, *The Better Part of Valor: Erasmus, More and Vives on War and Peace* (Seattle: University of Washington Press, 1962), 107, 171, and 298.

18.   "Citius fiat, ut nos degeneremus in Turcas, quam illi per nos reddantur Christiani." I cite the *Institutio principis christiani* in the edition of Otto Herding, which is included in vol. 4, part 1 of Erasmus's *Opera omnia*, ed. Jean-Claude Margolin (Amsterdam: North-Holland, 1974), 218. All translations of Erasmus are mine unless otherwise indicated.

19.   Erasmus, *De bello Turcico*: "Trahimur regnandi libidine . . . et ut dicam in

summa, Turcae pugnamus cum Turcis." I cite A. G. Weiler's edition, *Opera omnia*, vol. 5, part 3 (Amsterdam: North-Holland, 1986), 52. These arguments are all repeated in more or less the same language in the *Querela pacis*. See the edition of Otto Herding, *Opera omnia*, vol. 4, part 2 (Amsterdam: North-Holland, 1977), especially 80–82.

20.　"Nostris vitiis illi debent suas victorias." Erasmus, *On the Turkish War*, ed. A. G. Weiler, in *Opera omnia* vol. 5, part 3, 50. In *Crusading Commonplaces* Heath points to the contradictory clichés of anti-Turkish rhetoric that depict the Turk as both insatiably bloodthirsty and effeminately luxurious.

21.　I cite the translation of Margaret Mann Phillips in *Erasmus on His Times: A Shortened Version of the "Adages" of Erasmus* (Cambridge: Cambridge University Press, 1967), 135. The original reads: "Atqui quos nos vocamus Turcas, magna parte semichristiani sunt, et fortassis propiores vero Christianismo, quam plerique nostrum sunt," cited from *Adagia*, ed. R. Hoven, *Opera omnia*, vol. 2, part 7 (Amsterdam: North-Holland, 1999), 39.

22.　"Quum imperita multitudo Turcarum nomen audit, protinus concipit animo graues iras, et ad caedem inflammatur, canes et christiani nominis hostes illos vociferans; non reputans illos primum esse homines, deinde semichristianos . . . nec cogitans nullos esse perniciosiores ecclesia hostes, quam impios principes . . ." ["Whenever those in the ignorant multitude hear the word Turk, they immediately express great anger and are inflamed to slaughter, calling them dogs and enemies to Christians, not taking them to be first off men, then half-Christians, nor realizing that there are no more pernicious enemies of the Church than impious princes"]. *De bello Turcico*, 53. Erasmus's double logic, which both rejects and accepts the Turk, may be registered in his very lexicon. For as he attacks those who want to kill the Turks like dogs ("non aliter occidere quam canem rabidum" [*De bello Turcico*, 58])—an image to which we shall return in a moment—he describes their evil deeds as "latrocinia" (see, for example, pp. 40 and 42), a term that stems from the noun "latro" (thief), but that offers a long-standing Latin pun on the verb "latro" (to bark).

23.　"Si cupimus Turcas ad Christi religionem adducere, prius ipsi simus Christiani." *Querela pacis*, ed. Otto Herding, *Opera omnia*, vol. 5, part 3 (Amsterdam: North-Holland, 1977), 96.

24.　The contradictory relationship between ideals of charity and the crisis of European unity during the period is explored as well in the dialogue *Julius Excluded from Heaven (Julius exclusus e coelis)* of 1518, a text presumed to be by Erasmus but never published or claimed by him. Here Pope Julius II and Saint Peter have a dialogue before the gates of heaven, as Julius seeks entry. On the last page of the text, after having attacked Julius's worldly love of luxury, Peter criticizes him for having meddled in politics. Julius responds that Christendom would have collapsed and been overrun by Turks had it not been for his policies. Peter responds that the first church grew through the blood of martyrs, not through wars of conquest, but he never in fact responds to Julius's savvy evocation of the paradoxes represented by the Turkish threat. I have consulted the *Julius Excluded from Heaven* in Michael J. Heath's translation. It may be found in *Collected Works of Erasmus*, vol. 27, ed. A. H. T. Levi (Toronto: University of Toronto Press, 1986), 155–98. Erasmus's recuperation of the Turk as "semi-Christian" was, of course, not shared by all. For example, in several treatises on the Turkish question from the late 1520s, his friend Juan Luis Vives settled for simply attacking Christian disunity and lamenting the cruelty of the Turks.

25. For background on French relationships with the Ottoman Empire see Clarence D. Rouillard, *The Turk in French History, Thought and Literature (1520–1660)* (Paris, 1940; rpt. New York: AMS Press, 1973), 1–63 and 105–28. On Rincón's embassies to Suleiman see V.-L. Bourrilly, "Antonio Rincon et la politique orientale de François Ier," *Revue historique*, 113 (1913): 64–83, 268–308; as well as R. J. Knecht, *Francis I* (Cambridge: Cambridge University Press, 1982), 224ff. Rincón's embassy was seen throughout the period as somewhat of a scandal. Thus, for example, Giovanni Botero's *Della ragione de stato* (Venice, 1589) closes with a denunciation of Rincón as the example of a bad ambassador. The Turkish threat after the fall of Constantinople in 1453 was a frequent topic in poetry of the late fifteenth and early sixteenth centuries. Jean Marot, for example, wrote a "Complainte de Constantinople." For general background on the iconography of Francis as crusader see Anne-Marie Lecoq, *François Ier Imaginaire* (Paris: Macula, 1987).

26. Very little critical attention has been paid to this episode by scholars of Rabelais. However, for one reading that takes it as a kind of rewriting of Odysseus's recounting his adventures to the Phaiakians, see Gérard Defaux, *Le curieux, le glorieux, et la sagesse du monde* (Lexington, Ky.: French Forum, 1982), chapter 2.

27. It is certainly no accident that the sequence of episodes entitled "Of the Morals and Habits of Panurge," in which the character's predilection for lying is demonstrated, immediately *follows* his "true" account of his escape, with its play on conventions of prisoners' stories. For an account of the catastrophic attack on Mytilene, together with much information on French naval encounters with the Turks during the period, see Charles de la Roncière, *Histoire de la marine française* (Paris: Plon, 1914), 3:37–59.

28. On the relationship of rhetoric to alterity in history writing, see François Hartog, *The Mirror of Herodotus: The Representation of the Other in the Writing of History*, trans. Janet Lloyd (Berkeley: University of California Press, 1988), part 2, chapter 6.

29. Edwin Duval notes the limitations of Panurge's response in *Design of "Pantagruel"* (New Haven: Yale University Press, 1991), 67–68 and 91–94. He points out that it is precisely "piedad natural" ["natural piety"] that Panurge seeks from Pantagruel when he speaks to him in Spanish during their first meeting.

30. For Bersuire, Sodom is the "carnal life," while the mountain is the contemplative life of the Church. See his commentary in *Opera omnia* (Cologne, 1692), 1:9. Erasmus offers a similar interpretation of the same Biblical passage in the *Enchiridion*, but stresses that the mountain stands for spirituality in general. See *Collected Works*, vol. 66: 56.

31. The beaver image is first mentioned in Pliny the Younger's *Naturalis historia* 32.26. Rabelais's contemporary Lodovico Ariosto uses it in canto 27 of the *Orlando Furioso*. On the proverb about throwing one's bacon to the dogs, see Edmond Huguet, *Dictionnaire de la langue française du seizième siècle* (Paris: Champion, 1927–33), 2:265.

32. Castration, of course, is not the same as the removal of the penis. There are certainly images of castration in Rabelais, as ably analyzed by Lawrence D.

Kritzman, *The Rhetoric of Sexuality and the Literature of the French Renaissance* (Cambridge: Cambridge University Press, 1991), 111–26. On the relationship of Oedipus to the rise of the state see Gilles Deleuze and Félix Guattari, *Anti-Oedipus,* trans. Robert Hurley et al. (Minneapolis: University of Minnesota Press, 1985), part 2. For a study of this conjunction in the seventeenth-century theater see Mitchell Greenberg, *Canonical States/Canonical Stages* (Minneapolis: University of Minnesota Press, 1994).

33. Fredric Jameson, *The Political Unconscious: Narrative as a Socially Symbolic Act* (Ithaca: Cornell University Press, 1981), 82.

34. The metaphorical link between penises and "lardons" suggests another connotation to the appearance of the courtesan and the "little Turk" near the end of the scene. The courtesan knows that Panurge's literal member is unable to function. Since the strip of bacon is a metaphorical member, the "little Turk's" gesture of nibbling it suggests a simulated homosexual fellatio. This produces a conjunction of both meanings and bodies that is reinforced by the well-known cliché of anti-Turkish propaganda during the period, which cast the Turks as not only polygamists but also homosexuals. The cliché may be connected to Rabelais's own language through the expression "noce de chiens," (dog wedding), which was usd to describe sodomy. Luther evokes both the cliché of homosexuality and the notion of "dog weddings" in his treatise *On the War against the Turks* (see note 16, above).

35. Aristotle, *Nicomachean Ethics,* trans. W. D. Ross and J. O. Urmson, in *Complete Works of Aristotle,* ed. Jonathan Barnes (Princeton: Princeton University Press, 1984), 2: 1796.

36. Erasmus, *Adages,* 1: 5, 93 in *Collected Works,* vol. 32: 250. But see as well, André Thevet, *Cosmographie de Levant,* ed. Frank Lestringant (Geneva: Droz, 1985), 49: "The architects of our time apply the square, the level, or the plumb bob to the stone which they wish to carve. But they did the reverse, applying the stone to the square, or to other, similar, rulers, from which comes the proverbial phrase, 'The Rule of Mytilene,' which we use when we want to signify, without saying as much, that the order of Nature has been reversed, that we want to reduce facts to theory, and not theory to facts, the law to our behavior and way of living, not our way of living to the law" ["les Architectes de notre tems apliquent l'esquarre, le niveau, ou le plomb, à la pierre qu'ilz veulent tailler: mais ils faisoient tout au rebours, apliquans la pierre à l'esquarre ou autres semblables regles, dont est venu ce proverbe. La Regle de Metelin, duquel nous usons, quand voulons signifier couvertement l'ordre de Nature estre renversé, et que voulons reduire le fait à la raison, non pas la raison au fait: la loy à nos meurs, et maniere de vivre, non pas notre maniere de vivre à la loy"].

37. Jean de Léry, *History of a Voyage to the Land of Brazil, Otherwise Called America,* trans. Janet Whatley (1578; reprint, Berkeley: University of California Press, 1990), 126.

38. It is worth pointing out that the themes of charity and community were not lost on all travel writing during the period. Thus, in his account of his early fifteenth-century journey to the Holy Land, Bertrandon de la Brocquière insists, in terms that foreshadow both Erasmus and Rabelais, on the charity shown by the Turks to each other. "They are men of probity, and charitable toward each other. I have often observed, that should a poor person pass by when they are

eating, they would invite him to partake of their meal, which is a thing we never do" ["Ils sont moult charitables gens les ungs aux aultres et gens de bonnefoy. J'ay veu souvent, quant nous mengions, que s'il passoit un povre homme auprès d'eulx, ilz le faisoient venir mengier avec nous. Ce que nous ne ferions point"]. He goes on to stress the virtue of his own guide in the same terms: "This good man, whose name was Mohammed, had done me innumerable services. He was very charitable, and never refused alms when asked in the name of God. It was through charity he had been so kind to me, and I must confess that without his assistance I could not have performed my journey without incurring the greatest danger" ["Et là, je prins congié de mondit maleu qui avoit nom Mahommet, lequel m'avoit fait moult de biens. Et ce faisoit il par grant charité; et s'il n'eust esté je n'eusse peu faire mon chemin que à grant peine"]. I cite the *Voyage d'Outremer*, ed. Ch. Shefer (Paris: E. Leroux, 1892), 96 and 121. The English version is from *Early Travels in Palestine*, ed. Thomas Wright (London: Woodfall and Son, n.d.), 317 and 327. However, de la Brocquière's text is atypical. Rouillard (*The Turk in French History*, 40), notes that most travel writing demonized the Turks. In any event, as Rouillard also notes, de la Brocquière's text only circulated in manuscript form during the fifteenth and sixteenth centuries. Thus, it would be difficult to say whether either Erasmus or Rabelais would have known it. On the epistemological problems raised by the figure of the witness in Renaissance travel writing, see Andrea Frisch, "Novel Histories: The Figure of the Witness in Early Modern Fiction and Travel Narrative," Ph.D. dissertation, University of California at Berkeley, 1997.

39. For a somewhat different reading of this scene, which links the question of the witness to the definition of literary authority, see Andrea Frisch, "*Quod vidimus testamur*: Testimony, Narrative Agency and the World in Pantagruel's Mouth," *French Forum*, 24, no. 3 (1999): 261–83.

40. On the parallels between the two scenes, see Duval, *Design of Rabelais's "Pantagruel,"* 88.

CHAPTER THREE

1. Quoted in Donald R. Kelley, *The Beginning of Ideology* (Cambridge: Cambridge University Press, 1981), 17. Kelley's entire discussion of the atmosphere surrounding the Affaire des Placards is particularly clear and useful.

2. Kelley, *Beginning of Ideology*, 18.

3. Quoted in R. J. Knecht, *Francis I* (Cambridge: Cambridge University Press, 1982), 274.

4. The differences between the two books have been underscored by Michael A. Screech, in his *Rabelais* (Ithaca: Cornell University Press, 1979), 118–22; and Thomas M. Greene, in *Rabelais: A Study in Comic Courage* (Englewood Cliffs, N.J.: Prentice-Hall, 1970), 43. See as well the helpful notes by Gérard Defaux to his edition of the 1535 *Gargantua* in *François Rabelais: Les Cinq Livres*, ed. Jean Céard, Gérard Defaux, and Michel Simonin (Paris: Livre de Poche, 1994).

5. François Rabelais, *Oeuvres complètes*, ed. Pierre Jourda (Peris: Garnier, 1962); English translation by J. M. Cohen, *The Histories of Gargantua and Pantagruel* (Harmondsworth: Penguin, 1955). All subsequent page citations are to these editions.

6. The complexities of this form of representation have been discussed in par-

ticular by Michael Screech in *Rabelais* 218–20; Jerome Schwartz, *Irony and Ideology in Rabelais* (Cambridge: Cambridge University Press, 1990), 73–75; and Gérard Defaux, "Rabelais's Realism, Again," in *François Rabelais: Critical Assessments*, ed. Jean-Claude Carron (Baltimore: Johns Hopkins University Press, 1995), 19–38. The relationship between the war and Rabelais's father's affairs was first pointed out by Abel Lefranc, in his *Rabelais* (Paris: Albin Michel, 1953), chapter 3.

7. This dimension of humanism, and of Rabelais's work, has gone largely unexplored. One of the few discussions of politics in Rabelais is Nicole Aronson's *Les idées politiques de Rabelais* (Paris: Nizet, 1973), which concerns itself primarily with trying to pin down Rabelais's attitude toward the policies of Francis I.

8. Claude de Seyssel, *The Monarchy of France*, trans. J. H. Hexter (New Haven: Yale University Press, 1981), 132. The original French is from *La Monarchie de France*, ed. Jacques Poujol (Paris: Librairie d'Argences, 1961), 192.

9. I quote the *Biblia Vulgata*, ed. Alberto Colunga and Laurentio Turrado (Madrid: Biblioteca de Autores Cristianos, 1977). The English is the Revised Standard Version, from *The New Oxford Annotated Bible*, ed. Herbert G. May and Bruce M. Metzger (New York: Oxford University Press, 1977).

10. Erasmus is also concerned with this passage for philological reasons, suggesting that the Greek "parazeloso" means not "to emulate," but "to provoke to emulate." He says, "Let [the commentators] produce for us one passage where it is used in the sense of *aemulari*." Erasmus, *Paraphrase on Romans*, in *Collected Works of Erasmus*, vol. 42, ed. Robert D. Sider (Toronto: University of Toronto Press, 1984), 65. On the debates surrounding Paul's epistle in the Renaissance, see Jean-Claude Margolin, "The Epistle to the Romans (Chapter 11) According to the Versions and/or Commentaries of Valla, Colet, Lefèvre, and Erasmus," in *The Bible in the Sixteenth Century*, ed. David C. Steinmetz (Durham: Duke University Press, 1990), 136–66. Aristotle's discussion of emulation comes in the second book of the *Rhetoric*, 1388a-b.

11. Erasmus, *Paraphrase on Romans*, in *Collected Works*, vol. 42: 65. Here is the original paraphrase of the passage: "si qua fieri possit ut hac ratione provocem gentem meam, meam quidem affinitate generis licet fide alienam, ad aemulandum pietatem vestram, vel invidia quapiam ac livore, ut est zelotypum genus, atque ita si cunctos non queam adducere, saltem aliquot ex illis servem." I quote from *In Epistolam Pauli Apostoli ad Romanos Paraphrasis* (Basel: Froben, 1517), 121.

12. For an analysis of how these moral catagories are linked to positions in literary narrative see Fredric Jameson, *The Political Unconscious: Narrative as a Socially Symbolic Act* (Ithaca: Cornell University Press, 1979), 115.

13. The political topicality of the book has troubled even its best readers. Thus, for example, in an otherwise insightful treatment of the Picrocholine war Thomas Greene finds it necessary to allegorize the figure of Picrochole: "Picrochole in this chapter comes to represent not Charles V (as some would have it) but the frightful maw of human ambition revealed by modern warfare" (*Rabelais*, 44). I will argue that it is impossible to account for the complexities of Rabelais's rhetoric without taking into account the pressure on the text by current events, and the ideological problems raised by the conflict between humanism and emerging nationalism.

14. On the colloquoy tradition, see Michel Jeanneret, *A Feast of Words: Banquets and Table Talk in the Renaissance*, trans. Jeremy Whitely and Emma Hughes (1987; trans. Chicago: University of Chicago Press, 1991).

15. Erasmus, *Education of the Christian Prince*, in *Collected Works of Erasmus*, vol. 27, trans. Neil M. Cheshire and Michael J. Heath (Toronto: University of Toronto Press, 1986), 276; the Latin is in Erasmus, *Opera omnia*, vol. 4, part 1, ed. Otto Herding (Amsterdam: North-Holland, 1974), 207.

16. For a fuller explanation see the adage II, iv, 13, "Ad vivum resecare," Erasmus, *Adages, II, i, 1 to II, vi, 100*, ed. and trans. R. A. B. Mynors in *Collected Works*, vol. 33 (Toronto: University of Toronto Press, 1991), 196.

17. Erasmus, *Education*, in *Collected Works*, vol. 27: 315.

18. Erasmus, *Education*, in *Collected Works*, vol. 27: 286; *Opera omnia*, vol. 4, part 1: 218: "Nunc fere Gallum odit Anglus non ab iliud, nisi quod Gallus est ... Cur haec stultissima nomina magis nos distrahunt, quam conglutinat omnibus commune Christi vocabulum?"

19. The *Education of the Christian Prince*, and the *Complaint of Peace* may be found in volume 27 of Erasmus, *Collected Works*. The *Enchiridion* is in volume 66.

20. For a general comparative consideration of this generation of political thinkers, see Jack H. Hexter, *The Vision of Politics on the Eve of the Reformation* (New York: Basic Books, 1973), as well as Quentin Skinner, *The Foundations of Modern Political Thought*, vol. 1 (Cambridge: Cambridge University Press, 1978). It is unlikely that Rabelais was familiar with Machiavelli's treatise, and I mention it here merely to provide context.

21. Erasmus, *Education*, in *Collected Works*, vol. 27: 277. The Latin is in *Opera omnia*, vol. 4, part 1: 207.

22. Seyssel, *Monarchy of France*, 130; *La monarchie de France*, 190.

23. Seyssel, *Monarchy of France*, 132; *La monarchie de France*, 192.

24. Erasmus, *Complaint of Peace*, *Collected Works*, vol. 27:315 and *Education*, vol. 27: 275; *Opera omnia*, vol. 4, part 2: 90; vol. 4, part 1: 207. For a somewhat different analysis of the encounter, one linking it to the image of the devil throughout Rabelais's works, see Diane Desrosiers-Bonin, *Rabelais et l'humanisme civil* (Geneva: Droz, 1992), 171–85. Also, on the deployment of the devil image, see Richard M. Berrong, *Every Man for Himself: Social Order and Its Dissolution in Rabelais* (Saratoga, Calif.: ANMA Libri, 1985), 27–29.

25. On the topos of the discordant epic "enemy," see David Quint, *Epic and Empire: Politics and Generic Form from Virgil to Milton* (Princeton: Princeton University Press, 1993), chapter 1.

26. As Diane Desrosiers-Bonin has demonstrated, the image of the devil migrates across the whole territory of the book, becoming alternatively associated with Picrochole (who is assumed by Grandgousier to be motivated by the devil), with the monks in the Abbey of Seuillé, and with Gargantua's men. See Desrosiers-Bonin, *Rabelais*, 174.

27. See Quintilian, *Institutio Oratoria*, book 10.5. For a good discussion of the corporeal metaphors used to describe rhetoric during the Renaissance, see Wayne A. Rebhorn, *The Emperor of Men's Minds: Literature and the Renaissance Discourse of Rhetoric* (Ithaca: Cornell University Press, 1995), 218–40, as well as, more generally, Patricia Parker, *Literary Fat Ladies: Rhetoric, Gender, Property* (London: Methuen, 1987).

28. Later versions of *Gargantua* removed these oaths, under pressure, presum-

ably, from ecclesiastical authority. Cohen's Penguin translation deletes them, so this translation is mine.

29. For an insightful reading of ways in which the Parisian's curses evoke different dialects and geographical spaces, see Tom Conley, *The Self-Made Map: Cartographic Writing in Early Modern France* (Minneapolis: University of Minnesota Press, 1996), 152–55.

30. On the sacramental dimension of the scene, see Dennis John Costa, *Irenic Apocalypse: Some Uses of Apocalyptic in Dante, Petrarch, and Rabelais* (Saratoga, Calif.: ANMA Libri, 1981), chapter 5.

31. Erasmus, *Complaint of Peace*, in *Collected Works*, vol. 27: 309; *Opera omnia*, vol. 4, part II: 84.

32. On the ambivalent importance of the Erasmian dialogue for Rabelais's poetics, see Terence Cave, *The Cornucopian Text: Problems of Writing in the French Renaissance* (Oxford: Clarendon Press, 1979), chapter 1.

33. On the theology underlying Frère Jean's activism, see Screech, *Rabelais*, 234ff.

34. For the notion that the Evangelical message is given to all, regardless of social stratum or learning, see Jacques Lefèvre d'Etaples's "Exhortation" to the reader of his translation of the Bible (2d edition, 1525), reprinted in *The Prefatory Epistles of Jacques Lefèvre d'Etaples and Related Texts*, ed. Eugene F. Rice, Jr. (New York: Columbia University Press, 1972), 487–93.

35. On the history of the lily see Colette Beaune, *The Birth of an Ideology: Myths and Symbols of Nation in Late-Medieval France*, trans. Susan Ross Huston (Berkeley: University of California Press, 1991), chapter 7. For the various iconographic traditions surrounding the figure of Francis, see Anne-Marie Lecoq, *François Ier Imaginaire* (Paris: Macula, 1987).

36. "Never did Maugis the Hermit—of whom it is written in the Deeds of the four Sons of Aymon—wield his pilgrim's staff so valiantly against the Saracens as this monk swung the staff of his cross in his encounter with the enemy" (101) ["Jamais Maugis, hermite, ne se porta si vaillamment à tout son bourdon contre les Sarrasins, desquelz est escript es gestes des quatre filz Haymon, comme feist le moine à l'encontre de ennemys avec le baston de la croix" (112)].

37. The humanist texts relating to the magical frock are listed in Gérard Defaux's notes to his edition of *Gargantua*, in *Rabelais: Les Cinq Livres*, 216.

38. Erasmus, *Enchiridion*, in *Collected Works of Erasmus*, vol. 66, trans. Charles Fantazzi (Toronto: University of Toronto Press, 1988), 31. Here is the Latin: "duo praecipue paranda sunt arma ei, cui sit cum septem illis gentibus ... precatio et scientia. Semper armatos esse vult Paulus, qui sine intermissione iubet orare ... Sed precatio quidem potior, ut quae cum deo sermones misceat ...", cited from Erasmus, *Enchiridion*, in *Ausgewählte Schriften*, vol. 1, ed. Werner Welzig (Darmstadt: Wissenschaftliche Buchgesellschaft, 1968), 74–76.

39. See Lodovico Ariosto, *Orlando Furioso*, ed. Emilio Bigi (Milan: Rusconi, 1982), 11.50 and 29.60–62.

40. "civilitas civilitatem inuitat, aequitas aequitatem;" Erasmus, *Collected Works*, vol. 27: 285; *Opera omnia*, vol. 4, part 1: 216. I have amended the English to conform more closely with the original.

41. Erasmus, "Complaint of Peace," *Collected Works*, vol. 27: 321. Here is the original: "Nunc gratia gratiam pariat et beneficium beneficio inuitetur, isque re-

galior videatur, qui plus de suo iure concesserit." *Opera omnia*, vol. 7, part 2: 99–100.

42. Erasmus, *Education*, in *Collected Works*, vol. 27: 263; *Opera omnia*, vol. 4, part 1: 194.

43. Curiously, Grandgousier's rhetoric places the Saracens, elsewhere so present in the text, in a rejected past—as if the Turkish question were now settled and the most pressing concern were the disunity of Europe.

44. Erasmus, "Complaint of Peace," *Collected Works*, vol. 27: 310; *Opera omnia*, vol. 7, part 2: 84. For an insightful reading of the temporal shifts in both Grandgousier's speech and Picrochole's earlier harangue to his men, see Eric MacPhail, "Rabelais's Allegory of Prudence," *Etudes Rabelaisiennes* 30 (1995): 55–66.

45. "Non imaginibus et statuis, sed virtute et meritis prorogatur." Pliny the Younger, *Letters, Panegyricus*, ed. and trans. Betty Radice (Cambridge: Harvard University Press, 1969), 55.10: 452. The theological importance of the Plato passage on sedition is stressed by Screech, *Rabelais*, 234.

46. See 2 Corinthians, 3:1–4.

47. On the long battles over Brittany and Breton identity during the second half of the fifteenth century, see Emmanuel Le Roy Ladurie, *The Royal French State: 1460–1610*, trans. Juliet Vale (Oxford: Blackwell, 1994), 75–78.

48. In my discussion of exchange and utopia, here and below, I have profited from Richard Halpern's reading of *Utopia* in his book *The Poetics of Primitive Accumulation: English Renaissance Culture and the Genealogy of Capital* (Ithaca: Cornell University Press, 1991), chapter 4.

49. See, for example, the section in the *Education of the Christian Prince* on princely liberality, titled "De Beneficentia Principis," *Collected Works*, vol. 27:262–64.

50. St. Thomas More, *Utopia*, trans. Edward D. Surtz, S. J. (New Haven: Yale University Press, 1964), 94. The Latin phrase is, "ipsa benefacti conscientia, ac recordatio charitatis," cited from André Prévost's bilingual French/Latin edition (Paris: Mame, 1978), 520.

51. Edwin Duval, *The Design of Rabelais's "Tiers livre de Pantagruel"* (Geneva: Droz, 1997), 176. Screech's analysis comes in his *Rabelais*, 191–94. Gordon Braden has stressed the indebtedness of this description of human nature to traditions of Stoic writing, specifically to Cicero's blending of education and noble birth. See his *Renaissance Tragedy and the Senecan Tradition* (New Haven: Yale University Press, 1985), 81–85.

52. In this regard Theleme seems to follow the conventional function of Utopia which, in Halpern's felicitous phrase, involves the "negation of a negation." As he writes, "Utopian pleasure arises as the opposite of that which is forbidden, unavailable, or withheld, that is to say, as the negation of a negation" (*Poetics of Primitive Accumulation*, 148). For Rabelais, this means that the goodness of the Thelemites is the appetite that replaces the erasure of a negation of the appetite to throw off oppression. Erasmus stresses the importance of the Pauline image for Christian liberty in his *Enchiridion*. See *Collected Works*, vol. 66: 78.

53. Romans 11:14. I cite, as before, *Biblia Vulgata*.

54. Here is the Vulgate version: "Omnes honorate: fraternitatem diligite: Deum timete: Regem honorificate."

55. Gordon Braden, in *Renaissance Tragedy*, 82, has linked the notion of "honor" to traditions of Stoic thought. The courtly resonances of the term have been noted as well by Carla Freccero, in *Father Figures: Genealogy and Narrative Structure in Rabelais* (Ithaca: Cornell University Press, 1991), 118. Freccero notes that Screech's theological reading of the passage quite outrageously "translates" honor as the theological doctrine of "synderesis."

56. It may be because of the extreme pressure on images of community in *Gargantua* that Rabelais turns, in his third book, to locate the dynamics of Christian charity in the soul of the individual subject Panurge. Duval, in the *Design of Rabelais's "Tiers Livre,"* 172, notes that Theleme is a "virtual blueprint" for the type of education Pantagruel tries to impose on Panurge in the third book. And, indeed, after the prologue of the third book, the communitarian themes that are so important in *Gargantua* virtually disappear.

57. Both Freccero, in *Father Figures*, and Michel Beaujour, in *Le jeu de Rabelais* (Paris: Editions de l'Herne, 1968), 102, have also noted the "imperialist" underpinnings of Theleme.

CHAPTER FOUR

1. Franco Moretti, *Atlas of the European Novel 1800–1900* (London: Verso, 1998), 35.

2. Timothy Brennan, "The National Longing for Form," *Nation and Narration*, ed. Homi K. Bhabha (London: Routledge, 1990), 49. Brennan, like Moretti, is glossing M. M. Bakhtin's well known essay "Epic and Novel," from *The Dialogic Imagination*, ed. Michael Holquist, trans. Caryl Emerson and Michael Holquist (Austin: University of Texas Press, 1981), 3–40. On the question of narrative and space, useful insights are provided as well by Michel de Certeau's book *The Practice of Everyday Life*, trans. Steven Rendall (Berkeley: University of California Press, 1984), 115–30. On the multifarious intertwinings between literary discourse and the development of mapping in Renaissance France, see Tom Conley, *The Self-Made Map: Cartographic Writing in Early Modern France* (Minneapolis: University of Minnesota Press, 1996).

3. The Virgil passages come from *Aeneid* book 12: v. 896, v. 922. I cite the Latin and English text, ed. and trans. by H. Rushton Fairclough (Cambridge: Harvard University Press, 1978). My thanks to Albert Ascoli for bringing these passages to my attention.

4. François Rabelais, *Oeuvres complètes*, ed. Pierre Jourda (Paris: Garnier, 1962); English translation by J. M. Cohen, *The Histories of Gargantua and Pantagruel* (Harmondsworth: Penguin, 1955). All subsequent page citations are to these editions.

5. Certainly, on one level, Panurge's fable, with its linking of mapping and storytelling, brings to mind the great prophecy of Jupiter in book 1 of the *Aeneid* (and recalled in the last of Du Bellay's melancholy *Antiquitez de Rome*) in which Roman glory is seen to extend through time and space ("nec metas rerum nec tempora pono" [v. 279]).

6. See *Aeneid* book 1: v. 563–64, "res dura et regni novitas me talia cogunt/moliri et late finis custode tueri;" or, in Fairclough's translation, "Stern necessity and the new estate of my kingdom force me to do such hard deeds and protect my frontiers far and wide with guards."

7. The very origins of medieval romance, in fact, may be traced to the emergence of the aristocracy in the twelfth century as a universal class, rather

than a scattered group living on isolated farms. Romance is about how the aristocracy escapes its rural roots. See, for strong literary critical discussions of the relationship between romance and territory, Fredric Jameson, *The Political Unconscious: Narrative as a Socially Symbolic Act* (Ithaca: Cornell University Press, 1981), chapter 2, and R. Howard Bloch, *Etymologies and Genealogies: A Literary Anthropology of the French Middle Ages* (Chicago: University of Chicago Press, 1983) 194ff. More generally, see Marc Bloch, *Feudal Society*, trans. L. A. Manyon (1939; Chicago: University of Chicago Press, 1961), vol. 2.

8. *Don Quixote*, trans. J. M. Cohen (Harmondsworth: Penguin, 1950), 33. On the ideological function of romance as a definer of class identity in the sixteenth century, see David Quint's chapter "Tasso, Milton, and the Boat of Romance," in his *Epic and Empire* (Princeton: Princeton University Press, 1993). For a somewhat different interpretation of similar issues, see Richard Helgerson, *Forms of Nationhood: The Elizabethan Writing of England* (Chicago: University of Chicago Press, 1992), chapter 4. I have discussed the tension between romance and history as two literary genres which project different models of community and political engagement in my reading of *Don Quixote* in *Writing from History: The Rhetoric of Exemplarity in Renaissance Literature* (Ithaca: Cornell University Press, 1990), chapter 6.

9. Virtually all critical attention to the story has focused on psychological or even psychoanalytic concerns, to the exclusion of political, ideological, or literary-historical issues. One of the few critics to note, if only in passing, the presence of romance motifs in the tale is Patricia Cholakian, *Rape and Writing in the "Heptaméron" of Marguerite de Navarre* (Carbondale: Southern Illinois University Press, 1991), 88ff.

10. Citations will be taken from Michel François's edition of the *Heptaméron* (Paris: Garnier, 1967); page numbers will be included in the text. The English translation is by P. A. Chilton (Harmondsworth: Penguin, 1984). Chilton's translation is wonderfully readable. However, because Marguerite's text is not very readable, Chilton's version necessarily departs from a close reproduction of the French. Thus I have often altered Chilton's version to conform more closely to the language of the original.

11. I have here substituted my own translation altogether.

12. On the importance of Amadour's gaze in framing Floride, see Lawrence D. Kritzman, *The Rhetoric of Sexuality and the Literature of the French Renaissance* (Cambridge: Cambridge University Press, 1991), 47ff. Tom Conley argues that the names of the two protagonists of the tale are scattered through the text in a process of graphic fragmentation; see his essay, "The Graphics of Dissimulation: Between *Heptaméron* 10 and *l'histoire tragique*," in *Critical Tales: New Studies of the Heptaméron and Early Modern Culture*, ed. John D. Lyons and Mary McKinley (Philadelphia: University of Pennsylvania Press, 1993), 65–82.

13. For a good discussion of the relationship between doubling, narrative, and family identity in medieval romance, see Bloch, *Etymologies and Genealogies*, chapter 5. The structure of doubling that asserts the similarity of lovers is, of course, stronger in more classically inflected forms of romance than it is in medieval forms. However, even such an early text as Chrétien's *Erec et Enide* introduces its lovers through a formulaic repetition that stresses their similarity while making clear their social and sexual differences. Enide: "Never

was God able to form a finer nose, mouth and eyes. What could I say of her beauty?" Erec: "Never was greater prowess seen in any man of his age. What could I say of his virtue?" I cite the translation of D. D. R. Owen in *Arthurian Romances* (London: Dent 1987), 2,4.

14.   For an exploration of the relationship between the errancy of romance and the potential endlessness of narrative see Patricia Parker, *Inescapable Romance* (Princeton: Princeton University Press, 1979), chapter 1.

15.   The similarity between this courtly romance and La Sale's *Jehan de Saintré* has been noted as well by Lucien Febvre, *Amour sacré, amour profane* (Paris: Gallimard, 1944), 243. In a fine reading of the relationship between violence and gender in the story, Carla Freccero stresses the importance of Amadour's social inferiority. I would want to place equal emphasis on Amadour's geographical mobility, since this brings the questions of rape and social mobility into dialogue with the theme of geopolitics, which is central to the tale. See Freccero's discussion in "Rape's Disfiguring Figures," in *Rape and Representation*, ed. Lynn A. Higgins and Brenda R. Silver (New York: Columbia University Press, 1991), 227–47.

16.   The sense that the tale is working very self-consciously on romance clichés is underscored by the very name of Aventurade, which suggests a kind of generic brand of "romanceness." Romance thrives on the tension between the two senses of adventure, as both "exciting event" and "arbitrary occurrence." Aventurade is both the screen who makes possible the erotic "adventure" and the victim of "circumstance." Thus, fittingly, she gets a name that seems quintessential: "Aventurade" embodies the concentrated matter of romance as lemonade embodies the concentrated form of lemon.

17.   This question of rape is the central theme of Cholakian's *Rape and Writing*, but see, as well, Carla Freccero's entry on Marguerite de Navarre in *A New History of French Literature*, ed. Denis Hollier (Cambridge: Harvard University Press, 1989), 145–47.

18.   On this channelling of male desire into language in medieval romance see Geraldine Heng's essay, "The Woman Wants," *Yale Journal of Criticism* no. 5 (1992): 101–34.

19.   Niccolò Machiavelli, "Ritratto di cose di Francia," in *Tutte le opere*, ed. Mario Martelli (Florence: Sansoni, 1971), 56. My translation.

20.   On the semantic valences of "pays," as well as other terms used to define "country" and "nation," see the opening passages of E. J. Hobsbawm's *Nations and Nationalism since 1780* (Cambridge: Cambridge University Press, 1990). Even today, one uses the terms "pays" and "paese" in rural France and Italy to refer to one's village.

21.   Symphorien Champier, *La vie du preulx Chevalier Bayard*, ed. Denis Crouzet (1525; reprint, Lyon: Imprimerie Nationale, 1992), 183.

22.   Champier, *La vie du preulx* . . . 195; my translations. Bayard's international reputation is stressed again later, when he encounters Francis de Stirlingen, whose servant points out that Bayard "a couru par tous royaulmes chrestiens, et ne trouva oncques homme à qui il aye desnyé combat, soit Cyclien, italien, espaignol, ny aultre de quelle region que il fust, Angloys, Flamans, Ennoyers, Brebanson, Escoussays ou Dannoys et Souysses" (200) ["traveled through all Christian kingdoms, and never found a single man to whom he denied battle, be he Sicilian, Italian, Spaniard, or other, from whatever region—be it

English, Flemish, Dutch, Brabanter, Scot, Dane, or Swiss." My translation. Champier's text ends with a series of comparisons, à la Plutarch, between Bayard and great ancients (Theseus, David, Scipio, Hannibal, etc.). Bayard, of course, comes off as more heroic. In many cases this is because he died for his country ("la chose publique" [230]). I don't mean to suggest too close a connection between Amadour and Bayard, or to claim that Amadour is somehow based upon Bayard. Certainly the legend of Bayard stresses his moral rectitude no less than his martial heroism. Etienne Pasquier's *Recherches de la France*, for example, recounts how, visiting a bishop and being offered as company for the night a young girl whose indigent mother was selling her into prostitution, Bayard took pity on the girl, paid for her freedom, provided her with a dowry and sent her on her way. See Etienne Pasquier, *Les recherches de la France*, ed. Marie-Madeleine Fragonard and François Roudaut (1562; Paris: H. Champion, 1996), 1: 526.

23. Machiavelli, "Ritratto di Francia," 56. For Brantôme's anxiety about the dominance of the traditional aristocracy in state service, see his "portrait" of Francis I in vol. 3 of his *Oeuvres complètes* (Paris: Jules Renouard, 1869), esp. 255ff. For a good discussion of this aristocratic anxiety before the bureaucratization of the French administration in the sixteenth century see the opening chapters of Jonathan Dewald's *Aristocratic Experience and the Origins of Modern Culture* (Berkeley: University of California Press, 1993). On Francis's court as a turning point in the history of the imagery of the nobility, in which the courtier begins to replace the *chevalier*, see Michael Nerlich, *The Ideology of Adventure*, vol. 2, trans. Ruth Crowley (Minneapolis: University of Minnesota Press, 1987), chapt. 10. Nerlich's discussion is heavily indebted, as is my own, to the classic study by Norbert Elias, *The Court Society*, trans. Edmund Jephcott (1969; New York: Pantheon, 1983).

24. We have here, it would seem, a distant prefiguration of the famous Althusserian gesture of "interpellation," through which subjects are made subjects of power. See Louis Althusser, "Ideological State Apparatuses," in his *Lenin and Philosophy* (1969), trans. Ben Brewster (London: New Left Books, 1971), 121–73.

25. On the general question of the "exemplary" in Marguerite's text see the fine study by John D. Lyons, *Exemplum: The Rhetoric of Example in Early Modern France and Italy* (Princeton: Princeton University Press, 1989). Both Freccero, in "Rape's Disfiguring Figures," 235, and Kritzman, in *The Rhetoric of Sexuality*, 55, identify the moment at which Floride wounds herself as the inscription of a feminine writing on the text of history. I want to try to build on this insight in order to understand not only how that act asserts Floride's identity, but how it in turn locates that identity in the particular nexus of political, cultural, and social fields that make her identity possible in the first place.

26. It is worth adding that the shift from one world to another is incomplete, mediatory, and disposed, again, along lines of both gender and genre. Floride loses her beauty through age but remains morally pure, whereas Amadour, who never loses the youth of a conventional knightly hero, loses his beauty through moral turpitude. Her transformation is physical, suggesting the awareness of temporality that will later inform the discourse of the novel; his is moral, and recalls the allegorized metamorphoses of characters in romance.

27. The point is recalled yet again, following story 26, when we are informed that men and women have different forms of honor, "l'honneur des hommes et des femmes n'est pas semblable"(218). This question of different notions of honor has been noted by several critics—though none has traced how a whole courtly lexicon is dismantled. See, in particular, Freccero, "Rape's Disfiguring Figures," 235; Nicole Cazauran, *L'Heptaméron de Marguerite de Navarre* (Paris: Société d'édition d'enseignement supérieur, 1976), 200ff.; and Margaret W. Ferguson, "Recreating the Rules of the Game," in *Creative Imitation: New Essays on Renaissance Literature in Honor of Thomas M. Greene*, ed. David Quint (Binghamton: Medieval and Renaissance Texts and Studies, 1992), 153–188. For a general consideration of the "splintering" of language in the text, see Marcel Tetel, *Marguerite de Navarre's Heptaméron: Themes, Language, and Structure* (Durham: Duke University Press, 1973), chapter 4. For an analysis of the ways in which the rhetoric of friendship throughout the story is submitted to a similar fracturing, see Ullrich Langer, *Perfect Friendship: Studies in Literature and Moral Philosophy from Boccaccio to Corneille* (Geneva: Droz, 1994), chapter 4.

28. My translation.

29. On the connection between novella and exemplum, see Walter Pabst, *Novellentheorie und Novellendichtung* (Heidelberg: C. Winter Verlag, 1967).

30. In the decade between 1512 and 1521 alone, Navarre changed hands at least four times. Francis I's first military experience was, in fact, part of an unsuccessful action to win Navarre back to France (he performed without distinction). In 1520, Henri d'Albret, Marguerite's future husband, helped reconquer Navarre, though it was eventually ceded back to Spain at the peace of Crépy in 1543. The failure of the Cardinal de Tournon, who negotiated that treaty, to insist upon Navarre's restoration to d'Albret occasioned his fall from Marguerite's favor. See, for much background on this context, R. J. Knecht, *Francis I* (Cambridge: Cambridge University Press, 1982), 69–70, 105–8, 415. On the role of Navarre's neighboring border state Catalonia in the development of Franco-Spanish political identity, see Peter Sahlins, *Boundaries: The Making of France and Spain in the Pyrenees* (Berkeley: University of California Press, 1989).

31. This consolidation involves the beginnings of the famous notion of the "imagined community" that Benedict Anderson has offered to help explain the emergence of nationalism. See his well-known book, *Imagined Communities: Reflections on the Origin and Spread of Nationalism* (London: Verso, 1983), especially chapters 1 and 2.

32. The critical bibliography on the prologue is vast. Among the many studies of the relationship between the prologue to the *Heptaméron* and the prologue to the *Decameron*, I have consulted: Cazauran, *Heptaméron*, chapter 3; Glyn P. Norton, "Narrative Function in the 'Heptaméron' Frame Story," *La nouvelle française à la Renaissance*, ed. Lionello Sozzi (Geneva: Slatkine, 1981), 435–47; Ferguson, "Recreating the Rules of the Game"; K. Kasprzyk, "Marguerite de Navarre, lecteur du Décaméron," *Studi Francesi* 34, no. 1 (1970): 1–11; and chapter 1 of Gisèle Mathieu-Castellani's *La conversation conteuse: Les nouvelles de Marguerite de Navarre* (Paris: Presses Universitaires de France, 1992). No critic has commented on the political dimension.

33. For a somewhat different reading of this gesture of the gift, see Ferguson,

"Recreating the Rules of the Game," 168ff. On the general question of exchanges in the text, see Mathieu-Castellani, *La conversation conteuse*, 169ff.

34. For a consideration of the relationship between genre, subjectivity, and space, focusing on the domestic space of the novella tradition, see Daniel Russell, "Conception of Self, Conception of Space and Generic Convention: An Example from the *Heptaméron*," *Sociocriticism*, 4–5 (1986): 159–83.

35. Natalie Zemon Davis has suggested that carnavalesque reversals of gender roles functioned during the same period as a kind of safety valve for letting off steam, as a ritual that bolsters hierarchy (in her example, social hierarchy) while providing the vocabulary and opening perspectives for criticizing it. I would make a similar argument about the gender debates in the *Heptaméron*. See Davis's essay, "Women on Top," in her *Society and Culture in Early Modern France* (Stanford: Stanford University Press, 1975), 124–51. Joan Kelley-Gadol has made the point in a well-known article that the emergence of a newly centralized court society in the Renaissance worked to undermine, rather than affirm, the independence of women. One consequence of the increasingly constrained space of court society, I am suggesting, is that it both disrupts the aristocracy's traditional image of its function in society and, almost as a compensation, produces a *discourse* about the status of women. See Kelly-Gadol's essay, "Did Women Have a Renaissance?," in *Becoming Visible*, ed. Renate Bridenthal and Claudia Koonz (Boston: Houghton Mifflin, 1977), 139–64. This diminution in the relative mobility and power of women seems to recur at moments of transition to more centralized political systems. For an analogue in eighteenth-century France, see Joan Landes, *Women and the Public Sphere in the Age of the French Revolution* (Ithaca: Cornell University Press, 1988), 201ff. Landes points to the tension between the "universalism" of the masculinist Revolution and the "general" importance of that same Revolution for women.

36. Francois de Billon, *Le fort inexpugnable de l'honneur du sexe feminin* (Paris: Ian d'Allyer, 1555), 181. I would like to thank Professor Marianne Meijer for bringing Billon's work to my attention.

37. Marguerite de Navarre, "Les Prisons," in *Les dernières poésies de Marguerite de Navarre*, ed. Abel Lefranc (Paris: Armand Colin, 1986), 120–62, 150. My translation. For an excellent discussion of the contexts and structure of "Les Prisons," see Robert D. Cottrell, *The Grammar of Silence: A Reading of Marguerite de Navarre's Poetry* (Washington: Catholic University of America Press, 1986), chapter 9.

38. On the historiographical backgrounds to the text, see Laurence A. Gregorio, *Order in the Court: History and Society in "La Princesse de Clèves"* (Saratoga, Calif.: ANMA Libri) 1986. See, also, on the question of historical veracity in the text, Faith E. Beasley, *Revising Memory: Women's Fiction and Memoirs in Seventeenth-Century France* (New Brunswick: Rutgers University Press, 1990), 194–212.

39. References to *La Princesse de Clèves* will cite E. Magne's edition of Lafayette's *Romans et Nouvelles* (Paris: Classiques Garnier, 1970). The English translation is by Thomas S. Perry, revised by John D. Lyons for Lyons's Norton Critical Edition of the novel, *The Princess of Clèves* (New York: W. W. Norton, 1994). All page numbers will be indicated in the text.

40. Mme de Lafayette, *Correspondance*, ed. André Beaunier (Paris: Garnier, 1942), vol. 2: 63. My translation.

41. On the questions of verisimilitude and representation in the book, see Lyons, *Exemplum*, 198–99, and 234–36.

42. For a somewhat different reading of the appearance of Marguerite, which links it to the construction of a feminine literary history, see Beasley, *Revising Memory*, 220–21.

43. Citations of Brantôme come from *Les Dames galantes*, ed. Pascal Pia (Paris: Folio, 1981), 362. For a somewhat different treatment of the story of Elizabeth, see J. W. Scott, "The 'Digressions' of the *Princesse de Clèves*," *French Studies* 11 (1957): 315–22.

44. For a fine discussion of the story of Elizabeth as a "feminist pedagogy" see Beasley, *Revising Memory*, 212–25. For a less historically inflected account of the differences between representations of female and male desire in the novel see Naomi Schor, "The Portrait of a Gentleman: Representing Men in (French) Women's Writing," in *Misogyny, Misandry, and Misanthropy*, ed. R. Howard Bloch and Frances Ferguson (Berkeley: University of California Press, 1989): 113–33.

45. See Joan DeJean's *Tender Geographies: Women and the Origins of the Novel in France* (New York: Columbia University Press, 1991), 43–50.

46. Of course, as the novel unfolds, this geography becomes ever more "feminized," as key episodes take place far from the "masculine" eye of international politics. On the implications of this spatial displacement see Beasley, *Revising Memory*, 224–27, as well as DeJean, *Tender Geographies*, chapter 1. On the more general relationship between new forms of imaginative writing and new conceptions of political authority during the period, see Timothy Reiss, *The Meaning of Literature* (Ithaca: Cornell University Press, 1992), chapter 5.

47. Tony Tanner, *Adultery in the Novel: Contract and Transgression* (Baltimore: Johns Hopkins University Press, 1979), 100.

48. See Pierre de Bourdeille Brantôme, "Portrait du Duc de Nemours," in *Oeuvres complètes* (Paris: Jules Renouard, 1864–82), vol. 4: 168.

CHAPTER FIVE

1. Joachim Du Bellay, *La Deffence et Illustration de la Langue Françoyse*, ed. Henri Chamard (Paris: Didier, 1948), 188. All future references will be to this edition. My translations.

2. Du Bellay, *Deffence*, 186.

3. Benedict Anderson, *Imagined Communities: Reflections on the Origin and Spread of Nationalism* (London: Verso, 1983), 48.

4. Anderson, *Imagined Communities*, 49.

5. It is worth noting that the period of absolutism and court culture lying between the Renaissance rise of print capitalism and the emergence of nationalism proper in the eighteenth century is the one period of European history that Anderson's compelling discussion generally neglects.

6. Jacques Peletier du Mans, "Art Poétique," *Traités de poétique et de rhétorique de la Renaissance*, ed. Francis Goyet (Paris: Livre de Poche, 1990), 271.

7. Barthélemy Aneau, "Quintil Horatien," *Traités de poétique et de rhétorique*, 193. My translations.

8. Aneau, "Quintil Horatien," 193. For a discussion of the history of "patrie" in the period, see Liah Greenfield's *Nationalism: Five Roads to Modernity* (Cambridge: Harvard University Press, 1992), 102, and Jean Lestocquoy's *Histoire*

du patriotisme en France (Paris: Albin Michel, 1968), chapter 2. See also, on these debates, Gilbert Gadoffre, *La révolution culturelle dans la France des humanistes* (Geneva: Droz, 1997), 298.

9. See, on these processes, Norbert Elias, *The Court Society*, trans. Edmund Jephcott (New York: Pantheon, 1983), as well as Pauline M. Smith, *The Anti-Courtier Trend in Sixteenth-Century French Literature* (Geneva: Droz, 1966). On the question of "Italianism," in particular, see Jean Balsamo's study, *Les rencontres des muses: Italianisme et anti-italianisme dans les lettres françaises de la fin du XVIe siècle* (Geneva: Slatkine, 1992), as well as Eric MacPhail's *The Voyage to Rome in French Renaissance Literature* (Saratoga, California: ANMA Libri, 1990). On the relationship between Italianism and emerging national identity, see, as well, MacPhail's essay, "Nationalism and Italianism in the Work of Joachim Du Bellay," *Yearbook of Comparative and General Literature* 39 (1990–91): 47–53.

10. Henri Estienne, *La précellence du langage françois* (1578), ed. Edmond Huguet (Paris: Armand Colin, 1896), 27.

11. Henri Estienne, *Deux dialogues du nouveau langage françoys italianizé* (1578), vol. 1, ed. P. Ristelhuber (Paris: A. Lemerre, 1885), x. Balsamo's *Les rencontres des muses* features an excellent discussion of Estienne's text more generally. See his chapter 1.

12. François de La Noue, *Discours politiques et militaires*. Ed. F. E. Sutcliffe (Geneva: Droz, 1967), 208–9.

13. To offer yet another example, Etienne Pasquier's letter on the "language question," written in 1579 to his friend Querquifinen, considers the tension between courtly fashion and a French language that is "scattered" throughout all of the villages of France. See the *Oeuvres choisies* of Pasquier, ed. Léon Feugère (Paris: Didot, 1849), vol. 2: 230.

14. *Deffence*, 47–48.

15. "Ample Discours au Roy sur le Faict des Quatre Estats du Royaume de France," Joachim Du Bellay, *Oeuvres poétiques*, vol. 6, pt. 1, ed. Henri Chamard (Paris: Nizet, 1931), 197, vv. 65–74.

16. See Terence Cave, *The Cornucopian Text* (Oxford: Clarendon Press, 1979).

17. This economic imagery contrasts with the figural networks, such as architectural or horticultural imagery, that Du Bellay uses to describe the relationship between ancients and moderns. For good analyses of these images see Margaret W. Ferguson, *Trials of Desire: Renaissance Defenses of Poetry* (New Haven: Yale University Press, 1983), chapter 2, and Thomas M. Greene, *The Light in Troy* (New Haven: Yale University Press, 1982), chapter 11.

18. Joachim Du Bellay, *Regrets*, in *Oeuvres poétiques*, vol. 2, ed. Daniel Aris and Françoise Joukovsky (Paris: Garnier, 1993), sonnet 55. I have profited much from commentaries to a number of other editions of the *Regrets*, most especially, those of Henri Chamard and Henri Weber (Paris: Didier, 1970), and J. Jolliffe and M. A. Screech (Geneva: Droz, 1974). Given the brevity of the sonnet form, there is no reason to include line numbers in my citations of specific poems, so I will include only the numbers of the sonnets I am quoting. My translations.

19. I cite Gérard Defaux's edition of Marot's *Oeuvres poétiques* (Paris: Garnier, 1993), vol. 1: 87.

20. See Ullrich Langer, *Divine and Poetic Freedom in the Renaissance: Nominalist*

Theology and Literature in France and Italy (Princeton: Princeton University Press, 1990), 66–69, and François Cornilliat, *"Or ne mens": Couleurs de l'Eloge et du Blâme chez les 'Grands Rhétoriqueurs,'* (Paris: Champion, 1994), 330–38.

21.   Norbert Elias, *The Court Society*, 152. François Roudaut eloquently states that much of Du Bellay's unhappiness in the face of both the Roman and French courts seems to be related to an anxiety about "circulation": "ce n'est plus la conservation que est erigée en règle, mais la circulation, la mobilité: mobilité de l'argent . . . mobilité de la position social . . . circulation des femmes" ["it is no longer conservation that is the rule, but circulation, mobility: mobility of money . . . mobility of social position . . . circulation of women"]. See his discussion in *Joachim Du Bellay: Les Regrets* (Paris: Presses Universitaires de France, 1995), 40 ff.

22.   J. H. M. Salmon, *Society in Crisis: France in the Sixteenth Century* (London: Methuen, 1979), 97. Salmon's entire discussion of the social position of the Pléiade poets is very useful, as is Michael Nerlich's consideration of the problem of nationalism and epic heroism in *The Ideology of Adventure* (1977), vol. 2, trans. Ruth Crowley (Minneapolis: University of Minnesota Press, 1987), 290–95. More thematic and summary considerations of Du Bellay's discussion of language in the context of French nationalism may be found in Liah Greenfield's *Nationalism*, 102–7, and Lestocquoy's *Histoire du patriotisme en France*, chapter 2. For a good discussion of Du Bellay's other collection of Roman poems, the "Antiquitez de Rome," which inscribes its generic multiplicity into mid-sixteenth-century political contexts, see Cynthia Skenazi, "Le Poète et le Roi dans les *Antiquitez de Rome* et le *Songe* de Du Bellay," *Bibliothèque d'humanisme et Renaissance*, 60 (1998): 41–55.

23.   On the shifting depictions of the poet's role among Pléiade poets, see Grahame Castor's *Pléiade Poetics* (Cambridge: Cambridge University Press, 1964). My own analysis of Du Bellay's poetry will try to be especially attentive, given the poet's own insistence on the themes of ambition and disappointment, to the ways in which poetic authority is implicated in the notion of poetry as a "career"—a theme that needs much more attention than I am able to give it here. One might begin by tracing the poet's careful placement of himself in a field of cultural valuations, what Fredric Jameson has called a writer's "strategies of a well-nigh military character, based on superiority of technique and terrain, assessment of the counterforces, a shrewd maximization of one's own specific and idiosyncratic resources." See his revisionist discussion of the image of the heroic "great man" tradition of literary biography in *Postmodernism, or the Cultural Logic of Late Capitalism* (Durham: Duke University Press, 1991), 306–8. On Du Bellay's attempt to imagine a model of literary inspiration that would be free from metaphysical constraint, see Langer, *Divine and Poetic Freedom*, chapter 5.

24.   See Marot, *Oeuvres poétiques*, vol. 2, ed. Gérard Defaux, 29.

25.   See, for example, the fourth sonnet in de Magny's *Soupirs*: "Je n'estois pas assez en France tourmenté,/Sans qu'il fallust encor' venir en Italye/Sentir le traict/poignant de l'enfant d'Idalye,/Et m'asservir encore à quelque autre beaulté" ["I was not tormented enough in France,/So that I had to come to Italy/And feel the sharp point/Of the son of Venus,/And indenture myself to another beautiful woman"]. I cite the edition of David Wilkin (Geneva: Droz, 1978). In Michel Déguy's study, *Tombeau de Du Bellay* (Paris: Galli-

mard, 1973), several stimulating pages are devoted to the question of space in Du Bellay. However, Déguy deletes all historical or geographical specificity from his analysis, and turns the space of poetry into the space of language, in which, according to Heidegger (whom Déguy cites), the poet dwells "poetically." See esp. pp. 31–48. In an important recent discussion of the representation of subjectivity in the *Regrets*, Thomas M. Greene underscores the importance of Du Bellay's status as a *déclassé* aristocrat, concluding that his "nostalgia is essentially temporal rather than geographical;" that is, it is nostalgia for a medieval social order, which is vanishing. While I agree with Greene's assessment, I would stress that what is striking about the collection is precisely the ways in which temporal nostalgia is *represented* in spatial terms—an issue which his reading hints at, but doesn't discuss at length. See p. 3 in Greene's essay, "Regrets Only: Three Poetic Paradigms in Du Bellay," *Romanic Review* 84, no. 1 (1993): 1–18.

26. See Magny, *Soupirs*, sonnet #1. On the relationship of Du Bellay and Magny, see Henri Weber, *La création poétique au XVIe siècle en France* (Paris: Nizet, 1955), 443–51, and MacPhail, *Voyage to Rome*, 95–103. For a somewhat different reading of the loss of "ardor," which links it to aging and a kind of Petrarchan renunciation of early passion, see Roudaut, *Joachim Du Bellay*, 62.

27. For a useful discussion of the ways in which the language of praise in the Petrarchan tradition constructs a subject defined by lack, see the first chapter of Joel Fineman's *Shakespeare's Perjured Eye: The Invention of Poetic Subjectivity in the Sonnets* (Berkeley: University of California Press, 1986), esp. pp. 19ff. Fineman's larger consideration of the European lyric before Shakespeare, however, is a bit reductive. Still, it is useful to consider Du Bellay in contrast to Shakespeare, who applies the language of economics to the young man of the sonnets, and thus to the object of praise. Du Bellay uses it to describe the problematic position of the poet himself, thus making economics, rather than "desire" (in any psychological sense—though desire has, of course, its own economy), the starting point for discussing poetic subjectivity.

28. The relationship between Scève and Du Bellay needs thorough exploration. One consideration of the value of Scève's work for Du Bellay (though without reference to the specifically "emblematic" dimension that interests me) may be found in Dorothy Gabe Coleman, *The Chaste Muse: A Study of Joachim Du Bellay's Poetry* (Leiden: Brill, 1980), 27ff. A more dynamically intertextual reading, focusing on the "Olive," is offered by JoAnn DellaNeva, in "Du Bellay: Reader of Scève, Reader of Petrarch," *Romanic Review* 79, no. 3 (1988): 401–11. Floyd Gray has argued that the image of the "sun" in this poem may refer either to the lady, or to "a more general flame" that signifies poetic inspiration. This reading neglects the relationship to the Prince, which is clearly important in the poem. See Gray's otherwise insightful reading of the poem in *La poétique de Du Bellay* (Paris: Nizet, 1978), 81.

29. See Du Bellay, *Regrets*, ed. J. Jolliffe and M. A. Screech, 65.

30. Though see Marie-Dominique Legrand, "Le mode épistolaire dans les *Regrets*," *Nouvelle Revue du Seizième Siècle* 13, no. 3 (1995): 199–213, and, especially, Marc Bizer's "Letters from Home: The Epistolary Aspects of Joachim Du Bellay's *Les Regrets*," *Renaissance Quarterly*, 52, no. 1 (1999), 140–70.

31. For a good reading of sonnet #16 which stresses the importance of Du Bellay's exile as a rhetorical distancing of himself from Ronsard and develops

the contrast with Ariosto (without, however, exploring the formal issues that concern me here) see MacPhail, *Voyage to Rome*, 61–62.

32. Pierre Bourdieu, *Language and Symbolic Power*, trans. Gino Raymond and Matthew Adamson, ed. John B. Thompson (Cambridge: Harvard University Press, 1991), 57.

33. See Michael Screech's notes to Du Bellay, *Regrets*, ed. J. Jolliffe and M. A. Screech, 227, which send us to Erasmus's *Adagia*, 1.7.96. I have given a somewhat abbreviated reading of this same sonnet in a paper entitled, " 'Trafiquer la louange': L'économie de la poésie dans les 'Regrets' ", in *Du Bellay et ses sonnets romains*, ed. Yvonne Bellenger (Paris: Champion, 1994), 47–60. Marc Bizer explores the link between the epistolary nature of the sonnet and the humanist tradition of the epistle in "Letters from Home," 158–66.

34. Pierre de Ronsard, *Odes*, in *Oeuvres complètes*, vol. 1, ed. Jean Céard et al. (Paris: Gallimard, Bibliothèque de la Pléiade, 1993), 603.

35. Fernand Braudel, *The Structures of Everyday Life: Civilization and Capitalism, 15th-18th Century*, vol. 1, trans. Siân Reynolds (New York: Harper and Row, 1979), 417.

36. Francesco Petrarch, *Petrarch's Lyric Poems*, trans. Robert M. Durling (Cambridge: Harvard University Press, 1976), 486.

37. On the complex play of the themes of desire and glory in Petrarch, see Gordon Braden's fine essay, "Love and Fame; The Petrarchan Career," in *Psychiatry and the Humanities*, vol. 9, *Pragmatism's Freud*, ed. William Kerrigan (Baltimore: Johns Hopkins University Press, 1986), 126–58.

38. On the poem's sources, see W. A. Nitze, "The Source of the 9th Sonnet of the *Regrets*," *Modern Language Notes*, 39 (1924): 216–30.

39. I cite Petrarch from *Rime, Trionfi, e Poesie Latine*, ed. F. Neri et al. (Milan: Ricciardi, 1951), 804.

40. Thus, Petrarch begins with "Salve, cara Deo tellus sanctissima, salve" (804), while Virgil says, "Salve, magna parens frugum, Saturnia tellus." Virgil, *Eclogues, Georgics, Aeneid, 1–6*, ed. H. R. Fairclough (Cambridge: Harvard University Press, 1973), 128, v. 173.

41. See Marot's verse epistle, "Au Roy, du temps de son exil à Ferrare," in which a long list of rivals who have denounced the poet is followed by the conclusion that "France" has been "ingrate ingratissime/A son Poëte." In Marot, *Oeuvres poétiques*, vol. 2, ed. Gérard Defaux, 85. On the poetic and ideological stakes of Marot's exile in the history of religious struggle, see Ehsan Ahmed, *The Law and the Song: Hebraic, Christian, and Pagan Revivals in Sixteenth-Century France* (Birmingham, Ala.: Summa, 1997), chapter 2.

42. See Ronsard's "La Nymphe de France Parle," in *Oeuvres complètes*, vol. 2: 1130, and Du Bellay's "Prosphonématique au Roy Treschrestien Henry II," in *Oeuvres poétiques*, ed. Daniel Aris and Françoise Joukousky, vol. 1: 124. I am especially indebted, for my reading of this poem, to a very stimulating discussion provided by members of my Berkeley graduate seminar on Renaissance French poetry, in the fall of 1997.

43. In what is still probably the best general book on the *Regrets*, Yvonne Bellenger stresses the importance of the poet's distance from France for his idealization of it. See her fine discussion of the "myth" of France in *Du Bellay, ses 'Regrets' qu'il fit dans Rome* (Paris: Nizet, 1975), chapters 11 and 12, esp. 211ff.

44. Petrarch, *Rime, Trionfi, e Poesie Latine*, 804, v. 19; Virgil, *Eclogues, Georgics, Aeneid*, 1–6, 128, v. 173.

45. Petrarch, *Petrarch's Lyric Poems*, 95.

46. The citation is from "A Olivier de Magni sur les perfections de sa dame," in the collection of "Divers Jeux Rustiques," Du Bellay, *Oeuvres poétiques*, ed. Daniel Aris and Françoise Joukousky, vol. 2: 183. Aris and Joukovsky note the "Petrarchan" dimension of the figure of echo in their notes to sonnet 9, *Oeuvres poétiques*, vol. 2: 294. My research on the pairing of "antres et bois" has benefitted from the ARTFL website, originating at the University of Chicago. Of course, as my colleague Paul Alpers reminds me, the figure of the echoing landscape also calls to mind Virgil's first eclogue, in which the woods ring with the name of Amaryllis. For a fine reading of the psychological nuances present in the poet's privation see Greene, "Regrets Only," 10. On the history of the figure of France as mother, see Gadoffre, *La révolution culturelle*, chapter 11.

47. Marie-Madeleine Fontaine, "Des mots à la rime et de leur raison," *Du Bellay: Actes du Colloque International d'Angers* (Angers: Presses de l'Université d'Angers, 1990), vol. 1: 261–85. Fontaine contents herself with pointing out Du Bellay's citations of Marot, and stopping short of reflecting on their generic implications. For a good exploration of the whole problem of literary vulnerability in the Renaissance, see Jane Tylus, *Writing and Vulnerability in the Late Renaissance* (Stanford: Stanford University Press, 1993), chapter 1. Marot's translation of Virgil's first Ecolgue opens his first volume of poetry, the *Adolescence Clémentine*, published in 1530. It may be found in Gérard Defaux's edition of Marot's *Oeuvres poétiques*, vol. 1: 21–26.

48. See the prologue to the seventeenth canto of Lodovico Ariosto, *Orlando Furioso*, ed. Emiglio Bigi (Milan: Rusconi, 1982), in which the leaders of the Church are described as wolves, and *Petrarch's Lyric Poems*, 257.

49. Homer, *The Iliad*, trans. Richmond Lattimore (Chicago: University of Chicago Press, 1951), 83, v. 255.

50. See Du Bellay, "Sur le faict de ses quatres estats," *Oeuvres poétiques*, ed. Henri Chamard, vol. 6, pt. 1, v. 140ff. Ronsard employs the shepherd image in book 1, v. 128ff. of the "Franciade." See *Oeuvres complètes*, vol. 1: 1024.

51. Among the many critical discussions of Du Bellay's association of himself with the figure of Odysseus, of particular interest for my concerns is Klaus Ley's insistence on the journey to Rome as a kind of aborted ritual of aristocratic education ("eine Kavaliersreise"). See his discussion of the relationship between curiosity and disappointment in *Neuplatonische Poetik und Nationale Wirklichkeit: Die Uberwindung des Petrarkismus im Werk Du Bellays* (Heidelberg: Carl Winter, 1975), 239–47.

52. Most critical discussions of Du Bellay mention his debt to Petrarch, but usually in the context of the French poet's early collection of love sonnets, the *Olive*. Klaus Ley (*Neuplatonische Poetik*) focuses on the importance of images of political harmony taken from neoplatonic allegorizations of Petrarch. A good discussion of the use of rhetoric of contrast and comparison in the Petrarchan lyric may be found in Bellenger, *Du Bellay*, 91, and Gray discusses Du Bellay's manipulation of the sonnet form in his *La poétique de Du Bellay*, chapter 2. Roudaut (*Joachim Du Bellay*, 57), notes the importance of a "code Pétrarquiste," which appears intermittently in the collection. In his

Authorizing Petrarch (Ithaca: Cornell University Press, 1994) William J. Kennedy has shown persuasively the extent to which French lyric (though principally love lyric) during the period is indebted to the commentary tradition on Petrarch.

53. Mary Thomas Crane, *Framing Authority: Sayings, Self, and Society in Sixteenth-Century England* (Princeton: Princeton University Press, 1993), 145. Though centered on English literature, Crane's book offers interesting insights on the relationship between social groups and lyric forms that are applicable, with some adjustment, to France as well.

54. On the relationship between a rhetoric of refusal and literary authority see the seminal article by François Rigolot, "Du Bellay et la poésie du refus," *Bibliothèque d'humanisme et Renaissance* 33, no. 3 (1974): 489–502.

55. The secondary literature on Du Bellay's "satirical" voice is, of course, immense. Of particular use to me have been Floyd Gray's discussion in *La poétique de Du Bellay*, chapter 5, and Yvonne Hoggan-Niord's essay "L'inspiration burlesque dans les *Regrets* de Joachim Du Bellay," *Bibliothèque d'humanisme et Renaissance* 42 (1980), 361–85. Roudaut (*Joachim Du Bellay*, 52), points to the importance of the *pasquino* tradition, and of Francesco Berni as a possible model. For a general history of the pressure exerted on the Petrarchan sonnet by the satirical dimension of Du Bellay's poetry, see Walter Mönch, *Das Sonnet* (Heidelberg: Kerle Verlag, 1955) 121–26. Curiously, most of the pasquinades featured in the major modern collection of this form, *Pasquinate Romane del Cinquecento*, ed. Valerio Marucci et al. (Rome: Salerno Editrice, 1983), do not follow the traditional fourteen-line form of the Petrarchan sonnet, though both Du Bellay and Mellin de Sainct-Gellais refer to certain of their sonnets as "pasquins." Weber (*Création poétique*, 422), calls the transformation of the sonnet form away from the 8 + 6 model a move toward an "elegiac" form. This, however, seems too limiting a term to me.

56. On the political and historical background of the French legation at the Holy See, see Lucien Romier, *Les origines politiques des guerres de religion* (Paris: Perrin, 1913), vol. 1, chapter 3. On the position of the Du Bellays within the Roman context see Gilbert Gadoffre, *Du Bellay et le sacré* (Paris: Gallimard, 1978), chapters 2 and 6. On the problematic role of Rome in Du Bellay's writing, see Eric MacPhail, *Voyage to Rome*, 33–38.

57. Discomfort with the lavish rhetoric of the last poems has even led Michael Screech, in the introduction to the Jolliffe/Screech edition of the *Regrets*, to go so far as to claim (unpersuasively, in my view) that the final poems are not even part of the *Regrets* at all. Philippe Desan offers a more subtle perspective on the question when he argues that praise and satire are dialectically related in all of Du Bellay's work, that they constantly contaminate each other, and, thus, that Du Bellay's praise of the great is continually tempered by his awareness of the problematic nature of praise. See Desan's paper, "De la poésie de circonstance à la satire: Du Bellay et l'engagement poétique," in *Du Bellay: Actes du Colloque Intérnationale d'Angers*, vol. 2: 421–39. Roudaut (*Joachim Du Bellay*, 112) tends to take the praise straight, as a simple historical exigency. Bellenger is more appreciative of the poetic dimension of these sonnets and stresses the way in which they blend neoplatonic clichés about Marguerite's excellence with courtly rhetoric. See her *Du Bellay*, 157ff.

58. The image of the "espace vide" is evoked repeatedly by Déguy in *Tombeau de*

Du Bellay, as a way of linking the *Regrets* to a Heideggerian privileging of language as the place of being.

59. It is worth noting, as yet another point of contrast between Du Bellay and his contemporaries, that another of his friends, Jean-Antoine de Baïf, composed three books of love sonnets, without ever once moving beyond the analysis of his own erotic desire to engage the issues of national identity that one might think would be invited by the name of his "lady"—Francine. See Baïf's *Les Amours de Francine*, ed. Ernesta Caldarini (Geneva: Droz, 1966).

60. Ronsard, *Oeuvres complètes*, vol. 1: 1056. My translation.

61. Ronsard, *Oeuvres complètes*, vol. 1: 1176. "il ne peut estre parfaict sans l'aide des autres: car chacun jardin a sa particuliere fleur, et toutes nations ont affaire les unes des autres: comme en nos havres et ports, la marchandise bien loin cherchée en l'Amerique, se debite par tout ... Toutes Provinces, tant soient elles maigres, servent aux plus fertiles de quelque chose, comme les plus foibles membres, & les plus petits de l'homme servent aux plus nobles du corps." My translation.

CHAPTER SIX

1. "Plus que la moitié de la noblesse est perie. Quant aux soldats, il les faut conter par legions, le peuple diminué universellement, les finances sont espuisees, les dettes accreuës, la discipline militaire renversee, la pieté languissante, les moeurs desbordees, la justice corrompuë, les hommes divisez, et tout en vente." François de La Noue, *Discours politiques et militaires*, ed. F. E. Sutcliffe (1584; Geneva: Droz, 1967), 225.

2. "Les places de repos sont places étrangères,/Les villes du milieu sont les villes frontières." Agrippa d'Aubigné, *Les Tragiques* (1616), ed. Frank Lestringant (Paris: Gallimard, 1995), bk. 1, v. 225–26. For a good discussion of the representation of nations in d'Aubigné see Marie-Madeleine Fragonard, "La tragédie universelle: Images des relations entre les nations," in *Les Tragiques d'Agrippa d'Aubigné*, ed. Marie-Madeleine Fragonard (Paris: Champion, 1990), 145–66.

3. Quotations of Montaigne in English will come from Donald Frame's translation in *The Complete Works of Montaigne* (Stanford: Stanford University Press, 1967). The French text is from the *Oeuvres complètes* edited by Albert Thibaudet and Maurice Rat, in the Bibliothèque de la Pléiade collection (Paris: Gallimard, 1962). Montaigne produced three versions of the *Essais*, published in 1580, 1588, and 1595. Each new edition contained additions to the text, and by comparing the three versions we can trace the development of his thought. Thus in my references to the *Essais*, page numbers will be included in the text, along with the indication of which of the various main versions (indicated conventionally by a, b, or c) the passage is taken from.

4. La Noue, *Discours politiques et militaires*, 222. Jean Bodin mentions the topic as well, in his discussion of the transformation of popular republics into aristocracies. See Bodin, *Les six livres de la république*, ed. and abridged by Gérard Mairet (1583; Paris: Livre de Poche, 1993), book 4: 521.

5. For a good reading of "Of Evil Means ..." that links it to a series of other scenes of bloodletting in the *Essais*, see David Quint, *Montaigne and the Quality of Mercy: Ethical and Political Themes in the "Essais"* (Princeton: Princeton University Press, 1998), 85–88. My reading diverges slightly from Quint's in

its focus on the different ways in which community is depicted. On the shifting images of French community that characterize the period of the wars of religion, see Myriam Yardeni, *La conscience nationale en France pendant les guerres de religion (1559–1598)* (Louvain: Nauwelaerts, 1971). On Montaigne's representation of political chaos see Géralde Nakam, *Montaigne et son temps* (Paris: Gallimard, 1993).

6. Theodor W. Adorno, "The Essay as Form," in his *Notes to Literature*, ed. Rolf Tiedemann, trans. Shierry Weber Nicholsen (New York: Columbia University Press, 1991), vol. 1: 13.

7. "Dieu a meritoirement permis que ces grands pillages se soient absorbez par la mer en les transportant, ou par les guerres intestines dequoy ils se sont entremangez entre eux, et la plus part s'enterrerent sur les lieux, sans aucun fruict de leur victoire" (892b). I have slightly altered the translation. In an extensive discussion of the history of the Lucretian image Hans Blumenberg has shown how Montaigne turns it against its original Epicurian context. Whereas Lucretius stresses that the philosopher should actively seek pleasure by removing himself from strife, Montaigne takes pleasure in the fact that his very uselessness to the state has saved him from being a victim. He is nothing more than a witness to the suffering of his more capable countrymen. See Blumenberg's *Shipwreck with Spectator: Paradigm of a Metaphor for Existence*, trans. Steven Rendall (Cambridge: M.I.T. Press, 1997), 15–20.

8. Since I shall be speaking below about problems of citation, I note that the quotation of Lucretius introduced by Montaigne to illustrate his point about history is itself a misquotation. "Many poets sang other exploits besides the Trojan war and the fall of Troy," ["Et supera bellum Trojanum et funera Trojae,/multi alias alli quoque res cecinere poetae"] (692b), says Lucretius in Montaigne's citation. In fact, Lucretius claims that the fall of Troy *was* a unique historical event, the beginning of heroic history: "*No one* sang other exploits before the Trojan war and the fall of Troy" ["non alias alii quoque res cecinere poetae"]. I have consulted the Loeb Classics edition of Lucretius's *De rerum natura*, ed. Martin Ferguson Smith and trans. W. H. D. Rouse (Cambridge: Harvard University Press, 1982).

9. "Not only of particular events which fortune often renders exemplary and weighty, but of the state of great governments and nations, there escapes us a hundred times more than comes to our knowledge" (692–93b) ["Non seulement des evenemens particuliers que fortune rend souvant exemplaires et poisans, mais de l'estat des grandes polices et nations, il nous en eschappe cent fois plus qu'il n'en vient à nostre science" (886b)].

10. The value of the compass is underscored by Jean de Léry, one of the authors upon whom Montaigne drew for information about Brazil. Léry pauses, at the outset of his *Histoire d'un voyage faict en la terre du Brésil* (1578), to note the importance, for sea travel, of recent developments in navigational technique: "Let me say at this point that it is impossible to overestimate both the excellence of the art of navigation in general, and in particular the invention of the mariner's compass with which it is practiced—the use of which dates back only about two hundred and fifty years." See *The History of a Voyage to the Land of Brazil, Otherwise Called America*, trans. Janet Whatley (Berkeley: University of California Press, 1990), 8. The same topos is evoked by Lancelot-Voisin La Popelinière at the outset of his *L'histoire des histoires: L'idée de l'his-*

toire accomplie of 1599 as proof of modern superiority. See the reprint edition (Paris: Fayard, 1989), 2 vols., 2: 13.

11. Montaigne cites Lucretius's book 2: 1150 and book 5: 330–33.

12. See Hans Blumenberg, *The Legitimacy of the Modern Age*, trans. Robert M. Wallace (Cambridge: M.I.T. Press, 1991), 270ff. Both Blumenberg's discussion of the relationship between Lucretius and the rise of Renaissance skepticism and his concluding chapter on Giordano Bruno are extremely suggestive for thinking about Montaigne. For the influence of Epicurean cosmology on Montaigne's discussions of the New World see Giuliano Gliozzi, *Adamo e il nuovo mondo* (Florence: Nuova Italia, 1976), 209.

13. Bodin devotes a chapter to the question of defining the truth value of different historical narratives. The question of decline versus ascent is broached on pp. 223–36 of *Method for the Easy Comprehension of History*, trans. Beatrice Reynolds (New York: Columbia University Press, 1945). George Huppert's *The Idea of Perfect History* (Urbana: University of Illinois Press, 1970) offers a good study of Bodin's concern with endings and narrative directions. See Huppert's chapter 5.

14. Etienne Pasquier, *Les recherches de la France* (1562), ed. Marie-Madeleine Fragonard and François Roudaut (Paris: Champion, 1996), vol. 1: 254. The d'Aubigné passage is in the prefatory letter to the *Tragiques*, included in Lestringant's edition. See d'Aubigné, *Les Tragiques*, 54–55.

15. For the contexts of the late sixteenth-century French innovations in the philosophy of history see Huppert's *The Idea of Perfect History*, as well as Claude-Gilbert Dubois's *La conception de l'histoire en France au XVIe siècle* (Paris: Nizet, 1977), Donald R. Kelley's *Foundations of Modern Historical Scholarship* (New York: Columbia University Press, 1970), and Zachary Sayre Schiffman's *On the Threshhold of Modernity: Relativism in the French Renaissance* (Baltimore: Johns Hopkins University Press, 1991), chapter 2. On the importance of the new history writing for defining French identity, see Corrado Vivanti, "*Les Recherches de la France* d'Etienne Pasquier: L'invention des Gaulois," in *Les Lieux de Mémoire*, ed. Pierre Nora (Paris: Gallimard, 1986), part II, vol. 1: 216–45, as well as the same author's *Lotta politica e pace religiosa in Francia fra Cinque e Seicento* (Turin: Einaudi, 1974). Philippe Desan considers Montaigne's own reflections on himself as a Frenchman in the fourth chapter of his book, *Penser l'histoire à la Renaissance* (Caen: Paradigme, 1993).

16. The connection between Montaigne's classicism and his consideration of the New World, while central to "Of Coaches," is, of course, not limited to this essay. For an insightful reading of "Of Cannibals" that links the description of Brazil to civil unrest in France and to Montaigne's depictions of classical Stoic virtue, see Quint, *Montaigne and the Quality of Mercy*, chapter 3. On the importance of the moral superiority of the Aztecs, see the discussion of "Of Coaches" by Gliozzi in his *Adamo e il nuovo mondo*, 204.

17. Lucretius's discussion of the relationship of birth and death occurs in book 1: 250ff. On the use of the Lucretian metaphor to describe the movement of history see Huppert's discussion of Vignier in *The Idea of Perfect History*, 127.

18. See White's essay, "The Value of Narrativity in the Representation of Reality," in his *The Content of the Form: Narrative Discourse and Historical Representation* (Baltimore: Johns Hopkins University Press, 1987), 1–26. Also useful to me for thinking about the relationship between narration and event in his-

tory writing have been Paul Veyne's *Writing History*, trans. Mina Moore-Rin-volucri (Middletown, Conn.: Wesleyan University Press, 1984), chapters 3, 6, and 8; and the second section of Reinhart Koselleck's *Futures Past: On the Semantics of Historical Time*, trans. Keith Tribe (1978; Cambridge: M.I.T. Press, 1985).

19. Polybius, *The Rise of the Roman Empire*, trans. Ian Scott-Kilvert (Harmondsworth: Penguin, 1979), 43.

20. I cite Benjamin Jowett's translation of the *Timaeus* in *The Collected Dialogues of Plato*, ed. Edith Hamilton and Huntington Cairns (Princeton: Princeton University Press, 1961), 1158.

21. Bodin, for example, seeks a point of origin for the development of a "Universal Chronology" which could serve as the historian's equivalent of Ariadne's thread. See his *Method for the Easy Comprehension of History*, 300.

22. For the Atlantean invasion of Europe see Plato *Collected Dialogues*, 1158. For a general discussion of the importance of the Atlantis myth in Montaigne, see Gliozzi, *Adamo e il nuovo mondo*, 206–11. On the relativistic attitude advanced by some of Montaigne's contemporaries see Huppert, *The Idea of Perfect History*, 164–67, and Schiffman, *On the Threshold of Modernity*, chapter 1. Huppert links this attitude to the rebirth of Pyrrhonism. For a fascinating discussion of the rhetoric of skepticism in Montaigne see Terence Cave, *Pré-histoires: Textes troublés au seuil de la modernité* (Geneva: Droz, 1999), 23–39. For a discussion of the relationship between the subversion of narrative (in the form of biography) and the representation of the self in Montaigne see Timothy Hampton, *Writing from History: The Rhetoric of Exemplarity in Renaissance Literature* (Ithaca: Cornell University Press, 1990), chapter 4.

23. Montaigne's characterization of Aztec cosmology draws from contemporary sources, most specifically Francisco Lopez de Gómara's *Historia general de las Indias*, but it bears noting that Lucretius's *De rerum natura*, so present throughout the chapter, ends with a description of the plague that will destroy the world.

24. Bodin, *Method for the Easy Comprehension of History*, 302. On the role of apocalyptic rhetoric in late sixteenth-century historiography see Huppert, *The Idea of Perfect History*, 99. Tom Conley shows how Montaigne's text recasts its sources on the fall of Tenochtitlan and Cuzco to mimic the economics of New World exploration. See his discussion in *The Self-Made Map: Cartographic Writing in Early Modern France* (Minneapolis: University of Minnesota Press, 1996), 270–78. For a useful formulation of the semantics of decadence in historiography see Randolph Starn, "Meaning Levels in the Theme of Historical Decline," *History and Theory* 14, no 1 (1975): 1–31.

25. Henri Lefebvre, *The Production of Space*, trans. Donald Nicholson-Smith (1974; Oxford: Blackwell, 1991), 282. Lest my claim that Montaigne "frames" the essay with self-depictions seem exaggerated, I note that the entire first book of the *Essais* is famously constructed as a frame around the missing center—the sonnets of Montaigne's dead friend La Boétie. Such symmetrical structures are to be found all over Montaigne's text.

26. The problematics of the location of the "self" in the Renaissance have been elegantly and succinctly phrased by Timothy J. Reiss in a discussion of the breakdown in political and linguistic order during the late sixteenth century: "The sense of being, we may say, could . . . be 'fixed' only by situating it be-

tween some beneficent authority on the one hand and some alien antagonist on the other." See Reiss's *The Meaning of Literature* (Ithaca: Cornell University Press, 1992), 45. Still, part of the power of Montaigne's treatment of the New World stems from the fact that he complicates the distinction between the "beneficent authority" and the "alien antagonist." This is not to say, however, that he does so everywhere in the *Essais*. For a compelling theoretical discussion of the problematics of the "subject" in Montaigne see Reiss, "Montaigne and the Subject of Polity," in *Literary Theory/Renaissance Texts*, ed. Patricia Parker and David Quint (Baltimore: Johns Hopkins University Press, 1986), 115–49.

27. Royal entries like the one evoked in "Of Cannibals" frequently featured mock Roman triumphs in which New World natives were paraded as captives—a motif that connects "Of Cannibals" to both halves of "Of Coaches." For a discussion of one such entry and its implications for the representation of royal power see Stephen Mullaney, "Strange Things, Gross Terms, Curious Customs: The Rehearsal of Cultures in the Late Renaissance," in *Representing the English Renaissance*, ed. Stephen Greenblatt (Berkeley: University of California Press, 1988), 65–92.

28. For an extended discussion of the image of the fall in Montaigne see François Rigolot, *Les métamorphoses de Montaigne* (Paris: Presses Universitaires de France, 1988), 140–49, as well as the same author's "La 'pente' du repentir: Un exemple de remotivation du signifiant dans les *Essais* de Montaigne," in *Columbia Montaigne Conference Papers*, ed. Donald M. Frame and Mary B. McKinley (Lexington, Ky: French Forum, 1981), 119–34.

29. This is not to suggest, of course, that the two worlds do not resemble or even mirror each other in their violence. Indeed, this is Quint's persuasive argument in *Montaigne and the Quality of Mercy*.

30. On the dynamics of astonishment in the European response to the New World, see Stephen Greenblatt, *Marvelous Possessions: The Wonder of the New World* (Chicago: University of Chicago Press, 1991). On the image of the horse as a figure of transport and translation, see Patricia Parker, *Shakespeare from the Margins* (Chicago: University of Chicago Press, 1996), 137.

31. "Pour ceux qui les ont subjuguez, qu'ils ostent les ruses et batelages dequoy ils se sont servis à les piper, et le juste estonnement qu'aportoit à ces nations là de voir arriver si inopinéement des gens barbus, divers en langage, religion, en forme et en contenance, d'un endroict du monde si esloigné et où ils n'avoyent jamais imaginé qu'il y eust habitation quelconque, montez sur des grands monstres incogneuz, contre ceux qui n'avoyent non seulement veu de cheval, mais beste quelconque duict à porter et soustenir homme ny autre charge; garnis d'une peau luysante et dure et d'une arme tranchante et resplendissante . . . adjoustez y les foudres et tonnerres de nos pieces et harquebouses, capables de troubler Caesar mesme, . . . contez, dis-je aux conquerans cette disparité, vous leur ostez toute l'occasion de tante de victoires" (888b). I have slightly altered Frame's translation at the end of this passage. Frame omits the phrase about recounting the scene.

32. In one of the best stylistically based studies of Montaigne, Richard Sayce argues that this passage, with its grammatical convolutions, might be seen as characteristic of the style of the *Essays* as a whole. See his discussion in *The Essays of Montaigne: A Critical Exploration* (London: Weidenfeld and Nichol-

son, 1972), 310. Sayce does not, however, go so far as to consider the multiple perspectives it offers on the cross-cultural encounter it represents.

33. This question of the relationship between figuration and the representation of the Other has been explored, though from a slightly different perspective, by Eric Cheyfitz, in *The Poetics of Imperialism: Translation and Colonization from "The Tempest" to "Tarzan"* (Oxford: Oxford University Press, 1991). For a discussion of Montaigne, though without reference to the passage under consideration here, see Cheyfitz's chapter 7.

34. For a discussion of similar perspectival strategies in yet another invasion story, the episode of Aeneas's arrival in Italy, see Katherine Toll, "What's Love Got to Do with It? The Invocation of Erato, and Patriotism in the *Aeneid*," *Quaderni Urbinati di Cultura Classica* n.s. 33, no. 3 (1989): 107–18. Toll explores the way in which the question of the description of the stranger raises a whole series of problems involving the identity and nature of community. It is important for my argument about the crucial role of the essay in the description of alterity that Toll's discussion of the *Aeneid* focuses on how perspectival rhetoric emerges during an invocation to Erato, that is, at a moment at which the narrative movement of the poem is broken. There is, of course, a long critical tradition that links rhetorical "perspectivism" to the rise of the "Baroque style" in European art during the late Renaissance. While acknowledging both the interest and the limitations of this tradition of thought, I would want to insist on the particular political and social contexts within which given perspectival strategies work. For a fuller discussion of this question see my introduction to *Baroque Topographies: Literature/History/Philosophy*, *Yale French Studies*, vol. 80 (New Haven: Yale University Press, 1991).

35. For general discussions of the problems plaguing Montaigne's attempts to break away from his European perspective see Michel de Certeau, "Montaigne's 'Of Cannibals': The Savage 'I,'" in his *Heterologies: Discourse on the Other*, trans. Brian Massumi (Minneapolis: University of Minnesota Press, 1986), 67–80; Gérard Defaux, "Un cannibale en haut de chausses: Montaigne, la différence et la logique de l'identité," *Modern Language Notes* 97 (1982): 919–57; Tzvetan Todorov, *On Human Diversity*, trans. Catherine Porter (1989; Cambridge: Harvard University Press, 1993), 51–64; and the two-part essay by Frank Lestringant, "Le cannibalisme des 'Cannibales,'" *Bulletin de la société des Amis de Montaigne*, 9–10 (1982): 27–41 and 11–12 (1982): 19–38. Quint, in *Montaigne and the Quality of Mercy*, chapter 3, offers a fresh perspective on this problem by linking it to civil unrest in France and to Montaigne's representations of classical virtue.

36. Bartolomé de Las Casas, *The Devastation of the Indies: A Brief Account*, trans. Herma Briffault (Baltimore: Johns Hopkins University Press, 1992), 29.

37. For an influential reading of Montaigne's New World essays that takes a much darker view of the function of mediation, but also, I would argue, fails to account for the generic multiplicity of these texts, see de Certeau, "Montaigne's 'Of Cannibals': the Savage 'I' "; in his *Heterologies*. On the rhetorical problems that underlie the practice of ethnography in the West see James Clifford, *The Predicament of Culture* (Cambridge: Harvard University Press, 1988).

38. "Car il me semblait que je pourrais rencontrer beaucoup plus de vérité dans les raisonnements que chacun fait touchant les affaires qui lui importent, et

dont l'événement le doit punir bientôt après s'il a mal jugé." René Descartes, *Discours de la méthode*, in *Oeuvres complètes*, ed. André Bridoux, Bibliothèque de la Pléiade (Paris: Gallimard, 1953), 131. My translation.

39. On Montaigne and Descartes as travelers, see Georges van den Abbeele, *Travel as Metaphor: From Montaigne to Rousseau* (Minneapolis: University of Minnesota Press, 1991). Tzvetan Todorov notes that Descartes's "exile" from France is characterized precisely by an avoidance of any serious contact with alterity. See his discussion in *On Human Diversity*, 348.

CONCLUSION

1. Jean Bodin, *Les six livres de la république* (1583), ed. and abridged by Gérard Mairet (Paris: Livre de Poche, 1993), 417.
2. Carlos García, *La Antipatía de Franceses y Espanoles* (1617), ed. Michel Bareau (Edmonton, Alberta: Alta Press, 1979), 189. For a good background on the anti-Spanish pamphlet literature of the years around the turn of the seventeenth century, see Bareau's introduction to this volume.
3. Richelieu, Cardinal (Armand Du Plessis), *Testament Politique* (1668), ed. Françoise Hildesheimer (Paris: Société de l'Histoire de France, 1995), 296–302.
4. Pierre Corneille, *Polyeucte*, in *Théatre choisi*, ed. Maurice Rat (Paris: Garnier, 1961), 223, v. 209. My translations. For two interesting recent readings of this play that diverge from my own, while addressing similar issues, see John D. Lyons, *The Tragedy of Origins: Pierre Corneille and Historical Perspective* (Stanford: Stanford University Press, 1996), chapter 4, and Mitchell Greenberg, *Canonical States/Canonical Stages* (Minneapolis: University of Minnesota Press, 1994), chapter 4.

Bibliography

Abbeele, Georges van den. *Travel as Metaphor: From Montaigne to Rousseau.* Minneapolis: University of Minnesota Press, 1991.

Adams, Robert P. *The Better Part of Valor: Erasmus, More and Vives on War and Peace.* Seattle: University of Washington Press, 1962.

Adorno, Theodor. *Notes to Literature.* 2 vols. Edited by Rolf Tiedemann, translated by Shierry Weber Nicholsen. New York: Columbia University Press, 1991.

Adorno, Theodor, and Max Horkheimer. *Dialectic of Enlightenment.* Translated by John Cumming. New York: Seabury Press, 1972.

Agnew, John, and Stuart Corbridge. *Mastering Space: Hegemony, Territory and International Political Economy.* London: Routledge, 1995.

Ahmed, Ehsan. *The Law and the Song: Hebraic, Christian, and Pagan Revivals in Sixteenth-Century France.* Birmingham, Ala.: Summa, 1997.

Alamanni, Luigi. *Versi e prose.* 2 vols. Edited by Pietro Raffaelli. Florence: Le Monnier, 1859.

Allut, Paul. *Etude biographique et bibliographique sur Symphorien Champier.* Lyon: Scheuring, 1859.

Althusser, Louis. *Lenin and Philosophy.* 1969. Translated by Ben Brewster. London: New Left Books, 1971.

Anderson, Benedict. *Imagined Communities: Reflections on the Origin and Spread of Nationalism.* London: Verso, 1983.

Aneau, Barthélemy. "Le Quintil Horacien." Paris, 1550. In Goyet, 1990, 187–233.

Ariosto, Lodovico. *Orlando furioso.* 2 vols. 1532. Edited by Emilio Bigi. Milan: Rusconi, 1982.

Aristotle. *The Complete Works of Aristotle: The Revised Oxford Translation,* 2 vols. Edited by Jonathan Barnes. Princeton: Princeton University Press, 1984.

Armstrong, John A. *Nations before Nationalism.* Chapel Hill: University of North Carolina Press, 1982.

Aronson, Nicole. *Les idées politiques de Rabelais.* Paris: Nizet, 1973.

Aubigné, Agrippa d'. *Les Tragiques.* Edited by Frank Lestringant. Paris: Gallimard, 1995.

Augustine, Saint. "Faith, Hope, and Charity." Translated by Bernard Peebles. In *Fathers of the Church,* vol. 2. New York: Fathers of the Church, Inc. 1947–.

Baïf, Jean-Antoine de. *Oeuvres en rime.* 5 vols. Edited by Charles Marty-Laveaux. Geneva: Slatkine, 1965.

Baïf, Jean-Antoine de. *Les Amours de Francine.* Edited by Ernesta Caldarini. Geneva: Droz, 1966.

Bakhtin, Mikhail Mikhailovich. *The Dialogic Imagination: Four Essays.* Edited by Michael Holquist, translated by Caryl Emerson and Michael Holquist. Austin: University of Texas Press, 1981.

Balibar, Etienne. "The Nation Form: History and Ideology." In Etienne Balibar and Immanuel Wallerstein, *Race, Nation, Class: Ambiguous Identities*. London: Verso, 1991.

Balibar, Etienne, and Immanuel Wallerstein. *Race, Nation, Class: Ambiguous Identities*. London: Verso, 1991.

Balsamo, Jean. *Les rencontres des muses: Italianisme et anti-italianisme dans les lettres françaises de la fin du XVIe siècle*. Geneva: Slatkine, 1992.

Beasley, Faith Evelyn. *Revising Memory: Women's Fiction and Memoirs in Seventeenth-Century France*. New Brunswick, N.J.: Rutgers University Press, 1990.

Beaujour, Michel. *Le jeu de Rabelais*. Paris: L'Herne, 1969.

Beaune, Colette. *Naissance de la nation France*. Paris: Gallimard, 1985.

———. *The Birth of an Ideology: Myths and Symbols of Nation in Late-Medieval France*. 1985. Translated by Susan Ross Huston. Berkeley: University of California Press, 1991.

Bellenger, Yvonne. *Du Bellay, ses "Regrets" qu'il fit dans Rome*. Paris: Nizet, 1975.

Berrong, Richard M. *Every Man for Himself: Social Order and Its Dissolution in Rabelais*. Saratoga, Calif.: ANMA Libri, 1985.

Bersuire, Pierre. *Opera omnia*. 2 vols. Cologne, 1692.

Bhabha, Homi K. *The Location of Culture*. London: Routledge, 1994.

———, ed. *Nation and Narration*. London: Routledge, 1990.

Biblia Vulgata. Edited by Alberto Colunga and Laurentio Turrado. Madrid: Biblioteca de Autores Cristianos, 1977.

Billon, Francois de. *Le fort inexpugnable de l'honneur du sexe feminin*. Paris: Ian d'Allyer, 1555.

Bizer, Marc. "Letters from Home: The Epistolary Aspects of Joachim Du Bellay's *Les regrets*." *Renaissance Quarterly* 52, no. 1 (1999): 140–70.

Bloch, Marc. *Feudal Society*. 2 vols. 1939. Translated by L. A. Manyon. Chicago: University of Chicago Press, 1961.

Bloch, R. Howard. *Etymologies and Genealogies: A Literary Anthropology of the French Middle Ages*. Chicago: University of Chicago Press, 1983.

Blumenberg, Hans. *The Legitimacy of the Modern Age*. Translated by Robert M. Wallace. Cambridge: M. I. T. Press, 1991.

———. *Shipwreck with Spectator: Paradigm of a Metaphor for Existence*. Translated by Steven Rendall. Cambridge: M. I. T. Press, 1997.

Bodin, Jean. *Method for the Easy Comprehension of History*. 1566. Translated by Beatrice Reynolds. New York: Columbia University Press, 1945.

———. *Les Six livres de la république*. 1583. Edited and abridged by Gérard Mairet. Paris: Livre de poche, 1993.

Bornkamm, Heinrich. *Luther's World of Thought*. Translated by Martin H. Bertram. St. Louis: Concordia, 1958.

Botero, Giovanni. *Della ragion di stato*. Venice: Gioliti, 1589.

Bourdieu, Pierre. *Distinction: A Social Critique of the Judgement of Taste*. Translated by Richard Nice. Cambridge: Harvard University Press, 1984.

———. *Language and Symbolic Power*. Edited by John B. Thompson, translated by Gino Raymond and Matthew Adamson. Cambridge: Harvard University Press, 1991.

Bourrilly, V.-L. "Antonio Rincon et la politique orientale de François Ier." *Revue historique* 113 (1913): 64–83, 268–308.

Braden, Gordon. "Love and Fame: The Petrarchan Career." In *Psychiatry and the Humanities*, vol. 9: *Pragmatism's Freud*, edited by William Kerrigan. Baltimore: Johns Hopkins University Press, 1986, 126–58.

——. *Petrarchan Love and the Continental Renaissance*. New Haven: Yale University Press, 1999.

——. *Renaissance Tragedy and the Senecan Tradition: Anger's Privilege*. New Haven: Yale University Press, 1985.

Brantôme, Pierre de Bourdeille. *Les Dames galantes*. Edited by Pascal Pia. Paris: Folio, 1981.

——. *Oeuvres complètes: publiées d'après les manuscrits avec variantes et fragments inédits pour la Société de l'Histoire de France par Ludovic Lalanne*. 11 vols. Paris: Jules Renouard, 1864–82.

Braudel, Fernand. *The Identity of France*. 2 vols. Translated by Siân Reynolds. New York: Harper and Row, 1990.

——. *The Structures of Everyday Life: Civilization and Capitalism, 15th-18th Century*. 3 vols. 1979. Translated by Siân Reynolds. New York: Harper and Row, 1979.

Brennan, Timothy. "The National Longing for Form." In Bhabha, 1990, 44–70.

Burke, Kenneth. *Rhetoric of Religion: Studies in Logology*. Berkeley: University of California Press, 1970.

Carron, Jean-Claude, ed. *François Rabelais: Critical Assessments*. Baltimore: Johns Hopkins University Press, 1995.

Castor, Grahame. *Pléiade Poetics*. Cambridge: Cambridge University Press, 1964.

Cave, Terence. *The Cornucopian Text: Problems of Writing in the French Renaissance*. Oxford: Clarendon, 1979.

——. "Panurge, Pathelin, and Other Polyglots." In *Lapidary Inscriptions: Renaissance Essays for Donald A. Stone, Jr.*, edited by Barbara C. Bowen and Jerry C. Nash. Lexington, Ky.: French Forum, 1991, 171–82.

——. *Pré-histoires: Textes troublés au seuil de la modernité*. Geneva: Droz, 1999.

——. "Reading Rabelais: Variations on the Rock of Virtue." In *Literary Theory/Renaissance Texts*, edited by Patricia Parker and David Quint. Baltimore: Johns Hopkins University Press, 1986, 78–95.

Cazauran, Nicole. *L'Heptaméron de Marguerite de Navarre*. Paris: Société d'édition d'enseignement supérieur, 1976.

Certeau, Michel de. *Heterologies: Discourse on the Other*. Translated by Brian Massumi. Minneapolis: University of Minnesota Press, 1986.

——. *The Practice of Everyday Life*. 1980. Translated by Steven Rendall. Berkeley: University of California Press, 1984.

——. *The Writing of History*. Translated by Tom Conley. New York: Columbia University Press, 1988.

Cervantes, Miguel de. *Don Quixote*. 1605–15. Translated by J. M. Cohen. Harmondsworth: Penguin, 1950.

Champier, Symphorien. *Hortus Gallicus, pro Gallis in Gallia scriptus*. Lyon: Trechsel, 1533.

——. *La vie du preulx Chevalier Bayard*. 1525. Edited by Denis Crouzet. Lyon: Imprimerie Nationale, 1992.

Cheyfitz, Eric. *The Poetics of Imperialism: Translation and Colonization from "The Tempest" to "Tarzan."* Oxford: Oxford University Press, 1991.

Cholakian, Patricia Francis. *Rape and Writing in the "Heptaméron" of Marguerite de Navarre*. Carbondale: Southern Illinois University Press, 1991.

Chrétien de Troyes. *Arthurian romances/Chrétien de Troyes.* Translated by D. D. R. Owen. London: Dent, 1987.

Cicero, Marcus Tullius. *De Officiis.* Edited and translated by Walter Miller. Loeb Classical Library. Cambridge: Harvard University Press, 1913.

Clifford, James. *The Predicament of Culture.* Cambridge: Harvard University Press, 1988.

Coleman, Dorothy Gabe. *The Chaste Muse: A Study of Joachim Du Bellay's Poetry.* Leiden: Brill, 1980.

Comito, Terry. *The Idea of the Garden in the Renaissance.* New Brunswick, N.J.: Rutgers University Press, 1978.

Conley, Tom. "Montaigne and the Indies: Cartographies of the New World in the *Essais, 1580–88.*" In *1492–1992: Re/Discovering Colonial Writing.* Edited by René Jara and Nicholas Spadaccini. Minneapolis: Prisma Institute, 1989, 225–62.

———. *The Self-Made Map: Cartographic Writing in Early Modern France.* Minneapolis: University of Minnesota Press, 1996.

Corneille, Pierre. *Théâtre Choisi.* Edited by Maurice Rat. Paris: Garnier, 1961.

Cornilliat, François. "*Or ne mens*": *Couleurs de l'Eloge et du Blâme chez les "Grands Rhétoriqueurs.*" Paris: Champion, 1994.

Costa, Dennis John. *Irenic Apocalypse: Some Uses of Apocalyptic in Dante, Petrarch and Rabelais.* Saratoga, Calif.: ANMA Libri, 1981.

Cotgrave, Randle. *A Dictionarie of the French and English Tongues.* 1611. Columbia, S.C.: University of South Carolina Press, 1968.

Cottrell, Robert D. *The Grammar of Silence: A Reading of Marguerite de Navarre's Poetry.* Washington, D.C.: Catholic University of America Press, 1986.

Crane, Mary Thomas. *Framing Authority: Sayings, Self, and Society in Sixteenth-Century England.* Princeton: Princeton University Press, 1993.

Crinito, Pietro. *De honesta disciplina.* 1504. Edited by Carlo Angeleri. Rome: Fratelli Bocca, 1955.

Davis, Natalie Zemon. "Rabelais among the Censors (1540s–1940s)." *Representations* 32 (1990): 1–32.

———. *Society and Culture in Early Modern France.* Stanford: Stanford University Press, 1975.

Defaux, Gérard. "Un cannibale en haut de chausses: Montaigne, la différence et la logique de l'identité." *Modern Language Notes* 97 (1982): 919–57.

———. "Au coeur du *Pantagruel*: Les deux chapitres IX de l'édition Nourry." *Kentucky Romance Quarterly* 21 (1974): 59–96.

———. *Le curieux, le glorieux, et la sagesse du monde dans la première moitié du XVIe siècle: L'exemple de Panurge (Ulysse, Demosthène, Empédocle).* Lexington, Ky.: French Forum, 1982.

———. "Rabelais's Realism, Again." In Carron, 1995, 19–38.

Déguy, Michel. *Tombeau de Du Bellay.* Paris: Gallimard, 1973.

DeJean, Joan. *Tender Geographies: Women and the Origins of the Novel in France.* New York: Columbia University Press, 1991.

Deleuze, Gilles, and Félix Guattari. *Anti-Oedipus.* Translated by Robert Hurley, Mark Seem, and Helen R. Lane. Minneapolis: University of Minnesota Press, 1983.

———. *Kafka: Toward a Minor Literature.* Translated by Dana Polan. Minneapolis: University of Minnesota Press, 1986.

Bibliography

DellaNeva, JoAnn. "Du Bellay: Reader of Scève, Reader of Petrarch." *Romanic Review* 79, no. 3 (1988): 401–11.

Derrida, Jacques. *The Politics of Friendship*. Translated by George Collins. London: Verso, 1997.

Desan, Philippe. "De la poésie de circonstance à la satire: Du Bellay et l'engagement poétique." In *Du Bellay: Actes du Colloque Intérnationale d'Angers*. Angers: Presses de l'Université d'Angers, 1990, vol. 2: 421–31.

———. *Penser l'histoire à la Renaissance*. Caen: Paradigme, 1993.

Descartes, René. *Oeuvres complètes*. Edited by André Bridoux. Bibliothèque de la Pléiade. Paris: Gallimard, 1953.

Desrosiers-Bonin, Diane. *Rabelais et l'humanisme civil*. Geneva: Droz, 1992.

Dewald, Jonathan. *Aristocratic Experience and the Origins of Modern Culture: France, 1570–1715*. Berkeley: University of California Press, 1993.

Du Bellay, Joachim. *La Deffence et Illustration de la Langue Françoyse*. 1549. Edited by Henri Chamard. Paris: Didier, 1948.

———. *Oeuvres poétiques*. 12 vols. Edited by Henri Chamard. Paris: Nizet, 1931.

———. *Oeuvres poétiques*. 2 vols. Edited by Daniel Aris and Françoise Joukovsky. Paris: Garnier, 1993.

———. *Les Regrets*. 1557. Edited by Henri Chamard and Henri Weber. Paris: Didier, 1970.

———. *Les Regrets*. 1557. Edited by J. Jolliffe and M. A. Screech. Geneva: Droz, 1974.

Dubois, Claude-Gilbert. *Celtes et Gaulois au XVIe siècle: Le développement littéraire d'un mythe nationaliste*. Paris: Vrin, 1972.

———. *La conception de l'histoire en France au XVIe siècle*. Paris: Nizet, 1977.

Durling, Robert M. "The Epic Ideal." In *The Old World: Discovery and Rebirth*. Edited by David Daiches and Anthony Thorlby. London: Aldus Books, 1974, 105–46.

Duval, Edwin M. *The Design of Rabelais's "Pantagruel."* New Haven: Yale University Press, 1991.

———. *The Design of Rabelais's "Tiers livre de Pantagruel."* Geneva: Droz, 1997.

Eagleton, Terry. *Ideology*. London: Verso, 1991.

Elias, Norbert. *The Court Society*. Translated by Edmund Jephcott. New York: Pantheon, 1983.

Erasmus, Desiderius. *Ausgewählte Schriften*. 8 vols. Edited by Werner Welzig. Darmstadt: Wissenschaftliche Buchgesellschaft, 1968.

———. *Collected Works of Erasmus*. 66 vols. Toronto: University of Toronto Press, 1974–88.

———. *Erasmus on His Times: A Shortened Version of the Adages of Erasmus*. Edited by Margaret Mann Phillips. Cambridge: Cambridge University Press, 1967.

———. *In Epistolam Pauli Apostoli ad Romanos Paraphrasis*. Basel: Froben, 1517.

———. *Opera omnia Desiderii Erasmi Roterodami; recognita et adnotatione critica instructa notisque illustrata*. 9 vols. Series edited by Jean-Claude Margolin. Amsterdam: North-Holland, 1969–83.

Estienne, Henri. *Deux dialogues du nouveau langage Françoys Italianizé*. 1578. Edited by P. Ristelhuber. Paris: A. Lemerre, 1885.

———. *La précellence du langage françois*. 1578. Edited by Edmond Huguet. Paris: Armand Colin, 1896.

Febvre, Lucien Paul Victor. *Amour sacré, amour profane, autour de l'Heptaméron*. Paris: Gallimard, 1944.

———. *Le problème de l'incroyance au seizième siècle: La religion de Rabelais*. Paris: Albin Michel, 1942.

———. *The Problem of Unbelief in the Sixteenth Century: The Religion of Rabelais*. 1942. Translated by Beatrice Gottlieb. Cambridge: Harvard University Press, 1982.

Ferguson, Margaret. *Trials of Desire: Renaissance Defenses of Poetry*. New Haven: Yale University Press, 1983.

Fineman, Joel. *Shakespeare's Perjured Eye: The Invention of Poetic Subjectivity in the Sonnets*. Berkeley: University of California Press, 1986.

Fontaine, Marie Madeleine. "Des mots à la rime et de leur raison." In *Du Bellay: Actes du Colloque International d'Angers*. Angers: Presses de l'Université d'Angers, 1990, vol. 1: 261–85.

Fragonard, Marie-Madeleine. "La tragédie universelle: Images des relations entre les nations." In *Les Tragiques d'Agrippa d'Aubigné*, edited by Marie-Madeleine Fragonard. Paris: Champion, 1990, 145–66.

Freccero, Carla. *Father Figures: Genealogy and Narrative Structure in Rabelais*. Ithaca: Cornell University Press, 1991.

Frisch, Andrea. "Novel Histories: The Figure of the Witness in Early Modern Fiction and Travel Narrative." Ph.D. dissertation, University of California at Berkeley, 1997.

———. "*Quod vidimus testamur*: Testimony, Narrative Agency and the World in Pantagruel's Mouth." *French Forum* 24, no. 3 (1999): 261–83.

Gadoffre, Gilbert. *Du Bellay et le sacré*. Paris: Gallimard, 1978.

———. *La révolution culturelle dans la France des humanistes*. Geneva: Droz, 1997.

Gaguin, Robert. *Epistolae et Orationes*. 1498. Edited by Louis Thuasne. Paris: Bouillon, 1903.

García, Carlos. *La Antipatía de Franceses y Espanoles*. 1617. Edited by Michel Bareau. Edmonton, Alberta: Alta Press, 1979.

Gellner, Ernest. *Nations and Nationalism*. Oxford: Blackwell, 1983.

Giovio, Paolo. *Historia del suo tempo*. 3 vols. Translated by Lodovico Domenichi. Venice: Farri, 1555–57.

Gliozzi, Giuliano. *Adamo e il nuovo mondo*. Florence: Nuova Italia, 1976.

Goscinny, René. *Asterix the Gaul*. Illustrated by Albert Uderzo. Translated by Anthea Bell and Derek Hockridge. London: Hodder and Stoughton, 1969.

Goyet, Francis, ed. *Traités de poétique et de rhétorique de la Renaissance*. Paris: Livre de poche, 1990.

Gray, Floyd. *La poétique de Du Bellay*. Paris: Nizet, 1978.

Greenberg, Mitchell. *Canonical States/Canonical Stages*. Minneapolis: University of Minnesota Press, 1994.

Greenblatt, Stephen. *Learning to Curse: Essays in Early Modern Culture*. New York: Routledge, 1990.

———. *Marvelous Possessions: The Wonder of the New World*. Chicago: University of Chicago Press, 1991.

Greene, Thomas M. *The Light in Troy: Imitation and Discovery in Renaissance Poetry*. New Haven: Yale University Press, 1982.

———. *Rabelais: A Study in Comic Courage*. Englewood Cliffs, N.J.: Prentice-Hall, 1970.

———. "Regrets Only: Three Poetic Paradigms in Du Bellay." *Romanic Review* 84, no. 1 (1993): 1–18.

Bibliography

Greenfield, Liah. *Nationalism: Five Roads to Modernity*. Cambridge: Harvard University Press, 1992.

Greengrass, Mark, ed. *Conquest and Coalescence: The Shaping of the State in Early Modern Europe*. London: Edward Arnold, 1991.

Gregorio, Laurence A. *Order in the Court: History and Society in "La princesse de Clèves."* Saratoga, Calif.: ANMA Libri, 1986.

Halpern, Richard. *The Poetics of Primitive Accumulation: English Renaissance Culture and the Genealogy of Capital*. Ithaca: Cornell University Press, 1991.

Hampton, Timothy. " 'Trafiquer la louange': L'économie de la poésie dans les *Regrets.*' " In *Du Bellay et ses sonnets romains*, edited by Yvonne Bellenger. Paris: Champion, 1994, 47–60.

——. *Writing from History: The Rhetoric of Exemplarity in Renaissance Literature*. Ithaca: Cornell University Press, 1990.

——, ed. *Baroque Topographies: Literature/History/Philosophy*. Yale French Studies, vol. 80. New Haven: Yale University Press, 1991.

Hartog, François. *The Mirror of Herodotus: The Representation of the Other in the Writing of History*. 1980. Translated by Janet Lloyd. Berkeley: University of California Press, 1988.

Hay, Denys. *Europe: The Emergence of an Idea*. Edinburgh: Edinburgh University Press, 1957.

Heath, Michael J. *Crusading Commonplaces: La Noue, Lucinge and Rhetoric against the Turks*. Geneva: Droz, 1986.

Helgerson, Richard. *Forms of Nationhood: The Elizabethan Writing of England*. Chicago: University of Chicago Press, 1992.

Heng, Geraldine. "The Woman Wants." *Yale Journal of Criticism* 5 (1992): 101–34.

Hexter, Jack H. *The Vision of Politics on the Eve of the Reformation: More, Machiavelli, and Seyssel*. New York: Basic Books, 1973.

Higgins, Lynn A., and Brenda R. Silver, eds. *Rape and Representation*. New York: Columbia University Press, 1991.

Hobsbawm, E. J. *Nations and Nationalism since 1780: Programme, Myth, Reality*. Cambridge: Cambridge University Press, 1990.

Hoggan-Niord, Yvonne. "L'inspiration burlesque dans les *Regrets* de Joachim Du Bellay." *Bibliothèque d'humanisme et Renaissance* 42 (1980): 361–85.

Hollier, Denis, ed. *A New History of French Literature*. Cambridge: Harvard University Press, 1989.

Homer. *The Iliad*. Translated by Richmond Lattimore. Chicago: University of Chicago Press, 1951.

Huarte de San Juan, Juan. *Examen de ingenios para las ciencias*. 1575. Edited by Guillermo Serés. Madrid: Cátedra, 1989.

Huguet, Edmond. *Dictionnaire de la langue française du seizième siècle*. 7 vols. Paris: Champion, 1925–43.

Huppert, George. *The Idea of Perfect History*. Urbana: University of Illinois Press, 1970.

Hutchinson, John, and Anthony D. Smith, eds. *Nationalism*. Oxford: Oxford University Press, 1994.

Jameson, Fredric. *The Political Unconscious: Narrative as a Socially Symbolic Act*. Ithaca: Cornell University Press, 1981.

——. *Postmodernism, or, the Cultural Logic of Late Capitalism*. Durham, N.C.: Duke University Press, 1991.

Le jardin de plaisance et fleur de rhétorique. Paris: Antoine Vérard, 1501(?). Facsimile: Paris: Firmin Didot, 1910–25.

Jeanneret, Michel. *Le défi des signes: Rabelais et la crise de l'interprétation à la Renaissance.* Orléans: Paradigme, 1994.

———. *A Feast of Words: Banquets and Table Talk in the Renaissance.* 1987. Translated by Jeremy Whitely and Emma Hughes. Chicago: University of Chicago Press, 1991.

Jodelle, Etienne. *Oeuvres complètes.* 2 vols. Edited by Enea Balmas. Paris: Gallimard, 1965.

Kahn, Victoria. *Rhetoric, Prudence and Skepticism in the Renaissance.* Ithaca: Cornell University Press, 1985.

Kasprzyk, K. "Marguerite de Navarre, lecteur du *Décaméron.*" *Studi Francesi* 34, no. 1 (1970): 1–11.

Kelley, Donald R. *The Beginning of Ideology.* Cambridge: Cambridge University Press, 1981.

———. *Foundations of Modern Historical Scholarship.* New York: Columbia University Press, 1970.

Kelley-Gadol, Joan. "Did Women Have a Renaissance?" In *Becoming Visible,* edited by Renate Bridenthal and Claudia Koonz. Boston: Houghton Mifflin, 1977, 139–64.

Kennedy, William J. *Authorizing Petrarch.* Ithaca: Cornell University Press, 1994.

Knecht, R. J. *Francis I.* Cambridge: Cambridge University Press, 1982.

Koselleck, Reinhart. *Futures Past: On the Semantics of Historical Time.* 1978. Translated by Keith Tribe. Cambridge: M. I. T. Press, 1985.

Kritzman, Lawrence D. *The Rhetoric of Sexuality and the Literature of the French Renaissance.* Cambridge: Cambridge University Press, 1991.

La Brocquière, Bertrandon de. *Voyage d'outremer de Bertrandon de la Broquière.* Edited by Ch. Schefer. Paris: E. Leroux, 1892.

La Charité, Raymond C. *Re-creation, Reflection, and Recreation: Perspectives on Rabelais's "Pantagruel."* Lexington, Ky.: French Forum, 1980.

———. "Réflection-divertissement et intertextualité: Rabelais et l'écolier limousin." In *Textes et Intertextes: Etudes sur le XVIe siècle pour Alfred Glausser,* edited by Floyd Gray and Marcel Tetel. Paris: Nizet, 1979, 93–103.

Lafayette, Madame de. *Correspondance.* Edited by André Beaunier. Paris: Garnier, 1942.

———. *The Princess of Cleves.* [1678]. Translated by Thomas S. Perry, edited by John D. Lyons. New York: W. W. Norton, 1994.

———. *Romans et Nouvelles.* Edited by E. Magne. Paris: Classiques Garnier, 1970.

Landes, Joan. *Women and the Public Sphere in the Age of the French Revolution.* Ithaca: Cornell University Press, 1988.

Langer, Ullrich. "Charity and the Singular: The Object of Love in Rabelais." In *Nominalism and Literary Discourse: New Perspectives,* edited by Hugo Keiper, Christoph Bode, and Richard J. Utz. Atlanta: Rodopi, 1997, 1–10.

———. *Divine and Poetic Freedom in the Renaissance: Nominalist Theology and Literature in France and Italy.* Princeton: Princeton University Press, 1990.

———. *Perfect Friendship: Studies in Literature and Moral Philosophy from Boccaccio to Corneille.* Geneva: Droz, 1994.

———. *Vertu du discours, discours de la vertu: Littérature et philosophie morale au XVIe siècle en France.* Geneva: Droz, 1999.

LaNoue, François de. *Discours politiques et militaires*. 1584. Edited by F. E. Sutcliffe. Geneva: Droz, 1967.

La Popelinière, Lancelot-Voisin. *L'Histoire des histoires: L'Idée de l'histoire accomplie.* 2 vols. 1599. Paris: Fayard, 1989.

La Roncière, Charles de. *Histoire de la marine française*, 3 vols. Paris: Plon, 1899–1932.

La Sale, Antoine de. *Jehan de Saintré*. Edited by Jean Misrahi and Charles A. Knudson. Geneva: Droz, 1978.

Las Casas, Bartolomé de. *The Devastation of the Indies: A Brief Account.* Translated by Herma Briffault. Baltimore: Johns Hopkins University Press, 1992.

Lecoq, Anne-Marie. *François Ier imaginaire: Symbolique et politique à l'aube de la Renaissance française.* Paris: Macula, 1987.

Le Dantec, Denise, and Jean-Pierre Le Dantec. *Reading the French Garden.* 1987. Translated by Jessica Levine. Cambridge: M. I. T. Press, 1990.

Lefebvre, Henri. *The Production of Space.* 1974. Translated by Donald Nicholson-Smith. Oxford: Blackwell, 1991.

Lefèvre d'Etaples, Jacques. *The Prefatory Epistles of Jacques Lefèvre d'Etaples and Related Texts.* Edited by Eugene F. Rice, Jr. New York: Columbia University Press, 1972.

Lefranc, Abel. *Rabelais: Études sur "Gargantua," "Pantagruel," "le Tiers livre."* Paris: Albin Michel, 1953.

Legrand, Marie Dominique. "Le mode épistolaire dans les *Regrets*." *Nouvelle Revue du Seizième Siècle* 13, no. 3 (1995): 199–213.

Lemaire de Belges, Jean. *La Concorde des deux langages.* 1511. Edited by Jean Frappier. Paris: Droz, 1947.

———. *Les Illustrations de Gaule et singularitez de Troye.* 1512. Lyon: Jean de Tournes, 1549.

Le Roy Ladurie, Emmanuel. *The Royal French State, 1460–1610.* 1987. Translated by Juliet Vale. Oxford: Blackwell, 1994.

Léry, Jean de. *Histoire d'un voyage faict en la terre du Brésil.* 1578. Edited by Frank Lestringant. Paris: Livre de poche, 1994.

———. *The History of a Voyage to the Land of Brazil, Otherwise Called America.* 1578. Translated by Janet Whatley. Berkeley: University of California Press, 1990.

Lestocquoy, Jean. *Histoire du patriotisme en France.* Paris: Albin Michel, 1968.

Lestringant, Frank. "Le cannibalisme des 'Cannibales.' " In *Bulletin de la société des Amis de Montaigne* 9–10 (1982): 27–41, and 11–12 (1982): 19–38.

Ley, Klaus. *Neuplatonische Poetik und Nationale Wirklichkeit: Die Uberwindung des Petrarkismus im Werk Du Bellays.* Heidelberg: Carl Winter, 1975.

Lopez de Gomara, Francisco. *Historia general de las Indias.* 1553. Madrid: Calpe, 1922.

Lucretius. *De rerum natura.* Edited by Martin Ferguson Smith, translated by W. H. D. Rouse. Loeb Classical Library. Cambridge: Harvard University Press, 1982.

Luther, Martin. *Luther's Works.* 55 vols. Edited by Jaroslav Pelikan and Helmut T. Lehmann. Philadelphia: Fortress Press, 1955–67.

Lyons, John D. *Exemplum: The Rhetoric of Example in Early Modern France and Italy.* Princeton: Princeton University Press, 1989.

———. *The Tragedy of Origins: Pierre Corneille and Historical Perspective.* Stanford: Stanford University Press, 1996.

Lyons, John D., and Mary B. McKinley, eds. *Critical Tales: New Studies of the Hep-taméron and Early Modern Culture*. Philadelphia: University of Pennsylvania Press, 1993.

Machiavelli, Niccolò. *Tutte le opere*. Edited by Mario Martelli. Florence: Sansoni, 1971.

MacPhail, Eric. "Nationalism and Italianism in the Work of Joachim Du Bellay." *Yearbook of Comparative and General Literature* 39 (1990–91): 47–53.

———. "Rabelais's Allegory of Prudence." *Etudes Rabelaisiennes* 30 (1995): 55–66.

———. *The Voyage to Rome in French Renaissance Literature*. Saratoga, Calif.: ANMA Libri, 1990.

Magny, Olivier de. *Les soupirs*. Edited by David Wilkin. Geneva: Droz, 1978.

Marguerite of Navarre, Queen. *Les dernières poésies de Marguerite de Navarre*. Edited by Abel Lefranc. Paris: Armand Colin, 1896.

———. *L'Heptaméron*. Edited by Michel François. Paris: Garnier, 1967.

———. *The Heptaméron*. Translated by P. A. Chilton. Harmondsworth: Penguin, 1984.

Marienstras, Richard. *Le Proche et le lointain: Le drame Elisabethain et l'idéologie anglaise au XVIe et XVIIe siècles*. Paris: Minuit, 1981.

Marot, Clément. *Oeuvres poétiques*. 2 vols. Edited by Gérard Defaux. Paris: Garnier, 1993.

Marucci, Valerio, et al., eds. *Pasquinate Romane del Cinquecento*. Rome: Salerno Editrice, 1983.

Mathieu-Castellani, Gisèle. *La conversation conteuse: Les nouvelles de Marguerite de Navarre*. Paris: Presses Universitaires de France, 1992.

McKinley, Mary B. *Les terrains vagues des Essais: Itinéraires et intertextes*. Paris: Champion, 1996.

Mönch, Walter. *Das Sonnet*. Heidelberg: Kerle Verlag, 1955.

Montaigne, Michel de. *The Complete Works of Montaigne*. 1580–95. Translated by Donald Frame. Stanford: Stanford University Press, 1967.

———. *Oeuvres complètes*. Edited by Albert Thibaudet and Maurice Rat. Bibliothèque de la Pléiade. Paris: Gallimard, 1962.

More, Saint Thomas. *Utopia*. Translated by Edward D. Surtz. S. J. New Haven: Yale University Press, 1964.

———. *Utopie*. Edited and translated by André Prévost. Paris: Mame, 1978.

Moretti, Franco. *Atlas of the European Novel, 1800–1900*. London: Verso, 1998.

———. *Signs Taken for Wonders: Essays in the Sociology of Literary Forms*. Translated by Susan Fischer, David Forgacs, and David Miller. London: Verso, 1983.

Mukerji, Chandra. *Territorial Ambitions and the Gardens of Versailles*. Cambridge: Cambridge University Press, 1997.

Mullaney, Stephen. "Strange Things, Gross Terms, Curious Customs: The Rehearsal of Cultures in the Late Renaissance." In *Representing the English Renaissance*, edited by Stephen Greenblatt. Berkeley: University of California Press, 1988, 65–92.

Nakam, Géralde. *Montaigne et son temps*. Paris: Gallimard, 1993.

Nerlich, Michael. *The Ideology of Adventure: Studies in Modern Consciousness, 1100–1750*. 2 vols. 1977. Translated by Ruth Crowley. Minneapolis: University of Minnesota Press, 1987.

The New Oxford Annotated Bible. Expanded edition. Revised Standard Version. Edited by Herbert G. May and Bruce M. Metzger. New York: Oxford University Press, 1977.

Nitze, W. A. "The Source of the 9th Sonnet of the *Regrets*." *Modern Language Notes* 39 (1924): 216–30.

Nora, Pierre, ed. *Les Lieux de Memoire*. 3 vols. Paris: Gallimard, 1984–86.

Norton, Glyn P. "Narrative Function in the 'Heptaméron' Frame Story." In *La nouvelle française à la Renaissance*, edited by Lionello Sozzi. Geneva: Slatkine, 1981.

Pabst, Walter. *Novellentheorie und Novellendichtung: zur Geschichte ihrer Antinomie in den romanischen Literaturen*. Heidelberg: C. Winter, 1967.

Parker, Patricia A. *Inescapable Romance: Studies in the Poetics of a Mode*. Princeton: Princeton University Press, 1979.

——. *Literary Fat Ladies: Rhetoric, Gender, Property*. London: Methuen, 1987.

——. " 'No Sinister Nor No Awkward Claim': *Henry V*." Unpublished manuscript.

——. *Shakespeare from the Margins*. Chicago: University of Chicago Press, 1996.

Pasquier, Etienne. *Oeuvres Choisies*. 2 vols. Edited by Léon Feugère. Paris: Didot, 1949.

——. *Les recherches de la France*. 3 vols. 1562. Edited by Marie-Madeleine Fragonard and Francçois Roudaut. Paris: Champion, 1996.

Patrides, C. A. " 'The Bloddy and Cruell Turke': The Background of a Renaissance Commonplace." *Studies in the Renaissance* 10, no. 1 (1963): 126–35.

Peletier du Mans, Jacques. *Art poétique*. Paris, 1555. In Goyet, 1990, 237–346.

Petrarch, Francesco. *Rime, Trionfi e Poesie Latine*. Edited by F. Neri et al. Milan: Ricciardi, 1951.

——. *Petrarch's Lyric Poems*. Translated by Robert M. Durling. Cambridge: Harvard University Press, 1976.

Phillips, Margaret Mann. *Erasmus and the Northern Renaissance*. London: Hodder and Stoughton, 1949.

Plato. *The Collected Dialogues of Plato*. Edited by Edith Hamilton and Huntington Cairns. Princeton: Princeton University Press, 1961.

Pliny the Younger. *Letters, and Panegyricus*. Edited and translated by Betty Radice. Loeb Classical Library. Cambridge: Harvard University Press, 1969.

Polybius. *The Rise of the Roman Empire*. Translated by Ian Scott-Kilvert. Harmondsworth: Penguin, 1979.

Quint, David. *Epic and Empire: Politics and Generic Form from Virgil to Milton*. Princeton: Princeton University Press, 1993.

——. *Montaigne and the Quality of Mercy: Ethical and Political Themes in the "Essais."* Princeton: Princeton University Press, 1998.

——. *Origin and Originality in Renaissance Literature*. New Haven: Yale University Press, 1983.

——, ed. *Creative Imitation: New Essays on Renaissance Literature in Honor of Thomas M. Greene*. Binghamton: Medieval and Renaissance Texts and Studies, 1992.

Quintilian. *Institutio oratoria*. 5 vols. Translated by H. E. Butler. Loeb Classical Library. London: Heinmann, 1953.

Rabelais, François. *François Rabelais: Les Cinq Livres*. Edited by Jean Céard, Gérard Defaux, and Michel Simonin. Paris: Livre de poche, 1994.

——. *The Histories of Gargantua and Pantagruel*. 1532. Translated by J. M. Cohen. Harmondsworth: Penguin Books, 1955.

——. *Oeuvres complètes*. 2 vols. Edited by Pierre Jourda. Paris: Garnier, 1962.

Rebhorn, Wayne A. *The Emperor of Men's Minds: Literature and the Renaissance Discourse of Rhetoric*. Ithaca: Cornell University Press, 1995.

Reiss, Timothy. *The Meaning of Literature*. Ithaca: Cornell University Press, 1992.

———. "Montaigne and the Subject of Polity." In *Literary Theory/Renaissance Texts*. Edited by Patricia Parker and David Quint. Baltimore: Johns Hopkins University Press, 1986, 115–49.

Renaudet, Augustin. *Préréforme et humanisme pendant les premières guerres d'Italie*. 1916. Paris: Librairie d'Argences, 1953.

Richelieu, Cardinal (Armand Du Plessis). *Testament Politique de Richelieu*. 1668. Edited by Françoise Hildesheimer. Paris: Société de l'Histoire de France, 1995.

Rigolot, François. "Du Bellay et la poésie du refus." *Bibliothèque d'humanisme et Renaissance* 33, no. 3 (1974): 489–502.

———. *Les langages de Rabelais*. 2d ed. Geneva: Droz, 1996.

———. *Les métamorphoses de Montaigne*. Paris: Presses Universitaires de France, 1988.

———. "La 'pente' du repentir: Un exemple de remotivation du signifiant dans les *Essais* de Montaigne." In *Columbia Montaigne Conference Papers*, edited by Donald M. Frame and Mary B. McKinley. Lexington, Ky.: French Forum, 1981, 119–34.

———. *Poétique et onomastique: L'exemple de la Renaissance*. Geneva: Droz, 1977.

Romier, Lucien. *Les origines politiques des guerres de religion*. 2 vols. Paris: Perrin, 1913.

Ronsard, Pierre de. *Oeuvres complètes*. 2 vols. Edited by Jean Céard et al. Bibliothèque de la Pléiade Paris: Gallimard, 1993.

Rorty, Richard. *Contingency, Irony, and Solidarity*. Cambridge: Cambridge University Press, 1989.

Roudaut, François. *Joachim Du Bellay: Les Regrets*. Paris: Presses Universitaires de France, 1995.

Rouillard, Clarence D. *The Turk in French History, Thought, and Literature (1520–1660)*. 1940. New York: AMS Press, 1973.

Russell, Daniel. "Conception of Self, Conception of Space, and Generic Convention: An Example from the *Heptaméron*." *Sociocriticism* 4–5 (1986): 159–83.

Sahlins, Peter. *Boundaries: The Making of France and Spain in the Pyrenees*. Berkeley: University of California Press, 1989.

Saint-Gelays, Melin de. *Oeuvres complètes*. 3 vols. Edited by Prosper Blanchemain. Paris: Daffis, 1873.

Salel, Hugues. *Oeuvres poétiques complètes*. Edited by Howard H. Kalwies. Geneva: Droz, 1987.

Salmon, J. H. M. *Society in Crisis: France in the Sixteenth Century*. London: Methuen, 1979.

Sayce, Richard. *The Essays of Montaigne: A Critical Exploration*. London: Weidenfeld and Nicholson, 1972.

Schiffman, Zachary Sayre. *On the Threshold of Modernity: Relativism in the French Renaissance*. Baltimore: Johns Hopkins University Press, 1991.

Schor, Naomi. "The Portrait of a Gentleman: Representing Men in (French) Women's Writing." In *Misogyny, Misandry, and Misanthropy*, edited by R. Howard Bloch and Frances Ferguson. Berkeley: University of California Press, 1989, 113–33.

Schottenloher, Otto. "Erasmus und die Respublica Christiana." *Historische Zeitschrift* 210, no. 2 (1970): 295–323.

Schrader, Ludwig. *Panurge und Hermes*. Bonn: Romanisches Seminar der Universität Bonn, 1958.

Schwartz, Jerome. *Irony and Ideology in Rabelais: Structures of Subversion.* Cambridge: Cambridge University Press, 1990.

Scott, J. W. "The 'Digressions' of the *Princess de Clèves.*" *French Studies* 11 (1957): 315–22.

Screech, Michael A. *Rabelais.* Ithaca: Cornell University Press, 1979.

Scudéry, Madeleine de. *Artamène, ou le Grand Cyrus.* 10 vols. 1656. Geneva: Slatkine Reprints, 1972.

Seneca, Lucius Annaeus. *Moral Essays.* 3 vols. Edited and translated by J. W. Basore. Loeb Classical Library. Cambridge: Harvard University Press, 1935.

Seton-Watson, Hugh. *Nations and States.* London: Methuen, 1977.

Seyssel, Claude de. *La monarchie de France et deux autres fragments politiques.* 1515. Edited by Jacques Poujol. Paris: Librairie d'Argences, 1961.

———. *The Monarchy of France.* 1515. Translated by J. H. Hexter, with an introduction by Donald R. Kelley. New Haven: Yale University Press, 1981.

Shell, Marc. *Children of the Earth: Literature, Politics, and Nationhood.* New York: Oxford University Press, 1993.

Skenazi, Cynthia. "Le poète et le roi dans les *Antiquitez de Rome* et le *Songe* de Du Bellay." *Bibliothèque d'humanisme et Renaissance* 60 (1998): 41–55.

Skinner, Quentin. *The Foundations of Modern Political Thought.* 2 vols. Cambridge: Cambridge University Press, 1978.

Smith, Pauline M. *The Anti-Courtier Trend in Sixteenth-Century French Literature.* Geneva: Droz, 1966.

Starn, Randolph. "Meaning Levels in the Theme of Historical Decline." *History and Theory* 14, no. 1 (1975): 1–31.

Steinmetz, David C., ed. *The Bible in the Sixteenth Century.* Durham: Duke University Press, 1990.

Stephens, Walter. *Giants in Those Days: Folklore, Ancient History, and Nationalism.* Lincoln: University of Nebraska Press, 1989.

Strabo. *The Geography of Strabo.* 8 vols. Translated by Horace Leonard Jones. London: Heinemann, 1924.

Tacitus. *The Complete Works of Tacitus.* Edited by Moses Hadas; translated by Alfred John Church and William Jackson Brodribb. New York: Modern Library, 1942.

Tanner, Tony. *Adultery in the Novel: Contract and Transgression.* Baltimore: Johns Hopkins University Press, 1979.

Tetel, Marcel. *Marguerite de Navarre's "Heptaméron": Themes, Language, and Structure.* Durham: Duke University Press, 1973.

Thevet, André. *Cosmographie de Levant.* Edited by Frank Lestringant. Geneva: Droz, 1985.

Todorov, Tzvetan. *Nous et les autres: La réflexion française sur la diversité humaine.* Paris: Seuil, 1989.

———. *On Human Diversity.* 1989. Translated by Catherine Porter. Cambridge: Harvard University Press, 1993.

Toll, Katherine. "What's Love Got to Do with It? The Invocation of Erato, and Patriotism in the *Aeneid.*" *Quaderni Urbinati di Cultura Classica,* n.s., 33, no. 3 (1989): 107–18.

Tory, Geoffroy. *Champ fleury.* Introduction by J. W. Jolliffe. East Ardsley: S. R. Publishers; New York: Johnson Reprint Corporation, 1970.

Tracy, James D. *The Politics of Erasmus.* Toronto: University of Toronto Press, 1978.

Tylus, Jane. *Writing and Vulnerability in the Late Renaissance*. Stanford: Stanford University Press, 1993.

Urfé, Honoré d'. *L'Astrée*. Edited by Gérard Genette. Paris: 10/18, 1964.

Veyne, Paul. *Writing History*. Translated by Mina Moore-Rinvolucri. Middletown, Conn.: Wesleyan University Press, 1984.

Virgil. *Aeneid*. Rev. ed. 2 vols. Edited and translated by H. Rushton Fairclough. Loeb Classical Library. Cambridge: Harvard University Press, 1978.

———. *Eclogues, Georgics, Aeneid*. 2 vols. Edited and translated by R. Fairclough. Loeb Classical Library. Cambridge: Harvard University Press, 1973.

Vivanti, Corrado. *Lotta politica e pace religiosa in Francia fra Cinque e Seicento*. Turin: Einaudi, 1974.

———. "*Les Recherches de la France* d'Etienne Pasquier: L'invention des Gaulois." In *Les lieux de Mémoire*, edited by Pierre Nora. Paris: Gallimard, 1986.

Volosinov, V. N. *Marxism and the Philosophy of Language*. 1972. Translated by Ladislav Matejka and I. R. Titunik. Cambridge: Harvard University Press, 1986.

Weber, Henri. *La création poétique au XVIe siècle en France*. Paris: Nizet, 1955.

Weiss, Allen S. *Mirrors of Infinity*. Princeton: Princeton Architectural Press, 1995.

White, Hayden V. *The Content of the Form: Narrative Discourse and Historical Representation*. Baltimore: Johns Hopkins University Press, 1987.

Wright, Thomas, ed. *Early Travels in Palestine: Comprising the Narratives of Arculf, Willibald, Bernard, Saewulf, Sigurd, Benjamin of Tudela, Sir John Maundeville, De la Brocquière, and Maundrell*. London: Woodfall and Son, n.d.

Xenophon. *Cyropaedia*. 2 vols. Edited and with an English translation by Walter Miller. Loeb Classical Library. Cambridge: Harvard University Press, 1947.

Yardeni, Myriam. *La conscience nationale en France pendant les guerres de religion (1559–98)*. Louvain: Nauwelaerts, 1971.

Index